GLOBAL WARMING

THE FIRE OF PENTECOST IN WORLD EVANGELISM

An anecdotal history of
the work of Elim Missions
(1919 – 1989)

Peter Smith

GLOBAL WARMING

A catalogue record for this book is available from the British Library.
ISBN 978-0-9556085-0-6

Published by the Elim Pentecostal Irish Churches

Printed by Antrim Printers,
Steeple Industrial Estate, Antrim, BT41 1AB
Tel: 028 9442 8053

CONTENTS

FOREWORD 5

ACKNOWLEDGEMENTS 7

PREFACE 9

INTRODUCTION 13

Section One - Europe

Chapter

1. Albania 17
2. Armenia 19
3. Belgium 21
4. Elim Relief Association (ERA) 31
5. Europe (General) 39
6. Euroteams 51
7. Elim Women's Missionary Auxiliary (EWMA) 57
8. France 67
9. Greece 71
10. Spain 73

Section Two – Africa

11. Botswana/Bechuanaland 81
12. Belgian Congo/Zaire, Democratic Republic of Congo 83
13. Egypt 107
14. Ghana 113
15. Kenya 125
16. New Zealand/Zambia/Malawi 131
17. Tanganyika/Tanzania 135
18. Transvaal/South Africa 153
19. Zimbabwe/Southern Rhodesia 171

Section Three – Central and South America

20. Brazil 199
21. Guyana 213
22. Honduras 227

Section Four – India and the Far East

23. China/Hong Kong 233
24. India 245
25. Japan 273
26. Malaysia 277
27. Mongolia/Formosa/Taiwan 281
28. Thailand 295

29. Conclusion 303

FOREWORD

By Pastor John Glass
General Superintendent,
Elim Pentecostal Church

The Early Church was born amidst the flames of missionary zeal. In some cases, the fire generated had been first lit in an upper room on the day of Pentecost and blazed in as many combustible lives as would place themselves on the altar of service. On other occasions, the fire took the form of persecution as witnesses were thrust out to Regions that they would not normally have traversed had they not experienced the inferno fanned by ferocious enemies of the Gospel. As is so often the case, God causes the wrath of men to praise Him; and what was meant for evil turned out for good.

No period of history, however dark the age or dry the land, has been without its witnesses and it is to a small seventy year section of it, 1919-1989, that Peter Smith draws our attention in the pages that follow.

The author has 'earned the right to speak' as he has given many years of his life in dedication to the cause of world mission via his involvement in strategic planning on councils and committees, as well as direct engagement by visiting the Fields himself - applying his wisdom and teaching gifts to the benefit of the local churches.

You are about to read of lives propelled, not by the security net of financial guarantees but by a simple trust in a God who is bound to grant the means to sustain a call that He has placed upon the lives of His people. There will be countless others whose names are not recorded here but are indelibly printed in the pages of heaven's eternal audit.

Over time, the form that mission takes inevitably changes – yet its heart still beats to the same rhythms of grace and a call of God that never drops a decibel in its volume or a syllable in its challenge to reach a lost world for Christ.

Many mentioned here have already reached their reward. This text is not for them – they have no need of it. This book is for us. It transcends cold data and serves to inspire us to a higher level of commitment to the subject that is the nearest to God's heart and the purpose of the cross.

ACKNOWLEDGEMENTS

I am indebted to Pastor John Glass and the NLT for their encouragement and permission to use the reports in the *Elim Evangel* as the basis for much of the content in this book.

My thanks also to Pastor D. W. Cartwright, Elim's archivist and Mr. David Womersley of CAM for their help and input.

I acknowledge, with grateful thanks, the willing co-operation and help of missionaries, both serving and retired, together with the children of some who have passed on to their reward, who all responded to my search for information.

I have appreciated the unfailing support of my family who have put up with my long absences at the computer.

Last, and most importantly, I acknowledge the God of all grace whose eternal love has provided us with a theme for such a publication and for whose glory all that has been recorded and written was undertaken.

DEDICATION

To Janet
The love of my life
and the mainstay of my ministry

PREFACE

GLOBAL WARMING - ecologically and environmentally a potential disaster, but spiritually, an absolute prerequisite to the return of Jesus Christ. *"This gospel of the kingdom shall be preached in all the world for a witness unto all nations; and then shall the end come."* (Matthew 24:14)

God has presented Himself to us as fire throughout Scripture. He spoke to Moses from the burning bush. A pillar of fire during the wilderness wanderings signified His presence among His people. John the Baptist declared of Jesus that He would *"baptise with the Holy Ghost and fire."* (Matthew 3:11) The two disciples on the road to Emmaus testified - "Did not our hearts burn within us?" and, in more recent times, John Wesley's well-documented experience with God was that his "heart was strangely warmed".

It is interesting that, in the physical world, fire is sustained by a supply of flammable material and oxygen. So too, in the spiritual, the fire of evangelism rests on a supply of flammable material - willing, servant hearts, and the oxygen of the Divine Spirit.

Edwin Orr, in his appraisal of the Second Evangelical Awakening,[i] finds an abundance of both. He makes the interesting observation that "every revival of religion in the homelands is felt within a decade in the foreign mission-fields". He goes on to say that the revival of 1859 "helped to lay the foundations of the modern international and interdenominational missionary structure." Indeed, the period around 1859 gave rise to some of the most noted names in missionary endeavour - David Livingstone, George Grenfell, Mary Slessor and many others. Shortly afterwards, and as a direct result of the awakenings of those times, James Chalmers went to his martyrdom in New Guinea and James Hudson Taylor opened up the work in China.

Orr continues: "Only when the bulk of the foregoing material had been assembled was it possible to gain a comprehensive view of the Awakening and its relationship to the movement as of the fifty years following. It has been concluded that the fifty years following 1858 constituted a distinct and definite period of expansion of the Christian Church, in fact, a nineteenth century evangelical awakening comparable to its noted predecessor of the eighteenth century." It is his opinion that the Awakening of 1858-59 created new organisations of a permanent character and increased the efforts of all Christians to fulfil the Great Commission and carry the Gospel to every creature, at home and abroad.

The Welsh Revival of 1904 had also a remarkable impact on the work of spreading the Gospel overseas. Places as far removed as India, Madagascar and Patagonia responded to the Spirit's influences. Mainland Europe was not untouched. Africa, Asia and Australasia were all impacted by the revival. Eifion

Evans reports that the Christian and Missionary Alliance recorded, with reference to India, "The revival has given a new body of native evangelists and most of our native preachers have experienced a baptism of the Holy Ghost which has completely transformed their spirit and work". [ii]

It is against this background and historical legacy that the Elim churches responded to the challenge of the Great Commission. The founder of the Elim Pentecostal Church, George Jeffreys, was born in February 1889. He was born again in 1904, during the period of the Welsh revival and, in 1910, received his baptism in the Holy Spirit. Others have traced his life story, so it is not fitting that this should be repeated, except to say that, in a very short time, he began to preach locally in Wales and that signs and wonders followed his ministry. At the age of 24, he responded to an invitation to preach in Ireland and, subsequently, the Elim Church came into being. E.C.W. Boulton's book, *A Ministry of the Miraculous,*[iii] traces his career through to 1928 and it is evident that he was a gifted evangelist, on fire for God and committed to winning souls for Christ.

In his early years, George Jeffreys had a profound interest in overseas missions. His associations with the early Pentecostal pioneers of the twentieth century meant that he was open to developments in thinking relative to the evangelistic outreach of the churches with a Pentecostal ethos then in the process of being formed. Following on the principles adopted by Hudson Taylor and the China Inland Mission, Alexander Boddy and Cecil Polhill set up the Pentecostal Missionary Union in 1909. William K. Kay in his book, *Inside Story,*[iv] traces the development of this movement in its early years. He notes that the founding of the Congo Evangelistic Mission by William Burton and James Salter in 1915 "had the unintentional result of deflecting missionary finance to that field and away from PMU workers in China, India and the Tibet areas."

George Jeffreys' early Bible training came about indirectly as a result of the formation of the PMU. This was because the PMU used the Bible School set up by Thomas Myerscough at Preston and George Jeffreys went there in 1912, remaining until the following year. Willie Burton and James Salter were fellow-students. Boulton makes the point that "none would ever have dreamt of the potentialities and possibilities of that student class; in it were those whose influence has penetrated the whole world and whose names have been immortalised".[v]

My purpose in writing this history is partly to record for posterity, not only the names of those we have known, but the names also of the many hitherto unknown. Their efforts have often been unheralded and unsung but, without them, there would be no Elim missionary endeavour. It is also to register the broad effect that Elim has had on foreign missions. Its influence has been much greater than might be expected from its size and it is true that Elim is bigger abroad than it is at home.

This is due, in part, to the vision of successive leaders who have been open enough to see the potential in partnerships with other organisations whose ethos matches our own. This has meant that our sphere of influence has broadened considerably in the last two decades, although it should be noted that this record, because of limitations of reported material, will take the reader only up to 1989.

Pioneering missionaries have also reached out beyond their recognised fields to plant new works and encourage indigenous workers in developing their own ministries. From time to time, these efforts have been helped by short-term missions visits by people from the homeland whose skills have been beneficial to the work. All are to be commended in contributing to the health of the whole.

It is my prayer that the reader will be stimulated to prayer for the ongoing work and to feel a little of the excitement of being involved in a world-wide service for God that has, as its motivation, the warming of the hearts of millions and the hastening of the return of the King.

i Orr, Edwin J. *The Second Evangelical Awakening*, p. 106, 136. Marshall, Morgan & Scott, London, 1955.

ii Evans, Eifion. *The Welsh Revival of 1904*, p.160. Evangelical Press of Wales, 1993.

iii Boulton, E.C.W. *A Ministry of the Miraculous.* Elim Publishing Office, London, 1928.

iv Kay, William K. *Inside Story*, p.43,57. Mattersey Hall Publishing, Mattersey, 1990.

v Boulton, E.C.W., op cit. p.13.

INTRODUCTION

The effects of the Great War (1914-1918) and its aftermath were horrendous. The cost to the nation was enormous, running into billions of pounds. Consequences resulting from the conflict included not only the inevitable disruption of normal home and family life, but the economic and social fabric of society becoming so severely compromised that the nation had to endure years of food rationing and Government spending cuts that brought hardship to all.

During the war and in the years following, strikes for better pay and conditions were almost the norm. Munitions workers on the Clyde went on strike, the police, rail workers and miners all had their own struggles and Glasgow saw a General Strike in 1919.

At the declaration of war in August 1914, the Bank rate soared to 10% and queues formed at the banks as people tried to exchange bank notes for gold. Income tax was raised by 40%. Women were drafted into factories and worked 12 hour days, seven days a week. Twenty-four hour working became a way of life. Pay was £1.60 per hour for day shift and £3 for night shift!

By December that year, 100,000 British casualties had been reported while, at the end of the war in 1918, it was reckoned that 10 million had died, 750,000 from the UK, mostly servicemen. When hostilities ended, a major factor to be faced was famine in both Germany and Russia. At home, a crucial issue was a lack of employment for returning servicemen, many of whom had to take to street hawking to eke out a living.

By 1921, unemployment in Britain reached one million. The sense of frustration and disillusionment can be imagined, not to mention feelings of despair that, having fought for the nation, there should be no provision for resettlement in society.

Dickens's introduction to his *Tale of Two Cities* fits the bill – "It was the best of times; it was the worst of times." No doubt there was relief that the war was over, but the rebuilding of individual lives in the UK was no less fraught than that faced by the defeated countries.

It was against the background of such strife and uncertainty that the fledgling Pentecostal assemblies multiplied. Since the outpouring of the Holy Spirit around the turn of the century, Pentecostal phenomena had been in evidence across the globe, resulting in gatherings of like-minded believers joining together for fellowship and support in what was often a hostile environment.

Despite the troubles of the second decade of the century, much was achieved. 1915 saw the founding by George Jeffreys of the Elim Movement. Thomas Myerscough had opened his Bible school in Preston and many who were subsequently to become prominent in the Pentecostal Movement were influenced there. Among these were not only George Jeffreys and E.J. Phillips, but also Willie Burton who, in 1905, under the ministry of Torrey and Alexander in London, surrendered his life to Christ, and James Salter.

From his earliest days, Willie Burton was influenced in the direction of overseas missions. He had an uncle who planted churches for the Brethren in Switzerland while an aunt spent 20 years in China and just escaped before the Boxer Riots of 1900[i].

Although he applied to many Missionary Societies, he was turned down because he lacked experience. When his mother died in 1911, he thought he would go immediately to Africa, but in fact did not do so until 1914.[ii] In the meantime, he gave himself to full time ministry locally and was much used in the winning of souls. In May, 1914, God showed him that the time had come and he set off by ship for the Belgian Congo via South Africa, where he met the representative of the Pentecostal Mission of South Africa. He was joined in 1915 by James Salter.

Out of their association, the Congo Evangelistic Mission was founded as an independent mission in 1919. It was not until 1924 that the Assemblies of God was constituted, so the Mission became a vehicle for Pentecostal people to serve in the Congo, irrespective of denominational affiliation. It was to Congo that many Elim missionaries went in the first instance.

The challenge of Missions was well summed up by James Salter in an article he wrote for the *Elim Evangel* in December, 1919, some four years after his arrival in the Belgian Congo. He talked about a wide open door for the Gospel and the hunger in the hearts of the people.

One day, I was speaking of Christ Jesus to a chief. Side by side, we sat on a huge leopard skin. He seemed to listen attentively as I repeated the story of God's love for a lost world. There he sat, apparently deep in thought, with his chin resting on his breast. When I had finished, he deliberately lifted his head to the level of mine, calmly looked me between the eyes and said, "How long have you known this?" "About eight or ten years," I replied. "Did your father know about it?" he asked. On my replying in the affirmative, he asked, "And did his father know too?" "Yes," I said, "Our people have known for hundreds of years." He hung his head again for a few moments and then I heard him murmur, "Known for hundreds of years, and just come." Then with a glint of battle in his eyes and biting sarcasm in his tones, he exclaimed, "Yes, God is a white man." I knew what he meant. He continued, "God passed through our villages one night when it was dark. He did not want us. He came to you."[iii]

i Harold Womersley, *Wm. F.P. Burton,* p.22, Victory Press, Eastbourne, 1973

ii ibid, p.31,32

iii James Salter, Letter to *Elim Evangel*, Vol.1:1,p.6, December, 1919.

SECTION ONE

EUROPE

1. Albania 17
2. Armenia 19
3. Belgium 21
4. Elim Relief Association (ERA) 31
5. Europe (General) 39
6. Euroteams 51
7. Elim Women's Missionary Auxiliary (EWMA) 57
8. France 67
9. Greece 71
10. Spain 73

CHAPTER 1

ALBANIA

Albania had once been described as the most closed country in Europe as far as the Gospel was concerned. It had a mystique and challenge all its own. Surrounded on the continental side by foreboding, mountainous terrain, and guarded on the coastal side by mountains which drop into the warm, Adriatic waters, this intriguing country has, in a physical sense, a fortress-like defence against the rest of the world.

The geographical barriers which isolate Albania projected a more sinister barrier. For years, the authorities had, persistently and unashamedly, sought to extinguish the light and life of faith in its people. No religious activity was allowed within its frontiers. The Bible and all associated literature were defiantly banned. No church buildings were being used and there was no physical evidence that the Church even existed in this atheistic state.

For some time, Elim had been seeking permission to visit but telephone calls and correspondence had yielded nothing but silence. So, while involved in a 6,500 mile, five week fact-finding tour of the area in 1979, touching Yugoslavia, Bulgaria, Greece, Italy and Belgium, Brian Edwards, the European Director, presented himself at the Albanian border near the city of Ohrid. This was the main crossing of three from the Yugoslavia side.

Brian pleaded with the officials and more phone calls were made but all to no avail. He asked to be allowed temporarily onto Albanian soil to apply for a visa but was simply turned away. It appeared that the only people being allowed in were bona fide travellers on package holidays and they were always accompanied by official guides.

Albania, at that time, claimed to be the world's first state to have eliminated religion. Even to mention the name of God could place an Albanian in great danger. However, Albanian was spoken on the Yugoslav side of the border where there was a limited number of Albanian bibles. Christians there were praying that, from the few Albanian Christians in Yugoslavia, a Gospel advance into the hard-line Communist country would take place.

Later in the year, it became evident that the godless walls of this atheistic state were beginning to crumble. The underground church was growing and Scriptures were penetrating the closed borders. Suddenly, Albania was on the brink of economic disaster. Trade with its communist ally, China, had been broken off and, as a result, trade with the west was on the increase. Political leadership looked about to change.

With the changing political situation, a thrilling opportunity arose in 1981 to send more than 30,000 Gospels into the country. Because of the hard line taken against Christians, few details were given but Brian Edwards made it clear that Elim was not in the business of smuggling bibles. Confirmation had been received that the bibles had arrived and were being distributed eagerly.

While this ministry was a joint venture between "Action Europe" and a West German mission, Elim became involved in supplying some of the necessary finance. Strong requests were made regularly from Albania for more Gospels and this became a special project for the missions involved. At that time, each piece of literature was costing just 14p to produce, so little compared to the value it contained.

CHAPTER 2

ARMENIA

The major earthquake in Armenia at the end of 1988 was occasion for the Elim churches to bring their compassion to bear once again. The European Pentecostal Relief Association (EPRO), of which ERA[i] was a part, was actively involved in bringing aid to the area from the very first day of the disaster. By mid-January, $50,000 had been lodged in a bank account to be used by the churches for immediate relief.

In discussions with the authorities, EPRO had committed themselves to two projects. The first was to supply container homes to be used as dwellings, clinics or other essential shelter. The second was the supply of timber and other building materials from Sweden so that, once the weather had cleared, an orphanage could be built to provide for the many children who had lost parents.

In Swansea, a major appeal was launched by the Lord Mayor at the instigation of Swansea City Temple. The pastor, Ron Williams, had a great interest in Armenia and focussed the appeal on building a medical centre in Armenia and bringing 250 children to Wales for a holiday in the summer.

A report from around Christmas-time by Roland Nelsson and Lors Hornberg, workers with the Swedish Relief Organisation, Erikshjalpen, said they had never before seen anything like this emotionally on so many different levels. Roland described the scenes:

We had stopped near the partly demolished Baptist church and taken some pictures when the door of a sheet-iron container opened and a family came out. The oldest man in the family raised his cap to us, stretched out his hands to us and almost shoved us into his new, but temporary home. His family consisted of only seven persons in two generations, the rest lay buried under the ruins.

The walls were covered with thin, galvanised sheet metal through which they had installed a thin electric wire and, near the door, was an oil stove burning waste oil. There was no window and no ventilation. Two iron beds, cold as ice, could be seen along the walls and, between them, a small table with smoked meat, thin unleavened bread and coffee. Outside, it was ten degrees below zero. The catastrophe had struck them so hard, but they had not lost their hospitality or their warm feelings for strangers: "Please stop here and have a meal. Have a cup of coffee. . . "

We went on to central parts of Leninakan. This used to be a medium sized city, but now, most of the houses had collapsed or were heavily damaged. Nobody lived in the city centre any more. Women and children had been evacuated and men were searching the ruins along the streets, looking for survivors and for what remained of their old homes.

Suddenly, a group of people came out of a hole among the stones. With bare hands, they had taken away big lumps of concrete, scratched in the pebbles until they gradually reached into the small spaces that had been their apartments. They came out with clothes, textiles and other things to keep themselves warm. At another place, we saw an excavator, silent and still, as the workers listened for sounds of life.

This picture was repeated throughout the city. A man and his wife sat under a cloth tent that they had put up. In front of them was a fire made from demolished furniture. It had all been fine and modern until the 7th December at 11.41 a.m. After three weeks, the mother and father were still crying because they hadn't seen their two teenaged boys since that fateful night. As they left, they were approached by five or six women who asked what was to become of them. Absolute despair marked their faces as they contemplated the future.

The Baptist church, the supermarkets, the railway station, the hospital, the communist headquarters, the banks, the blocks of flats, the factories, the restaurants - all had to be levelled to the ground. But experience had taught us this - that life had to go on. Something new must be built and would be. Armenia, a country ravaged by disasters, occupations, wars and other evils would have to go on living.[ii]

[i] Elim Relief Association.

[ii] Report in *Elim Evangel*, Volume 70, Issue 9, Missions News.

CHAPTER 3

BELGIUM

In 1938, Belgium was described by Archie Scott, Elim's missionary there, as the Land of the Closed Book and the Open Door, so near to England but so far from Christ. His evaluation of the land and its people was quite perceptive but devastating. He described the people as having been brought up for generations in idolatry and priest craft, without any knowledge whatever of the love of Jesus, and denied access to the Word of God.

Because of this, darkness reigned supreme, but there was now an open door for evangelism. As the Gospel was preached, so the uplifted Christ drew people in who not only shook off the shackles of sin and the past, but were so filled with the love of Christ that they immediately began witnessing both to their families and from door to door.

Needless to say, such enthusiasm resulted in hardship and persecution. One of the difficulties faced by the young church was the effect of the Russellites[i] who had succeeded in influencing one of the young fathers in the church. Another area was the need to minister in homes where the husbands and sons had been lost in the forces. There was a peace that only God could give. In November, 1938, the war clouds in Europe seemed to have passed over but, of course, six months later, the whole scene was to change.

The Scotts had originally felt called to serve the Lord in the Belgian Congo and, for that purpose, went to Liege to study French. While there, Archie became greatly burdened with the needs of the people he saw around him because of their spiritual darkness. He was disappointed to learn that the door to Congo had closed but where he was, the door was wide open. God led him to La Louviere, a town where the Gospel had never been preached, where nearly the entire population had never seen a Bible and there was no conception of the love of God. The work started on 10th April, 1937. Rooms had to be found and a hall for meetings. This presented real difficulties but the Lord provided an answer.

On the opening day, after renovations had all been completed, there was great anticipation because invitations had been distributed house to house – but only four turned up! However, they persevered and the four became five, and then increased to fifty and sixty until the hall had to be enlarged. At the same time, a baptistery was added so that, with great joy, the new Christians could be baptised. At the second baptismal service, Miss Adelaide Henderson,[ii] accompanied by Miss Barbour, was present.

The following year, another work was started, this time in the town of Haine St. Pierre. Although there were 25 present for the first service, numbers dropped off when the clocks changed and the services were held in daylight. People were afraid to be seen making their way to the hall as this would have meant persecution and the possibility of losing their employment. In spite of this, God was active in saving souls and healing the sick.

The development of the work was, of necessity, personal. All those who had responded did so because of prayer and a personal witness. The legacy of spiritual darkness and superstition were difficult to deal with and it was recognised that only the Holy Spirit could make a difference. Archie told of one woman who had vowed she would never put her foot in the hall; she was born in darkness, steeped in sin and the worst blasphemer in the street. When God saved her, He gave her a new vocabulary. Her husband came to the Lord and the woman offered to clean the hall and light the fire. Her diligence meant that the place was always spotless and with not a chair out of place. Around this time, Archie met some English people who had stayed in Belgium after the last war, so a meeting in English was arranged once a week. Up to 25 attended.

God works in mysterious ways. The young father whom the Russellites had influenced started to send his young children to the Sunday school and the work continued to grow until the hall was packed to capacity. Nevertheless, there was unending effort expended in reaching people with the Gospel. A huge 20 foot arrow was erected pointing to the hall, door to door visitation was maintained and printed literature was posted directly to people to personalise the invitations.

Three radio stations were contacted with a view to obtaining air time for the Gospel. One reply was negative, one didn't reply at all and the third was positive. They wanted four hundred francs a month to play one hymn of a choir singing (on a gramophone record) and they would announce an invitation to the meetings once every day. The church agreed to raise the money sacrificially for one month and the hope was that eventually, a whole service could be broadcast.

Needless to say, the war had an adverse effect on the work so that, when Belgium was invaded in 1940, it was impossible for the Scotts to stay. Just one month after the radio broadcasts started, the country was invaded. There had never been a time before when Christian hymns were sung daily on air.

It was with sad and heavy hearts that they heard the sirens sounding on a Friday morning and knew that the work could no longer go on as it had. Men aged 16-35 were ordered into France immediately, leaving the church with no men, others having been mobilised previously. The advance of the enemy was so rapid and unexpected that a hospital at which Archie had been booked to speak was never even established. The door had closed!

The next few days were extremely anxious. The little church was scattered – the men to the colours, the rest to join the ever-growing stream of refugees – the shortage of food; the continuous drone of raider planes; the crash of falling bombs and buildings. What should they do? Meanwhile, back in England, a small group led by Pastor Douglas Gray was praying that God would bring the Scotts home safely. At precisely the same time, the decision to leave was made. On the Wednesday after the invasion, they were obliged to flee at 4 a.m., leaving all behind them. They too had become refugees. Their train was attacked three times, but it wasn't hit once although two stations were left in ruins, one just ten minutes after they had left it. At one stage, over 30 German bombers were overhead. Arriving in France, the weary travellers were met by British Tommies and welcomed as they travelled on to Dunkirk.

They arrived at Liverpool Street, London on the Saturday evening to be met by Pastor Joseph Smith. Despite being dirty and tired they were overjoyed at the welcome they received and the kindness shown to them. They went to live temporarily at Elim Bible College, Clapham and were constantly offered gifts of some of the necessities they had had to leave behind – a comb, a brush or a dress. But they didn't sink into despair or idleness and, before long, were itinerating round the churches with their story and their challenging and passionate appeal. At a meeting[iii] in the Elim Church, Clapham, Archie's message to a packed church was, "The time is short; it's later than you think!" Shortly after this, Archie set down his experiences in a book entitled, *The Curtain falls in Belgium.* In reviewing it, Pastor W.G. Hathaway said that Archie was no visionary, but had given an account of the grim realities of life in a war zone, gracious godliness and the outworking of the Providence of God in keeping His children safe.

Later in the year, Archie took over the Pastorate of the Elim Church in Salisbury and numbers began to rise immediately. The Spirit of the Lord was present in ever-increasing power. One particular feature was a Sunday evening service for troops followed by free refreshments. Many soldiers and airmen were richly blessed by the services.

In spite of war time difficulties, Archie had contact with believers in Belgium. One message said, "Elim of Haine St. Pierre all in good health, awaiting news of their pastor." The other said, "Awaiting news of their pastor. Sister Marie[iv] very ill with stomach cancer, pray for her. Holding meetings with evangelist Viquerat[v]. Bonjour to all."

Four years after Belgium fell, the Elim Foreign Missions Council was wondering about the work and how the believers had fared during the German occupation. Just four days later, news came to hand that thrilled them all. The headline in the Evangel report said, "Elim Church Survives German Occupation".[vi]

Fred Harrison, one of our Crusaders from the Elim Church in Bradford, now in the Forces, is the driver of Field Marshal Montgomery's Staff car. Driving one day through Haine St. Pierre where Pastor Archie Scott had opened an Elim Church, the car was brought to a standstill by the crowds. Belgians, overwhelmed by the joy of being liberated by the Allied armies, crowded round the vehicles, showering kisses and flowers on the occupants. Standing at the back of the crowd, Fred Harrison noticed a girl who seemed to be watching him. When the excitement had subsided, she came up to him and, pointing to his Crusader badge, asked him in French what he belonged to. Speaking French fluently, he replied that he belonged to the Elim Foursquare Gospel Church.

Then she told him that she too belonged to Elim. After the occupation of Belgium by the German forces, her father had taken charge of the Elim congregation and had continued throughout the whole period of the occupation.

After Pastor Archie Scott had left, the members, about fifty of them, continued to worship in the hall. In spite of the heavy bombing of that district in the ebb and flow of the earlier battles, the building had remained intact and provided a spiritual home for the converts of Mr. Scott's ministry.

Mr. Harrison, while in the district, was able to attend the church and minister the Word of God to them, being privileged not only to be a member of the Allied forces bringing liberation to that beleaguered district, but a member also of Elim bringing the glorious message of liberation to the captives in the matchless Gospel of the Grace of our Lord Jesus Christ. The little church at Haine St. Pierre is waiting for us to send them a minister now the country is free.

Such a speedy answer to the Council's wonderings and the account of the Lord's faithfulness to, and preservation of, the small flock brought a note of praise and a determination to see the Elim ministry functioning again in Belgium just as soon as was practically possible. But it was not until 1946 that Tom Evans, brother of Pastor W. Evans, went to Belgium to continue the work. At a farewell in Elim Woodlands,[vii] Mr. Evans told how some few years before, he had felt called to work for God in Belgium. When the war broke out, the door closed, but now, at last, it had opened again and he was going in obedience to the call. It was expected that his wife, Eva, and their two boys, Howard and Kenneth, would join him in a short space of time.

In the first instance, Tom Evans went to Verviers where he commenced a work. The building they had found served as both church and living accommodation and, following a week of special services, he commented that those days were not without encouragement. They had their share of difficulties, not the least of which was the weather. They also found themselves without furniture as theirs had been delayed for about five weeks. They had hoped to use their piano for the services but this wasn't possible just then.

They were helped in these early days by friends from the Assembly of God in Liege. On the first Sunday, a party came by Army lorry with two British soldiers and they brought a small harmonium which proved most helpful. There were four strangers present, three of whom had been converted in the Salvation Army some time before. They came to all the meetings and were keen to help and bring others along too. The following Tuesday, a party of young people came from Liege with their pastor and, although the temperature was nine degrees below freezing, they stood and witnessed for God in the open air, inviting others to come to the meetings. Their choice of meeting place for the open air was in a square where there was a monument to Protestant Martyrs. The three Salvation Army friends turned up and another three strangers appeared as well, one of whom was the Evans's next door neighbour. On the final night, three more strangers came with prayer requests and an invitation to visit them in their homes.

The services were limited to two services per week as the coal shortage prevented them from adequately heating the hall. In addition, the Ministry of Fuel had not granted them any allowance for the use of the hall during this period. Nevertheless, the church flourished and the work began to be consolidated.

Their work was not without its difficulties and challenges. Mrs. Evans reported that the estimated population of the town was 50,000 and that 80% of the marriages had disintegrated, which meant that thousands were living in adultery. Immorality was so common that it was treated with a measured indifference. So much so that they had to deal with a worker of some 20 years' standing who was living with another man's wife. He saw no problem with his lifestyle and said that God hadn't condemned him for it. The strong line based on Scripture meant that some left, but the work was strengthened.

In the spiritual darkness, while giving our tracts in the local market, Tom was approached by a lady asking him how much he would charge to say a prayer for her son who had turned to evil ways. A development in the work was the commencement of children's meetings. At first, these were well attended but soon, the numbers halved when it was clear that this was "the Jesus religion". The children who came reported that their friends' parents were not allowing them to return as the church "didn't believe in God or Mary, the Holy Virgin". The children who did come enjoyed the meetings and the singing of the choruses, entering into the joy of the Lord in their enthusiasm.

During the summer of 1947, an evangelistic outreach was held with Pastor Verlinden, of Mons, who came in a car equipped with a loud speaker and amplifier. People were converted in the meetings and one lady who had been saved brought a friend who, in turn, brought another. The atmosphere seemed a little warmer to the faithful few as people were led to the Lord. The following February, they intended to hold a special outreach with Pastor Douglas Scott who had been conducting campaigns in Italy and France with some success.

The campaign was judged a success as between twenty and forty attended each night. While there were no outward decisions for the Lord, there were some healings both during the campaign and afterwards. One man came in dragging his foot and saying that he couldn't sit down for more than a few minutes at a time. Mr. Scott prayed for him before the service started and he sat right through and after having hands laid on him the second time, he went away walking normally. Another little boy aged about three appeared to have meningitis and was rushed to hospital but, after prayer, made a complete recovery. His father had been studying to become a spiritist medium but afterwards confessed that his child was alive as an answer to prayer.

The development of the work was slow but sure. Believers were being baptised and ones and twos were finding Christ. Fellowship was being encouraged and the church would travel to nearby towns for Conventions. Open airs were held prior to the Gospel services so that others might be encouraged to attend and other towns were being targeted with the Gospel. Families were coming to faith in Christ and being set free from the benighted state that they had lived in for most of their lives.

While the Evans family was home on furlough in 1951, their place was taken by Miss Cynthia Partridge, then a candidate for Elim Missions, who stayed on for a period after their return. She had visited a home in one of the villages and heard about a small girl of four and a half years old who was in hospital dying from food poisoning. The child and her family were not known to the missionaries but they felt in their hearts that they should visit. Nine doctors had already said that nothing could be done to save her. The child was prayed for and immediately began to improve. She was sent home shortly afterwards and it was hoped that her miraculous recovery would provide an entrance into her home with the Gospel.

In 1954, Tom Evans was able to re-open the church at Haine St. Pierre. This had been started by Archie Scott but had closed shortly after the onset of hostilities during the Second World War, the congregation being cared for by a local brother. Since the War, the hall had been used for a variety of purposes, but the way had opened up for a resumption of church services. With the help of Christians from surrounding villages, the hall was prepared and services began again on 14th November. Some of the old members were still around and rejoiced at the renewal of the work.

Meanwhile, the work at Verviers was also experiencing a measure of blessing and souls were being saved in both places. While Tom was ministering in one place, his wife was looking after the other and they were being blessed in their labours.

In 1965, a young man from Essex went to Belgium to work and to seek to serve the Lord. He was Mike Williams, a 'graduate' of the Elim church in Pitsea where Bill West had taught and trained him since his conversion. His main contact in Belgium was through the European Evangelistic Society, but that ceased to function shortly after his arrival. As on all mission fields, the greatest challenges were in the areas of personnel and finance. For his first seven years, Mike worked full-time in a bank, commuting daily to Brussels and, for much of that time, pastoring four churches. He also served as Protestant chaplain at Belgium's largest prison at Merksplas as well as teaching at the American Continental Bible College (AoG) near Brussels. As the churches grew, so the Lord graciously added to the number of workers. Pastor and Mrs. Boer came from Holland to look after the fledgling Duffell[viii] work; Pastor and Mrs. Van Leeuwen (Belgian/Dutch) to pioneer in Brecht. In addition, workers had been raised up from among the Belgian converts to look after the dial-a-message programme, run the monthly, duplicated church magazine, manage the book shop, distribute literature on the ships in port and assist in the prison work.

While working on lines similar to those used in the British churches, there was a great deal of hostility towards 'heretics' and Bible believers. This was made known through persecution of work mates, the virtually complete opposition of unconverted parents to their children attending meetings, the refusal of hall owners to allow their buildings to be used for evangelistic purposes, often because they dare not do so, and the crippling cost of living.

They were not put off, but were pressing forward. Negotiations were in hand for the purchase of a shop in the centre of Antwerp's shopping area for use as a Christian book shop. They were also considering the purchase of a double-decker bus so that they could use the top deck as a chapel and the lower deck as a coffee lounge and bookshop where they could hold meetings and campaigns from village to village without all the frustration of obtaining halls and permits.

They anticipated consolidating their work among ex-prisoners, opening a centre where the men could go on leaving jail. Another centre was needed for drug addicts and others in need of long term rehabilitation. Finding premises was no problem; finding the staff to look after the projects was another story. However, it was expected that Pastor and Mrs. Van Leeuwen of Lier would take on this responsibility.

The summer of 1979 saw a flurry of activity in the Belgian Elim churches. A children's camp was held on a farm in July and, later that month, a young people's camp was organised in tents in Norway. In August, a Euroteam[ix] helped with evangelism in four weeks of activity and outreach. Daily open air meetings were held, sometimes with little or no response; at other times, there were crowds of hundreds standing listening. Over 20,000 Gospel newspapers were distributed and meetings were advertised by handbills and loud-speaker vans. Three campaigns were held using a film unit hired from Holland. There was little response recorded at the time, but in the following weeks, news came in of lives that had been changed.

By 1980, it was possible to give an overview of the development of the work. Belgium was seen as Britain's nearest mission field. It had a proportion of evangelicals to the population about the same as that in Asia. Its former colony, then Zaire, had two hundred times more believers than Belgium itself. At this time, there were seven prospering Elim churches in a land with a population of some 10 million. Fifty seven percent of the people were Flemish speaking, and the Elim work was concentrated in Flemish areas. The only Flemish Pentecostal magazine was published by the Elim church in Belgium.

Two years before, two brothers who were involved in the printing and newspaper industry had begun the *Icthus* magazine. While they were based on the assembly at Kortrijk, all the Elim churches helped with the costs and distribution. Each church was given a back page in succeeding issues so that they could highlight their local activities. A further milestone occurred in late 1979 when the Belgian government officially recognised the Elim churches and this gave pastors as well as churches additional rights in terms of hospital and school visitation.

Early in 1980, the dial-a-message ministry was recommenced and the ministry to sailors and lorry drivers was ongoing. A new Christian bookshop was opened in Antwerp and was doing a brisk trade from the beginning. It was on a central site and was close to four occult bookshops where satanic rites were practised. But the Gospel was not bound and people were being touched by it and the Pentecostal message, some for the first time in their lives.

One of the churches, in Duffel, was just about one hour's drive from Antwerp. In one of its quaint streets was a café called "The Saving Angel". But behind this innocent name lay a den of iniquity which was notorious for drink, drugs and many other questionable activities. But almost next door to it, another shop has been transformed and in its window there were Christian books about real angels, posters and tracts speaking about a Saviour for the world.

Inside was a room for Pentecostal worship and another became a Christian coffee bar reaching out to the needy customers next door. Further along the street, there was an exciting extension to the ministry. A rambling terraced three storey property, with a cellar and a large garden, had been set up for the rehabilitation of ex-prisoners. One of the early inmates was Raymond. He was an alcoholic who had not responded to medical treatment and had been incarcerated several times for violent behaviour.

It looked as though he would be returned to prison when he was excluded from his parents' home, but the police sent him to see Pastor Boer, the pastor of the Elim Church in Duffel, to see if he could help. He found Christ and was set free from drink and brawling, but he had another problem – epilepsy. One Sunday, he asked for prayer for healing. At the time, he had broken his leg in two places and was to be in plaster for a six week period.

Pastor Boer prayed for his whole body to be healed and, after prayer, Raymond showed that the cast on his leg had split. The next day, he went back to the hospital to have it renewed but before doing so, the hospital took further x-rays of his leg. The doctor said there was no need for a new plaster – his leg had healed. God touched his whole body and set him free from his epilepsy as well. In a campaign following this time, his brother, Vic, came to know the Lord and was baptised by Pastor Boer. Another baptismal candidate was a Russian immigrant lady.

Later in 1980, the ministry team in Belgium was augmented by Phil Gray, a young man from Wales. Phil's burden for Belgium led him to volunteer for one of the Euroteams and following that experience, his burden for the country had grown. Not only so, but while on the team, he met Barbara, a Glasgow girl who had been working as secretary to Mike Williams on a six month placement because of the shortage of Christian workers. Barbara became Phil's wife and they worked together in the towns of Lier and Nijlen. This area of the work was helped when EWMA[X] sent a new printing press for the production of Christian literature. A retired printer in the district used it to great advantage and it was seldom idle.

Euroteams continued to make an impact with groups once again, in 1982, going into the Belgian towns and witnessing to the Gospel. The centres were to be Lier and Antwerp and, in Lier, the authorities had given permission for a film truck to be parked in the centre of the town. Gospel film outreach would occupy the team for much of their time. The Belgian churches were continually looking for ways to expand the work. In April, 1982, a crusade in Roeselare encouraged the saints there while a further crusade was planned for Hoogstraten the following September.

Meanwhile, the work in Antwerp continued to present challenges to the church there. To meet some of those, a new building was required and in June, 1983, Elim in

Belgium found an 'old' new home. In a grand opening service, an alderman of the city brought greetings from the City Council, the first time ever that a Pentecostal church in Flanders had been given such recognition. Representatives of the fellowship that had once met in the building and had now amalgamated with the Elim congregation also took part, together with the International Missions Director, Brian Edwards.

This move, after only eight years in their former church, was brought about by a growth of 500% in the congregation so that they had standing room only on many occasions in the converted furniture shop they had used for a church. Searching for alternative premises had proved wearing because of the exorbitant prices of property in central Antwerp. Reluctantly, they were about to sign a lease on a dance hall, but God had other plans for them. Before they could sign the lease, they were approached by a group who didn't know them to ask if they would be interested in buying their building. Having inspected it, they liked what they saw, understood the Lord's leading and purchased it.

It was a 'real' church – not a converted shop or house, and that was very rare. At the time, it was just 50 years old and had ancillary rooms that made it a very desirable property, with seating for three hundred people. Although a little way out of the City centre, the transport service was excellent with buses and trams. Because the church's membership had dwindled and was now mostly elderly people, the building had been neglected and required extensive refurbishment, but the Elim members worked to make it right for the opening.

After the church moved into the building, they discovered that there were ties back to Elim from about 1926 when Pastor George Jeffreys had held a mission and the converts formed the nucleus of the church. However, contact seemed to have been lost during the late thirties, as did the Pentecostal experience and message. Another fascinating fact presented itself as well. It appears that the building was used by the occupying German forces for services, but what they didn't know was that they were being listened to by fugitive Jews who had been hidden in the attics by church members. The decline in church membership opened the way for Elim to have an excellent building just at the right time.

With the development of the work, there was always a need for workers and, in 1983, an appeal was made to young people in the UK to give a year of their time to help in the service of the Master in Belgium. Richard and Myrtle Clarke from the Ulster Temple in Belfast responded to this call and served for a number of years in Kontich, seeking to establish a work there while holding membership in the Antwerp church. Richard's practical skills had been extremely helpful during the renovations of the Antwerp building.

Leo and Hazel Maeckelberghe took over the works at Nijlen and Lier, while the Grays moved to the pastorate at Roeselare. Leo is Belgian and comes from Bruges, while his wife hails from Carrickfergus in Northern Ireland. They had pastored for some time in the UK before applying to the International Missions Board for a posting to the Continent. Initially, on their arrival, Leo held down a position with the largest transport and shipping company in Belgium, while Hazel upgraded her nursing qualifications by working eight nights per fortnight back in Dover. Such pressure can only be imagined, but it was not to last too long. Hazel returned full time to work in Belgium and Leo started teaching protestant religion in state schools. His job was peripatetic and he toured five different schools to teach ages 12-16. This meant that evenings and school holidays were now free and they looked to the Lord to do something new in Lier and Nijlen. Their desire was always to share the Gospel and the Lord opened the door for them to do this as they continued to serve Him.

i The early name for the Jehovah Witnesses.

ii The Missionary Secretary for Elim at that time.

iii It was a missionary box opening service addressed also by Miss Henderson making an appeal for funds.

iv Sister Marie was known in the church as The Fat Lady!

v Bro' Viquerat was a Swiss evangelist.

vi *Elim Evangel,* Volume 25, Issue 42, page 329. The date was October, 1944.

vii Woodlands was the official address name of the Elim Bible College in London.

viii See chapter on Euroteams for references.

ix See chapter on Euroteams.

x Elim Women's Missionary Auxiliary.

CHAPTER 4

ELIM RELIEF ASSOCIATION (ERA)

Elim missionaries have always been conscious of the need to minister to the whole man. That is why much of their labours have included schools, clinics and hospitals. While recognising the preëminence of the gospel, there has also been an acknowledgement that the hungry and distressed find it difficult to appreciate the spiritual when the physical is so pressing.

Against this background, it was felt by the IMB[i] that Elim should have its own relief arm for raising funds and distributing help when urgent needs presented themselves. The work of the ERA when it was launched after the Italian earthquake was indeed a new 'era' in Elim International Missions.

Following the Italian disaster in November 1980 that devastated southern Italy, there was a tremendous response from Elim people all over the UK. As a result, convoys of caravans were taken to the mountainous region around Naples. This was the earliest opportunity for the new venture. Brian Edwards, then European Director for the IMB, reported:

On the evening of Sunday, November 23rd, the seismological machines across the European earthquake belt jumped horrifically into action. Within seconds, the alarm was out - a major earthquake had taken place rating seven on the Richter scale in some places, but right off the scale at the centre. The news broadcasts indicated thousands dead, tens of thousands made homeless and countless people injured.

The ugly pieces of the jigsaw began to fall into place forming a picture of human misery, pain and bereavement. Then across the flickering screens of our TV sets came the first traumatic pictures of this, one of Europe's greatest natural disasters. Buildings, which moments before had housed precious Italian families, were now transformed into tombs. All that was left was a mound of rubble.

Meanwhile, the great Elim family had responded to the heart-rending news. A letter went to the churches telling of the many Pentecostal believers in that area who, in a moment, were now bereaved, homeless and broken. Offers of blankets, sleeping bags and clothing poured into the International office. At this stage, we did not know what would be the greatest need since reports in the media were confusing. No-one seemed to be really clear what the position was.

As soon as possible, I telephoned Rome and spoke with brother Francesco Toppi, one of the Pentecostal leaders in Italy. Very soon, we were in direct contact with Naples where an organising committee to relieve the Pentecostal victims was already being formed. Over a bad continental line, the picture began to take shape. What was needed most urgently was some form of instant house.

As I looked at the television pictures of the makeshift tented villages, it was obvious that this was far from adequate protection against the freezing and snowy wintry weather of southern Italy. The thought of caravans flashed across my mind and, within minutes, I was on the phone to Italy again with the suggestion that we should bring them homes on wheels and give them to the stricken families. The response was positive: "Just what we need", and so, "Operation Earthquake Relief" began to move into top gear.

After a quick consultation with David Ayling, the International Missions Director, it was agreed that we should proceed as quickly as possible. Phone calls to experts in the caravan market produced immediate help and soon eight caravans were ready to go. The big question was how to get them there in the shortest possible time. But we needn't have worried. Before very long, we had enough volunteers and vehicles to do the job.

To drive through Italy is expensive, not only because of the price of petrol but also because of the cost of the Channel crossing and toll roads in France and Italy itself. But the Lord was with us and we had good co-operation at all levels. The Italian embassy issued us with the necessary documents and a special letter of authorisation which meant we could travel all the way through France and Italy without paying any of the tolls. Townsend Thoresen, the Channel ferry company, offered to take the drivers and vehicles free of charge and so this major operation gained momentum. Other companies supplied necessary goods to take with us.

By Saturday morning, after four hectic days of preparation, we were ready to leave and soon a convoy of caravans was on its way to Portsmouth docks. The Elim Bible College minibus met us there, packed with relief materials. Boarding the Viking Venturer was the beginning of a 1500 mile drive to Italy and, for many, it was a first time for towing a caravan as well as for driving on the 'wrong' side of the road.

Conditions were extreme, with ice and snow covering some roads. All went well on the first day, but then disaster struck. One of the vehicles towing a caravan was struck by a gust of wind on the brow of a hill and went out of control, jack-knifed and was wrecked. The drivers were uninjured and the towing car was still drivable. It was a miracle that no-one else was hurt. Later, conditions worsened and we faced blizzards and freezing weather during the night. Finally, at 2 a.m., weary and exhausted, we stopped to rest.

Further down the road, we came across another of God's miracles as we met a family that had seen the pictures on television and were towing their own personal caravan to the area. It normally stood unused except for two weeks in the year, so they were donating it to help to meet the needs. Some time later, this same family stopped us to ask if they could join our convoy and donate their caravan to the people we were going to help. We had lost one caravan on the way and now the Lord was giving us a bigger and better one in its place.

After some 50 hours driving, we drew near to the disaster area and were beginning to see other relief vehicles. We began to see damaged houses, shattered roofs, just a foretaste of the devastation that was to confront us when we arrived in the main earthquake area south of Naples. It was so cold when we awoke in the morning that the insides of the caravan windows were covered in ice and we began to realise something of what it must be like for the victims.

At the end of the autostrada, we were met by the son of one of the leaders of the work who guided us across the city. It was an absolute nightmare taking the convoy through the narrow, potholed streets of this ancient metropolis. At times, the noise was deafening, first because of the traffic jam we were causing, but also because the people of Naples were thrilled to see this provision being made by the Pentecostal people of the UK. We eventually arrived at a huge factory belonging to a Pentecostal family. They had given it over for storage of materials and other help for the victims. They had also given up their homes to help. At 7 o'clock the following morning, on a gloriously bright day, although the temperature was well below freezing, we gathered to prepare to deliver the first group of caravans.

In the village of Caltiri, we saw the devastation at first hand. In places the road had been pulled away from the buildings and had sunk by about two metres. This was where families would now live in caravans for the remainder of the winter. As we travelled on towards the epicentre, the village of Lioni, we thought we had seen the worst devastation, but this village reminded us of scenes from the World War Two blitz. Vast areas were completely levelled. Four storey buildings had become just mounds of rubble. On the faces of the people we saw despair and anguish, some still waiting for bodies of loved ones to be removed.

This was our last call in a long and harrowing day as we drove through the streets with coffins stacked by the side of the road. It was a day none of us would easily forget.

The giving of the Elim family at that time amounted to over £38,000, a clear indication that there is a well of giving in the hearts of the Elim people that can be touched with the infirmities of others.[ii]

This was the first major demand on the new relief organisation within Elim. Following the visit of the caravan convoy, the story receded so far as the media were concerned. The deaths and broken lives became just another statistic. The German army that had worked so tirelessly to rescue and relieve the victims moved back to its base and even some relief organisations redirected their operations to new and demanding areas. At that time, Elim and Assemblies of God in the UK provided over £100,000 worth of aid. Over 300 families were left homeless and without possessions or clothing apart from what they wore.

For this reason, a relief committee was established to ensure that supplies reached their intended destination. A distribution centre was set up and a brother from Holland became the resident administrator. Sectional homes were found and transported speedily to Lioni on articulated lorries that were a nightmare to drive in the terrain around the village.

Once these had been delivered and erected, there was a thanksgiving service for all that God had done through the efforts of brothers and sisters in Christ. As a result of all the efforts, the Pentecostal testimony in Italy was greatly enhanced. So much so that the following year, the Chairman of the International Missions Board, Wesley Gilpin, was entertained by one family that had lost all but their faith in the disaster. They shared a meal in one of the caravans. It was small, but it was comfortable and it was home.

Later, in a visit to Conza del Compiana, he saw the shell of what had been the church where six people had died and six more had been pulled out alive. By then, a new church had been built and around 300 people were worshipping. The young Pentecostal pastor showed him around and asked him to thank the Elim people for their love and concern. "I was there and saw it," he said.

Some time later, in 1981, Brian Edwards visited Poland and was staggered by the desperate economic situation which had resulted in the widespread threat of malnutrition. Not only was there little or no food in the shops, but the military government was unable to supply the meagre rations that were introduced a few months previously. Before Christmas, the shops were already one month behind in supplying the family rations and it was, by then, almost impossible to obtain baby food or medical supplies. An appeal was made and, besides the response of individuals and churches, Johnson & Johnson supplied quantities of baby and medical supplies and Wyeth provided powdered milk. In consultation with David Ayling, a scheme was set up to send out food parcels. Brian described what he saw as he drove through the countryside:

Every town I drove through there were queues for food. I've seen queues before, but nowhere as big as these. There are ration books for just about everything. For many, there is no meat, cooking oil, margarine or flour. On some days, not even bread is available to buy.

In Warsaw, where goods are usually much easier to obtain, I saw a queue a quarter of a mile long which was four deep in places. They were lining up on the strength of a rumour that one of the shops was going to have a delivery of food.

Brian had taken with him a quantity of food from the Northampton church as well as from the International office. Because of his contacts, he arranged for the Elim food parcels to be distributed to Pentecostals by 46 pastors and church leaders. At the same time, a music group from the Portsmouth church arranged a tour of Poland and filled their coach with foodstuffs. By the time it was ready to leave (6th December in time for Christmas) six tons of supplies had been loaded and the church paid the costs involved in transport.

Despite the industrial and political unrest, the Polish church was continuing to grow. The pressure on the church and its leaders had diminished considerably. Each year, the Polish Pentecostals were allowed to print a number of Christian books and publications, although their proposals had to be agreed in advance. It was usual for the quota applied for to be reduced by half, but even this had eased and they were granted permission to print 100% of what they planned.

Sometimes we think of relief work as meeting only the physical needs of the people, but the experiences of the past two years showed that practical expressions of God's love often result in great spiritual harvests. It came to be seen that in meeting basic human needs, another evangelistic arm had been added to our outreach. In Lodz, 40 new converts were baptised.

The Polish people were always overjoyed to see lorries arrive laden with food and medical supplies. The local authorities were so impressed that when a pastor in the northern town of Koszalin asked permission to use the municipal swimming pool for a baptismal service, they readily agreed.

In 1983, the programme was taken forward by co-ordinating those who had an interest in Poland and were willing to help. A meeting in Graham Street church, Birmingham brought a number of interested individuals together and "Help Feed Poland" was born. The first convoy consisted of vans from Graham Street, Stirchley, Cardiff and the Portsmouth coach. John Coleman, then the pastor in Stirchley, tells of the adventures of their travels. He said:

This was the fourth visit of the Portsmouth brethren. Tribute must be paid to their tremendous sense of humour and dynamic enthusiasm for the cause of Christ. It was an education to me to see Terry(from Portsmouth) in action at border posts. What a Pompeyite can accomplish with limited German-Polish and glorious gesticulations accompanied by waving papers under the noses of bewildered border guards has to be seen to be believed.

One incident stands out. At the East German - Polish border[iii], some of us sat in the coach while waiting for the other members to deal with the paperwork required by the border officials. Facing the coach was a notice board on which was posted a map of Poland indicating the main roads and railways. Suddenly, Barry said, "Look at the Lord's face!" We followed the direction of his pointing finger. Amazingly, the black and red lines formed clearly, though unintentionally, the features of Christ with beard and crown of thorns as usually portrayed by artists.

In the following year, despite war in the South Atlantic and the Middle East, Poland continued to struggle. The situation there was growing worse all the time and it seemed that the Government and people were unable to cope. As always, the young, the old and the sick were most vulnerable. The media were reporting shortages of milk in many areas, lack of nutritious food coupled with an almost total lack of necessary medical supplies, like syringes and plaster-of-paris, antibiotics, pain killers and the most basic sterilised items necessary for surgery.

To date, ERA had supplied well over a quarter of a million pounds worth of medical supplies, food, clothing and footwear. The operations covered from the Baltic in the north to the Soviet Union in the east and Czechoslovakia in the south. The Polish authorities were always most helpful in allowing the material to be delivered where we proposed. Not only so, but this also resulted in tremendous spiritual blessing and help for churches in that land, as local congregations shared their benefits with neighbours throughout their cities and towns.

The people of Romania were no better off, and many were now facing tremendous shortages of food and many other commodities with all the suffering and hardship that famine in a modern society brings.

Although the Elim Relief Association was born out of need close to hand in Europe, it responded to cries for help in other parts of the world. The Honduran airlift helped to bring joy and relief to orphans housed in the orphanage at the Valley of the Angels near Tegucigalpa, the capital. This included food, clothing and toys as well.

On the continent of Africa, aid was airlifted to Ghana with drugs for the mobile clinics and essential foodstuffs. The possibility existed of developing an agricultural programme in conjunction with our sister fellowship, the Church of Pentecost. Equipment for hospitals was also on the shopping list.

An ongoing area of concern has been Ethiopia and Sudan, initially because of the ravages of drought, but lately, because of war and genocide, and help has been sent over a number of years. Rwanda also found itself in dire need after the war between the Hutu and Tutsi tribes and help was made available.

The story of the Rwandan Refugee will illustrate the nature of the need that ERA tries to help.

Abeli Gashagari[iv] was a tall, slim man with an Abraham Lincoln beard. His face, open and with deep-set dark eyes, beamed as he spoke with intensity in response to the many questions being fired at him. His brown suit was neat, if a little short in the leg, his shirt was clean, his tie subdued; his shoes showed signs of wear but were shining. Nothing externally marked the fact that these were the only clothes he possessed and that he was a tragic widower from the Rwandan war that had already created thousands of refugees.

As a pastor in a small group of Pentecostal churches, he had left home to find an organisation with which his churches could relate. He travelled through Kenya and Tanzania and came, eventually, to Tabora, just inside Tanzania near its border with Rwanda, where he met a pastor in the Elim Churches who supplied him with a copy of the church's Constitution. Having read it, he decided that this was what he had been seeking.

Tragically, while he was out of the country, violence erupted in Rwanda and when he sought to return, he got as far as Kigali and could go no further. The border had been closed and he was stranded. He was unable to gain any knowledge whatever of his family. After a few days, the border was reopened and the flood of refugees began. Rapidly, the landscape became dotted with sheets of blue UN plastics as people sought to establish themselves in an identifiable space.

Abeli began to make his way through the crowds looking for someone he might know, and members of his family in particular. He found his sister first and then he came across a nephew who was able to tell him that his wife and children were all dead, hacked to pieces, massacred by the Watusi. God gave him the grace to realise that he could do nothing for his natural family so he continued his daily forays into the camp looking for members of the church family. Within a short period of time, he came across six pastors and 77 church members, so he began ministering to them.

The Tanzanian church, although very poor itself, gave what help they could but against such a massive need, it seemed so little. Nevertheless, what was given provided an incentive to others and Abeli soon had organised a church in the camp. Within just a few years, there were over fifty churches scattered throughout the camps and help was given through Tanzania to get them established. These are the kinds of situations that ERA is involved in and the help given, although sometimes it seems relatively small, can make a tremendous impact on a needy people, not only in the natural, but in the spiritual as well.

The work of ERA is ongoing with ever greater demands being made upon it. The Elim people throughout the country continue to respond to the disasters that touch our world and we are able to target with a measure of precision those areas where our aid would be most useful.

i IMB – International Missions Board. The old Missionary Society was renamed.

ii This report appeared in the *Elim Evangel* Vol.62, Issue 3, p.6-9.

iii It should be remembered that Communism was still a vital force and the Berlin Wall still stood at that time.

iv The full story of Abeli Gashagari was featured in the *Elim Evangel.* It transpired that, in 2002, information became available that Abeli's wife had not in fact perished in the genocide. She had been misplaced in a Congolese refugee camp and returned with her two children to find that he had remarried. This obviously presented the Rwandan church with great disturbance and a difficulty which was dealt with by Ayubu Mgweno, then chairman of the East African region.

CHAPTER 5

EUROPE

In 1978, the International Missions Director, Leslie Wigglesworth, retired from office and, while doing so, made a proposal to the General Conference that a Missions Director for Europe should be appointed. The Executive Council, with the IMB, felt very much that the guidance and direction of the Holy Spirit were needed to find ways of meeting the great needs that were evident throughout Europe. The challenge of Eastern Europe, the rising influence in the remainder of Europe of anti-God political forces, the awakening as to opportunities in Spain deeply exercised the whole fellowship at that time.

So it was with a sense of God's clear direction that Brian G. Edwards, then minister of the Elim Church in Derby, was appointed full-time Missions Director for Europe. Brian was a man with Europe on his heart. A Council member for the European Evangelistic Society(EES)[i] and well-travelled throughout Europe on preaching and teaching tours, not least to Eastern Europe, he was well-fitted for the task. His own ministry in the homeland had been honoured by God since Bible College days in 1956 and he had been used to win souls and bring others into the Baptism in the Holy Spirit. His passion for Europe was well known and it was evident that God had been preparing him for this role.

The Executive presented this to the Movement as Eurovision[ii] and emphasised that it would be very much a pioneering work. For some years, the IMB had adopted a stance that overseas works should be fundamentally indigenous, and this was no less so in Europe. In most cases, therefore, the object would not be to open churches, but to support and facilitate those national works which were in sympathy with our aims and were happy for us to work in partnership with them. It was recognised from the beginning that the great need would be for Bible teaching and ministry. The prospects for development were exciting and deeply challenging, and the whole Movement was invited to participate by prayer and giving.

The primary thrust of the Mission, initially, was into Eastern Europe and a pledge was made to support and help brothers and sisters in the Soviet bloc countries. It was obvious that their needs were tremendous, while their resources were totally limited. In the midst of great darkness, there was an opportunity to shed the light of the Gospel.

The policy was to work with existing Pentecostal churches in East European countries, supporting them with Bibles, literature and other projects that presented themselves. A major consideration at that time was that the relationship between Church and State in many countries was better than it had been for some time. Doors which had been closed for ages now stood ajar; doors that had been ajar were now standing wide open.

One token of this openness was that Bibles were being supplied to believers in Russia, Romania and other countries with the full permission of the authorities concerned.

The intention was to continue to seek permission openly for such projects and then seeing them through by prayer and giving.

In June, 1978, John Wildrianne, Brian Edwards, John Cuthbert and Wynne Lewis undertook an extensive tour of Hungary and Romania. Their main purpose was to visit and minister to the churches in Romania and this they did with great acceptance. In two weeks they travelled more than five thousand miles by car over roads that were less than smooth. In all places they were impressed by the attitudes of the people and were greatly blessed by their reception. Summing up the visit, Wynne Lewis said,

During this visit, we didn't only visit the capitals and big centres of population, but we went to many small villages. There were no restrictions placed on our movements, we were free to meet and talk to the people. We questioned both people and pastors and found that they were not restricted at all by the authorities. They were free to preach the Word of God. It simply wasn't true to say that churches in Eastern Europe were full of elderly ladies. There were just as many men as ladies and, wherever we went, a large proportion of the congregations were made up of young people. Scores of children were also present in every church and in Margina, each of us had the added pleasure of dedicating a child during the service.[iii]

In late 1978, a new electronic organ was delivered to the site of the Sebastian Street church in Bucharest. This had been purchased by the Elim Youth Movement and served to enhance the fellow-feeling that existed then between Elim and the Romanian churches. The obvious joy and pleasure of the pastor and his people as the organ was unloaded brought tears to the eyes of those present, while the visitors from the UK were amazed to see young boys carrying wood for the building to the men who were putting on the roof on scaffolding 70 feet high. A team of old mothers were sitting there straightening nails to be used in the building of their church. When completed, this would be the first church built in Bucharest since the Second World War. The crowd included men and women of all ages. The fact that other believers, beyond the barriers and controls, cared enough to share in the burden of establishing this new church under such trying circumstances, gave new strength and vision for the tasks ahead. The new organ would be a fitting instrument for praise in the new sanctuary.

The visit to Romania also coincided with the commencement of the Bible College year, so the team were able to share in the opening services and joined the faculty for the Monday lectures. This section of the Romanian work was led by Professor Sandru, who was also the pastor of the church. The college then had 15 students training for ministry. Over the years, Elim had supplied this institution with theological books and other materials so that, at that time, there was a fairly substantial library available. All the students were supplied with a Thompson Chain Reference Bible, which was an invaluable study aid, and it was hoped that this ministry could be extended to other Bible students and pastors in Eastern Europe. Most were poverty stricken in many ways, including the basic necessities for Bible study, and appeals were made to churches in the UK to help to provide finance to further this work.

One of the greatest needs of the time was the provision of Bibles and an appeal was made for churches and individuals to supply the needed capital. Permission had been granted to import 7,000 Bibles, 2,000 Greek Lexicons into Romania as well as 25,000 Bibles and 5,000 Concordances into Russia. Needless to say, there was an exuberant response and the needs were met.

In 1980, the new church in Sebastian Street was completed and officially opened. Brian Edwards, the European Director, was present for the occasion and heard of the appreciation expressed for all the support and help that had been given from Elim in the UK. He was able to report that the outpouring of the Holy Spirit was continuing in the country and that churches were being opened and buildings erected in spite of, in many cases, opposition from the authorities. In five years, more than 200 churches had been established and in ten years, 20 new places of worship had been erected. Someone asked him why there was revival in such places. Could it be the result of persecution? Brian's reply was that the people were hungry for God and willing to give Him everything. Maybe that's a lesson we all need to learn.

The rich and evident blessing on the churches was not conducive to good relations with the government, however, and, within a few years, oppression increased and restrictions were being placed on the various churches. By 1987, visitors were being harassed at the airport and Romanian Bibles were confiscated. Churches were being denied development permission and planning approvals were becoming increasingly difficult to obtain. Hotel rooms were bugged by camera and microphone. A delegation representing CSI[iv] found themselves under inspection by the Secret Police and the local pastors were asking that their plight be publicised in the West, as that seemed to be the only thing that raised any kind of interest. The difficulties facing the Pentecostal churches were highlighted by the fact that there were 1000 congregations but only 200 ministers. The Government had allocated only three places to the Pentecostals at the Theological Seminary for the following four years. It was obvious that the Government was trying to deny the Church suitable leaders.

On another Elim delegation visit, time was spent with the Pentecostal churches of East Germany. It was the occasion of their Jubilee services, as they celebrated the founding of their church under a former regime when there had been a great deal of persecution. They were obliged to operate under the auspices of the Union of Evangelical Churches and, for many years, had experienced very little growth. There were very few full time pastors and this, in itself, was a hindrance to progress. But young men were being trained and their Pentecostal fire and testimony were evident even although they were often exposed to anti-Pentecostal teaching. In spite of all the problems, there were clear signs of blessing among the believers.

The church in Wilkau Hablau was packed to capacity for the services with many young people present. Elders who had helped to found the work gave testimony and one of these had been present in a seminar held in East Berlin on the subject of the Person and Work of the Holy Spirit. He exclaimed, "These seminars marked the beginning of a new Pentecost for our churches."

In a nearby town of Zwickau, there was a large house that had been converted into a church. The local congregation numbered around 300. The entrance area was used to display Christian literature and the main sanctuary was upstairs and had been beautifully arranged and decorated. Some fifty kilometres away was the city of Karl-Marx-Stadt with its ultra-modern centre; a bustling and important political venue. Some years previously, a church had taken over a building which began as a restaurant, but just recently had had to be extended. The congregation there had grown to over 200. Then pastor Hamble, a young man, told of a new move of the Spirit in the town. Once a month, over five thousand young people would meet on a Saturday night for a rally in a large Lutheran building right in the city centre. God was evidently moving despite all the limitations of the political scene and His Word was not bound. Recognising the needs of the situation, Elim churches responded to the call to provide resources to help to maintain the works in these needy areas.

One of the main changes made possible by Eurovision was that, whereas before, people could send support to Eastern Europe only through recognised agencies, which were usually not Pentecostal, they were now able to do so through our own agency, sure that their contributions were going to the Pentecostal people in Europe.

But the burden was not only for Eastern Europe. Many west European countries had not been fully exposed to the challenges of the Gospel. Many large cities across Europe had little or no evangelical witness and certainly no Pentecostal witness. The brethren in these countries had struggled to be faithful in the establishing of Pentecostal works and Eurovision meant support for them in their labours.[v]

The result of all this activity was that the Church was growing. Reports were coming in that buildings were being developed throughout Russia, Poland, East Germany, Hungary, Romania and Yugoslavia. It seemed that the Lord of the Harvest was opening doors and presenting the Church with unprecedented opportunities.

Because of this developing situation and the limitations of basic commodities, Eurovision supplied many of the practical needs to help the Church to grow. By 1979, the EES had ceased to operate and Eurovision and Action Europe[vi] were the only agencies then supporting the Pentecostal believers in Eastern Europe.

On a wider front, there were also major developments. Brian was visiting extensively and therefore able to supply firsthand information. A Conference for East and West European Church leaders was planned in Vienna, with Ron Jones as the keynote speaker. At home, plans were laid for Euroteams[vii] to make short term visits during the summer months to European churches and offer ministry and support. In Poland, some Pentecostal musicians and vocalists made a master tape from which records were pressed and the sales were a source of revenue for the very poor churches. Churches in the UK were invited to buy two, one for themselves and one to send back to Poland. The project of sending Bibles to Russia and Romania was going ahead and gifts were being received regularly to help with the costs.

In 1961, a young man from Poland, Edward Czajko, received a free scholarship to a college in Bristol and, while there, associated himself with the Bristol City Temple. He was quite clear that this had a significant impact on his spiritual well-being and he maintained contact with the Bristol ministers on his return home.

As a result, Ron Jones and Wynne Lewis, then minister in Derby, were invited to visit. Their tour brought them into contact with various groups of believers, including Brethren, Church of Christ, an evangelical church and two Pentecostal churches. They ministered throughout the country, beginning in Warsaw, then split up and travelled east and to the south-west. They were happy to see packed congregations and decisions being made on a regular basis. Services tended to begin at 6 p.m. with no closing time scheduled.

In 1981, it was a special joy for Ron Jones to meet again the young man he had pastored twenty years before as he met him at Warsaw airport Customs. Arriving at 5.10 p.m., Edward told Ron quietly that he was to preach at a service commencing at 6 p.m. This was held in the Pentecostal church's headquarters chapel at Zagorna. There were few empty seats, no hats and no music, but the congregation, keen for the Word of God, had many young people in it, some of whom responded to the invitation.

Later, Ron was to visit Gdansk, about 1250 miles north of Warsaw, where he met a 74 year old pastor who had spent two years in prison for his faith many years before. He had been pastor of the church since 1948. All told, at that time, there were about 60 growing Pentecostal assemblies in Poland with about 6000 believers registered. The main religion was RC, but where there was a Protestant church, it was usually Pentecostal. Although there were shortages of meat, sugar, butter and other foodstuffs, the old pastor declared that their greatest need was for the Word of God.

The Elim sponsored radio programme over IBRA radio was much appreciated. Bibles were being freely printed but the need was always growing. Euroteam visits were a great help and brought tremendous blessing as did also a visit by Portsmouth's music group, Sons and Daughters. The Polish church had its own Bible school and Ron was able to meet with and minister to some of the students on his itinerary.

Around this same time, Elim International Missions decided to become involved in practical ministry to those who were in desperate need, with children reaching advanced stages of malnutrition and old and young suffering indescribable hardships. Over a period of about eighteen months, this ministry grew and made a great impact on the Polish people at all levels of society, both locally and nationally. The result was that doors opened for ministry and outreach.

Subsequently, groups travelled to the country and took with them many tons of medical equipment and basic food supplies for distribution. The equipment included two respirators for children's wards in hospitals, and their handover was recorded on Polish national television. The effect of these visits and donations was that the Polish Government was very warm towards the groups and permitted them freedom in the country and on radio and television to preach the Gospel. They were keen to recognise the work done through ERA and the visits of the Euroteams and ministry groups. This was the second time a national government had given official recognition to the Work of ERA, the first being the Italian government at the time of their earthquake.

By 1988, there were then 90 assemblies and about 10,000 adherents. The work in Poland was lively and outward-looking. Developments took place on all fronts, not least in a work to help drug addicts. This occurred around 1970. A small group of Christians had a vision to open a centre in Slupsk, northern Poland, to help to free young people bound by their addiction to drugs before their lives were totally destroyed.

The Polish Government provided premises and also helped with the refurbishment of them. The task was to take a virtually derelict building and make it fit to live in, a task requiring both muscle power and finance. In course of time, the work was almost complete and the first addicts were admitted. The centre was officially approved by the authorities and a course of rehabilitation began. The Mayor of Slupsk had also given permission for council-owned premises in the centre of the city to be used as a Christian contact centre or reading room. There was a major push to reach the population and six thousand tracts were distributed, resulting in 50 enquiries. Throughout the project, there were visits by UK based helpers and UK churches became involved at various levels.

One of the targeted countries was Czechoslovakia where conditions were far from easy. Controls and restrictions were quite severe compared with other East European countries. On a visit here, Brian found a group of believers where the congregation had grown to around 250. There was a thriving Youth work and Sunday school. Asked about their greatest need, they replied that they had enough clothes, food and a home and they were able to rent an old Lutheran building to use for church. But they desperately needed Bibles in their own language.

On his return to England, Brian contacted the Bible Society and had the joy of hearing that the Czech authorities had given permission for Bibles to be printed in Czechoslovakia on condition that the UK supply the paper. The first print run was 30,000 and it was hoped that this might rise to 100,000. The challenge then was to raise the necessary finance, estimated to be around £100,000.

Two new activities arose out of the success of the Euroteams project the previous year - Euro-Service and Euro-Link. Participants would spend an extended period of time on the Continent working with an established assembly or helping to pioneer a church. This was expected to appeal to young people willing to give a year or more of their time and would be unpaid. Euro-Link invited churches to adopt a twin church in Europe and to support it by prayer and through personal contacts by mail. Such correspondence would help to develop fellowship between believers and churches.

The EPF[viii] had been at work in Europe for many years and, with changing political climates, its vision enlarged and increased. In the Spring of 1979, it had convened a Conference in Vienna, Austria, that brought together church leaders from both east and west Europe. In the autumn of 1981, the second Conference was held, again in Vienna, when 120 delegates attended. One brother from Romania was coming out of Eastern Europe for the first time in his life. He was the pastor of a church of 2000 meeting in a beautiful building the congregation had built themselves. He was a small man in his mid-60s, but was a giant in faith.

The delegates came from Hungary, East Germany, Poland, Bulgaria and Yugoslavia. Only the brethren from Russia and Czechoslovakia were prevented from attending and all costs were covered by churches in the West.

In all, 19 countries were represented and men brought greetings from their own fellowships. The reports indicated that God was moving in mighty ways all across the Continent. While the Conference was essentially for spiritual benefit, one decision was made that would have far-reaching consequences. They decided that a radio programme reaching into Poland would be beneficial and proposed supporting such a venture. Obviously, this would mean additional considerable expense, but it represented, too, an irresistible challenge.

The development of a regular radio broadcast meant that millions who had been denied the opportunity to hear the Gospel were now being ministered to. One letter said, "This evening we listened to your broadcast which proved to be so interesting to my wife and I. (sic) We would like you to know that there are many people who live in remote areas and for them the radio is almost their only spiritual food. One week ago, a young boy was baptised who had come to know the Lord through your broadcasts."

Victor was 17, living in one of the large cities of the Soviet Union. He loved nature and this led him to ask questions about its origin. His parents, being atheists, had no answers to give him. One day, his father bought a radio and as Victor was turning the dial, he came across the Gospel broadcasts. At last, he had found answers to his questions. He was able to contact some believers and gave his life to the Lord Jesus. He was baptised along with 50 others. Now he was burdened for the salvation of his parents. Letters were received from as far away as Siberia, underlining the tremendous power of the radio work.

In 1984, Brian was able to visit Estonia, one of the independent republics of the USSR. Around that time, there had been remarkable scenes of revival with many miraculous healings recorded. At one stage, people were coming from all over the Soviet Union to visit this place and carry back with them the revival blessing and spirit that was at work. The Authorities soon put a stop to it, however, but the work went on and the blessing flowed like a river.

At that time, it was reported that there were 400,000 baptised Pentecostal believers, 70% living in the Ukraine. There were more than 20 different branches of Pentecost, many of them unregistered although well organised. The brethren told of the history of the Pentecostal Movement there, when many were imprisoned, but they rejoiced in a great revival between 1976 and 1978 when mighty miracles of healing were seen, some through the laying on of hands, some by a direct touch from the Lord.

Many of the difficulties they now faced were the result of disagreements about Scripture interpretation and the application of Spiritual Gifts. But the meeting then developed into a seminar when some of these concerns were addressed. All testified to the benefit received as a result.

Leaving Estonia, Brian then travelled to Leningrad. It was mid-winter and the only heat in the night train to Leningrad was supplied by an old lady stoking up a wood-burning stove all night long. On top of that, the carriage window was broken and Brian had the top bunk. Outside a blizzard was blowing and, to some extent, it reached inside as well.

A difficulty to be faced on arrival was finding the believers. Because of the revival, the authorities had clamped down and the activities and movements of believers, especially Pentecostals, were severely restricted. A strong sense of anti-Christ pervaded the atmosphere. But the connection with the believers was made and, over a couple of days, they received fresh input into their lives that proved to be a blessing. In fact, on the second day, one man said he had been healed during the meeting on the first day. This brother had been invalided out of work, was often breathless and in great pain and unable to walk quickly or climb stairs. Now he was saying that when he arrived at the apartment block, the lift was out of order so he had run up ten flights of stairs without any pain or breathlessness! The concluding time in Leningrad was spent working out details of keeping in contact and ensuring a positive input into the work in the future.

Those who know Brian Edwards are aware that his life was always totally eventful. Wherever he went, no matter with whom, he could always tell of an unusual happening. No one could have imagined that he could go to France, one of the most developed countries in Europe, and still find a story to tell.

MIRACLE ESCAPE FOR MISSIONS DIRECTOR: When Brian Edwards pressed the bell of the Banque Nationale de Paris in Lyons, France, little did he know that just behind him was an armed bank robber. Using Pastor Edwards as a 'front' to gain access to the otherwise locked bank, the robber opened the way for a masked accomplice to grab cash from startled employees.

Pastor Edwards was blinded with ammonia and pushed to the ground, with a sawn-off shotgun aimed at his head. Waiting in the car outside, completely unaware of the danger which threatened her husband was his wife, Barbara. Bank employees were told that if they resisted, Mr. Edwards would be killed.

This was no idle threat. Three other bank raids in the area around that time had resulted in hostages being shot. In fact, the police expected him to have been shot and killed and had brought a van to take away the body! The Inspector of Police told Brian it was a miracle he had escaped with his life. Police thought the gang was part of a guerrilla organisation seeking to increase its funds.

In making their getaway, the robbers took Pastor Edwards' jacket containing his wallet and other belongings. After a visit to the hospital to have his eyes attended to, he was able to continue his journey, shaken but thankful to God for a remarkable deliverance.

He felt that his experience was a reminder that all missionaries face danger from time to time and claim an interest in the prayers of those who support them at home.[ix]

In terms of missions, then, Europe could then be divided into three distinct areas. First, there was the vast section overshadowed by the ever-threatening clouds of communism with anti-Christian ideology. In this section, more than 1.3 billion people lived which, if Euro-Asia is included represents 33% of the world's population.

Scandinavia, although part of the European land mass, is culturally and spiritually different from the rest of Europe. For the most part, it is strongly evangelical and has had a lively Pentecostal witness for many years.

The rest of Europe was dominated by Roman Catholic hierarchical influence that tended to stifle, wherever possible, the evangelical and Pentecostal witness. In some places, the Orthodox Church was extremely strong. In Greece, for example, it held sway and influence for a long time, resulting in much persecution for churches that preached the full Gospel of the Lord Jesus Christ. Preachers and missionaries were put in jail just for preaching the Gospel. In spite of this, the work in Thessaloniki led by Phil Sidiropoulos was blessed of God as people found Christ and were baptised. Some were filled with the Holy Spirit and the church was active in spreading the Word. At one stage, over 500 families had been visited and tracts, New Testaments and Gospels were given freely because of the tremendous need created by an almost total ignorance of the Gospel. Growth in the church pushed them to seek their own premises since the rent for the building they had been using had increased by 40%.

So often, the thought of persecution and imprisonment is confined to our ideas about the Eastern bloc countries. It is clear, however, that some communities were taking an increasingly hard line with evangelicals.

Apart from in Orthodox Greece, Elim was at work in some of the most militant Roman Catholic countries. In Belgium, Mike and Colette Williams and Phil and Barbara Gray, with an increasing number of Belgian pastors, were working through Elim Churches to spread the Gospel. The Antwerp church saw great growth and was able to begin ministry to East European countries as an outreach mainly through distributing literature to sailors in port.

One of the ramifications of the European Common Market was that the Republic of Ireland was seen as a European country and it was decided that it should come under the aegis of the International Mission Board. For a short period of time, therefore, the Missions Board took over the running of the work in the Republic of Ireland but, because of the nature of the existing long term relationship with Northern Ireland, this was not particularly successful and the Elim churches in Northern Ireland took back the oversight of the ministry there. This had always been seen as a missionary endeavour and financial support was drawn from the North over a long period of time. In recent years, this work has been becoming more self-sufficient and is working with its own field council under the general oversight of the Irish Executive.

There was a measure of co-operation with churches and personnel in France. For a time, a work was done among Tamil people in the Paris area and a work existed mainly among drug addicts and dropouts who congregated in their tens of thousands in southern France. This work was cared for by Gaston Claudel. Although this was in many ways a multi-national ministry, the vast majority of those helped were French nationals. Literally hundreds of lives were revolutionised and rehabilitated through the ministry.

Not so far away, in north-east Spain, Andy and Yolanda Smith were pioneering for Christ, helped for a short time by Isobel Stormont. Two churches were established, one at Figueras and the other at Llanca. They enjoyed input from the Euroteams. Still in the Iberian peninsula, the west European work continued in Portugal. The Portuguese work had input from the UK from time to time. Pastor John Fry regularly travelled to Portugal and had contacts there with Pentecostal believers and a Pentecostal evangelist who was willing to work to establish a local Elim Church. Subsequently, in 1981, Stephen and Maureen Huntly spent time there, following their involvement with the work in Brazil. Their base was in Carcavelos, about 20 minutes drive from Lisbon. Their outreach was targeted on an international community of some 50,000 drawn from about 88 different nationalities, thousands of refugees who had fled from Angola and Mozambique, NATO personnel and tourists. At that time, evangelical believers comprised just 1% of the population.

At that time, Elim was working in fellowship with three congregations at Oeiras, S. Domingo do Rana and S. Pedro. The intention was to start a fourth work in Carcavelos where there was no other evangelical witness.

Four churches were established and there was an extensive work especially among refugees from southern Africa. By 1988, Amilcar Rodrigues had the oversight and he, with Pastor Luis Travanca, cared for the fledgling work. The Apostolic Faith Mission (AFM) of South Africa took a measure of responsibility for this work at that time. The work was particularly demanding. The refugees were housed in a ruined asylum in conditions described as degrading. The Local Authority had more sympathy with the communist regimes from which the refugees had fled than they did with the refugees themselves. Then the support of Christian organisations that had been supplying food, medicines, clothing and milk for the children was removed and there was a recipe for disaster.

The situation was apparently hopeless as Pastor Travanca indicated that his church was seeking to help. He was impressed by the fact that the refugees never ever complained. But the church in Antwerp responded to the need under the auspices of EPRO,[x] sending a lorry load of powdered milk. Elim covered the cost of transport for this errand of mercy. It might be expected that refugees would live in substandard conditions, but this was also the case for many of Portugal's citizens. A report in 1988 by Pete Le Masurier[xi] expressed shock that many were living in third world conditions, some 350,000 in shanty towns around the capital Lisbon.

Such poverty and need provide a ready ground for the sowing of the seed of the Word of God. Obviously, reaching such numbers looked like a hopeless task but Amilcar Rodrigues, pastor of the Massama and Gouveia assemblies in Lisbon had harboured a desire to reach people through the media. He had moved from Mozambique and was instrumental in starting a regular Sunday television programme. Aired between 12 noon and 1 p.m. it was watched by between four and five million people. In the beginning, the programmes were just fifteen minutes long, but they were then extended to a full thirty minutes. The amazing thing was that Amilcar was appointed the producer so had full control over content. He maintained a strong evangelical influence but involved some 33 different denominations and over 1400 churches and Christian organisations. So God blessed the work.

It is clear that part of the reason for the development of the work throughout Europe was the increasing number of UK pastors who became involved in short term visits for teaching and preaching in the countries that were open to receive them. This itinerant role allowed for the support and encouragement of the churches and ministries which were continually being opened despite restrictions placed upon them. In our time, of course, we have seen the fall of the Berlin Wall and the reunification of Germany. The dissolution of the USSR has led also to an opening of some doors although who can tell when they may again close? The work in Europe has been helped over the years by the abilities of Elim people, not least Brian Edwards, and we give God thanks for all that has been accomplished.

i European Evangelistic Society, a joint venture between Elim and Assemblies of God.

ii Not to be confused with David Hathaway's later project title.

iii *Elim Evangel*, Vol.59. Issue 31, pp8,9. Issue 32, pp 6,7.

iv Christian Solidarity International; a group working for persecuted Christians worldwide. For a report by Mervyn Thomas see *Elim Evangel*, Vol.68. Issue 15, p.13

v Some individual works are considered after a general overview of Europe as a whole.

vi Action Europe was a support venture whose Director was John Wildrianne.

vii See separate chapter.

viii European Pentecostal Fellowship, a fellowship of churches from both east and west Europe.

ix Reported in the *Elim Evangel*, Volume 65, Issue 27, page 7.

x European Pentecostal Relief Organisation.

xi Report in *Elim Evangel*, Vol.69. 18.6.88, Pp6,11. Pete was working with the Belgian church in relief work in association with Fabien Vanquaillie.

CHAPTER 6

EUROTEAMS

The impetus given to the work in Europe – east and west – had an added boost when Euroteams were started. The philosophy was that young people should be encouraged and facilitated to serve short term in Europe.

Promotion of Euroteams was general but never more effective than at the General Conference. It was exciting to see young people in the Missions Rallies and to be able to give direction for service after the meetings closed. In Conference Late Night Specials, team leaders and members were able to share their experiences and challenge others to become involved. Some testified to a call to Europe but all agreed that their lives had been radically changed.

Mike Sherwood led a team to Germany in 1980. Heading for West Berlin, they had to drive through East Germany and had two border crossings to negotiate. Because of the Berlin Wall, Mike described it as "like being on an island, but surrounded by concrete instead of sea".

The group was there for two weeks and participated in church services, singing on the streets and inviting people to the meetings. They all lived together in Teen Challenge House in West Berlin and became involved in a Teen Challenge coffee bar service.

They met Frank who had escaped from prison, but had been cared for by local believers. They also were introduced to an Englishman said to be the only Christian working among 100,000 Turks in West Berlin. He was a graduate of Nottingham University and he, with his wife and two small girls, had worked in Turkey for a few years, bringing him into conflict with the Turkish authorities.

Disheartened, having just mastered the Turkish language, he was making his way back to England when a friend told him about the Turkish people in Berlin. For four years, he had been ministering to them, holding meetings in his own front room. He had seen little fruit, but a few converts had moved back to Turkey so they were trusting they would be able to witness there.

A team of 13 was sent to Thessaloniki in Greece, led by Vivian Thomas. The intention was to drive the 2000 miles overland over a period of five days and to pitch camp each evening. Unfortunately, rain played havoc with their plans and, on the first night, they just kept driving.

Passing through Yugoslavia, they had contact with local believers and became aware of the desperate needs of that land. On their way home, they met Radimir who had already spent two months in prison for preaching the Gospel. Nevertheless, he was pioneering a church and building in Pula involving a debt of £60,000 (£30,000 in tax!) for a derelict building and a further £30,000 for refurbishment. Their church had begun with three believers just three years earlier.

The following Thursday, they arrived in Thessaloniki to be met by Pastor Phil Sidiropoulos. Ministry involved taking part in meetings in churches in Thessaloniki, Athens and Katerini.

The high spot was an open air service on Thessaloniki sea front. At 9 p.m. they gathered at the foot of the huge statue of Alexander the Great to sing about an even greater King and conqueror of death. By the time Pastor Phil had finished preaching, the crowd had swelled to between 250 and 300 people, eager to hear about Jesus. The response was overwhelming.

It wasn't all 'hard work'. There were opportunities for relaxation and sightseeing, but the brief visit was described by Viv as a "real barometer of our commitment to the Lord and others".

The first Euroteam to Poland was led by Derek Green. The journey was via Germany and, travelling through East Germany, it was evident that appearances of progress and affluence were limited to the main street. Sadness and despair were written on the people's faces and there is a museum on the west side of the Wall telling how people have tried to escape.

Arriving in Poland, they felt like the clock had been turned back 35 years to the end of the war. They drove over cobblestone 'motorways', often not finding a petrol station for 150 miles. The very few restaurants were more like fourth rate transport cafés and there were queues everywhere for basic food.

Despite their problems, the Polish Christians were outstanding. Their welcome was tremendous. One lady, to bake some cakes for the visitors, had used a whole month's ration of flour. In one shop, they saw pieces of chicken costing about £8 in our money, yet one morning, two of the young people were treated to this luxury by the people they stayed with.

The group travelled hundreds of miles each day, visiting churches throughout the country and everywhere, they were filled with people praising God. In one church, the service ended with nearly everyone, including the team, in tears before the Lord.

The Belgian team was led by Eric Gaudion and comprised young people from Ulster, Guernsey, England, Wales and Scotland, each with a unique contribution to make. Ages ranged from 16 to an embarrassing 30 something and all had differing talents in music and speaking.

The team had fellowship with a group near Antwerp and were able to work in the area. This Flemish-speaking area of Belgium constituted a huge unevangelised mission field where Mike Williams and the Elim Church in Antwerp were seeking to make an impact. During their stay, the team was based in Duffel, a small market town just south of Antwerp. The work here included a rehabilitation centre for ex-prisoners as well as a bookshop and literature ministry.

Open air evangelism and meetings in various churches occupied the team's time. Their impact on the locality was reflected in an invitation to attend a reception in the office of the Burgemeister (Lord Mayor). Not only were the team members able to minister but each felt that they had been ministered to by the people of Duffel. Following the visit, two team members entered Elim Bible College.

For three weeks, Euroteam members to northern Italy were, to all intents and purposes, Elim's short term European missionaries. By linking themselves to others of a different culture and way of life, they enriched themselves no end and hoped, in days to come, to enrich the lives of others at home.

The church to which they were assigned in Udine was small but faithful. It was said that to open a church in the south was simple, but in the north, impossible. The older people were strong Roman Catholics. One old lady was heard telling a younger woman, "We don't need their Jesus Christ. We have the Pope." The young people are strong communists. One young woman was heard saying that they wouldn't stand a chance against the tanks she'd like to drive over them! This was the backdrop to the work in Udine.

There was a daily programme of morning and evening open airs, while afternoons were free. In the late evening, services were held in the church. Graham Murray, who led the team, said there had been no great miracles but even a small move of blessing was a miracle to the people of northern Italy.

The reason for the existence of the Euroteams lies in the statistics for some European countries. Belgium had a population of 10 million with only 0.6% Christian. Yugoslavia's population was 22 million but just over 0.2% believers. Greece, with a population of 9 million had not more than 0.2% believers and there were only 60 full time evangelical pastors in the country. Portugal had a population of 9.5 million and only 0.1% Christians. Some other European countries were even worse.

During 1981 therefore, teams were planned to visit Portugal, Greece, Belgium, Yugoslavia and Berlin. Because of the success of the venture, European pastors were writing to ask that the teams might visit them.

When Jimmy Ritchie led the Euroteam to Berlin, he discovered a city of sin with sex shops on every street corner, a city full of people of all nationalities trying to find employment. But there were also many signs of affluence that hid a deep spiritual need. The team was based on the Christian Fellowship Church in the centre of West Berlin and involved themselves in outreach using literature and singing, talking to people as they passed by.

Later in the evening, people would come for refreshments and to see films like the Cross and the Switchblade, and Fact and Faith films. There were a number of decisions, including a young American soldier who identified with Nicky Cruz, the hero of Cross and the Switchblade, because he was a Puerto Rican, brought up on the streets of New York. Michael was on heroin, a German who could speak just a little English. As he prayed, tears ran down his cheeks because he had just committed his life to Christ.

Kwame came from Ghana and knew about the Church of Pentecost. A young man from Ethiopia found it hard to believe that God could love him because of the terrible things he had seen in his own country. In all, 15 people surrendered their lives to the Lord during the team's visit.

Subsequently, two team members became full time Elim missionaries – Debbie Brown from Northern Ireland and Janice Edgar from Liverpool. She is now Janice Pate.

The Portugal team was led by Viv Thomas and was based in Lisbon where Stephen Huntly was then the pastor. The main thrust of their ministry was to show a series of Billy Graham films that had been dubbed into Portuguese. Some time was spent on the streets singing and distributing invitations to the films. Open airs were held in two nearby towns. There was a good response to the films with a crowd of 120 on the last night. Many contacts were made and people came forward at the end of the meetings, taking literature and signing up for correspondence courses.

The Greek team, led by Mike Sherwood, was accommodated in the homes of members of the church in Thessaloniki. The team's activities were similar to that of the previous year and, as they sang in the open air, a man introduced himself saying that he had come to know the Lord through the previous team's ministry.

The team had some time for excursions so visited some of the places mentioned in Acts as having been visited by the apostle Paul. Although the peninsula is beautiful, the team sensed the bondage that religion can bring and rejoiced in a message of a God who cannot be contained in buildings or man-made traditions.

The 1982 teams targeted East and West Germany, Poland, Czechoslovakia, Greece, Belgium, Spain and Portugal. The European Missions Director, Brian Edwards, reported:

In some places, the teams played a vital part in pioneer evangelism. For instance, a team led by Graeme Parkins joined with Andy and Yolanda Smith and me in conducting a crusade in the Spanish town of Figueras. As a result, some folks committed their lives to the Lord. As Andy and Yolanda continued the follow-up work through the succeeding months, the fruit became evident. They then had 18 committed members and often more than 20 meeting for the services.

The Portuguese and Greece teams travelled the furthest, totalling 3 and 5 thousand miles respectively. Even the journeys can become evangelistic. The Greek team stopped overnight at a campsite in Austria. While they were there, a holiday maker had a heart attack and died. The team leader, Jim Kay, was able to offer help to the wife of the man who died and share the Gospel with her. On their return through Yugoslavia, they visited the town of Osijek where they met with a group of Pentecostal young people and were able to encourage them in their church there. In Greece itself, they had a busy schedule of services, street work, literature distribution and a baptismal service at Lydia's river in Biblical Philippi.

The team to Portugal had a busy time too, participating in similar activities and encouraging the three churches north of Lisbon. They worked with Stephen and Maureen Huntly, reaching many hundreds of people in open air services for adults and children. A good number of people found Christ and a new children's work was started as a result of their visit.

In Yugoslavia, the team ministered to the saints in the new church in Pula on the beautiful Adriatic. Elim has had an ongoing involvement with this work since it had been pioneered two years previously. On this occasion, people came to know the Lord and local saints were encouraged.

The team with the least travelling went to Belgium. Their ministry was centred on Antwerp where they worked with Mike and Colette Williams. The second half of their time was spent in Nyjlen with Phil and Barbara Gray. Here they joined in a special film crusade and ministered to the people with much blessing.

Prior to each team going out, a training programme was arranged and those wishing to travel with a team were expected to attend. Teaching given included cultural orientation, the language and customs of the countries visited, the place of music, drama, personal and open air evangelism, the dynamics of working and living together as a team, encouraging a life of faith and the operation of the gifts of the Holy Spirit.

It will be obvious that the Youth Department and the Missions Board had sought to deal with as many eventualities as possible. The pastors who gave of their time to lead the teams were men of integrity and ability whose own lives were an example to the people they led. In all, the Euroteams programme ran for around ten years and the blessings accruing from their service will be fully seen only in eternity.

CHAPTER 7

ELIM WOMEN'S MISSIONARY AUXILIARY (EWMA)

Elim's new baby: Born between 3 and 4 p.m. on Tuesday of Conference week, 1966. To be called EWMA – Elim Women's Missionary Auxiliary.

There had been a gestation period! Earlier in the year, the Elim Missionary Council (EMC), with the approval of the Executive Council, invited Mrs. Gladys Gorton to attend a meeting with the idea of forming a women's missionary auxiliary. After discussion and some additions, Mrs. Gorton's plan was accepted and she was asked to become its first Secretary. The Conference subsequently ratified the agreement and on the Tuesday of that week, Gladys was presented to a ladies' gathering by Gerald Ladlow, a member of the Missionary Council.

Gladys reported on that time:

After I had finished, the meeting was opened for questions and while one or two were speaking, Leslie Wigglesworth, whispered to me, "This has just been handed in." He passed me a note from two sisters in Barnsley saying that they would give £25 each if we launched a fund for a jeep for India. We agreed to have an offering and then watched a miracle happening. Miss Marion Paint, missionary to India, stood up and said, "Our greatest need in India is a jeep. The one we have had since 1947 is falling apart." An appeal was made giving these details and the offering amounted to £70. By the Thursday missionary meeting, I had received in cash and promises, including £50 from Barnsley, £146/8/3.

Mrs. Caple, the wife of the Barnsley pastor, passed in that note. She had longed to get into the meeting but was hindered. God held her back so that we could see His confirmation of our plans. We also heard that two women in the north of England had set aside Tuesday to fast and pray that Elim would organise something to stimulate interest among women to aid our missionary cause. Nobody knew we would convene that meeting that afternoon; it was not on the scheduled programme. We did not know ourselves as nothing could be done until the Conference passed the proposal. This was another confirmation."

The jeep for India caught the imagination and the ladies rallied round, raising £450 in a very short time. Other gifts had been sent directly to Headquarters. It was decided that the response indicated the Lord's favour and arrangements were made to complete the transaction. Pastor & Mrs. D.C. Lewis[1] benefited greatly from their up-to-date transport and wrote thanking the ladies for their support.

But the cry from the country was, "What's our next objective?" The original idea was that ladies would generate funds to supply 'extras' to the missionaries, items not included in the official budgets. Jean Phillips of the Transvaal put it very well as she congratulated Gladys on the 'new baby' and said, "Many missionaries will greatly appreciate the little extras that they will now be able to enjoy. It costs so much now to feed, clothe and school children. Uniforms which have to be bought, bus fares, etc. make a big hole in a missionary's salary. I am sure missionaries are going to appreciate the 'new baby' more than you can ever think."

The EMC then asked for help to be given to Ghana. The establishment of a Bible school and a missionary residence was an immediate need, because there were many fine young men waiting for admission to a training centre for ministry.

At that time, Gerald and Margaret Ladlow were serving short term in Ghana and had advised that food and accommodation were extremely expensive, the cheapest house in Accra costing £50 per month to rent. So a target was set and the sum of £1013/11/6 was presented to the Missionary Secretary, Leslie Wigglesworth, at a great missionary rally in the annual Conference. This amount was raised in just six months. With the money for the jeep for India and food parcels sent to India and Africa, the ladies raised £2000 in the first year.

Each time a project was completed, there was an eagerness to know what the new direction would be. This time, the target would be Brazil, where the Jefferys[ii] needed money to complete their new church building in time for the visit of Pastor & Mrs. P.S. Brewster during the World Pentecostal Conference in Rio.[iii] Support was also needed for national workers and fresh personnel. Pastor & Mrs. John MacInnes[iv] in Guyana also had similar needs, so the target for the whole was a further £2000.

One of the difficulties experienced by EWMA from its outset was that not all churches involved themselves. A major activity on the part of the EWMA Secretary, then and subsequently, has been to attempt to involve more ladies' groups in EWMA ventures. While at church level, in some cases, there was a reticence to become involved, individuals throughout the country were enthused. One widow wrote that she felt she had nothing to give because she was on 'assistance', but the Lord showed her what she could do and she was then able to send in £25.

A young mother was asked by her Pastor to be responsible for EWMA in their church and her response was, "How would I find the time?" She also knew that there were many OAPs in the congregation and wondered how it could work. But she agreed and was touched by the fact that a blind lady wanted to know how she could help.

At a missionary conference, there were reports from around the globe and an overall picture emerged of needs in various fields. As a result, the focus of EWMA was directed to facilitating the production of literature and radio programmes and the setting up of Bible schools.

One report suggested that the lives of missionaries were spared by EWMA's efforts. Pastor and Mrs. Arthur Bull were threatened by a new tribe among whom they were working in Tanzania, but when they saw the EWMA parcels arriving, they decided to postpone the execution!

It was also considered providential that just as the target of £1000 for Ghana was reached, spacious premises suitable for a Bible school became available.

At this time, Pastor W.G. Hathaway promoted a scheme for the saving and selling of postage stamps. This came into being and continued until the early 2000s, raising much needed finance and augmenting the overall income. Some ladies are to be commended for their faithful work in this ministry over many years, as they soaked and peeled stamps from backing paper to make them suitable for selling to dealers.

The woman's touch was always very evident in the work of EWMA. The missionaries received birthday cards and cards and gifts at Christmas time, and this was much appreciated on the fields. Targets for Brazil and Guyana were met and made a huge difference. An idea was presented to 'adopt a missionary' and all were encouraged to do something to help, no matter how small. A generator for the new secondary school at Inyanga North in Rhodesia was next on the list and the ladies set about making this a reality.

At the end of the first two years, Gladys Gorton set out what she saw as the purposes of EWMA. These were –

1. Every church with an active EWMA.
2. Every EWMA member an intercessor.
3. Every member a soul-winner.
4. Every missionary or missionary family 'adopted'.
5. Every missionary, and their children, to receive a gift at Christmas, on birthdays and other occasions.
6. Every project given to the EWMA by the Missionary Council to be wholeheartedly supported and fulfilled.

She also indicated that the total giving for the period had reached almost £5000 and that the new project for 1968-69 would be SOS – Serve our Stations, for which £2500 was needed.

By this time, letters were being received regularly from those who had benefited from EWMA's efforts and telling of the blessing they had been. Two pastors from Tanzania received motor bikes and these had revolutionised their ministries, allowing them far more freedom to reach a wider area. Vera McGillivray in Hong Kong wrote saying how blessed she was to have had sufficient for Christmas that she didn't need to feel ashamed to invite her Canadian friends for a meal. Pastor David Tenobi from Ghana wrote to express appreciation for the funds that had made the Bible school possible. Other funds had been supplied that had put roofs on churches.

Jack and Grace Troke in India were on the receiving end of EWMA bounty and wrote saying how beneficial the gift of a typewriter had been to them. Their previous model had served them for forty years and was now obsolete, making it impossible to get parts to repair it. Such a small thing, in many ways, yet it made a world of difference to the Trokes in their service for the Master.

In its first four years of service, EWMA surpassed its target and, in 1970, were £1000 over what they had set out to raise, having produced the magnificent total of £4125. The two years of SOS project raised over £7000 and many mission stations were seeing the benefit. The next project was to be called 'Light through Literature' and this would be the means of providing the wherewithal to produce and spread Christian literature. So, printing presses, vehicles, paper – whatever was needed was the target and the £3500 required was in sight.

Minibuses would take the missionaries with their literature to the thousands who needed the Gospel. At Conference that year, the first minibus, a light blue in colour, was presented to Pastor Wigglesworth for David and Maureen Butcher[v] to take out for use in the Transvaal field. The second minibus was to go to Ghana and there was great encouragement to keep up the momentum by saving Green Shield and S&H (pink) trading stamps. This was presented to David and Margaret Mills[vi] for use in Ghana. In his word of thanks, David advised the gathered group at the Elim Church in Sheffield that he had talked to the proprietor of the garage where the bus came from, who told him that 1,676,800 stamps were needed to buy the bus and that if they had been put in line side by side, they would stretch to approximately 13.5 miles! What an achievement – stamps turned into a vehicle for missions.

When EWMA was five years old, Gladys Gorton reviewed what had been accomplished and noted the success of the venture. The ladies were encouraged to pray every midday for revival both here and on the fields. The Light through Literature project had exceeded all targets and negotiations were ongoing for the purchase of printing machinery. The SOS project was still being used for priorities. A new roof had been installed on a church in Tanzania; domestic electrical work was done on the house for Pastor and Mrs. Norton[vii] at Penhalonga because it had not been lived in for some time. Old Christmas cards were sent to India, Tanzania, Guyana and Ghana so that they could be used either for writing on – the backs – or for teaching – the fronts. Christian literature and Bibles were needed for India, Guyana and Ghana, and hymn books had been requested for Guyana and India. Food parcels had been sent to India and Tanzania and EWMA gave out information as to what could be sent. A third minibus was in prospect at a cost of 1250 Green Shield stamp books.

Reports given to the 1971 Conference showed the amazing extent of the work done by EWMA. Light through Literature funds had reached £5000 and each year, the target set for any given project had been exceeded. During this Conference, the MacInneses took delivery of a brand new Hillman estate car for their service in Guyana. This was not paid for with Green Shield stamps, but out of the funds raised through the South America project.

Just around that time, there had been a postal strike that had held up negotiations for the purchase of a Land Rover which was due to be sent to Rhodesia. In all, the report made for enthusiasm maintained and a great future for the work of the ladies overseas.

The next project was called Transmitting the Truth and brought EWMA into a new realm of service as thoughts turned to the advantages of using radio and electronic means to transmit the Gospel. This project made possible the communicating of the Gospel by tape cassette and would allow the purchase of tape players for evangelists in remote areas. They seldom had opportunity for personal teaching to help them and this was a way to minister to their needs as well as extending their usefulness in evangelism. There was a radio transmitter in the Seychelles that was used for sending the Gospel into India and the Far East where many people had short wave radios. The Bible College at Capel had a fully fitted studio where tapes and broadcasts could be prepared.

A story was told by Olive Garbutt, then missionary to Rhodesia, of a visit she made to a church while home on furlough. One of the problems EWMA people had was the high cost of sending goods to the fields and so, when missionaries came to visit, they were often asked to take things back with them. Obviously what they could carry was limited.

Olive was in Woolwich when she was shown a selection of items made by the local EWMA ladies, and invited to take as many as she could for her work. She chose a few items including one bright yellow cardigan trimmed with red. She felt it would be suitable for someone special.

Back on the field, she was inspecting a school at Imbeza. Susan, in Grade 5, had written a very good English essay about her home. In it she wrote: "We are a poor family, we don't have enough clothes, but we do have enough food so we are a happy family." Susan could not have known that Olive would visit her school that week or that she would read her essay. She had no knowledge of her need nor could she have picked her out of the class in any other way.

Olive thought about the winter season just beginning and a little girl shivering in class next term, so she asked where Susan was. The little girl did not have a school uniform. The head teacher confirmed her story that she came from a poor family. As Olive thought about the little girl, the yellow cardigan came to mind. A few days later, she took it to school and presented it to Susan as a special prize for having done the best, neatest work in class.

It was taken out of its wrapping, held up and admired then tried on with great delight. No one was jealous although there were probably others who were in just as much need. A few days later, a party of school children got on a bus at 6 a.m. to go to town for a sports event. Near Imbeza, some adults got on, surprised to see so many children at such an early hour. A teacher in charge heard one lady say to another, "They are from the Elim mission; it is a kind mission," – and the story of the yellow cardigan was told all over again. Who knows whether this witness will draw others into the house of God to hear the message of salvation?

In reviewing the progress of the work, it was noted that the Light through Literature project had provided a printing press for John Prentice[viii] in India so that thousands of tracts could be printed. The special evangelistic number of the Elim Evangel was sent in bulk to Guyana and Ghana, carriage paid for by EWMA and at the Emmanuel Press in Transvaal, Ron Gull was producing a four page newspaper entitled T.E.L.L.

The Transmitting the Truth project realised £5400 during the year and the proposal was to purchase time to broadcast from the Seychelles, Brazil and Ghana. Cassette tapes and literature were still being sent out on a regular basis.

In 1972, a seminar was convened in Brighton for those interested in EWMA. Approximately 130 attended including several missionaries on furlough or retired, and ideas and suggestions were exchanged. In the evening, the numbers were swelled by bus loads from nearby churches for a rally. Mrs. Ruth Walker, wife of the then President, preached and a great anointing was on the meeting. The whole day was described as an outstanding success and an inspiration.

As the T.T.T. project concluded, it was replaced by the '999 Fund.' Priority would be given to emergency situations. For example, where there was a drought or serious food shortage, the Fund would help. To some extent, the impetus for this project was a newspaper report that said that almost 1,000 million people lived in countries where there was not enough food to eat and drought was a real factor of life.

At a subsequent EWMA rally, there were reports of great benefits received on the fields as a result of EWMA efforts. In Rhodesia, the generator had improved life for schools, hospital and homes, while the bore hole water project supplied fresh water to the whole station at Inyanga North. In the Transvaal, an estate car purchased with green Shield stamps had improved accessibility to the remoter areas of the field and the gifts at Christmas had given a lift to spirits at that time. Zaire had received parcels of clothing that had been greatly appreciated and the radio works in Guyana and Brazil were still being supported.

In 1975, Gladys Gorton gave up the position as Secretary of EWMA and Mrs. Ruth Walker was appointed in her place. Ruth paid tribute to the more than nine years Gladys had led the work and the great achievements attained. She arrived in the middle of the 999 project and indicated that this had a target of £10,000 and would now be known as Missionary Essentials.

By 1978, the provision of goods and services had expanded in scope considerably. In Tanzania, clothing had been supplied to pastors and church members. Ghana had received a printing press and an IBM electronic typewriter. Books had been provided for a library in Taiwan and grants had been made for translation work in Brazil. Meanwhile, the work in Guyana had received a piano accordion, and in India, the costs of laying a foundation for a new house were given together with a printing press. A new typewriter and help towards the cost of a moped were given to Zaire plus, in various other locations, refrigerators, tapes, recorders, air conditioning and medical supplies were made available. The target for that year had risen to £20,000.

The 1978 project was called GOLD – Gospel Outreach and Literature Distribution. Much of this was centred on west and southern Africa. In 1980, the new target was £30,000 and was to Build a Church a Month. The cost was to be £2000 each in 12 different stations throughout the world. Countries involved included Transvaal, Taiwan, Brazil, Guyana, north and south India and Rhodesia. Some of these buildings had already been completed, while others were in the process of being constructed.

For a period of time, there was keen competition between the ladies of the home churches to see who could raise the greatest amount of money. This was highlighted at the annual Conference when EWMA totals were reported and new challenges given. New needs were always presenting themselves and the ladies always tried to be in a position to help. A good example was the donation given for a Cyclone Disaster Relief Fund for India and the help offered to Henry Joseph of Madras for his radio work. The encouragement to continue this work lay in reports of souls saved and lives transformed through the help that was given.

The 1980 project was called Speed the Word and, at the start of the 1981 Conference, only £29,000 had been raised but by the end of the Conference, the total of £40,000 had been achieved. This was seen as a milestone because EWMA had then reached 15 years old and in that time, had raised £200,000. Under Speed the Word, 10 students in North India were supported, money was given for a minibus in Taiwan, a duplicator was bought for Greece, a projector sent to Guyana, fridges to Transvaal, a minibus for North India, a Peugeot diesel for Ghana, radio support for Guyana, a car deposit for Brazil and a vehicle for Hong Kong. A roof was put on a church in Zimbabwe and there were plans to send similar goods to other areas as well. Mrs. Walker confidently believed that the £200,000 could be doubled within four years to continue the good work.

The next project was entitled Reach for God and the target set for that was £42,000. This was intended to help new missionary enterprises in Portugal, Honduras, Zaire and Thailand. David Ayling, then International Missions Director commented, "When we look back over what the Lord has helped the ladies of EWMA to do in the past, we can only say, 'How great is our God and greatly to be praised.' I know that it is under His good hand that the work has made this rapid progress and so to Him is all the glory."

This story was repeated year on year with targets rising higher each time. What had started out as a 'baby' had become a full-grown adult and, beyond providing some 'extras' to help the missionary's situation, was now being used to supply major capital items for the extension of the work. EWMA was now consistently raising between one sixth and one fifth of the total Missions budget.

The list of provisions under Keep Missions Moving in 1985 was intriguing: A V6B Diesel Land Rover went to Zimbabwe; a Peugeot 505 Familial G Diesel was sent to Ghana for Ruth and Lionel Currie; the Wilsons in Thailand received a Toyota Diesel truck with cabin and truck back for their work; a Mazda was purchased for Hong Kong; a renewal vehicle was supplied to Brazil for the use of the President of the churches there and Guyana was on the list for a replacement in the not too distant future. The purchase costs of all vehicles were fully met by EWMA.

In 1986, the programme was to Build the Kingdom and, once again, there was a list of items on the shopping list that was increasingly challenging. Payments were made to eight different countries and helped to evangelise, maintain workers, keep missionaries and national workers mobile, supply literature and help in Bible schools. Vehicle maintenance and running costs, plus tax and insurance, were also covered in some cases.

Although this record was amazing, it was always a source of some concern that at least 200 churches throughout the Movement never made any attempt to become involved. In some areas, there were inhibitions as to the type of things that might be done to raise funds; some judged themselves to be too small and in need of all the funds they could raise for their own needs; in others, the system was just to give, but at least some efforts were being made. Individual church members and wives of ministers tried to encourage others to share in the joy of achievement and in the knowledge that such work was being owned of God in the development of the Work.

By 1989, the financial goal was set at £100,000. Ruth Walker confessed that she felt a little intimidated by the amount and was almost tempted to reduce it and make it seem more attainable. But she stuck to her guns and went ahead and her ladies didn't let her down. It seemed fitting that, with a goal like that, the theme should be Going for Gold!

New projects were coming in all the time and the wherewithal was being made available to make a significant difference to the lives of those who had left home and loved ones to answer the call of the foreign fields. A back-up generator for the Curries in Ghana was necessary because of the frequency of power cuts, the Wests needed a vehicle as they went back to Guyana for a short term, the Bible school started by the Buxtons in Tanzania was progressing and help was offered to some students so that they could train for ministry. A major contribution was made to Brazil where the leaders of the work were so poor, that all worked for a living and most received nothing for their work for the church. In spite of that, many were building their own churches and using money earned to help both the church and the poor of the community.

In subsequent years, EWMA went through a series of changes. When Ruth Walker gave up office, Maureen Butcher became the National president of EWMA. Shortly thereafter, in conjunction with the IMB, the name was changed to Lifelink in the hope that this may have had more appeal to others who had not before been involved. One problem that this threw up was that, in Ireland, there were already two other groups using this name so, to avoid confusion, the Irish Conference decided to revert to EWMA. This presented no problem in the Province because people were accustomed to the Presbyterian connection with their PWA, which performed similar functions to our own ministry.

At the time of writing, a committee has taken over leadership for Lifelink.

i See chapter on India.

ii See chapter on Brazil.

iii See chapter on Brazil for details of the visit.

iv See chapter on Guyana.

v See chapter on Transvaal.

vi See chapter on Ghana.

vii See chapter on Transvaal.

viii See chapter on India.

CHAPTER 8

FRANCE

An immense contribution to the work in France in the early days was made by Douglas Scott, an early member of the Elim Church in Ilford. In 1930, he was led to minister as an evangelist on the Continent, particularly in France. His ministry was richly owned of God but, in 1939, he fulfilled a strong desire to work in the Congo, unaware that some months later, France would become occupied territory. In 1946, he went from Congo to Algeria before returning to France where, with the exception of several months in French-speaking Martinique and Quebec, he laboured prodigiously with untiring zeal until his homecall in 1967, his sixty-seventh year. He was buried in Chalon, near Paris and his funeral was attended by more than seventy French ministers.

Having established many Pentecostal churches in France, and being the instrument in the conversion of many men who then became ministers, he was recognised as the pioneer and father of the work in France. He was a remarkable man and a strong individualist who, with his wife, made a complete sacrifice of home and family life for the sake of the Gospel, refusing to accept any office in the French assemblies among which he accomplished so much. He exercised an apostolic ministry of signs and wonders among the people to whom he was called in France, North Africa and Congo. God answered both his faith and his faithfulness. He loved France and his many sermon notes were written in the language of those with whom he so closely identified himself. Despite being aware of fast-declining health, he continued to preach to the very eve of his departure from this life.

Many references to the work in France centre on the ministry of Miss Olive Routledge, a native of York, who was based in Lille in 1949. The work was developing slowly because of language difficulties and the influence of the RC church. But a regular prayer meeting was commenced and Sunday school was being well attended with new scholars appearing each week. People were being brought to know the Lord and there was encouragement for the workers. Olive herself was blessed in that, following a message in tongues in that first prayer meeting, she found complete freedom in giving the interpretation, although she had not done so before because of her inhibitions with the language. The interpretation pointed to sin in the midst and this resulted in a period when those present were constrained to confess those things in their lives that they felt were displeasing to the Lord. Blessing followed.

Following this time of evident renewal, one man and two women accepted the Lord as Saviour. There were no Protestant schools in the town so the church faced difficulties because of the influence exerted by the local RC church. Parents were brought under immediate pressure to catechise their children and prepare them for their first communion as soon as it was known that they had an interest in the Gospel.

Olive found soon that people were seeking her out for counselling and she was happy to be of service. One lady, living nearby, had asked for prayer as she had been an invalid for 22 years. Olive went to see her and pray for her and she then asked how much she would charge for her visit and her prayers. The lady testified to an improvement in health and promised that, when healed, she would attend the meetings.

The work continued to expand and special meetings were held in December of 1949 with the church conducting its first baptismal service using a large zinc bath as there was no proper baptistery. The Sunday school, which had started with fourteen children, was now about forty strong, all of them keen to be involved in the Christmas service. The building was packed to capacity and the highlight of the service was six tiny tots who sang the Christmas story in French with an English accent! Small presents were given to each child and this, in itself, was an innovation since the people were so poor that hardly any child ever received a gift at Christmas.

The church was richly blessed in seeing the Lord work in ways beyond their understanding. In the Sunday school there was a small boy with RC parents. He was not strong, having suffered from the age of sixteen months with a strange illness that the doctors couldn't diagnose. They said he couldn't live beyond seven years and although he had been in hospital several times and had been seen by three specialists, there was nothing to be done for him, humanly speaking. However, he used to attend the meetings regularly and was always cheerful, having given his heart to Jesus.

Then one day, he became desperately ill and was unable to move. The doctor said there was no hope whatever and his mother was heart-broken. Olive and the Pastor visited the home and instructed the parents about James 5:14; then they laid hands on the boy and prayed for him. A few weeks passed and the child lay between life and death, but prayer was offered continually on his behalf. Then the miracle happened. Suddenly, he began to get better and his body, which had become deformed through suffering, became absolutely normal. He began to eat without being sick and his thin limbs became strong and fit again. His mother was overjoyed and sent for Olive to visit at once. Imagine Olive's joy at seeing the boy running around playing with his little sister. The doctor came and was astounded, saying that he couldn't understand it, but the workers were able to point them to the wonder-working Christ. The following Sunday, the mother, grandmother and three friends all came to the service and accepted Christ as Saviour.

The work continued to progress in all departments despite local opposition and persecution. One of the special occasions that brought great joy to the little assembly was a visit in 1951 by the London Crusader Choir en route to Switzerland. During the summer months, Olive had permission from the town's mayor to hold children's services in the public park and she did so with great acceptance, using flannelgraph to provide visual impact to the Bible stories. This also provided opportunity to distribute Gospel literature to those who stood around and listened. On one occasion, her talk was listened to by a RC priest and a group of boy scouts and girl guides.

The work in France became largely indigenous with the passing of time. Local churches developed and organised and the input of expatriate missionaries declined.

In later years, following the appointment of the European Director, Brian Edwards, Elim had associations with groups representing, in some cases, immigrant communities, especially among the Tamil people of Sri Lanka. One of these groups formed the new Covenant Church in Paris which had a regular attendance of around forty people weekly. Mr. Deva Sinnathurai, with his wife, Anoma, took on the oversight of the Fellowship until Deva was officially recognised as its Pastor. New leaders were developing all the time and strengthening the work, not only in Paris, but also in Switzerland with Jenny Sinadurai. New premises were being sought because the Lord was confirming His Word with miracles as an almost weekly occurrence. Growth was evident and the Fellowship believed that nothing was too hard for the Lord.

Subsequently, the work continued to grow and remained indigenous, but associations with wider groupings of Pentecostal churches continued to be maintained and developed throughout the country.

CHAPTER 9

GREECE

In the streets and churches of Greece, the ancient idolatries known to the Apostle Paul still flourish, not now as in days gone by, but serving the icons of modern orthodoxy. Until 1974, to preach the Gospel openly, give out Christian literature and to seek to lead people to Christ was an offence for which you could be arrested and imprisoned. Many believers, with their pastors and evangelists, suffered great persecution in those days and the Pentecostal witness was suppressed. Although the power of the Orthodox Church has been limited by the introduction of new laws for religious freedom, the priests still exercise a powerful influence over the people.

There is still strong and often vehement opposition to any form of Protestant evangelism and particularly that of Pentecostal believers. It is reckoned that 95% of the population are under the influence of Orthodox religion so there are many possibilities for obstructing evangelism and the opening of new churches.

It is against this backdrop that Phil Sidiropoulos kept the faith and went to Britain for a period of Bible school training, returning to start a work for the Lord in Thessaloniki, in Macedonia in the north of the country. The Macedonian call of Scripture was repeated in the heart of our brother who, about two years previously, in 1977, stepped out in faith, sensing in his spirit a call from God to pioneer a new church in this city of a million souls. He began by inviting people to his own small apartment and holding meetings there. Soon, the numbers grew and he rented a hall with accommodation for about forty people.

Within two years, the congregation had grown to around 35 meeting week by week under his leadership. Many people were contacted through personal evangelism and the distribution of Christian literature. New Testaments were delivered to interested people at a rate of about forty per month, and the Living Word was implanted in the hearts of Greeks in this needy area. The church was made up of people who, though not rich in this world's goods, were nevertheless rejoicing in the new found joy and life in the Spirit. This was real to them because the area was subject to earthquakes when homes were damaged and people were forced to live in tents.

Sophia Assaridou, who also completed Bible school training in Britain, was also working in the city heading up the door-to-door work in an 'Evangelism Explosion' style of programme. She was also ministering through women's groups, among the young people and helping with evangelism in the surrounding towns and villages. There was a work among boys and girls that was growing and a thriving Sunday school had been started to train children in the ways of the Lord.

The work was helped in 1984 during a mission conducted by Pastor Edwards, when a young boy was brought for prayer. He was awaiting major heart surgery, but when hands were laid upon him in the name of Jesus, he was completely healed. His parents were freed completely from the fear that he might damage himself when he ran or jumped and the specialists had confirmed that he was now perfectly fit and well.

Elim Missions had committed to go and help because Phil was having to hold down an almost full time job in order to support his family and himself as well as supporting the baby church in its infancy. As well as a small amount of money being sent on a regular basis through the Eurovision project, the church benefited from the visits of three Euroteams.[i] The ultimate desire of course was to see brother Sidiropoulos released into full time care for the church and the evangelism that burned in his heart.

The strategic positioning of this work was not lost on the Missions department, recognising its proximity to Yugoslavia, Bulgaria and Turkey, with Iran not too far distant. In light of the upsurge in Islam, the country of Greece was regarded as a key factor and of paramount importance in the end times.

i See Euroteam chapter for details.

CHAPTER 10

SPAIN

George Henry Thomas and Maud Elizabeth Whitty Thomas (nee Evans) were both from in Dowlais, South Wales. Born in 1892 and 1893 respectively, they married in 1917. At that time, they were worshipping in a "dead" Church of Wales church so, in 1920, when George Jeffreys arrived in town and they saw the many miracles of healing and demonstrations of the power of God, they joined the newly formed Elim Alliance church. They very soon became involved in the "Spanish work", a ministry to Spanish immigrants in the town. It is perhaps not surprising that hearts so on fire for God should sense an almost immediate call to further service and so, when the Elim Bible College opened in Clapham, London, in 1925, they were among the first to enrol. Having completed their course, they then set sail for Mexico in 1926.[1]

It appears that the Thomases associated themselves with a small number of American missionaries and, in effect, sought to begin a work for Elim at that time. This was not as successful as expected and so, a little later, they moved to San Diego where they commenced a Bible school for Mexican Bible students, remaining there until 1932, at which time they moved back to Europe, arriving in Ronda in Spain in 1933. Their time was spent on literature distribution and evangelism and a church was planted in Ronda.

George was in the habit of leaving Bibles with the people but these were quickly confiscated by the RC priest who followed him around to undo his work. One lady was known to have wrapped her Bible in dough and put it in the oven so that it wouldn't be taken away. Such was the hunger for God that many people put their jobs on the line just to find out more about the Gospel. The work continued until the Thomases were forced to leave the country because of the Spanish revolution.

In 1935, George described Spain as a 'land of darkness'. In one village, one woman refused to accept a leaflet because it was being offered to her without price. She adamantly declared that it must be of the 'enemy', although George was never able to discover who the 'enemy' was. One young boy, hearing the commotion she was causing, tore up the literature he had just received. Spain had become a republic some four years earlier and, as a consequence, the power of the Roman church had been diminished, but George saw that power being restored. The feast of Corpus Christi was celebrated but, at the same time, the little band of believers gathered together for a time of real praise and worship. Meanwhile, the work continued without abatement as the workers moved into the towns and villages distributing Scriptures and tracts.

What they discovered was extreme poverty so that the people could not afford the small amount of ten centimos, but they made sure that the Word was given. In another village, they were invited into a home that was more like a stable, so poor were the people, so that they could read to the woman from the tracts. There were children in the house who were naked because they had no clothes. The challenge the missionaries heard often was, "How could God be a God of love to allow some people to live a life of luxury while others did not have enough to eat or wear?"

Besides the opposition of the RC church, there was also a negative response from communists that they met, who ridiculed and laughed at the truths of the Gospel. However, after some conversation, they became more serious and were left with something to think about. Others were more kindly disposed and some even were happy to report that they still had the books they had been given twelve months previously.

Conditions in the country deteriorated rapidly as the Fascists declared a revolution, the military leaders being the prime movers in the revolt. By the following day, there were reports of deaths as a result and the workers took possession of the town, searching the houses of the better-class people and seizing all firearms. It was felt wise, in the circumstances, to suspend the services until the situation became clearer. There was no opportunity for communication with the outside world.

As time progressed, the situation worsened as more people armed themselves and patrolled the streets, some with rifles, pistols, shot guns and sticks. One RC church was completely gutted by fire and all the images had been removed into the streets for burning. Not a member of the regular police was to be seen; the workers were in control. On the third day, a train arrived in Ronda bringing in more workers to reinforce those already there. Houses were searched for firearms, but the Thomas household was never touched.

There was a total lack of communication – no newspapers or mail; just a little spasmodic reporting via the radio. Cars and trucks were commandeered for the workers' use and servants in homes were told to leave so that their employers might be obliged to do their own work. George said it was unusual to see proud Spaniards going to market with shopping baskets. He also found it was impossible to send a telegram as he had wished to advise Headquarters of the situation.

About a week after the Revolution started, George discovered that all the British subjects had left the town. The British Consul at Malaga had sent two cars to take the British subjects to safety, but the Thomases had been overlooked. Each night was disturbed by the sounds of gunfire and, each morning, there was news of others who had been caught and shot. In spite of the mayhem, they were able to hold a communion service and a number of believers attended. George was finally able to get a telegram off to Headquarters advising that all were safe.

News came through that a British warship was at Malaga waiting to take British subjects away, so George immediately went to the communist Mayor of the town to obtain the necessary travel documents. They left at once carrying only one suitcase each and the journey was fraught with danger as they were stopped at road blocks all along the way and not released until their papers had been verified. When they arrived in Malaga, they found somewhere to stay for the night, but in some trepidation because the place had been a battle ground and the houses of the main streets had been burned to the ground. In the morning, they saw the British Consul who advised them that there was a warship standing by and that they would leave for Gibraltar in a few days. While they were there, the town was bombed by the rebel forces. The following day, three RC priests were shot and killed and there was another bombing raid. Ultimately, 52 refugees were taken to Gibraltar having first proved they were British as many Spaniards were trying to leave at the same time. They left on the destroyer, HMS Bulldog and, by six that evening, were safe once again under the British flag in Gibraltar.

Some four months later, George discovered that it was possible to travel within Spain again, via Gibraltar so he made the journey with the approval of the brethren at Headquarters. His travels were once again anything but smooth as he had to seek out the necessary permits and papers to allow him free passage. There was only one train per day to the interior so he had to stay overnight and be ready to move early the next morning. The train was filled with soldiers and young men dressed as Fascists. Along the way, walls and buildings were covered in slogans – "Long live Spain"; "Long live Christ the King"; "Long live the army" together with statements from speeches by Mussolini.

After about five hours travelling, he arrived at his destination and discovered that the house was untouched, with the British flag still nailed to the wall. The little car in the garage had not been interfered with either, which in itself was a miracle as all vehicles seemed to have been commandeered. The church had not been entered or damaged in any way while the workers or Government forces were in control, but when the rebel soldiers and Moors succeeded in entering, the signs outside the building had been ruthlessly torn away and destroyed, the building itself forced open, the texts on the walls torn down and then, later, everything movable was taken away, leaving the place completely empty. They not only took the piano and chairs, but the reading desk and the electric light fittings as well.

Much of the town had been destroyed because the rebels had bombed it several times before advancing to take it over. On hearing of their advance, about three quarters of the population that was left fled in whatever transport could be made available. Meanwhile, the town was running with blood as the civil war continued on its course. No quarter was given and, as quickly as the local jail was filled, it was emptied by taking the prisoners out and shooting them. In the midst of all this, George went about his business and was able to pack up his belongings and get them to Gibraltar where he put them in store. Then he returned to Spain to seek to recover the goods that had been removed from the church. He was successful in finding the piano but was told he would need to look for the chairs himself. Fighting continued without ceasing as the Government forces tried to retake the town, but were unsuccessful. As can be imagined, George was more than happy to get on the train back to Gibraltar.[ii]

Having returned to the homeland, George was appointed Missionary Secretary for the Movement in 1944. He resigned in 1957 and was called into the Presence of the Lord he had loved and served in 1970.

The Spanish Civil War and, in a very short time thereafter, the Second World War meant that Elim's input to Spain was severely curtailed and effectively nothing further was done until around 1980 when Brian Edwards travelled throughout Spain and Portugal seeking contacts on which to base an evangelistic work. But in October, 1981, after completing their studies at Elim Bible College, Andy and Yolande Smith accepted the challenge to go and pioneer the work. Andy planned to use his qualifications as a language teacher to obtain a foothold in Spain to begin the work.

Although Andy was a son of the manse in Elim, he had in fact been saved in Mexico, Yolande's homeland. Consequently, they entered the work in Spain without the backing of a local assembly in the UK and this presented them with added difficulties in that they were virtually unknown to Elim's UK constituency and therefore personalised support was not forthcoming. They felt the lack of a pastor and the backup a local church could have given and this left them often with feelings of isolation on the field.

Nevertheless, God miraculously opened a door of opportunity for them in Figueras where there was a British Language Institute. This was a strategic and important town of 30,000 in the Province of Girona in the north-east. They started holding meetings in their flat which was convenient to the centre of town and began to reach out with the Gospel. The plan was to establish the work in Figueras and then use it to reach out to other areas. It was also the intention to send Euroteams to help with the outreach.[iii]

Just one year after they first set foot in the country, Andy and Yoly took Brian Edwards to the fishing village of Llanca. The previous year, one of the Euroteams had paid a visit there and a thriving children's work was started. At this time, there were about 40 children and young people involved, meeting each week in the home of one of the new Christians, a former English language student who, with her daughter, came to know the Lord through the ministry in Figueras. They ran a hairdressing business in the town and, with a couple of other believers, had a real vision for the development of the work in that place. Happily, the Lord had wonderfully provided premises for them to meet.

In 1984, Isobel Stormont, the daughter of Pastor and Mrs. Philip Stormont, went to Spain for a period of ministry. She worked alongside Andy and Yoly in Figueras. At the time of her leaving in 1987, Isobel said,

I smile as I look back at the changes I've seen; five new babies and two more on the way. The last was a surprise to us all as the doctors believed that Manoli would never conceive again. But God healed her in a wonderful way. As wonderful as the physical births, are the spiritual ones, as well as the growth of those who were babes-in-arms when I first arrived. The family unit remains strong in Catalunya, and it's a miracle to see the family nature of God being expressed in our relationships with Him and with each other. Not only babes, but also grandmothers, brothers, aunts and cousins are being grafted in simultaneously, being sewn together in a new dimension of love, prayer and commitment. Miguel is back from National Service, Silvia from Bible school and two of our families living on the coast have now moved into Figueras so as to add strength to the main church body. . . Rafael, a one time student of Andy and me, is responding after years of witnessing and turning from his atheistic views to know God.

An encouraging development of the work was the commencement of a prison ministry. This came about because a personal friend of some of the church brethren became involved in a family feud and was forced to spend some time in the local Penitentiary Centre. This opened a door the church had been praying about and, after going through the obligatory paperwork, they were able to start a Bible Study group on Sunday afternoons. Ironically, the first day they went in, their contact was released, leaving them almost without an audience, but over the weeks, the numbers grew to between ten and 15 regulars eagerly waiting for the huge barred doors to swing open and then to greet the teachers enthusiastically before heading for the library where the group met. In a ten month period, eight conversions were registered, one of whom was on day release and was about to be baptised.

One prisoner, a 34 year old man, was known throughout the Province for mainly violent drug-related crime due to his heroin addiction. He was then serving a total of 17 years with 14 lawsuits still awaiting trial. His testimony was a tribute to the work being done and to the change Jesus can make in the life.

What I'm going to tell you about is something I wouldn't have dreamed possible a short time ago. For quite a time now I've been feeling different. I've done just about everything in my life. I started smoking 'hash' out of curiosity, then went on to LSD and finally got hooked on heroin without realising it, and needing to 'shoot' up to 2 grams a day. I've robbed banks, innocent people and deceived anybody and everybody to get my hands on drugs, a downward spiral that finally led me to the point of suicide. Whatever it was that brought me to this place, I truly thank God for letting me within these walls because in this prison I've found my salvation.

Needless to say, such testimonies were a source of much encouragement to the four men who were engaged on what was a difficult ministry. One can only imagine the joy felt by those faithful friends as another prisoner was allowed out of prison to go through the waters of baptism in testimony to his faith. Much red tape had to be untangled to make it happen and eventually, Manolo was baptised to the great joy of the gathered church despite having his hands handcuffed in front of him. No doubt the guard who had brought him heard something to his advantage as well that day.

The development of the church was such that in July 1987, Andy was able to leave his secular employment and work full time in the church. In the December, they had their first vacation home to the UK and began a strenuous itinerary around the UK churches. While on furlough, they left the church in the charge of the two elders, Antonio and Valentin. On his return from furlough, Andy had the happy task of commissioning Valentin Saavedra as pastor of a daughter church that had been planted from Figueras.

Valentin was converted as a direct result of the first Euroteam mission in 1982 and went to a local Pentecostal Bible College. There he met his wife, Sara, who shared his desire for evangelism and the discipling of believers.

The work in Spain was never easy, but the church grew and three churches were planted with plans for more and greater development. The Smiths, who left the field in 1997, were helped by John and Val Knox who gave themselves to the work. Local people became committed workers as time passed including Emilio and Yvonne Sevilla and others who intermarried within the churches. Pastoral care at the present time rests with John Knox and Emilio Sevilla.

i I am indebted to Mrs. Jewyl Shellard, the Thomas's daughter, for early insights.

ii These events were reported in detail in *Elim Evangel*, Vol.17. Issue 33, pp. 545-547; Vol.18. Issue. 5, pp65-67

iii See details in chapter on Euroteams.

SECTION TWO

AFRICA

11. Botswana/Bechuanaland 81
12. Belgian Congo/Zaire, Democratic Republic of Congo 83
13. Egypt 107
14. Ghana 113
15. Kenya 125
16. New Zealand/Zambia/Malawi 131
17. Tanganyika/Tanzania 135
18. Transvaal/South Africa 153
19. Zimbabwe/Southern Rhodesia 171

CHAPTER 11

BOTSWANA, Bechuanaland

The origins of the work in Botswana are not clear, but in 1973, W.H. Francis[i], an Elim missionary to Transvaal, had contact with a number of Pentecostal assemblies and a Pentecostal Bible school in Gabarone, the capital. At that time, young men were being saved and, sensing the call of God on their lives, were training in the Bible school to fit themselves for service.

The later work[ii] with which Elim had a connection, although it was never under Elim's auspices, was centred on Francistown, which is some 80 miles from Bulawayo in Zimbabwe. This was a work being done by Lance Corker who hailed originally from our Elim church in Harrogate, and whose family had connections with Hull City Temple.

Lance and his family had lived and worked in Africa for many years doing contract teaching in secondary schools. The foundation of this ministry lay in the school in Francistown. There was an obvious need for a work in the schools of the area. There were also great social needs because of alcoholism and marriage breakdown.

While many were coming to know Christ, there was little follow-up or aftercare. This led to the commencement of a Saturday night service for the whole group of believers, but schools ministry was carried on all through the week. In this, children of secondary school age were encouraged to evangelise the primary schools. There was also a vigorous prison ministry and older believers were encouraged to involve themselves in this.

By 1988, a plot of land had been purchased with a view to building a church and hopes were high that this would be fruitful.

As a nation, Botswana is relatively undeveloped although there are tarred roads. Most townships are situated near the railway, but the population is sparse.

Problems facing the church were both cultural and natural, drought being a major difficulty. There is poverty and a shortage of printed material in the local language, which is Setswana, but potential is unlimited.

i See W.H. Francis in chapter on Transvaal.

ii During the 1980s.

CHAPTER 12

CONGO/ZAIRE/DEMOCRATIC REPUBLIC OF CONGO

In an article published in *Christianity Today* (24.3.06), Grant McClung makes the point that "from the earliest inception of the Pentecostal Movement, our mission has always been missions. Indeed, Pentecostalism cannot be understood apart from its self-identity as a missionary movement raised up by God to evangelise the world in the last days."

The Elim Missionary Society was not formally organised until 1929, so any Elim people who felt called to a missions work had to go with organisations already functioning. This meant that many who went to the Belgian Congo did so under the auspices of the Congo Evangelistic Mission (CEM) founded by Wm. Burton and James Salter in 1915. Indeed, the minutes of the Elim Missions Board, when constituted, indicated that candidates for Congo were often advised to make application directly to the CEM leadership.

This arrangement worked well, as missionaries to Congo were required to raise their own support and their activity on the field was regulated on the Field by the Field Council, the home Board dealing more or less with administrative affairs. They also provided a Court of Appeal should disputes arise.

The closeness of fellowship was clearly demonstrated by the amount of material published in the *Elim Evangel* in subsequent years. Mr. Burton regularly sent home news items as well as articles for publication. Mr. Salter, likewise, was a prolific writer as time permitted and much of the early information about Congo came from the pens of these two brethren. In course of time, others directly associated with Elim went to the Field and began to record their experiences.

March 23rd, 1922 was a significant day for Elim Missions when Miss Adelaide Henderson of Belfast, accompanied by Miss Elsie Brooks of Tunbridge Wells, set sail for Congo after much waiting on God for His release. In a farewell letter, she thanked people for praying and expressed gratitude for the practical support that was making the journey possible.

Their trip was not without incident for, at 1 a.m. on the morning they were due to dock in Capetown, they were rudely awakened with cries to be prepared to abandon ship as their ship had run aground. There was no panic as the ship's lifeboats had been lowered but, in the end, tugs were able to pull the ship off the rocks and she steamed into harbour without any of the passengers or crew suffering injury.[1]

Sadly, just two months later, in June, Miss Elsie Brooks contracted malaria and died very quickly after just one day's illness. At the time, the party was travelling on a boat up river to Congo. James Salter was in the party and he conducted a funeral service. Miss Brooks was buried in a piece of land donated by a local chief.

Miss Henderson herself was far from well, suffering a severe bout of malaria, but was nursed by Mr. and Mrs. Salter until she recovered. Thus the arrival at the mission station in Mwanza was not what had been anticipated, but through the sadness, Miss Henderson's view was that 'God must have some lesson through it all'.

As she began to involve herself in the work, she became very much aware of the conflict between light and darkness. She had watched as Mr. Burton dealt with the kazunji – an idol used by the witchdoctor to bring healing, but more usually to entice the people to part with their goods. The effort resulted in the witchdoctor being shown up for what he was and the whole village became interested in the Gospel. Nevertheless, shortly after this event, the baby of one of the young men who had helped Mr. Burton became seriously ill and was expected to die. The village looked upon this as the witchdoctor's revenge. But prayer was made without ceasing and the baby revived. The following Sunday, the church was crowded and the young man was asked to bring his baby to the front so that all might see what God had done.

One of the earliest Elim missionaries to the Congo was Dr. Cyril Taylor. His reports contained much detail on the continuing fight against the darkness of heathenism and idol worship. He and his wife were very concerned about the spiritual welfare of the boys working around their house, so they decided to have special prayer with them in the early morning. Despite feeling tired, she responded to the boys' reminder and was rewarded to see them being filled with the Spirit as the fire of God fell on them while they prayed. One after another fell down prostrate, speaking in tongues and prophesying as the Spirit gave them utterance.

On one of his visitations, Cyril spent a week with some Methodist missionaries and ministered to them. Shortly after his return to his own home, he received a letter telling him that the Holy Spirit had fallen on the Methodist mission station and they were asking him to return to teach them concerning Pentecost.

Reports were also received regularly from Pastor Burley. He was a statistician in his own way and reported that in one quarter alone, meetings had been held in 1159 kraals, 12,758 people were present and 49 decisions were recorded. In many cases, the converts were chiefs of the kraals, so that the influence of their conversion was great in the locality.

At that time (1924) he was concerned that there were many ladies on the field but that few men were volunteering their services. His point was that pioneering was heavy work, needing strong men to carry it out, but that if the men were not forthcoming, the women would have to do it, at some cost to themselves, no doubt.

There was a strong work among the fishing villages that lay around the lakes and many had trusted the Lord. Imagine the blessing of baptising and being baptised in a crocodile-infested swamp. The Lord gloriously blessed one such gathering as they baptised a crippled boy and watched him come from the waters completely healed. At the praise time following, the Holy Spirit broke in upon the company and many spoke in other tongues. The natives from the village were amazed at what they saw and heard.

Teddy Hodgson was another stalwart of the early days in Congo. His story is told by Colin Whittaker in his book, *Seven Pentecostal Pioneers*.[ii]

James Mullan of Belfast was a member of Elim's Evangelistic Band. He too felt the call of God to missions and sailed for the Belgian Congo on 30th April, 1926 and remained in the country until 1934, when he transferred to South Africa. When he arrived at the main station in Mwanza, almost overwhelmed by the new sights and sounds, he found a warm welcome not only from the native population, but also from Mr. and Mrs. Burton. The following day, all the missionaries from the region met together to decide where he should begin work and they agreed that he should go with Harold Womersley to pioneer a new work in Busangu.

Leaving Mwanza, the journey to Busangu took about a week by bicycle (where possible), over valleys, crossing streams and mountains. Mr. Burton joined them very shortly afterwards to help with the planning of the new station, and finally taking the plans to Kamina for approval. James stayed with the 'stuff' while Wm. Burton and Harold Womersley went to deal with the authorities.

Busangu was a fairly large village set on a plateau at 3,700 feet above sea level. They spent some time cutting back the jungle to make roads and boundaries for the mission station. They cleared enough space for their tents as they contemplated building a proper house, and were glad to be a little above the village and thus removed from village sounds to the peace of the forest. Meetings for the Gospel were a little slow because many of the men of the village were away working on a new road or burning the bush to trap animals. But they were expecting a rich harvest of souls in due time.

House building began on August 13th and depended on mud and wattle for the walls with a roof of bamboo poles covered in thatch. The house provided them with two bedrooms and a dining room in between, and measured 30 by 15 feet. On a couple of occasions, James came very close to danger as he grasped a snake while clearing out a hole for one of the wall poles. He let it go very quickly, which was fortunate since it was poisonous. A little later, he quietly left a black mamba to sleep as he had no weapon with which to deal with it.

Meanwhile, spiritual work was not neglected. Mr. Womersley held a meeting every morning for the workmen and any others who came along. On Sundays, they held a communion service for the Christians in the morning and went into the village in the afternoon with the Gospel. A special highlight of the month of August was the delivery of six letters from home and an *Elim Evangel*! Within a short time, however, he was transferred to the station at Kisanga as the lady missionary there had gone away to be married, and the work was to be placed in the care of Mr. Mac and Mrs. Irene Bradshaw (née Clarke).

The Bradshaws continued to serve in Busangu where Mrs. Irene Bradshaw, a skilled midwife, was much used for the benefit of the native population and the proclamation of the Gospel. Sadly, after only about two years on the field, when the Bradshaws were ready to go on furlough, Mrs. Bradshaw contracted blackwater fever and died very quickly. Since Mr. Bradshaw's health had not been good, they had decided to take their furlough in Capetown rather than make the long journey back to the UK, and there, friends from the Apostolic Faith Church were looking after them. The memory of Mrs. Bradshaw's sweetness and devotion to the people of Busangu would not be soon forgotten.[iv]

James was involved at this time with James Salter who had made preparations for his arrival, but who soon was to begin travelling around the region, leaving James on his own. From time to time, there were opportunities for fellowship with other missionaries and it was a great joy to James when Mr. and Mrs. Taylor[iii] with their baby son, Eustace, visited. There was much catching up to do with news about other Elim folks both at home and abroad, and the ministry of Mr. Taylor in the village was much blessed of God. Mrs. Taylor, too, made a positive contribution as she spoke with freedom and fluency. Her message was accompanied by great blessing. However, their departure left James feeling somewhat lonely and the house empty.

The Taylors, based in Ngoi-Mani, were experiencing rich blessing in their ministry as people were being saved and the Lord was working among them with signs and wonders. Their strength was increased by the arrival of Mr. and Mrs. Garfield Vale from Kasongo Mule. Mr. Vale had charge of about six of the meetings and schools at the nearby out-stations.

It is difficult to imagine the time and distances involved in carrying out the work of the Lord in Congo. Without roads or proper transport, much of the work was done on foot, with native carriers and sometimes, by boat on the rivers. Teddy Hodgson told of nearly arriving at a planned destination when the bearings on the motor of their boat collapsed for lack of lubrication, so forcing them to go with the flow, back down river. Cyril Taylor reported that a trip round the outstations had taken him a month. A note in the *Elim Evangel* highlights some of the pressure:

I thank you for your gentle hint about writing more often for the Evangel. I too have been disappointed that so few have written to me. It would have been a great joy and encouragement to my soul if the folks in Elim had written a few lines now and then. Sometimes the loneliness out here is felt, and one has been nearly three months without seeing a white skin, and it is in such times that one looks and longs for a cheery letter from the brethren at home.[v]

James Mullan, while reporting some of his experiences after a year in the country, told of the difficulties involved in facing Satanic powers, idol worship, wild animals, including elephants, snakes and lions and tramping knee deep in water to make a journey. In this context, he felt constrained to utter a word of warning:

I write you these details because I know there are many of you at home who seem to think that the missionary's life out here is a bed of roses, and also because I feel there are many, not knowing the difficulties we have to labour under, who would talk of coming out here without counting the cost to the full. I have found that those who are out here do not complain about their difficulties, trials and troubles, but take them cheerfully as part of the day's work for God[vi].

The following months saw James totally involved in the work of the Mission as he travelled many miles, in the most horrendous of conditions, to bring the Gospel. He moved house from time to time and, two years after his arrival, saw him in the north at Kipushya. On the whole his health remained good except for one very bad case of fever when he had to send for Cyril Taylor to come and pray for him. Both Cyril and the native Christians held fervent prayer and, the following morning, he was anointed with oil and his condition improved. He was taken then to Mwanza for a period to recover and was treated like royalty.

Early in 1928, the team was enhanced by the arrival of Mr and Mrs. Allan McIntosh. Mrs. McIntosh was known to Elim folks as Miss Marjorie Phair. They farewelled from Clapham in February and found their way to Congo via Dar-es-Salaam and Lake Tanganyika, by car to Lake Kion where they waited ten days for another boat. Finally, their luggage was placed on the heads of carriers and they set off for their final destination. There is virtually no further reference to them in the archives or in published reports.

In 1930, James had his first furlough and spent time travelling around the churches. He also took the time to find himself a wife, when he married Miss Mary Paynter, one of the brightest and most earnest Brighton Crusaders. As they contemplated a return to Congo in October that year, the then Missionary Secretary, Pastor Charles H. Coates, made a special appeal to help them with their equipment. He stated that they would need special equipment beyond the normal because they were going to a very remote region. It was also recognised that the Government in Congo was now frowning on natives being used as bearers, so a lorry was proposed. A further £100 would be required to provide them a house to live in. Altogether, the necessary items would come to £750 to cover the next few years on the field and readers of the *Evangel* were asked prayerfully to consider how they might help. The point was well made that Mrs. Mullan would be considered as a fully accredited Elim missionary in her own right. It was a major encouragement when, at their farewell service, the offering which had been designated for the building of their house came to £80.

Once they had returned to Congo, the work went forward. Their time was divided in so many ways as they sought to reach the furthest villages with the Gospel, all the time battling the forces of evil and wicked men, facing opposition from chiefs and Roman Catholic priests who did their utmost to disturb the work.

Mary Mullan and Marjorie Taylor found much to occupy them. Mrs. Taylor had two small children, but nevertheless went about praying in money to start a work among the women. When the Lord answered, she made arrangements for a women's conference at a central outstation. They left home at 3 a.m. and travelled for three days, one day's journey being in a huge native canoe down the Congo River. Ultimately, some 86 women attended and, out of that experience, Mrs. Taylor realised the great need there was for girls and women to have teaching and the ability to read. When she arrived home, she set about preparing accommodation for women to come for teaching and, when this was ready, eighteen turned up and came for an eight week period as they learned to read, to sing and to pray.

Subsequently, the women came, often unannounced, to receive teaching and instruction, as well as for fellowship, something previously unheard of since it meant some of the women travelling for up to four days from their homes. One young lady had just finished learning to read. To her, it was like being the first to swim the English Channel or reach the North Pole. She was just about to marry a young evangelist, so the expectation was that she would be able to support him in his work by teaching other women.

Mrs. Mullan, meanwhile, was teaching a class of evangelists who were being trained and came once a month for classes. They spent some time with the Lord and then turned to teaching so that the evangelists could go back to their areas better equipped to win souls. In addition, she found herself conducting children's meetings in the nearby village with some success as children asked the Lord to save them.

Life and ministry continued to be a round of struggles with climate and customs, as well as the necessary travels far and wide to the various outstations, each with its own selection of challenges and blessings. Personal health was always under threat, but God's servants were undaunted in their efforts to reach the lost and to move further and further afield with the Gospel.

In the course of travel, there were many encouragements. At times, a baptismal service would be conducted in one of the local streams or rivers and, often, as they did so, the power of the Holy Spirit came upon the gathered crowd. Many were filled with the Spirit and spoke in other tongues, while several were heard to prophesy. As they challenged the forces of darkness, they saw God at work in miraculous ways and His name was glorified among the people.

The measure of effectiveness of the ministry and the maturity of those who had trusted the Lord was in evidence all the time. Mrs. Mullan reported the case of Patishio, one of the native evangelists who had been persecuted for his faith and witness, as he described his experiences to the church:

It is wonderful to see how God keeps us from day to day. When we leave the Mission and its blessings behind us each month, we have to lean wholly on the Eternal One, and He is ever faithful in His care for us. Even so it was with me when, in His Name, I went to the new villages on the road to Kabinda. The Catholics have taken such possession of these places that nobody would leave their houses to hear my words about Jesus Christ. At last I stood in the middle of the road in a village which was so large that it took a whole day to traverse to the middle of it. Then it seemed that everyone was shouting and screaming at once as down from each end of the street came hundreds of people, led by the Roman Catholic catechist at the head of each crowd, and they were shouting to me to clear out, and that they didn't want the devil there, and that I must return to the eternal fires. Soon they were upon me, beating and kicking me, flinging goats' refuse into my eyes and mouth and hurting me dreadfully.

I could never have fought them single handed had I wanted to, but God had left no anger in my heart. . . Eventually I was too weak to stand, and as I fell, someone hit me over the eye with a stick. The persecutors were giving me a bad time of it, and at last, I stuttered out: Kill me if you like, only hurry and do it quickly. But the Catholic catechist replied: No, we do not intend to kill you because you would haunt us. Besides that you are a friend of the Mission and if they knew we had killed you they would have us put in prison.

Later, they wearied of their sport and left me. I was so stiff and bruised, I could not move and my left eye was swelling fast and becoming very painful. However, out of a hut crept an old man and he carried me to his bed and cared for me. God will surely bless that man who gave me such pity and love.[vii]

The following month, he returned to the village, taking his four year old daughter with him. There he was met and warmly greeted by a stranger who proved to be an overseer of the Catholics and was anxious to make peace with Patishio. He said he had heard of the ill-treatment and those concerned had been severely dealt with. His greatest marvel was that Patishio had not reported those involved to the authorities at Kabinda. From that time on, Patishio was welcomed and became loved as he remained to work among the people there.

Early in 1935, the work was dealt a major blow by the sudden and unexpected death of Cyril Taylor while he was home on furlough. There had been no indication of illness. This was a man who had great human potential. He was a student at Cambridge where he took an MA and had brilliant prospects. However, he renounced a life of comfort and refinement so that he might carry the message of redeeming love to darkest Africa. When he went to Congo in 1920, he left behind him, in the hearts of those who knew him at home, the memory of a man who counted it a living joy to be a servant of Jesus Christ, who cared not what the future held of toil, privation, pain or loss, so long as his Divine Master used him in bringing perishing souls to His feet. His success on his station at Ngoi Mani will be known in full only when the great day of accounting comes, but we are sure that there will be hundreds of souls there to give praise to God for his faithfulness.[viii]

Just under one year later, Mrs. Taylor returned to the Field, taking her two youngest children with her and leaving behind in the homeland the four older children. Once returned, she began to make preparations for continuing the work she and her husband had been engaged in, so that now, instead of simply concentrating on training young women, she became busily involved with the training of evangelists and teachers as well.

In 1933, Leslie Wigglesworth had responded to the call of God and went to serve in Congo. He had been studying French in Belgium when he met up with Fred Ramsbottom and they attended an interview together, hoping to be accepted for the work, and knowing that acceptance depended on their ability with the language. Success found them travelling to Congo where, for a time they worked together.[ix]

In 1939, Leslie married Ruth Boulton, daughter of E.C.W.Boulton, and they both returned to the Field. Ruth was a trained nurse so her contribution was likely to be significant. The Wigglesworths were based at Katenta, with an area stretching from north to south and requiring six days to cross it. One of the challenges regularly put to Leslie by the natives while on trek was the question as to why the missionaries would always keep to set paths when, in the bush, there were thousands who had never ever heard the Name of Jesus. Eventually, despite all possible sorts of delays, Leslie managed to reach such an area and found great acceptance of the message, with requests for a soon return. Despite much prayer, there were always official restrictions on sending native evangelists into those areas but, just about one week before he was due to leave on furlough, permission was granted and the work opened up.

One of the great difficulties they faced was in persuading the womenfolk to accept Christ. Leslie wrote: Unless the women are won for Christ, there can be little hope for a godly family life among the Basongo peoples. One evening, after our village open air meeting, two mothers with young children in their arms came to ask that we would pray with them. If you could realise how much harder the women are to win than the men, your hearts would bound with joy as ours did. In school, we have the priceless privilege of helping to shape the characters of the future men and women.[x]

At the same time, Alice Wigglesworth, Smith Wigglesworth's daughter was also serving on the station at Kabondo Dianda. She had gone as a missionary to Angola in 1913 and then moved to South America after she married the British and Foreign Bible Society's representative there, Rev. S. Smith. They worked in South America until his premature death, but in 1920, she then entered Congo as the wife of James Salter.

An energetic and lively woman, she became thoroughly involved in the work and, in spite of having served in Angola, found much in the Congo that was fresh and new. Within about three months of her arrival, she found herself occupied in a six week training programme for native evangelists and teachers.

Alice died in 1966 and her funeral took place in the Bradford Elim church where she had been brought up and was well known for thirty-five years. Many recollected her fiery preaching and Spirit-filled ministry. Representatives attended from CEM, Assemblies of God and Elim and Harold Womersley and Bessie Swettenham paid tribute to her labours on the Congo Field. Harold, himself, died in 1986 at the age of 84. He was buried in Bedford after a funeral service attended by several hundred, in which tribute was paid to a Christian statesman and faithful warrior for the Gospel. It was stated that "his competent exemplary work drew recognition from the Congo government and he received several civil honours."[xi]

1939 saw Elim headquarters beginning its publication of a small quarterly broadsheet entitled *Elim Missionary Courier*. This was a four page document carrying information and news from the fields and seemed to be distributed as an encouragement to prayer. It was also possible to publish more detailed information than in the pages of the *Evangel*. 1939 saw also the beginning of the Second World War and the storm clouds had their effect on those wishing to go to the mission field.

One such individual was Tom Nosworthy who had felt a call to missions some twelve years before but now, in 1939, found himself, with his wife, on board a ship bound for South Africa, en route to Congo, in a convoy accompanied by destroyers. Although far removed from the scenes of conflict, the missionaries discovered that there was a knock-on effect and that prices, especially of food, were rising rapidly day by day. As a result, they sought to be as self-sufficient as possible by growing their own.

A letter written to W.G. Hathaway[xii] soon after their arrival is very telling:

I thought I would write you from time to time and let you know something of the work here. We are so happy in the work to which God has called us, and from the very first day, we knew this was the place; there was not the slightest tinge of strangeness. It seemed as if we had always been here and although we are tucked up in one room, with mud floor, mud ceiling and mud plaster on the walls and having come without any kind of furniture, no beds, no towels, no cutlery or any sort of household goods and not even a wash stand or basin or bucket, in fact nothing but a few clothes that we managed to buy at Selfridges the very morning we left, yet we are as happy as 'sand boys' - the centre of God's will is happiness and contentment.

The missionaries here loaned us two camp beds, two small tables, a couple of native cane chairs and a frame-work of bamboo canes to hang clothes on, some native straw mats for floor covering, so until our things arrive from England and my purchases arrive from Elisabethville, we shall be 'fixed up nicely'.

Having received only one letter from England it is difficult to know how things are at home, but we pray that you are all safe; we pray for you every day without fail and believe that He will keep you all safe at this time.

I wrote to Mr. Corry[xiii] and told him of our experiences on the ship; we shall never forget them. Did you know that our ship was actually waiting to be broken up when war was declared and the ship that should have sailed a fortnight previously was taken over by the Admiralty and that meant that hundreds of South Africans were stranded? So they brought this ship into service again; the poor old thing was rusty, its maximum speed was just 10 knots, we were packed six to a cabin with the portholes closed, we were running out of fresh water. As we passed along the Channel, surrounded by battleships and aeroplanes, the sea seemed to have the atmosphere of danger and at one place, we noticed it was covered with oil and one of the officers told us a tanker had been sunk. Then we were left alone on the high seas; no destroyers, no aeroplanes, no convoy; you see, the war had commenced only a few days previously. At a place when we were so far from land, the nearest being the bottom of the ocean, we noticed a black, thin-like object just protruding above the water. It was coming for our course; it must be the periscope of a U-boat. Our ship turned sharply off course, passengers preparing for the worst. What could our poor old boat do? But it turned out to be just a sea buoy that had broken adrift.

Instead of taking only 17-20 days for the journey, it actually took us four weeks and one day. Weren't we glad to get off the boat and take the long journey through sand and forest across Africa until we stepped off the train at Kabondo Dianda, not far from the Mission station? There was nobody to meet us. The telegram I had sent from the border was carried on the same train as we had travelled on! Fortunately, there was a trader there who spoke French. He told us that the missionary in charge was away recovering from malaria, but he agreed to take us to the Mission where we found two sisters in charge and they gave us something to eat and two camp beds to rest on.

Since arriving, I have visited Mr. and Mrs. Bradshaw at Busangu, Mrs. Taylor at Ngoi-Mani (about six days' journey from here), also Mr. and Mrs. Burton at Mwanza, Mr. and Mrs. Hall at Kisanga, Mr. and Mrs. Hodgson at Kikondja, all by bicycle - this is gruelling work especially when, without water and miles from a village, the natives are very hospitable with water and peanuts, but it's the forest, rocks, roots and tree stumps, climbing and carrying the cycle - It's a totally different life from that in the Homeland. A PS to his letter said "We hope you will not mind this letter coming via Glossop. Only it costs 5d each letter from here"!

The territory to which they were assigned, Kabondo Dianda, stretched seventy-five miles to the south, forty-five miles to the north and twenty-two miles each way east and west, and there was a Government ruling that they must visit the villages once every three months. There wasn't much time for sitting on their hands! Before their departure, someone gave Dora Nosworthy a piano accordion which did sterling service but also created such amazement that sometimes, the folks forgot to sing. They had never seen a 'breathing instrument' before. Her guitar was much more 'ordinary'. Wherever they went, they found a strong welcome from believers, and interest in the Gospel shown by others who wondered why the white people had come so far to tell them about Jesus.

One of the necessary chores for all missionaries is to become proficient in the language. Tom and Dora Nosworthy had to study the very difficult Kiluba language and were expected to pass exams to show their understanding. At exam time, Tom gained 94% in Paper 1, 92% in Paper 2 and 85% in Paper 3; Dora scored about 5% less in each paper. Not content with knowing the language, Tom also spent time during one of his furloughs to attend the Missionary School of Medicine in London. There he graduated top in his class, with T.W. Walker coming second. Tom was 39 at the time and one of his fellow students was John Phillips of the AoG.

This furlough took place in 1944, while the war was still on and Tom was booked to speak at Elim churches around the country. He visited East Ham, Leyton and Croydon. While visiting Wimbledon, Islington, Kingston and Ilford, the flying bombs could be heard and felt. He was impressed that, in spite of the restrictions, with flying bombs dropping, and destruction and the effects of blast in evidence everywhere, there had been no suggestion that the meetings should be cancelled. His commendation was that a missionary visiting the Elim churches could feel the atmosphere that was charged with holy zeal and passion, while every minister endeavoured to make the missionary feel welcome and did all in his power to make the meeting a success. One wonders if the same might be said today!!

Fluency in language obviously makes for better communications. The end result was an ability not only to preach the Gospel but also to engage in the daily business of village life. The whole range of human experience was there, from witch doctors drawing blood and presenting charms as the answer to needs, to dealing with local chiefs on matters of law and policy. But one of the great encouragements they found was when village chiefs or headmen found Christ as Saviour.

They were at Kavukwa and had opportunity to preach the Gospel. All the old men of the village sat on a tree trunk in front of Tom as he spoke from John 3 and found great liberty in explaining how God wanted a sacrifice and that His Son had come to meet the need. He asked who would honestly make a stand for salvation – no shams, only genuine converts, not to follow the white man, only the Saviour, Jesus Christ. Up shot the hands of the chief. They prayed together and closed the meeting. Just as they were leaving, the chief stood up and commanded them to sit as he wished to speak. He said, "Relatives, Jesus Christ shed His blood to save me and today, I am the only one who will accept Him in this village. It doesn't matter – I am going to follow Him and I want to see all my people follow Him as well. Years ago, I was a slave in Angola, but after freedom came back to Congo and found the Saviour. I bought this chieftainship and put God behind, and other things of earth first. Many have been the times that His servants have visited this village and I refused to return. To-day I have heard the voice of God and want to worship God and read His Word, for years ago, I learned to read."

Needless to say, the struggles and difficulties of the journey – the worst yet - became as nothing compared to the joy of seeing fifteen souls, including the chief, respond to the Gospel.

It was quite marvellous how God intervened in so many ways to show Himself alive and involved in the affairs of men. The Hodgsons were stationed at Kikondja. Mrs. Hodgson reported that she had left the station to travel to Johannesburg "with a black heart" – thus did the Africans describe a feeling of dissatisfaction. She didn't want to be away, partly because she was heavily pregnant with her first child and the journey was tiresome. However, in Johannesburg, she found herself in the care of a Mr. and Mrs. Bennett. Mr. Bennett came from Yorkshire, so she felt a little better at that. While there, she gave birth to her son, John Michael, and realised that God's timing was perfect. Her return to the Field was in a much lighter heart, especially when, at Ndola station, she was helped by the station master who provided her with tea and arranged for her to have access immediately to the train which was not due to leave for several more hours. She saw the hand of the Lord in her journeys.

In the work, too, God was clearly at work as they were able to report miracles of healing under the ministry of the African evangelists. One was called to a home where a child was very sick. The child was in a very bad way with blood pouring from nose and ears, and it was vomiting so much that the whole bed was just a red pool. Also, whenever someone touched its body, it started to bleed. The Evangelist prayed over the child then went home and continued to pray in his house. When he returned the next day, the child was well.

Another Christian girl gave birth to a baby that was blind. The relatives – heathens – said the child should be allowed to die, but the Evangelist, a young, recently-converted boy, took charge of both mother and baby, declaring that the baby would not only live, but would also receive its sight.

The girl's father was away at the time, but when he heard about his daughter, he came home, bringing with him his charms and native medicine, but the girl stood firm in her faith and rejected them all. Each day, the Evangelist knelt in the home and prayed for the child, thanking and praising God for the wee life. God heard and honoured their faith and, at the end of a month, the baby had a pair of beautiful eyes.

In another village, a believer had a dream in which the Lord challenged him about giving thanks for his food. When he arose in the morning, he took special care with the food that had been prepared the previous evening, and discovered that someone had placed a deadly poison in it. They too thanked God for His preserving power.

Mrs. Harold Berry (née Wigglesworth, Leslie's sister) reported that she was fully engaged on the same station as the Hodgsons in working with the girls and women of the village. She was most keen to see that the women and girls understood the reality of their faith and that Jesus had died for all, not just for the men. She recognised that the women didn't have a very exciting future before them, in the normal way of things, but she was determined to help them to make the most of their opportunities by offering them training in reading, writing and homemaking, among other things.

After her first year, she reflected that life in Congo was just so much different. She contemplated riches, and thought that a missionary needed the riches of patience and perseverance. A rich native would possess a charcoal iron, a suit and a hat of some kind, a boat if he was a fisherman, a spear and a gun if he was a hunter, a few francs, a wife and some children. He was rich until the day of catastrophe. She saw fire devour the village and watched as women screamed for their children who might be in the huts; the rich man became poor instantaneously, but in his poverty was led to know the riches that are to be found in Christ Jesus.

She thought about honour and confessed that, most of the time, the missionary was honoured, with children standing by to do small deeds for the white lady. But a greater honour was to be stopped by a woman with a sick child who was seeking help. What an honour to stand under the open canopy of heaven and bring such needs before the Great Physician and feel certain of His answer.

Dora Nosworthy found herself in similar circumstances, but realised that God is a God of wonders who can turn around things that seem impossible otherwise. It would be wrong for us to imagine that the missionary's life was filled with miracles every day. There were dry times and times of deep frustration and testing. At Busangu, there had been no decisions for some time and, feeling rather "dry", the mission house was opened for times of special prayer. At one point, Tom Nosworthy prayed that if the people wouldn't come in to hear the Word of the Lord, then the Lord would speak to them directly, even in their dreams.

Two days later, one of the young men came and told them that Asa's mother had had two wonderful dreams and was now converted. They didn't know Asa had a mother living. Oh, yes, but she is old and ill and lives away back in the forest. Without more ado, they went looking for the old lady and found her, a very old woman sitting on a grass mat under a small palm frond shelter, naked except for a dirty piece of sacking around her loins, eyes that could hardly see and limbs that were terribly swollen because of dropsy.

They greeted her and asked her about her salvation. In a feeble voice she told them that a messenger in white had visited her and told her the story of the Cross. She had argued with him and refused to listen. He came back the next night; at first she refused him but then she believed and now, she said, my heart is white; I'm rejoicing; my heart is white.

As they listened to her story, Tom remembered someone praying, "Lord, we know You are in heaven, but Your footprints are here on earth." It was humbling to think of someone so insignificant, so poor, housed in a shack not fit for animals and with nothing of this world's goods, yet the Lord of glory had come to visit her and brought joy and gladness, salvation and hope and a glorious expectation of a wonderful future.

Dora said:

And so we see them, the women of dark Congo, downtrodden, ignorant, debased, but many, thank God, lifted by His grace to sit in heavenly places with Christ Jesus. With hearts changed, lives transformed, they are faithfully and earnestly letting their lights shine in the midst of the darkness of unspeakable sin and wickedness. Many, too, are suffering the bitterest persecution from heathen husbands, fathers and relatives, but are ready to lay down their lives rather than deny the Lord that bought them with His own blood, and that raised them out of the filth and the mire to the clean, pure, happy life of the child of God. We thank God for every one of them.[xiv]

One of the interesting things about the Congo work at that time, even although the Elim Missionary Society had been in existence for over ten years, was that Burton and Salter were treated with great esteem in the Elim churches they visited while on furlough. There was no impression of their being something apart from the Elim work in any way. Indeed, on one of James Salter's visits, he was accompanied round the Elim Churches in London by Pastor Joseph Smith who spoke of his joy at such an opportunity. In his own inimitable way, he said, "It is well known among preachers that whilst it may be possible to give the members of a congregation a very thrilling time, yet to thrill the heart of a preacher every time you minister is something to which very few will lay claim. But I must confess that my soul was thrilled every time I listened to the ministry of Mr. Salter."

Equally interesting was the fact that, for the previous twenty-five years, on average, two churches were opened every five weeks and a fresh native preacher was sent out into the work every two weeks in the same period.

The passing of the years brought many and varied experiences to each of the missionaries on the field. Their lives were filled with joy and sorrow, blessing and not a little cursing on the part of those who couldn't find it in their hearts to wish them well. Sadly, persecution came as much from other religious bodies as it did from heathen sources. They saw sinners converted and young men and women giving themselves wholly to the work of God, despite great opposition within their own families or villages. Baptismal services were sources of joy and celebration, and the putting away of idols brought a sense of closure to a former life and an assurance of life everlasting through the Lord Jesus Christ.

Everyday life was anything but tedious or boring, with something new each day to challenge and stretch the imagination and ingenuity of the workers. Trekking to distant villages was often fraught with dangers from the terrain, wild animals and hostile natives. Journeys were taken by bicycle, motor cycle and motor boat as well as on foot. Roads being few and far between, motor vehicles were not always the best way to travel. Longer journeys were sometimes made by train. One of the difficulties identified by Leslie Wigglesworth was the developing desire on the part of the natives for material wealth. While the Government officials considered this a good omen for the future of the race, the grasping lust for wealth pushed out the desire for spiritual things. Worship and the desire for prayer vanished to be replaced by a rampant materialism.

Because of this change in the attitude of the people, the Wigglesworths felt that they could no longer stay to minister in that area. When they threatened that this would be their response, the people were aghast and concerned, but it had absolutely no effect on their way of life. They therefore moved away to Mutengwa, where they found large villages and multitudes of people ready to hear the Gospel. After the strain of their previous station, the work here was a joy, despite requiring a great deal more in terms of effort and time commitment.

At one stage, they had sixty evangelists together for training and what was true here, was also true right across the land wherever the missionaries laboured. The intention was to equip as many young men as possible to do the work of an evangelist. In one case, the study had been on the judgements and the students were required to take turns in preaching what they had learned. One young man, an able speaker, took a different tack. He brought in the local tyrant from the village and preached to him everything he knew about judgement. The man squirmed and trembled and the following Sunday, came to church looking to be saved.

Tom Nosworthy concluded his missionary endeavour in Congo in 1943. During 1944, while home on furlough, he undertook training at the Missionary School of Medicine in London and, in 1945, returned to Africa, this time initially to South Africa and then to Tanganyika.[XV] In 1946, he and Arthur Tate, with whom he was pioneering in Tanganyika, paid a short visit to his old station in Congo where they received a tumultuous reception. As they travelled through the country, they were given many opportunities for ministry and the Evangelists in each district showered them with gifts of chickens, eggs, manioc, sweet potatoes, corn, peanuts and pineapples, etc. There were hundreds of questions repeated over and over, not least among them – Where did you get the motor car? and, Will we see you again?

The Wigglesworths, who had also been on furlough after six and a half years on the Field, returned in 1947 for a further term, accompanied by their two children, Brian and Joyce. Their first stop was at Kipushya, where they were to remain for a period. Imagine their joy to arrive and hear that the past two years had been times of revival and reaping, and that many they had gone home praying earnestly for, were now soundly saved and serving the Lord. The old chief, for whom they had prayed for many years, was one of the first to greet them.

One of the problems they had to face was the tropical storms, always accompanied by lightning. Houses in the village were set on fire and in the neighbouring village of Mutengwa, the house where they used to live was struck by lightning and destroyed completely, leaving Elton Knauf[XVI] and his wife with their two small children homeless and deprived of their possessions.

The following year, Kipushya was the venue for the Field Conference. This lasted for ten days and catered for some fifty missionaries and their twenty-three children. Two missionaries were missing because of illness, but otherwise the whole complement attended. The days were filled with Conference sessions, fellowship meetings and planning meetings, including travelling to other sites to investigate the possibility of erecting church buildings. Efforts were made to translate Mr. Burton's Bible Studies from Kiluba into Kisongo. These had been used in the Bible School at Mwanza for many years to great effect. Bible translation into local dialects was an ever present activity and one which goes on into the present day.

In 1949, the half ton truck they had been waiting two years for was delivered. They had to collect it from Matadi and drive it 1600 miles back to the mission station.

Leslie's complaint was that petrol was very expensive – four shillings (20p) a gallon!! How times have changed, but they saw the vehicle as a tool for reaching the outstations, some of which were 150/200 miles away.

With the passing of time, modern civilisation was penetrating to the very interior of the country. Metalled roads were being built and mud huts were being replaced with brick buildings. Most of the major villages were now accessible by road and short cuts were being constructed to save wear and tear on the five-ton lorries that were the mainstay of transport in the region. Distances were thus being cut and the missionary's work and travel were being helped in a measure.

After they left the field in 1953, Leslie and Ruth returned to the UK and, in course of time, Leslie became Elim's Missionary Secretary after George H. Thomas. During his time in office, he not only presided over missionary departures and returns, but was often found in print updating the missionary news and seeking to stir up support in the homeland for those he knew so well on the various Fields. A broad overview of his time in Congo was contained in an article he wrote for the *Elim Evangel* entitled, Pioneer Trails. (Vol.63, Issue 29, pp. 6, 7) This writer remembers him telling of an occasion when, lost in the bush, the only way to find a direction for travel was to reach some high ground. This was impossible in that area, so Leslie climbed to the top of a tree so that he could see over the forest and establish where they were.

With the end of the Second World War, missionary endeavour, which had been somewhat curtailed, began to flourish once again. Donald Gee reported that, at the end of 1947, Elim had thirty-seven missionaries on the various Fields, located in India, Congo, Egypt, Belgium, Tanganyika and other fields.[xvii] One of those was Olive Garbutt, who went in 1947 and left at Independence in 1960. Olive hailed from North Yorkshire and, after conversion, was associated with the Bridge Street church in Leeds. The call to missions came to her at the farewell service for Leslie Wigglesworth in 1934, when James Salter presented the challenge and she rose to her feet at the end of the meeting, along with a number of other young people similarly touched. Nursing training followed and then she became a Queen's District Nurse, in preparation for her future work. She resigned from nursing in the January and, while waiting for her visa, she studied at Elim Bible College. The visa was not obtained until the December because the application was lost when the Belgian Government transferred its offices back from Leopoldville to Brussels. This meant that it was 1947 before she was able to leave Leeds with blessings showered upon her and the prayers of her many friends following her as she travelled first to Antwerp, then on to Congo, to Kabondo Dianda.

Her first appointment was to the mission station at Mwanza where she would work alongside brother Burton and his wife, but before going there, she was sent to Kashiukulu to work for nine months with Sister Grace Clement who would help her with the language. She also discovered the joys of cycling through the Congo forests. Her arrival in Mwanza was filled with excitement because there was an intention to build a new hospital, and they had waited until her arrival to consult on the plans. Because it was the start of the rainy season, they decided just to erect a temporary shelter, but as soon as this was done, the work started, sometimes with over 100 coming for treatment each morning.

Another lady was Cynthia Partridge, who was on the Field from 1952 until 1959, and was stationed at Kikondja. Cynthia was fully engaged in hospital work as well as ministering in the churches and villages. Sometimes, she would see as many as 300-350 patients in a day. They would come looking for injections for syphilis and bilharzia, and there were cases of leprosy and TB to be treated. She also had a full case load treating sores, ulcers and abscesses as well as looking after patients with 'flu (which could be deadly) and pneumonia. This work provided excellent opportunities for preaching the Gospel although those who came seemed to be more interested in their bodies than in their souls.

During that same year, 1952, James Mullan, formerly one of the missionaries there, paid a visit and, after so many years in South Africa, still retained a memory of a fair amount of the Bekalebwe vocabulary and was able to communicate quite well. He stayed for five days and, during that time, met old friends and ministered powerfully, bringing with him something of the revival that was then touching South Africa.

Over the next few years, others joined the ranks in Congo. Ruby Grimwade served from 1955 until 1959 and in 1959, Catherine Picken ventured into the Field. Cath was a native of Southend on Sea and, in 1940, she was evacuated from home to find herself billeted in a drunkard's home. This drove her to her knees but, while living there, she led her first soul to the Lord. She took teacher training during her evacuation and, after qualifying, returned to Southend.

She was baptised in the Spirit at a Youth Camp and felt the call of God on her life to go to Congo. The way didn't immediately open up, so she undertook Bible correspondence courses to prepare herself. Finally, the way opened on condition that she took a teacher's diploma course in Belgium. This was a very intensive course, but she found that God's callings are also His enabling and, at last, the needed diploma was obtained.

After sailing from Southampton, she was then stationed at Kabondo Dianda where she began more intensive study in the local language, Kiluba. This was necessary because although the school work was in French, the students knew only Kiluba, so the two languages were necessary for effective communication.

Sadly, Cath was to be in Congo for just one year, because of the growing unrest in the country as the native population began seeking independence. For many years, Congo had been an oasis in a continent in turmoil, but one journalist commented, "Twilight is fast falling in the Belgian Congo." The wave of terrorism that had swept other nations was now drawing near to the Congo borders and although the Belgian authorities had committed themselves to granting independence, there were those in the nation who wanted it *now*.

Cath and Olive Garbutt were the two Elim missionaries in Congo at the time of Independence in 1960. They were evacuated to Southern Rhodesia where they made contact with Archie and Agnes Nicholson in Penhalonga. They stayed there for a few weeks, waiting to see if there would be any possibility of a return to Congo, but when this seemed to be impossible, they began to work with the Rhodesia team and continued their service there.[xviii]

An editorial by Aubrey Hathaway in the *Elim Evangel* (41.31.484) reported that Miss Garbutt and Miss Picken were safe in Southern Rhodesia, together with many other of the Congo missionaries, including Mr. Burton. Word had also been received that several were at Kamina awaiting evacuation, but some were still unaccounted for. The comment was made that there seemed to be a likelihood that the Congo Republic may split up into a number of separate states – virtually a return to the tribal divisions of past days. *While the ordered transition of power to indigenous rulers is an inevitable and logical conclusion to an enlightened colonial rule, the hasty and ill-advised nature of the transfer of power in the Congo to a people so little trained in the art of government, and with so few men capable of handling the affairs of state, must have a disastrous effect not only in Congo, but also on other nations now seeking autonomy.*

History has demonstrated the accuracy of such a judgement. But something for which all were truly grateful was the fact that the leaders of the Congo mission had had the foresight to lay good foundations for the work and kept the indigenous principle to the fore. Only thus would the work remain when expatriate missionaries were withdrawn.

At Kabondo Dianda, Independence Day was celebrated by the Church with meetings for praise, worship and communion, while the unsaved in the village went on a spree of drunkenness and dancing.

Towards the end of the year, James Salter reported that Teddy Hodgson and Elton Knauf were reported missing. Initially, there was little concern since James Salter had himself been 'missing' for three weeks with Teddy Hodgson some two months previously. However, three days later, a further cablegram was received notifying of their martyrdom. The UN reported that their bodies were 'unrecoverable'.[xix]

A memorial service was held in Preston – Mr. Hodgson's home church – and another in London for friends in the south. The London meeting was chaired by Donald Gee and involved representatives from all the Pentecostal groups in the UK. The final speaker was James Salter who told of his last nightmare journey with Mr. Hodgson a few months previously, when they were both fortunate to get out alive from Kikondja in a convoy under UN protection. Mr. Hodgson had later accompanied Mr. Knauf on an errand of mercy back to the latter's station with milk and supplies for needy people. They had disappeared on the way and it was later discovered that a band of fanatical youths, urged on by witchdoctors, had captured and murdered them. Their death was witnessed and reported by a few heart-broken Christians who were powerless to prevent the atrocity. Subsequently, a statement was issued by the CEM and the Overseas Missions Council of the Assemblies of God outlining the situation in Congo.[xx]

After Independence, the situation settled down somewhat, although there was always an undercurrent of unrest. But in 1968, the work took a new turn when two of the

African leaders of the Congo work visited the UK. Othniel Beseka, Chairman, and Jonathan Ilunga (Secretary-general) visited East Ham Elim church and gave thanks for those who had gone to their country with the good news of the Gospel. They said that the first white men had come in 1910 and dug into the mountains for precious stones. Two years later, more white men came and told them they must worship the queen of heaven. The Congolese, who had yearned to know God, flocked in thousands to these services in order to find God, but how disappointed they had been. They had religion but no life. They were thirsty but had no water to spring up into everlasting life. But in 1915, more white men came who told them of Jesus. Those who received Him were saved, set free and perfectly satisfied with the well of water ever springing up within. Changed lives were the best testimony and now there were thousands rejoicing in a living Saviour. At that time, they reported that there were 1400 churches established in fellowship with CEM.

The following year, Jonathan Ilunga was elected Chairman and Wilson Mutombo was elected Secretary. They reported to their Conference that, in the previous year, 25,000 had made decisions for Christ with 12,180 having been baptised and received into membership. The number of believers was now almost 100,000. During the Conference, which was attended by 3000, sixty-seven testified to having received the Baptism in the Holy Spirit and no fewer than 533 testified to a healing touch from the Lord, ninety of whom were long standing cases of serious illness. One national pastor said, "This is not the fruit of our labours, but of the labours and sacrifice of brother Knauf who gave his life for this land nine years ago."

Despite having retired some years before, Willie Burton continued a ministry of travelling and preaching. He was a prolific writer of both books and articles, and the *Elim Evangel* published several of his teaching articles from time to time; his artistic ability was legendary. In January 1971, he was staying with friends in Pretoria. He had preached every night for a week and was just about to be taken for a drive in the countryside. As the car was being made ready, he returned to the house for his camera and, on his way back to the car, collapsed and died.[xxi] A tribute was paid to him by Leslie Wigglesworth who confessed, "Eulogising a personality who deprecates any personal praise presents difficulties." Such humility characterised the man who once, when asked to open a meeting in prayer, and being likened to the great Dr. David Livingstone, said in a small voice, "I am only a tramp preacher willing to tread the forest trails so that I might preach Christ. I am plain Willie Burton. Shall we pray?"[xxii]

The next year saw the home call of James Salter, Willie Burton's lifelong partner in pioneering. Having completed his work in Congo, he became the Home Director for the Mission. J.T. Bradley, then Elim's Secretary-general, remembered an occasion when brother Salter visited the Elim church in Halifax during the war. He recalled that a group of soldiers had been brought into the Gospel service by the church workers. Mr. Salter preached with his usual humour and pathos. Then he made an appeal. As men streamed to the front of the church, they thought of how James Salter was always the missionary, whether in Yorkshire or the Congo. Eric Dando, at his funeral in Bedford, saw him like Barnabas: *he was a good man and full of the Holy Ghost.*

Even though the Founders had been promoted to glory, the work still went ahead and God continued to lay his hand on dedicated lives that might be useful to Him in the foreign fields.

From 1971 to 1997, Congo was renamed Zaire and the CEM also was renamed ZEM to reflect the new situation. 1971, therefore, saw Jennifer Quirie going to Zaire where she laboured until 1976, when she returned home to Bradford to be married. She had one furlough and then returned to work in Kipushya, teaching and doing translation work. At her farewell, an offering was taken that raised £240 which Jennifer said she would use to buy a motor scooter to assist her with travel on the Field. Having purchased a Peugeot moped with the money, her first visit took her 30 kilometres to another village.

The journey was not completely without incident. Accompanied by a secondary school pupil who was returning home for the weekend, she left at 8.30 a.m. on roads that were quite sandy, so the wheels were prone to skid. At 8.45, she had to stop and balance her load. She was continually hailed by the natives as she presented an unusual sight. Hens scattered from her path, while dogs came to keep her company. Children came to run alongside as she almost panicked and said, "Go away! I'm only a learner." At 9.00 a.m., the student's load, consisting of blankets and a camp bed, began to slip and needed attention urgently. At 9.10, she felt the bike swaying and, looking down, discovered that she had a flat tyre. After walking about two kilometres back to the nearest village, pushing the moped uphill most of the way, the puncture was mended and they were on their way again by 10.15.

As they started out again, they met some choir members who were also going to the village for a special weekend, so they travelled together. Soon, they turned off the main road onto a bush path. It seemed easier to walk. But, parking the bike against a tree trunk for a rest, Jennifer's leg touched the hot exhaust and she ended up with quite a nasty burn. They decided it would be safer to walk for a while, pushing the moped. By 11.30, the road was much better so one of the choir members became chauffeur until, five minutes later, they hit the root of a tree and went flying through the air. They walked from then until the road became wider and then it was possible to ride the rest of the way. Once arrived at the village, she was treated like royalty; her sore feet were washed; she was given a chair to sit in that had been brought from elsewhere in the village. Despite the journey, the weekend services were blessed as seven young people accepted the Lord on the Saturday, and three more came to Christ on the Sunday.

In 1981, a need arose for a teacher in Zaire and the appeal was responded to by Joan Caudell who was then teaching English at Elim Bible College. Joan had served in Southern Rhodesia from 1961 to 1977, but now she was willing to go back to the Field and serve in Congo. One of the things that spurred her on was the knowledge that there were young African men and women waiting to be taught the Word of God, so that they could teach future generations in Zaire.

The country was in a state of dire poverty so that the Government was looking for help from the West. The Marxists were just waiting to take over. She felt that the door of opportunity was standing open and Christians must do their part in bringing in the Word of God. Joan served in the Secondary and Teacher Training schools until she left in 1983 because of ill health.

Gordon McKillop was a young man in the Motherwell Elim church. A holiday in one of the Scottish Youth Camps transformed his life as he surrendered fully to the claims of Christ. Did he know then that he would become one of today's outstanding missionaries to Zaire? He, with his wife Sybil, undertook training at Elim Bible College in Capel, Surrey before going out to Zaire. Anyone who has met Gordon knows that, physically, he is a big man, but he's also a 'big man' when it comes to the Work of God. They travelled out to Zaire in 1982 and from that time, Gordon's consuming passion has been to do the work of God and to reach the Africans with the Gospel. His practical skills have meant that he is never idle, always on call to meet a need. On one of his furloughs, his description of his work was such that one church member was heard to ask, "Is he a surgeon?" No doubt, he has fallen into the mould of the pioneer missionary who had to become all things to all men.

There was always sensitivity to atmosphere. Sometimes, the precious fragrance of the Holy Spirit pervaded; at others, there was a real sense of evil and attempts of the enemy of men's souls to hinder the work. On one occasion, a young pastor was conspicuous by his absence from a seminar. His ministry was in a small village and he had seen few results. His reason for non-attendance was that he was depressed, so the brethren felt they should visit his village and encourage him. A group set off the next morning on their bicycles, pushing them, riding them and carrying them through forests, swamps and across rivers.

They came to a large, fast-flowing river that was spanned only by a tree, its bark crumbling and falling away, and covered in slippery moss. Gordon began to cross with his bicycle on his shoulder when almost immediately, he was confronted by a large, black spitting cobra. Edging back to the bank, some of the pastors felt they should turn back, but Gordon was convinced they should go on. Taking a machete out of his pack, he went out onto the log. The cobra began spitting its venom with deadly accuracy. Covering his eyes with his hand, he moved nearer to the snake and, when close enough, he swung the machete, cutting off the snake's head and tossing its body into the river. Everyone then crossed in safety.

On arrival at the village, they sensed evil abounding and the old chief was very antagonistic. But they invited him to the afternoon meeting where they preached on the Lordship of Christ. Testimonies were given and, at the end, the old chief presented himself at the front of the church and asked for salvation. That night, there was great rejoicing in the village and almost the whole village turned to the Lord.

While Gordon enjoys such episodes, Sybil stays behind looking after the hospital. A qualified midwife, she finds plenty to keep her occupied. In addition, she had responsibility for dispensing the medicines to the bush dispensaries, so had to visit them from time to time to ensure things were being done properly. Somewhere in their hectic lives, Gordon and Sybil produced three fine children, Bobby, Gordon and Susan.

Furloughs provided marvellous opportunities to fire the enthusiasm of young people in the homeland for the work of missions. As a result of a visit to Vazon, Guernsey, about twenty young people caught the glow and began raising money to purchase a bicycle to be sent out to Zaire. This was a tremendous effort. Nowadays, it is often easier to supply money, as most goods can be purchased locally, saving the costs of transport. That particular furlough was somewhat limited in scope because Gordon had to be referred to Care for Mission[xxiii], as it was discovered that a parasite had entered his blood. He was soon given a clean bill of health and the whole family prepared to return to Zaire. On their return, they were to have a new Toyota Land Cruiser, a necessary vehicle for the types of roads on which it would be used.

Unfortunately, there were difficulties with South Africa at that time and it looked as though the vehicle would have to be shipped directly to Zaire, a much more expensive route, possibly requiring the payment of taxes, insurance and import fees of anything up to £42,000. Happily, most of these envisaged costs were avoided and the Land Cruiser quickly became an essential part of the team. A letter from Gordon indicated that it had a wide sphere of service. It had been used as an ambulance for the sick, in children's evangelism, for hospital and prison visitation, carrying necessary goods and materials for building and once, it was used as a hearse!

It will be obvious that this story has no end. Although this chronicle finishes in 1989, the story goes on. In subsequent years, others went to Zaire. These included Debbie Howard and Linda McAuley. After 1997, the country renamed itself again - Democratic Republic of Congo. As a result, ZEM then became CAM - Central African Mission, not only because of the nation's change of name but also to reflect the widening stream of witness as they began to work also in Zambia and Ethiopia. Eternity alone will reveal the rich harvest gathered in through the faithful work and witness of so many precious saints of God who counted not their own lives dear.

i Adelaide Henderson, Letter to *Elim Evangel,* Vol.3:7, pp106,107, July, 1922.

ii Colin Whittaker, *Seven Pentecostal Pioneers.* Marshalls, Basingstoke, 1983.

iii It is interesting to note that the Taylors' last child, Cecil, was born a short time after his father died. He has been involved in the development in recent times of the new technology academies and was knighted for his services to higher education.

iv Mrs. Bradshaw's last letter was published in the *Missionary Courier* of December, 1940.

v *Elim Evangel,* Vol.8. Issue 13, p.197.

vi *Elim Evangel,* Vol.8. Issue 15, p.225.

vii *Elim Evangel,* Vol.15. Issue 8, p.123.

viii A tribute by Adelaide Henderson was printed in the *Elim Evangel,* Vol.16. Issue 6, p.91.

ix Fred Ramsbottom, *African Plenty.* Marshall Pickering, Basingstoke, 1987.

x *Elim Evangel,* Vol.22. Issue 2, p.18.

xi *Elim Evangel,* Vol.67. Issue 38, p.16.

xii Then Missionary Secretary. A full account was given in *The Elim Missionary Courier* No. 4, December, 1939.

xiii Then Principal of Elim Bible College situated at Elim Woodlands in Clapham, London.

xiv *Elim Evangel,* Vol.23. Issue 23, pp. 265,266.

xv See chapter on Tanganyika.

xvi A missionary from New Zealand who was martyred with Teddy Hodgson in the time of Independence.

xvii Donald Gee, *The Pentecostal Movement,* Assemblies of God Publishing House, Luton, 1949, pp.220,221.

xviii *Elim Evangel,* Vol.61. Issue 40, pp13,14. See chapter on Zimbabwe for further information.

xix Colin C. Whittaker, op cit. See chapter on Teddy Hodgson.

xx *Elim Evangel,* Vol.42. Issue 29, p.459.

xxi Colin Whittaker, op cit. p.169.

xxii See also the tribute paid by his niece, Pat Barton in *Elim Evangel,* Vol.52. Issue 11, pp.6,7.

xxiii A medical facility in the Scottish Borders specialising in tropical medicine. All returning missionaries were required to have an examination there.

CHAPTER 13
EGYPT

ALICE & LILIAN MARSHALL

In 1913, the Lord baptised Alice Marshall in the Holy Spirit and the following year, she was asked to help in the Free Pentecostal Mission in Gravesend, Kent. George Jeffreys had been invited for a mission and there was a mighty anointing on his ministry. In the final Sunday morning breaking of bread service, Alice had a remarkable vision.

A group of dark clad women were appealing to the Lord Jesus for help. Instinctively, she knew that she was to be the answer to their prayer and she called on the Lord to show her where they were. Immediately, in large gold letters on a bright red sky she saw the word: EGYPT. It was so real and clear that she felt she would have been out of God's will to have gone anywhere else.

The whole assembly prayed earnestly that she might be guided aright during the days to follow, because World War I had just begun and travel was severely restricted. Alice's age group was expected to be engaged in some kind of war service so she volunteered to care for war orphans. She served in Shrewsbury and Bournemouth and, by the spring of 1919, those busy years had practically drowned the vision of Egypt.

As soon as she was free of her war duties, she went to stay with friends who ran a mission in Shrewsbury. After only a few days with them, the Lord gave her an exact repetition of her earlier vision. This time, however, there was an added message. She was to prepare at once for Egypt, but it was another eight months before a passage became available.

In February, 1920, Alice stepped ashore in Port Said. God had opened a door for service, English was needed in a girls' school and home for destitute children. At the same time, she was able to learn the language. The following years gave opportunities to visit remote villages and it was then that she met the women she had seen in her vision. The years of preparation had been so necessary.

Any converts made during that time were encouraged to fellowship in the existing evangelical church of the country, because they were only a few women proclaiming the gospel. But after furlough in 1926, Elim took over the work and Alice was overjoyed at the thought that all the Elim family was now standing behind her. However, her position was not to change as Elim didn't start to send out missionaries until 1938 at which time she became an associate missionary. Until then, all her support had been through voluntary gifts from individual friends.

Once again, God's timing was perfect as friends could no longer send out money because of the onset of the Second World War. Elim, as a recognised Missionary Society, was able to transfer funds regularly through a bank and Alice was thus accepted as a full-time missionary.

Lilian Marshall, Alice's younger sister, recalled happy days in early childhood that prepared her heart for a life of service on a mission field. She was born again under the ministry of Gypsy Smith in 1903 and had a Sunday school teacher who took an interest in overseas missions. This activity all grew into a desire to serve the Lord.

In 1913, she too received her baptism in the Holy Spirit and was led in many different ways that she felt prepared her for her life's work. Eight years later, early in 1928, the door opened for her to join Alice in Egypt. A new work had been started in the Nile delta, but after only a few weeks together with her sister, Alice was called to the Headquarters in Port Said. Lilian stayed on in the village with a few young Egyptian helpers, working hard to learn the new language. They opened a school for any children they could persuade to come and held meetings for women.

Several small, delicate children were received into the home and this made openings for them to visit relatives. From this station, they were able to reach other villages, either by walking through fields or travelling by donkey.

The country folk were very hospitable, even though a man's wage at that time was only £1 a month. Very few were able to read, but they loved to listen to the Word of God. To openly confess Jesus as the Son of God, however, meant a big price to pay.

In 1937, she took over the orphanage in Port Said and became mother to 47 girls and three small boys too young to be sent to the boys' orphanage, all aged from three to 15 years. This she saw as a tremendous privilege. The work had grown through the years and was now given over to the Filadelfia Church of Stockholm. They sent out a missionary and his family and so the Church of Peace was formally recognised by the Government.

In this work, Moslems, Syrians and Copts all lived together harmoniously under her care. Like any other mother, her days were packed full of activity beginning at 5.30 a.m. and not finishing until bedtime at 9 p.m. She had one woman to help her, the first orphan received into the home some 23 years before. Each girl had set duties and some were being taught dressmaking skills.

The most precious time of the day was bedtime when a visit to each child gave opportunity for the personal touch and a sharing of a helpful word of scripture that might address some of the problems of the day. Lilian's desire was that the children should see the establishment as a home and not as an institution.

There was a clear association with church life and baptismal services were held for those professing salvation. These were held separately for men and women. Immediately after the baptisms were conducted, time was given to waiting for the Baptism in the Holy Spirit. In less than ten minutes, a fourteen year old girl was baptised in the Holy Spirit and this led to a number of others seeking the Lord as Saviour. Later, two workers from an outstation at Dekernes sought prayer, one for healing. She was anointed with oil and received such a mighty touch from the Lord and the other was baptised in the Holy Spirit.

This led to an interpreter seeking and receiving his baptism, an unconverted man getting saved, and the cook in his white apron seeking a blessing. While all this was going on, the bigger boys rose from their beds and came down, pouring out their hearts to the Lord. The presence of the Lord was so real that they just asked and immediately received. Long before daylight next morning, a Pentecostal prayer meeting was being held in the girls' dormitory. One girl who had been the subject of much prayer for many years broke down and yielded her life to God.

During the morning recess, many of the day girls joined in prayer; one was baptised in the Holy Spirit, and several were saved. One of the lesson periods in the school was turned into a prayer meeting and the workers had the great joy of seeing fruit for their many years of labour.

Alice's great burden for Egypt was that it was a nation requiring deliverance from oppression by the forces of evil. She said she found strength in a rendering of Psalm 84:5-7 that she had found – *Blessed are they whose strength is in Thee: when they go through the vale of tears, they transform it into a place of fountains, and their strength increases according to their going.*

The response of the people brought encouragement. One lady laid her burden down at Jesus' feet. She was known to the sisters for years. She seemed to be indifferent to the message but had recently been coming to the meetings and heart-hunger was written on her face. The change in her life was a blessing to behold. One of her daughters was already saved; a son was recently restored and baptised and her younger daughter then made a public confession.

But there was still a challenge to faith with multitudes in crowded villages needing to hear the story of redeeming grace. Because of the ongoing work in the orphanages, there was opportunity to visit some who had left to start their own homes and families. As homes were visited, lives were challenged, strengthened and encouraged. These people, in turn, began to share their faith with their neighbours, pleading with them to yield themselves to the Lord.

There were many encouragements at that time (1941), as many were coming to Christ and seeking water baptism. The Baptism in the Holy Spirit was sought fervently and Lilian talked of one lady who had such a longing for God that she took off all her gold (this means much to an Eastern woman), so that nothing would hinder her in following the Lord wherever He might lead.

Church life was very full. A Bible study taking up 100 hours was undertaken with much blessing – during the hottest month of the year – and there were meetings in homes every evening. Special prayer had been made for a breakthrough in the women's side of the work and they saw this answered as seven women dared to take the step of confessing the Lord in baptism, while some others were still waiting for permission from their husbands. One evangelist even built a baptistery at his own expense and the Lord was still filling people with the Holy Spirit.

In a report to a Conference while on furlough in 1946, Lilian said that their day had been set for about eight years with a prayer meeting at 5.30 a.m., Bible study at 7.00 a.m. and a service every evening at 7 p.m.

These faithful servants of the Lord had a varied ministry that included the very important work of training the native Christians so that they would, in turn, become pastors and evangelists to their own people. In this way, forces were multiplied and a foundation was built on which the work could become indigenous and self-supporting.

The assembly work was still enjoying a measure of blessing as people were saved, baptised and filled with the Spirit. Spiritual gifts were in operation and new centres were being opened to meet the needs. Another side of the work, not generally seen, was their ministry to English speaking troops in Egypt because of the war. Many service men – Army, Navy and Air Force – found their way to the meetings conducted by the missionaries. Only God knows what benefit accrued to those so far from home as they heard familiar hymns and stories from Sunday school days. Alice also engaged in first aid at times and told a story of how, requiring a suture, she actually took a horse's hair, sterilised it and used it for this purpose.

Alice and Lilian returned to England on furlough in 1946 and a special welcome service was convened in Bloomsbury Central Baptist church, London to celebrate the occasion. In the service, Alice reported that there had been difficulties and testings but that God was still on the throne. She said that out of a population of 17 million, only 1 million were born again.

In the following year, Lilian returned to the field, but Alice remained behind in England to look after an invalid loved one and also because of her own health. While little is known of her activities in retirement, there are nevertheless references to her involvements in the homeland with EWMA[i] as she sought to encourage others to become involved in this support arm for Elim Missions.

In 1948 there was a cholera epidemic but thankfully, Lilian was not affected. There were, however, significant changes taking place in the country that would affect the work and make life for the missionaries increasingly difficult. There were manifestations of intolerance and persecution directed towards the Christian church. But God was still blessing the preaching of the Word. Indeed, a report stated that in recent times, there had been a wonderful wave of revival and many were saved. Two workmen employed on repairs to the outside of the mission house were saved, one bringing his family along to the meetings.

It was noted that the power of Islam was growing stronger, making missionary work more difficult. Palestine was also becoming a major issue and it was becoming more difficult to get about in an Arab town, but the people were coming to them.

By now, Moslem children were being forbidden to hear the gospel. Parents were pleading with the teachers of mission schools to take their children, but they were not allowed to do so. Visitation of homes became crucial because, in some cases, the women were not allowed out to the meetings. Although many hesitated to become followers when they realised that they must leave all and follow Him, often they returned weeks later, such was the hunger of their hearts.

Baptismal services were held regularly and provided excellent opportunities for witness. In spite of difficulties when the baptistery leaked, the people came to a joyful understanding of salvation and others trusted when they saw the evidence of changed lives.

Despite a very cold winter in 1949, the work in the Sunday school saw great increase, not only in children but also in teachers as well, many of whom had once been residents in the orphanage. There were still many children who could not read or write, never having been to school, but the mission was trying to help in this. Some adults who started learning to read just a few weeks previously were making good progress and were longing for the day when they could read the Word of God for themselves.

It was becoming increasingly evident that time was growing short. Islam was becoming more and more militant, even to the extent of trying to close down the Christian Church. A Church Court settled the matter and the church was left in peace for the time being. But there was increasing persecution of believers and, understandably, some became faint hearted and turned back.

One disappointment was to hear of a Moslem convert of over 20 years, married to a converted Copt, with a happy little family, who left her husband and married again to a wealthy Moslem. The husband then had the two boys, but the law claimed that the religion of the State is Islam so the boys should be handed over.

Lilian had visited a home in Cairo and saw one of the girls who was saved in the orphanage some years ago. She was standing firm for the Lord. In another home, she met with a lady who was a bright Christian and member of the church. Her family was poor and they could not pay school fees for their son to attend a non-Moslem school, but he could go if the mother renounced her membership and returned to a lifeless church. The husband, not being saved, had made it very hard for them as she had refused to give up her membership. Her testimony was shared by many others: Salvation has brought me joy and a new life.

By contrast, two baptismal candidates were middle aged women. When their names were brought before the church, all were free to comment on their suitability for baptism. Their daughters-in law were most encouraging. Both were radiantly happy that the Lord had answered prayer; they not only had saved husbands, but saved mothers-in-law as well and they spoke of blessed times of fellowship in the home, as well as in the church.

Each of the homes of these two families consisted of one room hardly big enough for all to stand up in at the same time. There was no window to let light in and certainly nothing outwardly to bring them joy, yet they were rejoicing in the Lord because the entrance of His word brought them light.

In 1981, Alice celebrated her 90th birthday and a number of friends gathered with her for the occasion. These included Pastor Leslie Wigglesworth, Pastor Ron Chapman and Pastor and Mrs. Eldin Corsie. The evening was an opportunity to reminisce of the years in the Lord's work in Egypt and to rejoice in His faithfulness. All present were challenged by the dedication of these two sisters. In 1982, Alice passed into the presence of the Lord she had loved and served for so many years. For many years while in the homeland, she, with Lilian, had supported EWMA by sewing and knitting. Even although she was in indifferent health, and EWMA wanted to ease her burden, she wouldn't hear of being left out when prayer partners were being sought. Nothing was too much for them and even when they were too old to labour overseas, they never eased up on their service, always finding something for their hands to do.

i EWMA: Elim Women's Missionary Auxiliary, commenced in 1966. See separate chapter.

CHAPTER 14

GHANA

Elim's introduction to Ghana was in 1966 at the invitation of the Rev. David Tetteh Tenobi, a former correspondence student with Elim Bible College, London, who asked for missionaries to serve in the thirty-six churches in his fellowship. When missionaries arrived, they discovered that most of the churches were independent and had joined Rev. Tenobi because he had promised the pastors that Elim would pay their salaries. This was not known beforehand and when no money was forthcoming, thirty-one pastors and churches left the group.

The nation was then in the throes of change because of a military coup which had sought to set the country on its feet after a period of instability under the former regime. Help was being supplied by the USA and the UN in sending essential foods; there was a scarcity of money and goods were in very short supply. Nevertheless, the Elim delegation felt that there was the possibility for a flourishing work and were determined to become involved, although this would necessitate supplying personnel and money to help the work.

For five years, between 1966 and 1971, David and Margaret Mills and Gerald and Margaret Ladlow sought to establish and build the work. They had five churches to work with and some two hundred members, centred on Koforidua. Brother Tenobi was still involved at this point. At a very early stage, Pastor Gerald Ladlow, a member of the Missions Board and minister of the Elim church in Motherwell, went to try to deal with a problem that threatened the stability of the work but, unfortunately, he felt that his input had been unacceptable. Shortly afterwards, however, he was assured of a warm and sincere welcome by a delegation from the first church that had been planted at Nkurakan.

Koforidua is the capital of the Eastern region and, in the Government Commercial College, meetings were held for young people. As David Mills gave his testimony and Gerald Ladlow preached the Gospel, over twenty teenagers responded. The area had six such colleges as well as other educational and vocational establishments, so the potential for reaching thousands of young people was huge. A fine hall had been offered at a modest rent and they were anticipating holding a pioneer crusade to reach the district.

In January 1967, they had visited the village of Plewa Odortom by invitation. When they arrived, they found almost the whole village waiting for them and, before long, the chief was offering them land on which to build a church and a primary school. A Ghanaian teacher was available and it was felt that he could be supported by local funds since many of the people were farmers. No time was lost in preparing the ground and soon a temporary building had been erected, with some spare land being set out as playing fields.

By Whitsun, there was a viable church and a Whitsun convention was organised. This was well attended and several people were baptised in the Holy Spirit. At the opening of the Primary school, about forty pupils attended and some older young people, who had not had the opportunity for formal education, were seen to be eavesdropping on the lessons. The intention then was to widen the bush path so that the missionaries could drive their car down to the village.

The day eventually arrived when a baptismal service was to be held. This was an occasion for much rejoicing and singing as the candidates followed the Lord through the waters of Baptism. The service was to start at 9.00 a.m. but, with African time, began at 10.30 and lasted for about four hours. Ultimately, more than sixty adults and fifty children were present to hear the Word of God and to watch the proceedings.

The work was enhanced in 1968 when Brian Cheal from Caerphilly, a qualified mathematician who had accepted a post as Principal of a college in Ghana, arrived and hoped to be of help to the missionaries during his time there.

As part of the development of the work, it was felt that a Bible school was needed, so a search was instituted for suitable premises. Mr. Tenobi found a place in Koforidua that was considered eminently suitable and negotiations eventually agreed a rent that was acceptable. Beds, desks and tables were constructed and advertising was done to find students. Initially, there were seventy replies and thirteen applications. On the day of the interviews, only one applicant reported, and he was not interested in a full time course. The next day another applicant arrived, but he had no money for fees.

The dilemma was solved by making space available to the Wycliffe Translators' team who had been ordered out of Nigeria. They stayed for two months and the fellowship engendered was precious to all. Interest in the school developed gradually and, finally, a course for church leaders was started, running five days a month. Out of this, the work of the Bible school commenced.

One of the major challenges in the Ghana work was to reach the children and so Margaret Mills started a Sunday school in Koforidua, helped by Agnes Amiyo who acted as her interpreter. Such was the response that it was reported that the work had *multiplied* rather than simply being added to! A school that started with ten scholars was soon catering for more than 200, although on the day of the anniversary, almost 300 children attended. While the Sunday school work in the villages could not produce results on the same scale, nevertheless the work was ongoing and fruitful.

Another developing area was in the supply of Scripture throughout the country. The first request came from a boy over 200 miles away, although no one knew how he had obtained the Bible school's address. But a portion of the Word was sent and following this, over 550 similar requests were received from far and wide. It became obvious that most letters came from schoolboys who had learned to read, but their replies indicated that the Lord was doing a work in their lives as a result.

Pioneer evangelism was also high on the agenda as the missionaries ventured into obscure villages with the Gospel and had the joy of leading many to the Lord, who worked with them confirming the Word with signs following. At the end of the short mission in

Agogo, there were many testimonies of miraculous healing, Baptism in the Holy Spirit and, as a result, a water baptism service was conducted even although the river was at its lowest level. A viable church was established with its own pastor and their first priority was to find a suitable place for worship since their present canopy of bamboo and palm leaves would be insufficient when the rains came.

Some four months later, Gerald returned to the church to find it in good heart with adequate teaching from the Pastor. They took time to visit a local family that owned land to see if they could purchase enough for a church building. The outcome of this was that after much palaver, with repeated offer and counter-offer, the old patriarch of the family, said to be 100 years old, pronounced his verdict. This resulted in the church being allowed to buy the whole plot of land for the equivalent of £10 sterling and the members set to with a will to clear the land and erect a building without further ado.

Early in January 1971, a new minibus was sent to Ghana for the work. This had been purchased under the Green Shield Stamp scheme, through the efforts of both EWMA and EYM[1] and others. There was an immediate service of thanksgiving and dedication as the church rejoiced, not only that the minibus had arrived, but that the Government of Ghana had waived import duty and purchase tax.

It wasn't long before the vehicle was pressed into service. A number of seats were removed to make way for an amplifier and stocks of literature so that a team could travel to one of the markets with the Gospel by proclamation and the printed page. In a four hour visit, over 1300 portions of the Word of God were distributed and David Mills paid tribute to the United Bible Societies whose supplies of the Scriptures made such evangelism possible. Later, the minibus did duty as a hearse following the death of a young boy from one of the churches.

Delivery of the minibus also coincided with the first anniversary celebrations of the sisterhood work in Ghana. The sisterhood had been the vision of Margaret Ladlow, so the service was tape recorded for her as she had, by now, returned to the UK. Throughout the year, the ladies had been able to testify to the working of the Holy Spirit among them as lives had been changed and the sick had been healed in answer to prayer.

THE CHURCH OF PENTECOST

The Founder of the work in Ghana which came to be known as The Church of Pentecost was James McKeown, a native of Portglenone near Ballymena, Northern Ireland. He first went to Ghana in 1937 under the auspices of the Apostolic Church and subsequently, because of difficulties experienced on the field, set up his own church, the Church of Pentecost. The story of its beginnings was told in the book, *A Giant in Africa,* written by Christine Leonard and published by New Wine Press in 1989. For this reason, it will not be appropriate to examine this in further detail at this time. This work was already well established on an indigenous basis but with James McKeown as its leader, and a close link developed as the Church of Pentecost became recognised as a sister Fellowship to Elim with a reciprocal agreement regarding Executive involvements in the two Fellowships. Over a period of time, various Elim personnel were based in Ghana to give input to the ongoing work. This included the Bible school and the radio work, as well as outreach in remote areas and support for mobile clinics and a small hospital.

In 1969, just before their first furlough, the Church of Pentecost gathered in Koforidua for their annual convention. David and Margaret Mills became aware of the event as the population of the town doubled overnight. They attended the meetings and David was invited to sit on the platform with other leaders. James McKeown preached for over an hour and, at the end of the service, asked David to preach the following night. David could hardly believe his ears! He was a virtual stranger to James McKeown, yet he was being asked to participate in a service with about 35,000 in attendance. The response to the Word was staggering as 167 came forward for salvation and over 2000 Church members came forward to signify their obedience to the message.

At the end of the Convention, James took those who were in the Executive Council off for a special meeting and suggested the rest spend the time listening to David and asking him questions. When James returned, he said to the Council, "Well, now you have heard David. He represents Elim. Last year you said you would like to have an affiliation with a church overseas, so you would feel part of something bigger. How about an affiliation with Elim?"[ii]

The result was a meeting in Elim headquarters in Cheltenham in which an agreement was reached as to affiliation and fellowship. From then on, the work, which was very strong and had a vibrant missionary outlook, continued to grow exponentially, and David and Margaret Mills became close friends of James and Sophia McKeown.

In 1973, David and Margaret Kilpatrick joined the Mills family, facing six months of language study before moving north to the Volta Region. Their appreciation of Ghanaian worship knew no bounds as they entered into the very joy of it. A few months later, the Women's section of the church held their bi-annual convention at Sekondi. Some 7000 sisters came together and there was great rejoicing at the testimonies and ministry.

One sister told of being on a boat on the Volta which went on fire and many people jumped overboard to escape the flames; others were being burned on the boat. She cried to the Lord in her trouble and He heard her and showed her a place in the stern that would be safe. She and her three children, together with a few others, sheltered there but some wanted to jump overboard as they watched the flames approaching. She told them with confidence that her God would deliver them. As they looked into the water and saw the bodies floating like dead fish, they decided to stay with her. As the flames came dangerously close, *they just went out!* A rescue boat picked up six out of a party of over one hundred. Her testimony brought about much soul searching in the Convention as might be imagined.[iii]

The growth of the Children's Movement necessitated visits to all eleven regions of Ghana by Margaret Mills, Assistant National Leader. In an itinerary lasting several weeks, she was able to review the labours of many who had committed themselves to reaching the young. She was amazed to find one Sunday school with three hundred pupils being run by one teacher. In no church did the numbers fall below one hundred. A thirteen year old girl in one of the schools was able to recite the whole of Mark 15 and, for her efforts, they presented her with a Bible in her own language. Throughout the journey, seminars were held to train teachers and supply them with teaching and visual aids for their work. Margaret was told that, in one church, a children's prayer meeting was in progress and, hearing children's voices, a passing school teacher went in to find out what was going on. As a result he gave his heart to the Lord. In one of the Kumasi schools, the children had learned to tithe and were then asking about breaking bread.

In 1975, a Children's Movement Convention was held with about 1700 children attending. The Ladlows were back in Ghana for a visit and Margaret Ladlow was excited to see the children taking part the Convention services. They sang, recited, gave testimonies and sermonettes and acted in short plays. It was a weekend of prayer, praise and fellowship.

This was also the year that the Executive of CoP asked Gerald Ladlow to take over the organisation of setting up a radio programme. The following year, with financial support from EWMA, "The Pentecost Hour" was inaugurated. This went out regularly on a Monday at 9.45 p.m. Gerald became the Radio Pastor and had responsibility for answering the letters and enquiries that arrived from all over the country.

Because of the wide variety of languages within the nation, English was used as the primary language for broadcasting in order to gain the widest coverage. Before very long, the manager of the Ghana Broadcasting Company offered the church a second period at peak listening time – 8.45 p.m. each Tuesday.

Soon, there was a significant response to the broadcasts from far and near. One school teacher in a village wrote, "I have taken a delight in your weekly programme and any time that I have missed it, I have felt that I have really lost something precious." This was typical of the scores of letters that arrived at the office daily. Another man wrote, "I am a man of 29 years of age and have never been inside a church since I finished school twelve years ago. I was busy in my room when your programme came on the radio and I was arrested by the singing and could not help but listen. By the end of the broadcast, I knew that I needed a saviour. Please help me." From the north of the country, there was a plea from six schoolboys who had heard the programme on their school radio and had decided to accept the Lord as their saviour. "We are only twelve years of age and have no Bibles and no Christian books to help us. We have no money to buy any; can you send us some booklets or papers that will show us how to be true Christians?" Needless to say, there was an attempt to meet these needs, but resources were very scarce and appeals were made to the churches in the UK for materials to use for follow up work. Over the succeeding years, there were multitudes, too numerous to report, who traced their conversion to hearing the Gospel presented on the radio.

Such was the development of the Church of Pentecost that it was no strange thing for high ranking members of the Government to attend their proceedings. In 1976, General Ignatius Kutu Acheampong, Head of State and Chairman of the Supreme Military Council attended the annual Church Council of the Church of Pentecost in Winneba on the coast of Ghana. He read from the Scriptures and was presented with a Bible, after which James KcKeown prayed for God's blessing on the Head of State and the nation. Following this, he preached from 1 Corinthians 1:33 and 2:7, 8, making the point that Jesus is supreme over all. The General stayed to the end of the service and appreciated the ministry. This situation has been repeated many times since then with the Church enjoying good relations with the Government of the day.

One of the outstanding features of the Church of Pentecost is its burgeoning growth and many have wondered at the reason. Anyone who has been to Ghana would be quite ready to exclaim that the Ghanaians are the most generous people they have ever met. James McKeown was not long in the country when he sat down to a meal in a humble home and realised that the people were giving him of their own food. But he learned that day a Ghanaian proverb that became for him a way of life for almost forty years, the African way of saying, *"Give and it shall be given unto you, good measure, pressed down, shaken together and running over shall men give into your bosom."*

It is this spirit of generosity that makes the Ghanaians want to share with others the things they possess and accounts, in a large measure, for the constant growth of the Church. Although it all began with a handful of believers won in the open air through the witness of the missionary and his wife, such was the passion for sharing the good things of God that the work grew. There were no funds from overseas to pay for salaries of pastors and evangelists, there were no material incentives for men to leave secular employment, but at the call of God they went forth with the good news.

But how God blessed! Today the Church is active in every continent and is continuing to see the hand of God blessing their efforts for Him. In 1975, the women in Ghana held 220 rallies and won 1803 converts; the Youth Witness Movement held 379 rallies at which 5903 decisions were recorded and over the borders in neighbouring countries, more than 200 churches were established. By 1977, just forty years after its inception, The Church of Pentecost was estimated to have a membership of 100,000 with 1500 churches.

One pastor, so on fire with the Gospel, had a burden to reach the men in his local prison. In a three year period, he saw more than four hundred men accepting Christ and, in effect, a church was begun within the prison walls. One of the prison warders was the presiding elder for the prison church and his deacons were inmates who had surrendered to the Lord. Many had been baptised and regular services for three hundred men were held on a Sunday, with two Bible studies and a prayer meeting conducted weekly. The local pastor, I. Adu-Mensah, was known to the men as 'The Bulldozer' because of the energetic way he preached and conducted the services.

In mid 1977, Keith and Joyce Baynham with their sons, Wesley and Matthew, were sent to Ghana by the International Missions Board to set up a printing facility for Church of Pentecost. A Rotaprint press was sent from the UK and Keith had the job of commissioning it, but things didn't run smoothly. The machine arrived at Tema docks and it took time to process the paperwork for its release. Unfortunately, as it was being lifted onto the lorry, the fork truck driver needlessly reversed, bumped over a railway line and the crate holding the machine fell from about five feet in the air. The disappointment can well be imagined and it was necessary to encourage themselves once again in the Lord to see some good in the situation. There were no spare parts in Ghana and obtaining them from the UK would take months, so there was nothing to do but wait. Such occasions, although frustrating to say the least, were useful in developing patience. In fact, it took a further eighteen months before the system was up and running. Once installed, no time was wasted and four helpers became involved in production, layout, photography and follow-up. Thousands of pieces of Gospel literature were pouring from the press each month and reaching areas hitherto untouched.

The input of expatriate missionaries was of inestimable value. While the Church was well organised and well run, with a fully developed indigenous leadership, the preaching/teaching ministry of David Mills, the editorial and radio ministry of Gerald Ladlow and the design and printing expertise of Keith Baynham all contributed to the forward move and the development of these functions within the Church itself and were complementary to the evangelistic drive and spiritual vision of the Ghanaians.

In August,1978 Gerald and Margaret Ladlow retired from the work in Ghana and returned to the UK. At a farewell service in the Sophia McKeown Temple in Accra, attended by over 2000 people, Rev. G. Egyir Paintsil, General Secretary, on behalf of the Church of Pentecost Executive, paid warm tribute to the work they had both accomplished during their time there. The radio work had reached such a high standard that over 200 letters per day were being received. In addition, the *Pentecost Fire* magazine was given a new format and was being read widely in Universities, Secondary schools and by many church members even beyond those of Pentecostal persuasion. Mrs. Ladlow's work among the young people in Sunday schools and in the training of Sunday school teachers was recognised, as was her general ministry of singing, preaching and writing. Today, those areas of activity are continuing at a professional level. The CoP has a televisions studio, often hired for use by professionals, while the Press turns out virtually all of the materials required by the Church in addition to some commercial work as well.

It will be appreciated that, from its inception, the Church of Pentecost has been a church with a strong missionary vision. From the beginning, it reached out to the neighbouring countries and planted churches wherever possible. But such work was not without its tears and challenges. The work in Togo began in 1950 but in 1980, the Togolese

Government decided to restrict the number of churches it would licence. Church of Pentecost was not one of them, despite having over 5000 members and 147 churches. Because of the restrictions, some believers would slip over the border into Ghana for fellowship. One pastor was recognised in Ghana and asked to preach but on his return to Togo was arrested and imprisoned. Nothing was heard of him over the next six months and there were fears for his life. Appeals to the President of Togo fell on deaf ears and all the church could do was pray. Today, this situation no longer obtains and CoP has a viable work in the country.

Development of the work in Liberia was significant. There were only 15 members when Pastor Fred D. Walker went there, but within three years, there were 240 members and about 55 children in the Sunday school. With increasing numbers, the church had moved from a room in a house to a school classroom until, eventually, they were able to buy their own plot of land and erect, first of all a zinc shed, and then a church building. The work continued unhindered until, in 1988, Pastor Michael Kwabena Ntumy, with his wife, Margaret and their family, was appointed a missionary there to assist the resident Missionary. Shortly after their arrival, there was war in the country which resulted in, among other things, a grievous oppression of Christians. The Ntumy family was separated, imprisoned and suffered terrible hardships, sometimes despairing of the possibility of a family reunion and even of life itself. The story of those eventful times was recorded by Michael Ntumy[iv] who subsequently became the Chairman of the Church of Pentecost.

The Church of Pentecost has, over the years, been tremendously blessed by the stature of its leaders. The pattern was set by Pastor McKeown in his many years as Founder and Chairman. Then Pastor F. S. Safo, initially the Superintendent of the Ashanti Region but later to become Chairman, was an outstanding man with deep spirituality. Pastor Paintsil, the General Secretary for over 30 years, left his mark on the Movement and so, when he was called home in 1981, the whole Movement mourned his passing. In addition to his administrative duties, Pastor Paintsil continued to be the Regional Apostle for Accra, with over 100 churches in his care. He was also Chairman of the National Council of the Bible Society of Ghana and President of the Ghana Pentecostal Council. The wake-keeping saw a crowd of some 20,000 gathered, including Government ministers, heads of churches, missionaries, at least 200 pastors and a multitude of ordinary folks. Pastor McKeown, at the funeral, discussing his important role in the life and development of the Church, said, "I had no one like minded".[v]

When David Ayling was International Missions Director, he visited Ghana and, while there, had a series of fruitful consultations and discussions on the subject of primary health care in rural areas. The consequence was that, in 1979, the Church of Pentecost took the bold decision to set up PENTWAS – the Pentecost Welfare Association whose aims were to include the Church's teaching on accountability towards God and service to man. Land was acquired to launch large scale agricultural projects incorporating oil palm plantations, cash crops, poultry and animal husbandry. In 1982, a mobile clinic was inaugurated in Dunkwa-on-Offin, commissioned by Pastor F. S. Safo, then General Secretary. Helping to set this up and get it going were Janice Barrett and Pam Weston. On arriving in Ghana, they stayed with David and Margaret Mills for five months in Kumasi, doing their orientation course for nursing, spending time in clinics and learning about the Ghanaian way of life and some of the Twi language.

In a very short time, the Ghanaians had built a bungalow for the girls and they found themselves settled in very acceptable accommodation. They became the recipients of typical Ghanaian hospitality and generosity to the point of embarrassment, but were made to understand that this was the Ghanaians' way of saying 'Thank you' for their presence there. Their mobile clinic was a Peugeot 505 pickup with a hard top, so that drugs and equipment could be safely stored inside and kept secure. With the arrival from England of their equipment, their work began almost immediately as they travelled round the villages.

That such a venture was necessary was highlighted by a survey that showed that one in 14 people was dying per year and that one in 20 under-fives was so severely malnourished that, had they contracted measles, for example, it would have meant certain death. Because of the military control of the country, drugs were in short supply or unobtainable, so the work of the clinic was indeed a Godsend. Elim was sending money and/or drugs but the fear was that this would dry up and this needy work would not be sustained. But so long as they were able, the team, led by Janice Barrett, continued to meet the needs of many who, otherwise, would simply die for lack of care.

Linda Hughes joined Janice as an Elim Pathfinder and, in 1983, was present at the commissioning of a second mobile clinic. This was supplied by the Canadian High Commission – Mission Administered Fund, which provided £8000 for the purchase of the vehicle. Tear Fund also gave £1000 for medical equipment for the first clinic. Some three months later, Jayne Lacey from Keynsham gave up her job in Bristol as a midwife to become an Elim Pathfinder and to go and work in the mobile clinics.

January, 1983 was a significant month for the Church of Pentecost with the death of Sophia McKeown, wife of James and 'mother' to the church. James and Sophia had retired to Ballymena, Northern Ireland, so she was buried from the Elim Church there. Many tributes were paid to a lady who had demonstrated a great love for the Ghanaian people and who, in retirement, had maintained the glow of her spirituality to such an extent that the local church was significantly blessed by her presence.

In September, 1983, Ruth and Lionel Currie, who had become very friendly with David and Margaret Mills, travelled to Ghana for a short visit. What they saw and heard made a tremendous impact on them as they were exposed to the great contrasts between Ghana and the UK and they became aware of the deprivation being suffered by the people. Some fourteen months later, Lionel with John Lancaster spent three weeks ministering to the Apostles and Prophets of the Church of Pentecost, as well as ministry around some of the churches. In June, 1984, Lionel and Ruth Currie left Northampton Elim church and went to Ghana for a year while David and Margaret Mills were on furlough. Lionel became

Acting Principal of the Church of Pentecost Bible School at Madina. By 1985, they had been asked by the International Missions Board to stay on as permanent replacements for the Mills family as they returned to the UK. In addition to his work as Bible school Principal, Lionel was the Secretary to the Medical Committee, responsible for the ordering and issuing of all drugs and medical supplies for the two mobile clinics.

David and Margaret Mills, who went to Ghana in 1966, left for England in 1985 to oversee their family's education needs. Their farewell was attended by 6000 people and over 1200 went to the airport to see them off. Such was their standing in the Church and with the people. David's contribution to the Bible school and wider ministry, and Margaret's involvement with the Women's and Children's Movements meant that their ministry had far reaching effects on the work as a whole.

In July, 1987, news was received in Cheltenham of the home call of Pastor Safo, the Chairman of the Church of Pentecost in Ghana. In a tribute to him, Pastor T. W. Walker said that he had been a man of God from his earliest days, and was described by Pastor James McKeown as 'a preacher all his days'. In the 1960s, he had been sent to deal with problems in neighbouring Togo, although he was unable to speak French. Nevertheless, he established the work on the principles which were foundational to the Church of Pentecost, thus ensuring a stable work for the future. In the mid-seventies, he returned to Ghana and became Superintendent of the Ashanti region, then on to headquarters to become Acting General Secretary in 1981.

When Pastor James McKeown retired the following year, Pastor Safo was appointed to the prestigious role of Chairman. His induction was on 10th October, 1982. Although hindered by lameness for his last fifteen years, he never failed to apply himself to the task in hand and to fulfil all the demands of his office. At his death, he was only in his fifties, but he had done so much and inspired so many that his contribution to the work of God was second to none. Needless to say, both the wake and the funeral were attended by thousands as they marked a huge outpouring of appreciation for this man of God, whose impact on the Movement had been enormous.

At the end of 1987, there was a special celebration of Pastor James's fifty years in ministry. It took place in the Ballymena church and was attended by members of Pastor James's family as well as the International Missions Director, Brian Edwards, and the Irish Missions Secretary, Pastor William Mullan. The service was conducted by the Ballymena Minister, Pastor William McCandless and there were taped messages from various members of the Executive Council in Ghana. As will be well understood, the tributes to fifty years of faithful ministry that had culminated in a work such as the Church of Pentecost were glowing and there was a challenge to younger people present to consider the commitment and challenge in following in the footsteps of such a servant of the Lord.

In late 1987, the writer, with Pastor John Lancaster, had the privilege of ministering to the Apostles and Prophets at the Aburi Gardens retreat in Ghana. This was a time of wonderful fellowship and eye-opening exposure to the solid nature of the work of the Church of Pentecost, not only in Ghana but throughout the world. After the retreat, we ministered in different churches across the country and appreciated the hospitality of Ruth and Lionel Currie for the duration of our stay. At that time, Pastor Safo had died and the church was deliberating on who should become chairman. In due course, the following year, the honour was bestowed on Pastor Yeboah.

POST 1989

The Curries were later replaced by John and Trish Waller who served most acceptably for many years. Pastor Yeboah served for many years until ill health caused him to retire. His place was taken by Pastor Michael Ntumy.

i Elim Women's Missionary Auxiliary and Elim Youth Movement.

ii *A Giant in Ghana,* Christine Leonard, New Wine Press, Chichester, 1989. p.155.

iii Reported in *Elim Evangel,* Vol.54. Issue 49, pp. 10, 11.

iv The record is preserved in the book, *Flamingo, the Camp of No Return,* by Michael Kwabena Ntumy. Published by the Pentecost Press, Accra, 1994.

v David Mills' report in *Elim Evangel,* Vol.62. Issue 24, p.5.

CHAPTER 15

KENYA

TOM AND HILDA JOHNSTON

The tentmaker role in missions has ever been beneficial to the work and never more so than in Kenya when, in 1948, Tom Johnston, a native of Northern Ireland, went to the country in Government service. He had applied to Elim to become a full time missionary but was advised that there were no funds to accept him at that time. However, if he should find himself in Government service in Kenya, Elim would willingly recognise him and supply him with an honorary missionary credential. He was therefore officially regarded as an honorary Elim missionary and his wife and children, Cecil, Audrey and Ruth, remained in Northern Ireland until suitable arrangements could be made for them, a period of about fourteen months.[i]

Tom disembarked at Mombasa and immediately went to Nairobi where he met up with several believers who had been studying Pentecostal doctrine and were looking for someone to offer them teaching. Within a very short time, he found himself in a remote wild game reserve supervising 130 natives in building projects. He was the only white person among them and had no knowledge of Swahili, as most of them had no knowledge of English either. Nevertheless, he found a native Christian who could speak English and act as an interpreter, so he wasted no time in arranging his first meeting for the natives. Twenty eight people attended. Before long, in ones and twos, the interpreter brought others to Tom's hut to receive Christ. What joy there was in seeing fruit for his labours!

With the arrival of the family in 1949, Tom moved into Nairobi as his centre of operations. There the Johnstons felt they wanted to open their home to passing missionaries and, before long, they were playing host to missionaries of all denominations. They arranged a missionary prayer meeting and had about twelve missionaries gathering to pray for the work. Meanwhile, they were associating with an African assembly and seeing the Lord work in mighty ways as the Holy Spirit moved among them. In one service, the Spirit moved so powerfully that the time was taken up with weeping and confession of sin as men and women made things right with the Lord and each other.

Within a forty mile radius of Nairobi, there were numerous groups of believers who were seeking teaching on Pentecost and Tom had been asked to help. As time allowed, he began the general oversight of five of these groups although his Government work necessitated work days of long hours. Nevertheless, finishing work at noon on Saturdays, they set off after a quick lunch to minister. Their travels took them from one place to another so that weekends were always extremely busy. In the evening after their return, they would hold a prayer time for the houseboys and had the joy of seeing some of these respond to the Gospel.

In 1950, they held their first Convention and were encouraged to see more than 150 Africans attending. It was an in-house activity as the Africans provided their own music and Tom preached. Because of the development of the work, he decided that he would be in a position to baptise several who had professed faith, after examining them in detail as to their faith.

As the work grew, Tom felt that there was a need for an African evangelist to reach out to the areas where he was able to go only at weekends. He recognised the need for visitation and regular teaching to enable the believers to grow.

On one occasion he was invited to speak at a church on a coffee farm. No white man had ever been there before and conditions were quite primitive. But he and Hilda enjoyed the fellowship of about 100 people as he brought the good news of the Gospel. The service lasted about four hours with the people sitting on seats made from trees cut in half longwise and placed on other stumps fixed in the mud floor. After the service, they were able to distribute garments that had been made by the ladies of the Lurgan church to the women and children.

Easter in 1951 was a special time for the Johnstons. They started Easter Sunday with an early morning service at the Post and Telegraph Training School, where there were about 120 students ranging in ages from 16 to 21. These boys represented many tribes and each made a contribution to the service in his own language. After this service, forty believers gathered for a Breaking of Bread service. When the meetings were over, the school Principal greeted them and expressed his appreciation for their weekly input to the lives of the boys. In the afternoon, another service was held among the Maragoli tribe and the Lord blessed yet again.

Hilda was very much involved in the work. She wrote:

I do praise the Lord that the time has arrived for starting a women's meeting. I go to the African location on Wednesday mornings, leaving the house at eight o'clock for the meeting at nine. Since we have no mission station, we have to take the Gospel out to the people. I have to travel about five miles, but praise the Lord, the rewards are great for there in the house of one of the African elders I gather about seventeen women and their eighteen children, all squatting on any available space. I combine Bible study with a sewing class and hope to get a blackboard to teach the children the letters of the alphabet while their mothers are sewing. I feel this is a further effort to bring these dear souls to the Saviour. It seems to me that the women are neglected, their husbands, generally speaking, believing they can do nothing of benefit.

Hilda used to travel around Nairobi and the surrounding area on a little scooter. The sight can be imagined, not to mention the intrepid way she would brave the African roads to carry the Gospel.

In 1952, there were serious disturbances in Kenya with tragic loss of life because of the uprising of the Mau Mau secret society, and this gave rise to concern for the missionaries working there. Just how close they were to the conflict was highlighted by the news that the Mau Mau had held an oath-taking ceremony not more than 100 yards from their back garden. This society was anti-Christian and anti-European and many Christians suffered for their faith as a result. In the midst of the trouble, however, there was still blessing and souls were being saved and baptised.

In spite of the unrest, there was still work to be done. A special area of concern was for the children who attended the Sunday morning service. It was decided, after much prayer, that they should be taken into another room and there they would have their own Sunday school. This would be taught in Ki-Swahili and, since most of the children spoke Wa-Kamba, it would present a learning situation for them.

Meanwhile, Tom's area of influence was increasing all the time as he made contact with various people through his work. Invitations were received to address meetings of diverse groups, all of which allowed him opportunities to preach the Gospel. There was a strong feeling that the time available for the ministry of the Gospel might be short, so Tom set in motion plans to allow the work to become as indigenous as possible.

It became increasingly obvious that the unrest in the country would only escalate and, sadly, following a massacre at one village, the Johnstons found themselves visiting the local hospital to pray with and try to comfort those who had become victims. Their descriptions of the wounding and maiming, as well as the brutal killing that had occurred were too horrible to contemplate, apart from the realisation that these were the works of people who had no knowledge of God.[ii]

But the Lord continued to bless! A Kikuyu Instructor in the Post and Telegraph School came out for Jesus. Previously, he had been a Postmaster, greatly addicted to drinking and smoking, but God made a great change in his life. One of the reasons for the joy in his testimony was that he was a Kikuyu, and the majority of this tribe are members of the Mau Mau and therefore despised.

As Tom travelled to various services on a Sunday, he had to go through Kikuyu territory and always wondered if they would be ambushed by terrorists, but they came to no harm and praised God for His protection. Their joy was to know that, despite the negative factors of being a Kikuyu, the Lord was reaching them and many were turning to Him. It was, perhaps, significant that the Nairobi City Council allocated a site for the building of a Pentecostal church in the location of Bahati, an area almost 100% Mau Mau. Building operations produced a beautiful cut stone building with a red tiled roof which would comfortably seat 400 people. At the opening baptismal service, many Africans risked their lives to be present and they were encouraged to find about twenty five white people there too. These included missionaries as well as National Service men and others from the Forces. The church stood as a Lighthouse in a very dark place.

Hilda was asked to set the Scripture exams for the local African day School, where she had two classes. The results demonstrated the thirst in the children for knowledge and the things of God. Among the children in the school were a number of Roman Catholics and the prayer was that they too would be won to the Lord. It was a source of joy for Tom to be able to supply the students in the Post and Telegraph School with copies of the Coronation Bible, donated by the British and Foreign Bible Society. He had also been asked if he could supply the Kabete Technical School, but was having to await further supplies.

This school was the location for a regular service and 42 students attended. They were aged from sixteen to twenty-four and came from Tanganyika, Uganda and Kenya. It was a great opportunity to tell them of Jesus in the hope that what they had heard they would take back to their own countries. Unfortunately, many believed that because they had taken a new name, that made them Christians.

The effectiveness of the work was enhanced by the provision of a film strip projector and, in the showing of The Pilgrim's Progress, there was much interest. As a result, three souls came to know the Lord, one of whom had been very hardened against the gospel, feeling that he was too well educated to surrender his life to the Lord. But he came through, as did his wife and he testified to the change in his life immediately. He was chief clerk in one of the schools and his conversion resulted in his asking the school Principal for forgiveness for things done in the past.

The political situation continued to present major difficulties for the Gospel. Civil unrest and massacres were almost daily occurrences, but God was sovereign and he reached into the darkness so that Tom had the joy of leading members of the Mau Mau to find peace with God. Danger was a daily companion as the society had vows that denounced Christianity, although most of their atrocities were against their own people. Even in addressing the 300 students at the Kabete Trade school, the Kikuyu were being reached and the witness was going forth, knowing that the increase lay with God.

An example of the danger was reported by Tom:

The power of Jesus to save was recently manifest in Nairobi. An African Christian wearing a "Jesus saves" badge was suddenly faced with a gun in the hand of a Mau Mau who said, "Let's see if Jesus saves" and at the same time shooting the African brother in the face. The gangster fled believing that he had killed the Christian. Fortunately, he didn't die because the bullet passed through one cheek and out through the other without touching his teeth and he recovered. He knew that man who had shot him and if he had reported him to the police, the gangster would certainly have been hanged since carrying a gun was punishable by death.

One day the Christian and the Mau Mau came face to face in Nairobi and, as might be expected, the latter almost fainted at seeing what he thought was a ghost. He was about to run away when the Christian caught him and preached Jesus. They continued to see each other every day and the Christian's persistence was rewarded when the man responded to the Gospel and proved that Jesus certainly does save.[iii]

While on furlough back in Northern Ireland, Tom's children settled well into the local environment, free from the anxiety of the political situation in Kenya. They asked if it were not possible to stay, but Tom and Hilda had known the call of God and, despite the troubles, were convinced that Kenya was where the lord had placed them. There were encouragements in the country and testimonies from Kikuyu people to the saving power and grace of God strengthened their resolve to return.

One of the main areas of activity was among the children, a work particularly developed by Hilda. The politicians had described 1960 as a year of destiny for Africa, and Hilda saw that being fulfilled in the lives of the boys and girls in her Sunday schools. She wrote:

Sunday afternoon at 1.30 finds me on my way, on my scooter, to take the Gospel to the Kikuyu children. As I travel along the road, stretched out before me are ever-present reminders that this is 'Kikuyuland'. On either side of the road is the fascinating Kikuyu countryside, baked hard by the tropical sun, with its banana trees and mealie shambas (maize gardens).

As far as the eye can see are hundreds of African huts. These are located in new villages set up by the Government for the Kikuyu people. It is from many of these homes that the children come to Sunday school. There are usually between 140-150 children each week, in all states of dress, but all are welcomed.

It may well be that some of them will be future leaders in Kenya and this is the time to plant the good seed of the Word of God; if we are faithful, this could have far-reaching effects.

Hilda's expectations for her Sunday school scholars were seen to have relevance when considering the outcome of earlier witness to students in the Posts and Telegraph School. With the restoration of order in the nation, the work developed and expectations grew as to the blessing of the Lord. One happy event was a reunion of some of the students who had been contacted in the Posts and Telegraph school. Some were from Uganda and Kenya, and some had been saved as far back as 1951 and 1954. The one from Uganda now held a responsible post with the Uganda Post office as an engineer, and was on fire for God. Others were in responsible positions in the Nairobi General Post Office. One who had been a leading figure in the services when Willard Cantelon had visited was now Director of Postal Services for East Africa. This work continued with students from as far away as Malawi. It was observed that, when independence came to Kenya, some of those appointed to responsible positions were former students who had received Christ. Their appointment was not because of their superior educational abilities but because they had recognised standards of truth and uprightness.

While Hilda spent much of her time in teaching day school, a Sunday school had been started by their daughter, Audrey and, when Audrey went to the Royal College of Nursing in London, her younger sister, Ruth continued the work. So the ministry was very much a family affair, and the Lord was pleased to bless. All this time, Tom was holding down a Government position and was in charge of building secondary schools and teachers' residences throughout Kenya. This often required him to travel hundreds of miles to supervise the schemes. Hilda was doing her own housework in addition to her teaching roles and Ruth was a full time teacher of shorthand and typing in a Nairobi Commercial college.

By 1972, the Johnstons had moved on from Kenya to Zambia, and were based in Ndola. After being there only a few weeks, Tom was asked to teach Scripture in an African government secondary school about five miles from his home. He readily accepted the challenge and began teaching three times a week in Chifubu School which had about 600 students attending. The students were aged from 14 to 18 and had very limited knowledge of Scripture. There were very few Bibles or New Testaments at that time and supplies were slow to arrive.

It will be understood that Tom Johnston's ministry did not lead to the establishing of churches in the name of Elim. But there were many other missionary organisations working in the country and churches existed under their auspices. A young couple from Cardiff, Mervyn and Sheila Thomas, who had been working as Elim Missionaries in Tanzania, had moved into Kenya and were associated with one of the churches connected with the Pentecostal Assemblies of Canada. In 1973, Alex Tee was invited to conduct a major evangelistic crusade in Nairobi. Although lasting for only one week, the results were amazing with over 500 decisions recorded and many healings reported.

With the Thomas's departure to Canada, the Elim work in Kenya virtually dried up until recent developments when the work was started again under the leadership of Simon Githigi, a Kenyan. This now continues as an indigenous work which itself has a missionary outreach into Ethiopia.

i Tom's story is set out in the *Elim Evangel*, Vol.41. Issue 36, pp.568, 569.

ii Reported in the *Elim Evangel*, Vol.34. Issue 19, p.218.

iii *Elim Evangel*, Vol.36. Issue 16, p.185.

CHAPTER 16

NEW ZEALAND/ZAMBIA/MALAWI

The establishment of the Elim Church in New Zealand resulted in an ongoing missions outreach developing.

ZAMBIA: In 1982, the Executive of the New Zealand churches, in response to letters from Africa, sent Pastor Les Covic and Brian Storey, an elder, to investigate the situation. They met with Pastor Felix Mwranza and ministered in several churches in Zambia. On their return, the Executive indicated its unwillingness to be involved but the local church at Hamilton caught the vision and began to support the African work.

A further visit revealed that Pastor Felix was a Youth Pastor with the Assemblies of God. Consequently, this contact was broken and efforts were made to establish a work based on the Elim Constitution. The work began in a small way, but the potential was great.

In 1987, a third visit was made and contact was established with Charles Mumba, a trained Baptist minister who was then working with the Prisons department in Zambia. He was Spirit-filled, could speak five languages including Chichiwa, and he was appointed as Superintendent of the work, which developed throughout the country to some 60 centres.

Charles Mumba was used in teaching seminars as the New Zealand leaders pioneered a work in neighbouring Malawi. Ultimately, the New Zealand influence was removed, but Mumba stayed on as superintendent. Around 1995, an application was made to Elim(UK) and Zambia was incorporated into the work of Elim International Missions.

MALAWI: In 1984, Pastor Les Covic with Bryan Johnson, an elder, went to Malawi at the request of the New Zealand executive. They travelled via Zimbabwe where they met with Peter Griffiths, the Field Chairman, Brian Edwards, International Missions Director and Pastor David Tsvamuno.

Encouraged by the visit, they made contact with Pastor Samuel Paul a leader of some 40-50 churches throughout Malawi. This work was centred on Blantyre so, in response to a good report, the New Zealand Executive agreed to work there.

Meanwhile, a New Zealand minister, David Beaumont with his wife, Vicky, was working in Zimbabwe with World Outreach. They had been there since 1981, church planting and training national leaders. Around 1986, their work permit expired and renewal was refused. World Outreach had no suitable alternatives to offer them but, in God's perfect timing, they were asked in February 1987 to go to Malawi. There was a limitation on the time available because their children were getting older and needed to return to New Zealand for education. But they settled in Limbe, on the outskirts of Blantyre, and began work.

They were busy times as churches were established and a City Bible School was set up. The work grew to about 80 churches and pastors were regularly sent for training. A church was defined at that time as having 30 or more adults meeting regularly.

At the end of a two year period, the Beaumonts returned to New Zealand and their place was taken by Les and Isobel Covic, with their 12 year old daughter, Angela. While the Beaumonts returned to plant a church in Whangarei, the Covics gave two years to the work in Malawi and saw it develop to around 100 churches. They returned to New Zealand in May, 1991, and opened an Elim Church in Christchurch.

Les Covic tells of a time in Malawi when a seminar for pastors was held in premises owned by the Roman Catholic Church. On the first occasion, the resident priest spoke to pastors who were not used to such buildings –

When you use the toilets, do not stand on the seat tops.

When you use the showers, please remove your clothes and shoes.

When you go home, please leave the sheets on the beds!

River baptisms were commonplace and sometimes they had the added adventure of a crocodile looking on. On one such occasion, a pastor came out of the church dressed in his wife's white nightdress to perform the ceremony in a muddy stream.

Pastor Henry Thom with his wife, Nellie, then took over the work. A teacher by profession, Henry was First Secretary of the South African Consulate in Wellington and well versed in African affairs. Under his leadership, the work continued to develop and grow. The Thoms gave four years to the Malawi field, to be replaced in 1995 by Russell and Margaret Knight, who served until December, 1997, when they returned home.

The Knights gave themselves to evangelism, church planting and the training of national leaders, while also involving themselves in social, medical and educational activities. Although the political situation was relatively stable at the time, there was much lawlessness resulting in attempted robbery, burglary and regular gun shots in the night.

One of the highlights of ministry was the Easter convention. Several hundred Malawians had gathered in Benali village under the shadow of the Zomba Mountain. Many had arrived on foot, having travelled 35-40 miles. Some came on bicycles or by taxi. Others came on huge trucks carrying 70 or 80 people at a time. They brought with them all they needed for the weekend – goats, bags of maize, ready to enjoy fellowship under hot, clear skies.

On the Saturday, 54 were baptised in the local river, without the help of the indigenous water dwellers – snakes and other nasties. The Sunday services were disturbed towards the end of the evening by the truck driver, who had spent most of his time in the local beer shop, deciding it was time to be going home. He sat revving his engine and leaning on his horn until, getting no response from his passengers, he took off for home without further delay.

It took a chase by the missionaries and the help of the police to stop him and bring him back for his passengers. Unfortunately, night had now fallen, the truck had no lights, but the driver drove as if he could see in the dark. No doubt, prayer lives were enhanced by the experience.

Following the withdrawal of the New Zealand input in both Zambia and Malawi, the New Zealand churches concentrated their missions endeavour on Cambodia, the Philippines and other countries more accessible to New Zealand. The consequence of this was that the work was transferred to Elim (UK) and Trevor and Maggie Mackriell became overseers of what was predominantly an indigenous work.

During Russell Knight's time of ministry in Malawi, he was able to purchase a large plot of land at Ndirande, a suburb of Blantyre. An A-framed church was built on the site using whole eucalyptus trees and banana leaves for a roof. This stood until just a few years ago when a new, brick-built City church was erected and is a credit to the work.

Margaret Knight had her ministry too as she taught women in rural areas the rudiments of hygiene and simple health matters. She travelled with an interpreter and had many opportunities to preach the Gospel. She was also able to teach many Muslim children in one of the expatriate schools using her music. Scripture in Song originated in New Zealand and Margaret used her own brand which the children learned and then sang back in their own homes. Who knows what the Holy Spirit can do with such seed?

Between 1998 and 2000, the New Zealand churches raised NZ$25,000 each year to assist with the development of the work that had now been transferred to Elim (UK).

CHAPTER 17

TANGANYIKA/TANZANIA

Subsequent to a decision by the Elim Missionary Society to open a field in Africa, Tom Nosworthy, who was at home from his work in the Congo and seeking a new direction for his ministry, with Arthur Tate, set out to pioneer in Tanganyika. At that time, they were commissioned by Pastor E.J. Phillips in 1946, "Leave no stone unturned until Elim has been established in central Africa." The pair travelled by air to Lisbon before taking a cargo ship for the rest of the journey round the west coast of Africa to the east. The journey was via Lisbon, Funchal on the island of Madeira, a further twelve day sail to the island of S. Tome and then on to Luanda, the capital of Angola. From there, they sailed to Lobito where they stayed for three days "taking on coal". Ultimately, they arrived in Capetown but, shortly thereafter, Arthur succumbed to a bout of malaria. Fortunately, his travelling companion, Tom Nosworthy, was able to look after him. The final destination in their voyage was Laurenço Marques (Maputo) in Mozambique where they disembarked and travelled overland to Nelspruit in the Transvaal. This gave Arthur an opportunity to meet Hubert Phillips and to see the work in which he was engaged.

They then travelled by train to Johannesburg where they bought an ex-army truck. Their journey then took them north to Congo, passing through Rhodesia, Nyasaland and over the Congo River to Busangu. From there, they went to Lake Tanganyika and crossed over to Kigoma, where David Livingstone died. It had taken three months without any contact from the home base but, eventually, Arthur set up a home in Morogoro where he and Peggy later lived.

It will be readily understood that a missionary's early days can be fraught with great trials and loneliness. In Arthur's case, he was separated from Tom Nosworthy, who had malaria and was in hospital some forty miles away. Arthur himself could speak no Kiluba, so he was very much isolated. However, he had a good serving boy who was able to communicate sufficiently to make life bearable.

While they were in Congo, and shortly after Tom's return, there was great excitement when the Mission Hunter at Busango arrived with an elephant's tail in his hand, declaring that he had killed an elephant and they needed to go and collect it! This meant a journey through the forest accompanied by about one hundred natives, all armed with knives. After some hours of walking and stumbling, they found the 'kill', a mountain of flesh and bone. In about one hour, they had the beast chopped up into manageable pieces and were ready to carry the meat back to the village. Arthur counted over eight hundred pieces of meat and the mission took home fifty sacks.

An area of ministry that appealed to Arthur early on was a work among the young people. There was great hilarity in the teaching of Elim Choruses to African children and sometimes the tunes had to be manipulated some to make the words fit. Opportunities also opened up for ministry in the local prison where, out of 36 inmates, only five had ever before heard the gospel.

Some three months later, the Missionary Council announced that Miss Peggy Priddis had been accepted as a missionary candidate and would be travelling to Tanganyika. It was also reported that she was to marry Arthur Tate. Thus, in September, 1946, Peggy Priddis set sail for Tanganyika but the journey, this time, was through the Suez Canal rather than round the West African coast. Her destination on this route was Mombasa and thence, two days by train to Moshi in the shade of Mount Kilimanjaro. The onward journey was to Morogoro which was in a beautiful situation near the mountains and surrounded by trees. The local livestock was interesting too, for a new arrival, and Peggy had to come to terms with snakes, hyenas and monkeys as neighbours. Rats were a problem but she didn't see too many spiders. The ones she did see were enormous. Before very long, she found herself involved in the work and was warmly welcomed by the African women to their homes and to the work.

Tom Nosworthy left the field for South Africa in 1947 with nothing finalised as to areas of operation. The following year, the team was augmented by the arrival of Pastor and Mrs. Jimmy Lochore and their children. They travelled from Johannesburg, via from Laurenço Marques by ship up the coast to Dar-es-Salaam. From there, their baggage was placed on the lorry and Arthur and Peggy, accompanied by Mrs. Lochore and the baby, set off on the 120 mile journey to Morogoro. Pastor Lochore with the three other children travelled by train overnight and arrived at 5.30 the next morning, to be awakened by a welcome from Arthur announcing their arrival.

Within a short time, Arthur and Jimmy had discovered for themselves the joys of driving in Africa as they tried to move through the bush in the old lorry with, often, no roads and many times, no bridges. Fortunately, there always seemed to be a number of Africans nearby to lend a hand and get them out of trouble. The Lochores left again in 1948 because of the lack of schooling opportunities for their children.

About one year later, Arthur and Dorothy Bull with their daughter, Heather, set out for Tanganyika. They took over what the Tates had started at Morogoro, while the Tates moved on to Kondoa. We often think of lady missionaries as teachers or nurses, but Dorothy Bull's background was interesting. In her early days, she had been a cabaret dancer until she was convicted of sin, born again and called by God to work in Africa. She gave up the footlights and took up nursing, serving in an East London hospital during the blitz in the Second World War.[1]

At this time, she was engaged to Arthur, then serving in the Forces and having no interest in the things of God. While she told him of the change in her life, she omitted to say anything about working in Africa. Arthur, as a young soldier, was always in trouble of some kind. He was peeved at the change in his young lady but, eventually, surrendered his life to Christ after attending a number of Elim meetings. Soon afterwards, his unit was posted to West Africa and, while there, he sensed the call of God to serve in East Africa.

He returned to the UK but shortly afterwards, was posted to East Africa where he took up medical work, training for which was provided and paid for by the Army. He conducted meetings and was able to preach to the local people so that, when he went as a missionary, he was already about four years in advance of a new missionary's situation because of his Army experience.

Someone had asked Arthur(B), before he left England, what would be the first thing he would do in commencing a pioneer work. His reply – Build a mud house! So it was, when he set out to pioneer in Kinonko, he left his wife and baby behind while he lived in a tent and began to build his mud house. Before long, however, he brought the family to a tent behind his building. At this time, the local people were not over friendly and they suffered with thieves who stole most of their personal belongings. As soon as was practicable, they settled themselves in the mud kitchen until the main house was complete.

While this was a good temporary measure, they knew that to establish a proper mission station, they would have to build more permanent buildings to house a school, hospital and the family. A dispensary was opened and was much used but had to be closed when Dorothy Bull had to have two operations and then contracted malaria. Once these were out of the way, the dispensary reopened, only to find an outbreak of typhus in the area. This was successfully dealt with. There were times when medicine was in short supply and the missionaries were cast on the Lord in prayer. Happily, they saw the Lord answer and His name was exalted as a result. Spiritually, the work developed as well and a number trusted Christ, having been made fully aware of the change in lifestyle that would be expected.

The work in Tanganyika was essentially pioneering for the Gospel. At Kikilo, Arthur(T) and Peggy literally had to create a home out of the bush, cutting down trees to build a house and planting a vegetable garden to supply them with food. Their water supply was two miles away. The language of the local people was just some unintelligible guttural sounds, but gradually, they were able to communicate and a work began. The primitive nature of the tribes required that Arthur make himself quickly aware of their customs and he was surprised to discover that much of their activity centred on blood sacrifices. They found themselves in demand for medical help although much of this was carried out according to tribal customs by the local witchdoctor.

The presence of missionaries in such a remote area couldn't help but draw attention and, before long, Arthur(T) was appointed to the Kondoa District Education Committee and was asked to present plans for the educating of the children at Kikilo. Agreement was reached that Arthur would build at Kikilo and the Government would build at Bereku, some nine miles away. Classes had already been started for reading and writing and about fifty people were attending the clinic for medical help daily.

The Tates were joined a little later by Miss Meta Topping who gave herself to the study of Kiswahili so that she could work by herself in the clinic. Arthur himself used Kiswahili for preaching but was also trying to learn Kifiome, an unwritten language but one used by many in the area. In the short time she had been there, Miss Topping had recorded 7000 visits, many of which might have been admitted to a hospital had there been one nearby.

Miss Topping's involvement took her to Kinonko to serve with Mrs. Bull in a ministry at the Kingolwira Prison, some twenty-five miles away. Several of the women there had become Christians, including one charged with murder, and the work was very satisfying as it reached to the darkened hearts. Arthur Bull conducted a simultaneous service for the men and had a full attendance.

In the same period of time – almost one year – only two people had responded to the Gospel in Kikilo. Many were counting the cost of discipleship, and were holding back because they had several wives and this presented a problem in the light of Scripture.

Life was not without its humour, albeit touched with sadness. Because of a famine, one woman brought her sister to Arthur, offering for her to become his wife in exchange for three cows. The marriage laws there set girls up for marriage at age twelve, all arranged by the men of the tribe, and a man could have as many wives as he could support.

But faithfulness brings its rewards and the work became established, with a foundation laid on which to secure a permanent work for God. The local people began to come for salvation and demons were cast out to the glory of God. Building work made progress with thousands of bricks handmade and fired for the construction of the school, which was reckoned to be the largest in the district.

1952 was a year of progress for the mission. Arthur Bull told of reaching out to remote areas where there were many Africans from many different tribes working on a plantation. There were some 3000 labourers in the area working on the sisal estates who had come originally from Tanganyika, the Congo Border and Portuguese East Africa (now Mozambique). After much prayer, a place was found for an evangelist, but there was no meeting place. The Christians among the labourers told Arthur that if he could find a suitable place, they would build a church. Thus it was that Africans from different tribes, after a hard day's work, gave themselves to creating their own church building, demonstrating their earnestness for the things of God.

The newest missionary to arrive at Kikilo was Ron Gull[ii]. He had been working in Africa from some time, employed by Sir Alexander Gibb & Partners, a well-known firm of Consulting Civil Engineers. He had a good grasp of the language, so that his addition to the team was a means of strengthening the work. Having missed the train he should have been on in Dar-es-Salaam, he set off by road, overtook the train he should have caught, and then continued his journey to Dodoma. From there, he travelled the remaining 150 miles to Kikilo on his Matchless motorcycle, arriving to the cheers of the school children and the welcoming smiles of the Tates. He was accustomed to inspecting his surroundings and his description of the Kikilo station was enlightening.[iii]

Kikilo Mission stands on a hill. A ridge of the hill known as Kikilo forms the site, on which are dotted the buildings which form our headquarters. The Mission house looks over the Bubu valley which, four years ago, was wild country, unsettled and untamed. Today that same valley is covered with a patchwork of unfenced fields and studded with the low earth-roofed huts of the Waasi folk. Beyond the Bubu River are the new settlements that have caused almost tribal war in the last few months and shimmering in the haze beyond them rise the low hills that mark the beginning of the rolling Mangati plains. Farther away to the north lies the smoky-blue mass of the extinct volcano, Hanang, which dominates the whole district with its steep 11,000 feet high peak. Behind the house, the ground slopes down to a low flat valley, beyond which another range of hills marks the edge of the escarpment and the ground falls abruptly several thousand feet to the famous Massai Steppe. To the South, a vista of hills leads one's glance to another mountain known locally as Ghost Mountain. It stands not far from Kondoa Irangi, on one side a sheer wall of white limestone rock that shines like a cloud in the heat haze of the day. This is the area in which we work.

In 1955, Arthur Tate's sister, Betty arrived and she and Ron were married in Dar-es-Salaam. They served with the Tates until Peggy Tate's death in 1958[iv] and later relieved the Bulls at Msolwa during their furlough in 1960, returning to Kikilo in 1961 to enable Arthur and his girls to return to the UK. The Gulls left the field in 1964, but subsequently returned to work in South Africa.[v]

With the growth of the work and the establishing of good foundations, it was possible for the workers to venture further afield in their work of evangelism. They found a willingness to listen to the Word especially when they turned up in the village with their 'black bag' that was able to make people well. This meant that the Tates and Ron Gull and the Bulls with Miss Topping were now seeing fruit for their labours. Many long miles were travelled seeking out new avenues and spheres of service and the Lord was gracious in leading and protecting them in their work.

Development of the work demanded additional meeting places for both services and schools and, in this, Ron Gull was a great help with his surveying and drafting ability. The need was also increased by a bush fire that almost destroyed the station where the Bulls were. Fortunately, only the roof of the teacher's kitchen burned.

The development of buildings sent a message of permanence to the local people. They realised that the missionaries would not be just here today and gone tomorrow. On the fifth anniversary of the Tates' arrival in Kikilo, the Mission Station was well established. It comprised the main mission house, a guest house and office; a workshop, a church building, the primary school, accommodation for the African teachers and a school garden. The erection of school buildings was an important task which facilitated the reaching out in evangelism to the surrounding districts.

A tool for evangelism that presented itself to them came about when the station was visited by Miss Joy Ridderhof. This lady was the Founder and Director of Gospel Recordings Incorporated. She spent time with the missionaries as they made a total of eighteen records, with Ron and Arthur translating from English to Kiswahili and then various converts translated form Kiswahili into local dialects. The Sunday school provided a musical background. There was excitement as the team waited for the records to arrive and they had hopes of obtaining cheap record players so that the Word could be more widely disseminated.

Furloughs for the missionaries were not so regular in those days and it was about ten years before the Tates returned to the UK and to their home church at Leicester. But they arrived home in time to attend Elim's annual Conference in Harrogate and were delighted to be presented with a brand new Land Rover by Jack Hywel-Davies, the National Youth Director. Following on from this, Rochester Sunday school fulfilled a promise they had made by presenting Arthur with a case of carpenter's tools which he had said, on a previous visit, were necessary for the work.

Meanwhile, back on the field, Betty Gull had started a Women's Bible Class which was meeting with some success. There was also a sewing class and a reading class, while religious teaching periods in the school were rewarding, a number of the scholars having accepted Christ.

In November, 1957, a young man from Cardiff, who had been trained at Elim Bible College, had a combined ordination and farewell service. He was Mervyn Thomas, moving out to Tanganyika in obedience to God's call. Arrived in Africa, he initially worked with Arthur Bull at Kinonko, deep in the bush, but not too far from the capital city of Dar-es-Salaam. There he became involved in all aspects of the work – evangelism, medical and school work, and learning to do practical things like cutting hair, pulling teeth and repairing vehicles.

Later, he moved to Kikilo to work with Arthur Tate, a station much further removed from civilisation in the central highlands. He was joined in 1959 by Sheila, his wife who, because she was a nurse and trained midwife, found herself fully engaged in medical work among the people.

During his time in Tanganyika, Mervyn was active, not only in local evangelism, but regularly sought to keep the needs of the field before the believers at home. His articles published in the Elim Evangel[vi] challenged those who might be 'at ease in Zion' to stir themselves and recognise the responsibility they had for reaching the lost. His call was for rededication of each life, regular prayer for the heathen, giving for the work and, should God call, going into the harvest field. He also threw the spotlight on the development of national evangelists. The growth of the work demanded that the new converts be instructed and encouraged to reach out to their own people and this was effective in carrying the Gospel to those who perhaps would be discouraged by hearing it from the white man.

One of the areas in which Mervyn's expertise was particularly useful was in the installation of electricity at the Kikilo station. The 'Lend-a Hand' Land Rover had been delivered and now, another youth activity was coming to fruition. "Send-the-Light" had provided an electric generator to supply electricity to the remote station at Kikilo. There was much preparatory work to be done as the area was wired for power. Overhead pylons were constructed from trees and concrete and wires were installed in walls, with switches and fuse boxes.

Once the work was complete, it was a matter of time until the generator could be collected from Nairobi. Fortunately, it fitted into the Land Rover – just! Despite its weight and the lack of any kind of heavy lifting equipment, the unit was installed on its plinth, ready for action. Sadly, it didn't work and, to the dismay of the missionaries, they discovered that it had been sent out without an injector unit. But this was soon remedied and, before long, there was light in the house. The next step was to dig trenches to carry wires to the church so that there, too, the power could be used.

The whole station was so lit up that the main mail plane for South Africa flew low to see what it was all about. As can be imagined, the people were excited and the work was greatly enhanced. The Africans were now calling it the 'white man's moon'.

Together with the ongoing joys of winning souls and seeing lives transformed, there was the daily business of maintaining life, a situation challenged continually in the bush areas by the incumbent wild life. Sometimes, there were leopards stealing chickens, at others, there were snakes ranging from puff adders to pythons. On one occasion, Dorothy Bull opened her chicken house to be confronted by a huge python with bulges along its length indicating it had already made a meal of some of the chickens.

She recorded her encounter –

I took a somewhat nervous aim at the snake's head (it was beginning to sway ominously) and my bullet landed beyond its head, but immediately next to the main artery, injuring but not killing the snake. It reared its head, stabbing the air viciously with its long tongue and began to uncoil as it moved towards me, fixing its eyes balefully on me. It took three shots to kill it (I could have done with something more than a .22 rifle for this occasion.). . . The snake was 14 feet 8 inches long and none of the Africans who had come for medicine would skin it so I had to do it myself after the day's work was done. . . .The carcass was left in the bush with the hope that the hyenas would eat it and the dead fowls were thrown away for the leopard. Unfortunately, the leopard preferred live meat and another chicken was taken.[vii]

The ladies on the field were very active, Betty Gull being also fully involved in the work among the women. Their evangelistic thrust used a team of eight women and was helped by the use of records supplied in local languages by the vision of American Gospel Recordings Inc. The gramophone on which they were played was, in itself, a unique tool, as many of the local people had no idea how the sound could come out of the box.

In 1960, Alan and Anne Renshaw moved from Zimbabwe, where they had been serving for about one year, to work with the Mission. This was a fulfilment for Alan who, when he was a Regular in the Royal Navy, docked at Dar-es-Salaam and knew then that this was the country to which God had called him. It was to be some years before he saw this in reality, after training in the Elim Bible College and then serving for a time in pastoral ministry in the UK.

But the day finally came, and he found himself labouring in evangelism, church planting and using his many practical skills while Anne, a school teacher, involved herself in school work as well as the wider aspects of ministry. This was a fairly difficult time for the Renshaws as they felt the frustrations of shortage of finance, tensions between workers and the strain of settling into a new situation. They remained in the country for just over three years before returning to Zimbabwe in October, 1964.

Easter Sunday, 1963, was an auspicious occasion for the church in Tanganyika. *"I, the undersigned, Rev. A.D. Bull, representing the Elim Missionary Society in Tanganyika, do hand over to the local church the following property, namely the church building and pastor's house, built on native authority land adjacent to the Elim Mission, Msolwa."* The document was signed and the local church began to stand, maybe weakly, maybe with doubts, but it began to stand. Under the leadership of Pastor Joseph, the council of elders had received the church and shown their willingness to 'begin to stand.'

Although representing a beginning, this was the culmination of the work of many over the years. Pastor Bull had started the work that led to the opening of the church and dispensary at Msolwa. It continued under the good hand of the Gulls while the Bulls were on furlough. On their return, they were ably assisted by Pastor Thomas who was in charge of the Bible school to train local workers. Shortly after Bible school finished, the Thomas family went to pioneer the work at Kondoa, while their place was taken by the Renshaws.

It was Alan's responsibility to do the actual building of the church and pastor's house, a demanding work because of the nature of the soil in the area. Because of this, rather than building with burnt bricks and cement, they erected a timber-framed construction and covered it with corrugated iron. Instead of foundations, the building was set on concrete "feet". Unfortunately, there was a problem with white ants, which loved to eat timber! So all the wood had to be thoroughly treated with creosote – a long, smelly and dirty task. But the frames were eventually made and the building erected with a floor area of 48' x 24'. Because of a shortage of water, they decided to make concrete slabs for the floor; 300 would be required. Gravel was hauled in the Land Rover from the nearby river and, just before the official opening and handing over ceremony, the work was completed.

One area of concern for the missionaries was that, while Africans were being converted and called into their ministry, they were being ordained into a Pentecostal church without a Pentecostal experience. This situation led Ron Gull to make an appeal through the Elim Evangel that there might be specific prayer for these young men to be filled with the Spirit. Before long, there was a report that God had graciously heard and answered and the Holy Ghost granted mighty baptisms of power. Things that before had been impossible now became gloriously possible; problems that had once seemed insurmountable now became stepping stones to greater service.

These things represented a development in the church in Tanganyika indicating a desire for independent growth and the missionaries wisely recognised the growing maturity of the African brethren as they sought to conduct their own affairs without totally relying on the missionary. Meanwhile, the missionaries were giving themselves to the preparation of tracts and booklets, and also in translation work. The national church was learning to go ahead and was looking to God for His guidance, supply and support.

TANZANIA

What was happening in the church was, in some measure, a reflection of the transitions within the country. In December, 1961, Tanganyika had become an independent nation but, in January, 1964, there was an amalgamation with Zanzibar creating the new nation of Tanzania. Julius Nyerere, who had been Prime Minister of Tanganyika, remained as Prime Minister of the newly created state.

Following a short furlough in the UK, Mervyn and Sheila Thomas returned to Tanzania, disembarking at Mombasa in Kenya where they stayed overnight with Tom and Hilda Johnston. But instead of going west to Haneti where, initially, they were to pioneer a work, they travelled south to Tanga on the coast.

The latter part of the Thomas's ministry was in the city of Tanga where they saw the hand of God at work in mighty power as signs and wonders followed the preaching of the Word. The blind, deaf and crippled and lame were made whole and a church was established, a building erected and paid for by the youth in the UK. Mervyn and Sheila found this superb preparation for their future ministry which took them to Nairobi in Kenya.[viii]

The Tanga work had been started by Jack and Jewyll Shellard. The Shellards were independent missionaries, Mrs. Shellard being the daughter of Pastor George Thomas, previously Elim's Missionary Secretary. The work was small but had great potential. The town had a population of some 65,000 souls and there was a desire among the believers to reach out to their community. Despite having their home ransacked and virtually all their belongings stolen on the night of their arrival, the Thomases got right down to work. They planned a Bible training centre, began an intensive literature distribution programme and sent out evangelists equipped with bicycles supplied by the Jersey Elim churches. It was the intention to visit every home, no matter what religion or race. Ultimately, of course, Tanga became the headquarters church and offices for the church in Tanzania.

The ongoing work in Tanga had five priorities – the training of national workers, the erection of national buildings to obviate the need to rent, the development of a full literature programme, the use of films as an evangelistic tool and the development of an input to schools and student bodies. Africa was, at this time, in a state of turmoil and Christians were very aware that the Soviet Union, with virtually unlimited funds, together with many and varied false religions, was flooding the continent with subversive literature.

The desire, therefore, was to seek in some measure to combat this onslaught by disseminating good Christian literature as widely as possible. As part of the strategy on Elim's part, Ron Gull had translated a basic correspondence course for beginners into Kiswahili and, when funds became available, this was sent out from Tanga to all parts of the country.

Elim's presence in Tanga was like a city set on a hill – it could not be hid! One night, two Anglican missionary ladies arrived at the home of Mervyn and Sheila Thomas. One was a doctor, the other a nursing sister. After a somewhat prolonged conversation, they indicated that they had felt the Lord's leading to come and they asked that they might receive the Baptism in the Holy Spirit. So Mervyn and Sheila taught them from the Scriptures and then they began to pray. However, the sister was filled with fear and so they left, asking that they be remembered in prayer.

The following morning, they returned and the sister told them that the Lord had taken away her fear in the night. So they arranged another time of waiting on the Lord. They were joined at this time by Mr. Edwin Johnston, a member of the Ulster Temple in Belfast, who was then working with the Tanzanian Government in the local high school. There followed a time of testimony and worship and, although the sisters did not receive the Baptism, they were greatly touched. That night, back in their accommodation, the nursing sister began to speak in other tongues as the Spirit gave her utterance. Subsequently, this lady wrote to say that on her mission station, people were being baptised in the Holy Spirit and they were seeing conversions and healings. At this time, there were further reports of Lutheran, Episcopalian and Presbyterian missionaries all being filled with the Holy Ghost.

The growth of the work in the Tanga area depended, to some extent, on the Volkswagen Kombi van that was used extensively for film evangelism. Many thousands of miles were covered visiting outlying mission churches and, as the films were shown, many people came into a living relationship with the Lord who loved them. Despite the hardships of travel on poor roads, far from civilisation and without adequate sleeping or feeding arrangements, nevertheless Mervyn and his family sought for souls far and wide and were rewarded by a harvest that would glorify the Lord.

A perennial problem for missionaries was the supply of necessary finance. Usually they had to work on tight budgets, often made out about one year in advance with little possibility of increase, even if unexpected difficulties arose. For this reason, the Missions Department at home had always to be on the lookout for ways and means of raising funds. A letter published in the Elim Evangel from Mervyn Thomas[ix] highlighted the dreadful needs of the mission fields, not only Elim but missions in general. One comment was telling. He said,

"We will readily turn out the old clothes cupboard and send our unwanted garments to clothe the needy, yet we would not give even the value of the stamps on the parcel to aid the programme of evangelism overseas. . . Why is it that appeals for maize and corn and farm implements can draw in thousands of pounds, yet the general funds of missions dedicated to the spread of the Gospel cry out for money but receive only the meagre donations of the committed few?"

One can well appreciate his frustration and, although things have improved somewhat in latter years, the need still exists.

Over the years, the young people of the Movement were harnessed to some activity or other that would not only raise money for missions but, hopefully, would also inculcate in them a vision for the work. With this in view, the Elim Youth Movement (EYM) was encouraged to help with the building of churches in Africa. Drawings taken from architects' plans were enlarged and copies were sent out to the churches. Sunday schools and other youth departments were asked to 'buy a brick' and as these were purchased at a given price, a small brick was pasted onto the plan. At that time, a brick cost threepence (3d) and a tile cost sixpence (6d). The older groups of Crusaders[X] were given a selection of items they could buy including pews, chairs, tables and other items of furniture. The scheme was to run for six months, by which time, the church building would be complete. At the other end of the scale, the Swansea Sunday school raised £65 for a complete building in one of the outstations. Elim's young people have always risen to such challenges as will be readily seen in the various countries in which we labour.

Over the years, faithful sowing was producing harvest and young men were not only being saved, but were responding to God's call to ministry. In 1968, an ordination service was held at Msolwa, conducted by A.D.Bull and M.O.Thomas, for young men who had been identified as evangelists and pastors. One young man, ordained at that time, was Ayubu Mgweno, later to become the chairman of the church. He had come out of a Moslem background and although his early years had been fraught with difficulty and challenge, he had remained faithful, learning many lessons in how to live the Christian life.

Another young man was Eliya, an evangelist, who also testified that religion had failed him. His Roman Catholic background had not stopped him from becoming a witch-doctor. He had become well known for driving out spirits; this he did by the drum, the frenzied dance, smoke and calling on the ancestral spirits. He found Christ through a young lady, claimed by her family to be demon possessed. The spirit in her was stronger than Eliya's spirits and his life was changed. Eliya was at this time supported in his ministry by the sisterhood at Bournemouth.

The third young man ordained in this service was Emmanueli, who had been a pagan without knowledge or care for God. Now he was an evangelist. There were two years between his and his wife's conversion, difficult years in which his faith was severely tested, but he remained faithful and, in spite of many drawbacks and trials, was happy serving the Lord and leading others to faith in Him.

A happy occasion for the church at Msolwa was a visit from Elim's president, Leslie Green in 1968. There were many interesting experiences awaiting him. He had lunch with a former cannibal and asked him, "What would have happened if I had come to your house a few years ago?" "You would not have got out," was the cheerful reply. There were many others – a man who had been demon possessed; a man who used to have four wives; a man who used to be a witch doctor. The only complaint during the visit was that it was not long enough, just one week before going on south to other fields.

The visit to Africa was the fulfilment of a dream for Leslie Green, who had long cherished the idea that one day he would see Africa. He landed in Nairobi to be met by Pastor Tom Johnston and the next day, travelled to Tanga where he opened the new church building. This was a special occasion that was attended by the deputy to the President of the country as well as the local mayor. At the opening, Moslems were asking about being saved and some were converted, while others were baptised in the Holy Spirit. Thereafter, he went to Morogoro and Msolwa to see the work being done by Arthur and Dorothy Bull. His cup was full to overflowing with impressions and experiences.

The development of the work advanced rapidly, to the extent that the reports stated that there were not enough workers or money to keep pace with growth. In one period in 1969, shortly after the Bulls returned from furlough, they saw over 100 Masai women turning to Christ in the Msolwa region. One aspect of what was described as a revival was the number of miracles of healing reported. In one of the mountain outstations, Pastor Joseph met a blind man who had been led to the church by a small child. After prayer, he cried, "I am healed! I am healed!" Shortly afterwards, he found salvation. A Masai woman had to be carried into the church but, after prayer, jumped up joyfully and walked the many miles to her home. Despite the fact that many witch doctors were actively standing against the missionaries and their Gospel, people were being converted and filled with the Spirit.

For several years, Arthur Bull had held the position of Field Chairman, but now believed that it was time for the Africans to take charge of their own affairs. Time was therefore taken to pray and seek the Lord for a successor and the decision was made that Pastor Joseph, who had been a witch-doctor's son, should be installed in the position. Joseph Ibrahimu was saved in 1955 and, at this time, had served as an evangelist for five years. One of the first of his tribe to be converted, he had suffered persecution and abuse, but he and Arthur Bull had worked tirelessly in the area to reach the lost, first among his own tribe and then, with Arthur, to other surrounding tribes people.

On the day of his installation, he said, "Pray for me. I am nothing and nobody." He spoke of the tremendous debt he felt he owed to the Elim Missionary Society and to the missionaries and said, "I take this opportunity to send our thanks and our greetings to our brethren in the United Kingdom who have made it possible and who still maintain our missionaries here today."

As the work continued to expand, the need for buildings was ever present. The great challenge to each group of believers was to build a 'Jesus house'. Then the local people set to with a will and they were joined in a partnership with the EWMA in the UK who supplied the money for corrugated iron roofs.

Having seen the work to which God had called them prosper under His hand, the time came for the Bulls to take a furlough. So, in 1972, they left Africa with a promise that, though thousands of miles apart, they would pray for the African church at 3 p.m. every day. The work had now been committed to faithful African brethren and, under their guidance, progress continued to be made in all directions. When the Bulls returned from furlough, they picked up where they had left off and moved right back into their routine once again. Many people had been touched by the Gospel and there were many experiences to be recounted.[xi]

In the course of time, there were new challenges for the work, since the nation was vast and the tribes widely scattered. For some time, there had been a growing desire in the hearts of the national evangelists to reach out to other Masai tribes, particularly those in the north east on the Kenya border. Plans were therefore made for evangelist Kazimoto and Arthur Bull to travel into their area with a view to starting to work among them. On their second probing visit, they came across a circle of seated elders who were in discussion with their witch-doctor about the lack of rain. They were not the slightest bit interested in the missionaries, but one was persuaded to leave the group and a conversation led him to invite them to meet with a larger group about one week later. The result of that meeting was an agreement that Kazimoto should live among them to tell them about Jesus and a grass church was erected for the purpose with a small room for the evangelist.

A significant visit took place in 1978 when Pastors T.W.Walker and J.C. Smyth, representing the International Missions Board, visited Tanzania and met with the African members of the Tanzanian Executive, accompanied by Arthur Bull. A major part of their discussions was concerning a Constitution for the church in Tanzania. The church would then be known as K.E.P.T. – Kanisa la Elim Pentecoste Tanzania. The visitors were impressed with the maturity of the work and the balanced way in which the African brethren were seeking to develop the whole ministry with Bible schools and churches, as well as caring for social needs as they presented themselves.

The growth of the work continued apace and the Missions Board asked Arthur Tate with his wife, Yvonne, to return to Tanzania. Arthur's earlier experience in the country, together with his ability to speak the language, made him an excellent choice. The Tates were shortly afterwards followed by the arrival of Pastor R. (Dick) and Mrs. Tesne Davis, just released from the Elim Bible College in the UK. They were headed for Tanga to work with the Tates, having been collected from the airport at Dar-es-Salaam by Arthur Bull.

When Arthur Tate revisited Kikilo, the whole area erupted with joy as he was welcomed back into the region. Indeed, one old man introduced him to his married son. The boy had been helped into the world by the Tates at the time of his birth and had been given the name, 'Tatey'. So the cry rang far and wide – "Tatey's back! Tatey's back!" Remarks flew back and forth to the effect, "Yes, it is he," and "Truly, he is still alive". The response to the man who had first introduced the people to reading and writing was phenomenal and there was great rejoicing over the whole neighbourhood. Thirty years later, Arthur Tate, one of the two original pioneers, felt he might have responded to E.J. Phillips's comment with the reply, "Task almost completed" as he surveyed the measure of development and maturity he now saw in the Tanzanian work.

It will be readily appreciated that the work of the missionary would be impossible without an adequate vehicle for transport. For many years, the mission had used a Land Rover which was now very much getting "past it"! But in the UK, the Green Shield Stamp system was still at work and, by co-ordination through Elim Headquarters, sufficient stamps were collected to purchase a new Land Rover, which was deemed to be the best vehicle suited to the terrain. This was delivered in 1978 by a Russian ship. It was liable for a £5000 import tax but the Government graciously granted an exemption. Within a very short time, therefore, the miles were clocking up and in just a few short months, there were over 5000 miles registered.

At a slightly lower level of activity, but with no less commitment, the Leicester Sunday school provided three bicycles for the use of pastors. These were presented to Arthur Tate at the Leicester church while he was at home on furlough. This was followed, on their return to the field, by a day of dedication, attended by Pastor and Mrs. T.W. Walker and Pastor David Ayling, the International Missions Director. They all took part in a great service of thanksgiving as a new Bible school was opened, the bicycles were presented for use among the Masai and the youngest son of Pastor Ayubu was dedicated. The leader of the Women's work thanked Mrs. Walker for all that EWMA had done in supporting the work in Tanzania over the years.

Another area which saw help coming from the UK was in the HELPS Scheme. This was a scheme, operated through Headquarters, whereby individuals agreed to give £1 no more than twice per year, usually to help with the establishing of a new church after a pioneer Crusade. At the instigation of Ron Jones, Secretary General, and Wynne Lewis, then Evangelistic Secretary, there was a suggestion that the latest appeal be sent to build church buildings in Tanzania. Churches could be built in rural areas for £50 and in town locations for £500; thus the response to the appeal could result in new church buildings being supplied for congregations that were unable to fund a building themselves. Needless to say, this was an enormous encouragement to both the Africans and the missionaries in their work.

For six months, from January to June, 1980, Alan Renshaw was released from his church in Grimsby to return to the field to deal with matters that "required wisdom and spiritual far-sightedness." Subsequently, he returned in 1981 for an extended period of service that stretched to 1998, when he retired. On that occasion, he found himself with something of a dilemma. The Renshaws were supposed to disembark at Kilimanjaro airport near Arusha, but the pilot decided he couldn't land there since the airport fire engine was out of order. But Arthur Tate, shortly to return to UK, decided to go to the airport just in case. As it turned out, the pilot decided to make an unscheduled stop at Kilimanjaro and the Renshaws were spared the onward trip to Dar-es-Salaam where there would have been no-one to meet them. Initially, they went to work in the interior area of Babati where there was a full range of ministry waiting including Bible teaching, Sunday school and other church duties as well as teaching in the all-age day school.

February 1986 saw the induction of a new field Chairman, Pastor Ayubu Mgweno and also a welcome to the newest missionaries, Richard and Rajindark Buxton at the church in Nguvumali, Tanga. Richard's main activity was to oversee the Bible school so he had the responsibility of setting the syllabus, arranging for the translating of lecture notes into Swahili and organising all that was necessary to make this a school of excellence for the training of young men for evangelism and ministry. The record indicates that he did a magnificent job that was much appreciated by all concerned.

But in addition to their work in the Bible school, the Lord opened a door for ministry to some of Tanga's Asian population. Richard describes what happened[xii]:

Until a few weeks ago, there was only a small handful of Asian Christians here. While most of the Africans in Tanga are Moslem, the Asians are virtually all Hindus, including Sikhs. One of these Asian Christians, feeling burdened for his own people, organised a city-wide campaign. The Lord moved in mighty power resulting in many conversions, miraculous healings of the blind and lame and, in particular, many of the Hindus, whose lives revolved around the worship of idols and demons, resulting in demon-possession being a common problem, were delivered. A number of them burned their idols and charms. . . The result was that the young Indian evangelist was left with a sizeable congregation on his hands.

Rajindark was asked to give her testimony one night, telling of her conversion from Sikhism to Christianity. There were many Sikhs there that night on whom the testimony made a big impression and who wanted to talk with her afterwards. After the mission, I was asked to do a number of Bible studies for the new converts. The mission had been held in a local Hindu community hall but, when it was discovered that many Hindus had turned to Christ, they shut the doors to our using the hall. So when we turned up for the studies, there was nowhere to meet, so we held them on a playing field next to the hall.

The next day, with timing clearly that of the Lord, the Indian pastor was supplied with a meeting place to hold services any night of the week. The people rejoiced and the only problem was that the building was not quite complete, being in the final stages of construction. Our intention is to maintain contact with the new, independent church, an advantage to all being that their main language was English.

This association with the Asian church developed as Richard was asked to run a weekly discipleship course for the leaders. This was done on a house meeting basis where there was Bible teaching as well as opportunity for the leaders to prepare their own teaching material. This had the benefit of them both learning as well as fulfilling their desire to reach their own people.

The Bible school was also developing apace, to the extent that they outgrew their accommodation. Back in the UK, the Missions Board and the Youth Committee had accepted plans that would lead to an extension of the Tanga Bible School and the Executive Office building. As a result of a visit by David Butcher, then a member of the International Missions Board, the Gloucester church, with many others, began to seek to raise £7000 to build an extension. This was completed in good time as young people became excited about the project and cars were washed, slims, walks and runs were sponsored and undertaken. A "Drive for Tanga" was instituted as a number of cars planned to drive around England, calling at as many Elim churches as possible. The idea was to publicise the Tanga project far and wide. Someone cleaned the windows at Headquarters in Cheltenham, the young people of Long Eaton held a Gospel concert and two young boys from Derby offered a dog-walking service. The bulk of the money came, however, through direct giving on the part of the church members.

By the time the Buxtons were ready for their first furlough in 1988, the Bible school was well established. At that time, there was a record enrolment, with students coming from all over the nation. The first batch of eight students had completed their two year courses and received their certificates at a special Bible School rally held during the Conference of that year. As an extension to the work, it was also planned that, in the following term, the ministry of the School would be taken into the regions for the teaching and training of pastors who were unable to attend the School in Tanga on a residential basis.

At that time, the Field Chairman, Ayubu Mgweno, reported that delegates had come from the farthest reaches of the nation. Stephen Mwayahila[xiii], the General Secretary challenged the gathering with the church's vision – to have a work in every district within two years. There were then 120 churches with about 3000 members. It was at this Conference that the first Women's President was elected. She was Mama Raheli and her appointment was greeted with great delight by the assembled ladies.

The outlook for the work in Tanzania was bright as various visitors from the UK called and then, on their return home, were able to present the vision. Perhaps the most regular of these were Pastors Mervyn Tilley and Patrick Rose, whose ministry was always acceptable. The Lurgan church undertook the building of a new church in Arusha, and Pastor William McCandless, on a visit with the writer, was able to unveil the foundation stone. A new Land Rover was supplied to the Renshaws, as well as an off-road motorcycle for one of the district Superintendents. Given the state of the roads, where they existed at all, this was a good choice of transport.

While this record finishes in 1989, the Renshaws remained in position until Alan's retirement in 1998. The Buxtons moved from Tanzania back to the homeland, but were soon involved in the work in Malaysia as a consequence of the Lord's dealings with Rajindark's brother[xiv].

i See *Elim Evangel* Vol.41. Issue 17, p.262 for details.

ii A fuller record of Ron's introduction to Mission work is given in an unpublished personal account – Chapter Three: In Azania, A pivotal point – from 'Soils' to Mission.

iii *Elim Evangel.* Vol.34. Issue 45, p.533.

iv Peggy was buried in Arusha. She left three small girls, aged 3, 5 and 7.

v See chapter on Transvaal/South Africa for further details of the Gulls' ministry.

vi See, for example, *Elim Evangel*, Vol.44. Issue 9, pp.136-138.

vii Reported in the *Elim Evangel*, Vol.40. Issue 25, p.396.

viii See chapter on Kenya for further comment.

ix Paralysed by Poverty. *Elim Evangel*, Vol.49. Issue 15, pp.15,16; Issue 16, p.245

x One of the Youth Departments – section into Junior and Senior.

xi Both Arthur and Dorothy Bull were prolific writers and the *Elim Evangel* regularly carried stories from the field, too many to be retold in detail in this work.

xii Reported in *Elim Evangel*, Vol.67. Issue 25, p.13.

xiii Pastor Stephen Mwayahila subsequently undertook training at Regents Theological College in Nantwich, gaining his Masters Degree in Theology and remained to pursue a Doctorate. The intention was that he would return to become the Principal of the Bible School in Tanga.

xiv See chapter on Malaysia for details.

CHAPTER 18

TRANSVAAL/SOUTH AFRICA[i]

Because of the worldwide nature of the Pentecostal revival at the turn of the 20th Century, there was already a strong Pentecostal witness in South Africa, with connections across the world to leaders of other works. Thus when missionaries went to Africa from the UK, they often had occasion to make contact with settled churches in South Africa as they transited to their chosen field. It was a regular occurrence for them to disembark at Capetown and then travel via Johannesburg to countries in the north. Sometimes they would remain on board ship until they reached Laurenço Marques (now Maputo in Mozambique) in Portuguese East Africa for onward travel to countries to the west and north.

The missions work in South Africa, which was under way before Elim missionaries ventured there, tended to reach out to those working in mines or farms throughout the region. These enterprises were usually run by white people, either Europeans or Afrikaners, with camps alongside to house the black workers. The camps became the focus of missionary activity and developed their own character of worship and witness.

This work was led by a Mr. Burley who, with a diverse body of missionaries, worked along the south eastern boundary of the Transvaal Lowveld, opposite what was then Portuguese East Africa (now Mozambique) and Swaziland. Their main Mission station was at Mbuzini, situated on the high land to the east of the malarial Komati River valley, and they called themselves the Lebombo Pentecostal Mission. There must have been some contact with Elim because reports and letters from Mr. Burley were featured in the *Elim Evangel* of those days. Because of the unhealthy nature of the area, particularly during the rainy season, some of the missionaries removed to Komatipoort around 1922.

In 1928, Hubert Phillips[ii], who hailed from the Letchworth church, arrived on the South African field. Hubert's wife, Jean, travelled to Transvaal as his fiancé in January 1929, and they married in February the same year. Jean passed into the presence of the Lord in 1977. She was an outstanding missionary in her own right.

His early association was with the Lebombo mission which had a small number of workers together with several native evangelists. But in 1929, a division arose and a number of likeminded individuals met in Nelspruit to form a new body they called Emmanuel Mission. Hubert was elected Chairman and the headquarters were in Nelspruit, at that time a European village with a station on the railway line from Johannesburg to Delagoa Bay. Then, the chief occupation was citrus fruit farming and the village comprised a few shops, two banks, Post Office, Farmer's Hall, and Dutch church, but today it is a bustling modern city.

Hubert identified those involved. The first on the field was Mrs. Larsen (Denmark), who was in full charge of the work at Koomatipoort and the surrounding countryside. Next to arrive were Miss Edith E. Hobbs (1921) and Miss Waymouth, both from UK. Miss Hobbs worked at Headquarters while, in 1930, Miss Waymouth was due to go home to England on furlough. Miss Lokken (Norway) was working hard in Laurenço Marques and the Vice Chairman was a Mr. Willmer, then working in a government department in Northern Transvaal. There was also a Miss Johannson (Sweden) and Mr. and Mrs. Bromberger (South Africa).[iii]

The challenge facing the missionaries is seen when you hear of a boy who travelled from 40 miles away to ask for a teacher to come to his area. He was one of sixteen who were interested, but he lived at a mine where there were over 1000 employed. This was the fourth or fifth call that had recently come in.

Hubert wasted no time on his arrival and immediately began to build a church which was accomplished in about fourteen weeks. The opening took place on 3rd September, 1928 and the doors were opened by Mrs. Willmer. The effect of opening the new building was that they were able to conduct evening school classes on three nights a week and it was encouraging to see boys learning their letters and beginning to read the New Testament. They were also seeing numbers of new people attending the services.

This work was to be left in the charge of Miss Hobbs and Miss Waymouth, while Hubert was moving on to Kaapsche Hoop where there was an asbestos mine employing some 1000 people with another nearby, allowing a ministry to over 1500 people. In the course of time, churches were opened in several places with strange-sounding names. In 1929, a church was opened at Mataffin, with about 70 souls, and another at Joes Luck. It is clear that much use was made of local evangelists in the development of the work.

At Mataffin, the local people built their own church and felt a sense of ownership in it. They were asking for their own teacher-evangelist too and were willing to help with his support. Further afield, there was a church at Tonetti where an evangelist, Isaya Tumbu, was in charge and he had three branch churches with local preachers to help him. In the mining area of Noordkaap, another evangelist, Hezekiah Kossa, with local preachers was doing a great work and also had branch works under his care.

By 1931, a Bible School had been opened and the works in Nelspruit and Komatipoort were developing. At the Christmas convention in Komatipoort, Hubert baptised several of the converts while a white man stood guard over them with a gun in case of crocodiles approaching. Later, at Nelspruit, they held a Watchnight service lasting for three hours and experienced great blessing. Each year, they brought the evangelists and teachers into the Bible school for a week of Bible study and training. At night, the evangelists would preach in public meetings and saw the Lord move. Day schools were also running successfully at this time.

Extension work was going on all the time, with a work at Karino, where there was a church building, but no one to run it. A new opening presented itself at Koedoeshoek, where a group of people wanted to see a church established and had already collected some money to pay for it. Water baptismal services were a regular feature of the lives of the missionaries.

A further development in the work was the setting up of a printing press for the production of Gospel literature. Known as the Emmanuel Press[iv], originally situated in Nelspruit, but later relocated in White River, it was set up in 1929 by Hubert Phillips and Austin Chawner[v]. In a report dated 1962, Hubert indicated the scope of the Press's work. He said:

For months now our Kelly press has been rolling out two-coloured tracts from 6.30 a.m. until 10 p.m. daily. These are then cut and folded and dispatched to many African countries, from Cape to Cairo. Reply slips come back to us daily, amounting to thousands in a year. The work of a press like this must be equal to the work of hundreds of individual missionaries. . . In schools, some tracts have been used for reading sheets and in one school, a whole class of boys accepted the Lord as their Saviour. Saved men have received a new vision for service and send to us for regular supplies. Follow-up Bible studies are always available to converts in their own language. God wonderfully overruled in the dispatch of 250,000 tracts to Congo so that they arrived at their destination the day before the railways were blown up![vi]

Thursday, June 16th, 1932, was an auspicious day for Pastor W. H. Francis[vii], as he farewelled from Clapham en route to South Africa to work with the Emmanuel Mission. Within two weeks of his arrival, he, with the help of Hubert and the students, had built his own house and helped with the building of one of the churches. All he had to do then was to make his own furniture! Then it would be time to move in and settle down to intensive language study.

Koedoeshoek Mission station in the Crocodile River valley west of Montrose was opened at the end of 1933 under the leadership of Pastor Francis. It was closed in 1935 when he moved to Pilgrim's Rest after his marriage to Miss Lynch in the January. In the April of that year, he established a new Station in his new location. Miss Lynch was a member of the Brixton Full Gospel Church, Johannesburg. In 1938, the Francis family, now augmented by the arrival of baby Geoffrey, left Pilgrim's rest for a well earned period of furlough in the UK.

In course of time, an opportunity presented itself for Hubert to visit a local jail in the Nelspruit area. A convict was appointed interpreter and about 1250 persons attended. Later, they went to the hospital and ministered to about thirty people there. This was followed by a 'big' meeting with 383 present. At this service, there was a convict choir and a community hymn was sung, while the warders sat around the edge on high stools watching the group. After this meeting, Hubert travelled four miles to the prison farm where there were about seventy prisoners, all with life sentences and judged to be the worst characters in the Transvaal.

Letchworth also played a part in the sending of the next missionaries to South Africa. They were Mr. and Mrs. Blythen with their daughter, Dora. They had sensed a call some nine years earlier, but the doors hadn't opened until now. They travelled to Africa with Miss Hobbs and Miss Stacey, and were assigned to Witbank where they found a small group of believers. This work had been started in 1921 by someone who had received his Baptism in the Holy Spirit in the revival that broke out in Komatipoort. He remained faithful and after some time had elapsed, he moved to Witbank to work in the coal mines. There he commenced to hold meetings among his fellow-workers and night school classes to help them to read and study the Bible. The numbers grew to about eighteen regular followers. The Blythens then undertook further Bible training on the Witwatersrand before finally establishing themselves at Witbank in 1937 where they erected a permanent house for the princely sum of £700. In 1939 they were able to report blessing and encouragement from their labours in Witbank and the church was well established with its own building seating 120 and a membership of 89 people. Brother Blythen laboured unstintingly among the Africans for almost twenty-three years until his home-call in July, 1958.

An opening on the Leydsdorp Gold Fields in the Murchison Range of hills was considered and investigated during 1935, but it was decided that it would be more strategic to establish a Mission Station in Tzaneen town slightly further to the north. Mr. and Mrs. James Mullan who had been working in the Congo with CEM arrived in South Africa in 1935 and were appointed to Tzaneen, establishing themselves there in January 1936. (RGD)

Unfortunately, the first service they tried to hold was fraught with difficulty as they couldn't find an interpreter. James tried with the smattering of languages he had, but none seemed to work. Finally, a big man offered and did a good job. It was discovered that he was the sergeant of police in the district. The following Tuesday night, there was a violent storm and a native hut was struck by lightning and set on fire. They thought the house was vacant but discovered afterwards that the policeman had been struck by lightning in the hut and killed. The outcome was a turning to the Lord by several people, including the policeman's wife, who had been a backslider.

Development of the work in Tzaneen saw the central services being taken by Mrs. Mullan while church planting and outreach were taken out into the bush areas with a measure of success. The names tell their own story, since much of the work was focussed on those who worked on local farms. So there were works at Pearlman's, Botha's, Piencer's, Meiser's, Bennet's and Union Citrus. There was also a work at a lumber camp, Middle-Kop, but this had to be closed because of transport difficulties and no local evangelist to look after the services.

In 1938, the church in Tzaneen opened its own building. About three hundred attended the opening, including Mr. Chawner Senior and his son. The local magistrate attended with his wife and both brought words of encouragement to the assembly.

Back in the homeland in this same year, a decision was taken by the Missions Council to enlarge the scope of its work. They intimated that they would now recognise Associate Missionaries who, although not supported financially by the Council, would have access to the churches to raise awareness of their call and to invite support from the congregations. Their reports would be published from time to time and every encouragement would be given to them in seeking to establish indigenous works overseas.

In 1940, Mrs. Bessie Christie and her daughter, Faith[viii], travelled from the UK to Pilgrim's Rest. A Mr. and Mrs. Richards also arrived then and took the oversight of the church while Mr. and Mrs. Francis were on furlough. It was reported that Mrs. Christie had built a house at Pilgrim's Rest at her own expense. A Mr. Delport also went to South Africa at that time and was assigned to work in the Emmanuel Press. He left again in 1941. (RGD)

An important aspect of the work was that, in addition to serving the Africans, there were also calls to minister to the Europeans. This proved to be a fruitful area of labour for all the missionaries to a greater or lesser degree. Mrs. Jean Phillips ran a Sunday school for white children and in later years, Ron Gull reaped the benefit when looking for permission to enter certain areas, as he found those he was dealing with had 'history' as former pupils in Jean's Sunday school. He obtained the permission he needed.

James Mullan made an interesting comment. It was 1941, and speaking about their travels to distant farms, etc., they found themselves receiving good offerings from the white farmers. This was beneficial and his comment is telling. "Thus our petrol is paid for by the Europeans. The cost of running a car now (with petrol 2/3 [11p] a gallon) is awful, and one has such distances to go; we spend our 'all' on the old car!"

A further development in the work was the growing numbers of Spirit-filled native evangelists whose ministries were being continually released and proving extremely fruitful. Both William Francis and James Mullan were reporting news of ever-widening doors of opportunity to minister throughout their regions. Hardly a month passed without a call reaching them from some distant or remote area, where people wished to hear the Word of God. The African Christians had been taught for many years to manage their own affairs as much as was possible against the day when the missionary might no longer be present. The wisdom of this was now being seen as the local people were taking on the responsibility for the support of their own evangelists, who alone could reach the masses.

There was much to encourage, but equally, there were times of great tension. One day, they saw several large lorries full of men and women. They discovered there had been a 'rising' among the employees of the huge Letaba Citrus estate, some fourteen miles away which resulted in the dismissal of four hundred workers. The disturbances were inter-tribal and the strangers were all being returned to their own land in disgrace.

The following Sunday, James Mullan and his evangelist went to the estate in trepidation, only to find the believers gathered together as usual, enjoying the sweetness of God's Presence. The Compound Manager gave them a large shed for their meetings and school as their former hut had become too small. The development of the work into various areas went ahead as doors opened at mines and farms. Meetings were being held monthly for Europeans and a regular visit to Pietersburg was organised, where they called at houses with tracts and booklets, reaching out to African and European alike.

After a number of years of faithful service in Tzaneen, Pastor and Mrs. J. Mullan felt led to move to a new field and commenced a work in East London in the Cape Province in 1944. Their leaving had a profound effect on those left behind, and one confessed that he had not fully realised what it would mean for 'his mother and father' not to be returning. This dear brother recognised that his own feelings must have been the same as those who had seen the Mullans leave Congo some years before. The Lord graciously set His seal upon their move, however and, within a very short time, they were able to report that fifteen souls had been won. This in spite of the fact that James wrote that his new area was 'the worst place we have ever seen or heard of . . . a wicked place where the people are careless, self-indulgent and with no thought of God or eternity.'

They arranged an evangelistic mission with evangelist Nicholas Bhengu, a name that was often to be described as 'the Billy Graham of Africa.' Their report made thrilling reading. Over one hundred professed salvation on the first two nights and eighty-three on the Friday. Healings took place – two blind men received their sight. The meetings were attended by all classes; those attired in rags seated with smartly dressed soldiers; some dressed in the latest European styles – all patiently standing for hours as Bhengu spoke.

Shortly after the Mullans left Tzaneen, Mrs. Christie and Faith left Pilgrim's Rest to take the oversight there, staying until 1947 when they moved on to Phalaborwa to pioneer a new station in that area. It was expected that mining operations would result in the creation of a new town and already, the influx of African labour had produced several huge new townships. But initially, the station was in the bush, primitive and remote from any kind of facilities and prone to attack by stampeding elephants!

In 1945, the Blythens took a furlough in England after having been on the field for eleven years. When they returned in 1946, they left their daughter, Dora, behind them working for Letchworth Printers, the Phillips' family firm.

In 1947, Tom Nosworthy who had served with CEM[ix] in Congo and, for a short time, with Elim in Tanganyika, came to Tzaneen. Ruby Simms from the Elim Church in Hove, and Frieda Grossen, also arrived in that year. Initially, Frieda was stationed at Nelspruit where she worked among the Asian and Coloured people as well as with the local African people, specialising in children's work and Bible teaching. Ruby's destination initially was Tzaneen where she would join Mrs. Christie and Faith, but there were plans afoot to move from there to start a new work at Mica from their new base in Phalaborwa. Some two years later, the first meeting was held at the Railway compound at Mica and they had a good response.

At this time, Hubert and Jean Phillips were continuing to see steady growth in the work and a developing ministry through the printed word. In addition, Jean Phillips, with the help of CEF[x] workers, Mr. and Mrs. Wright, established a midweek meeting for English-speaking children in Nelspruit.

Meanwhile, Pastor and Mrs. Francis in Pilgrim's Rest and Pastor and Mrs. Blythen in Witbank were experiencing the blessing of the Lord on their labours. In one service in the Sabie district near Pilgrim's Rest, Pastor Francis was unable to continue with his message because of a move of the Spirit on the congregation that resulted in many people making their way to the front, weeping and confessing sin.

The Blythens continued to make much use of the native evangelists attached to their station. In an outstation, thirty-eight miles from the Blythen home, two evangelists saw the Lord working mightily as a result of an all-night meeting that started on Saturday evening and continued until 5 a.m. on the Sunday. The two preachers saw many souls saved and then they were praying for the sick and seeing miracles until 6.30 a.m. At 9.30 a.m. they conducted a baptismal service in the local river for a boy and a seventy-eight year old woman. Afterwards, they returned to the church and continued the service. On the Monday, they went from village to village and from kraal to kraal visiting people and they were much blessed in healings and deliverance from demon possession. Many people were saved in two villages because of the evident blessing on their ministry.

Permission had also recently been obtained for the starting of meetings at two of the new coal mines situated about 25 miles from their home. The following month, they were expecting to begin a new work in Pretoria and district, some 65 miles away. There was a desperate need for more workers as the Lord blessed. Over one hundred children were then in school.

Some four years after they moved to Port Elizabeth, the Mullans were able to report excellent growth following a very hard start. Some three and a half years earlier, they had seen revival as a result of the ministry of Nicholas Bhengu. Their first meeting had started with just eight people present, but eventually, the hall was filled, and sixty people professed salvation. This was just the beginning and, some three years later, they were able to talk of churches established in Swaziland and Natal as well as in the Transkei. In each centre, fine men were identified and trained as elders so that the works could be self-supporting and indigenous. The Mullans themselves moved from Port Elizabeth some two hundred miles to East London where, again, they pioneered the work. Some work had been done by the Mullans and by Nicholas Bhengu, but a local elder, Evangelist Dlamini had been left in charge and was able to report blessing and growth despite the two main pioneers being absent.

An innovation at Tzaneen, reported by Mrs. Nosworthy, was the conducting of a Women's Convention. This was much appreciated by all who attended and it was significant that, early on the Sunday morning, the women 'invaded the Tzaneen Location' and held stirring open air meetings before the men could get themselves drunk! The women showed great zeal for the work. One young girl, Melita, who worked in the store of one of the European believers, was amazed one day when a man to whom she had testified, came with a company of people "to hear the words of God". She asked them to wait until she shut the store, then preached to them 'Jesus'. That night, six souls found Christ. What was happening at Tzaneen among the women was being repeated in many other centres and reports of blessing on the ministry of women were being received regularly.

The Nosworthys left Tzaneen and Emmanuel Mission in 1950, resigning from both the Assemblies of God (SA) and Elim UK to join the Baptist Church, serving first in Roodepoort and then moving to the United States of America. As a result, Miss Grossen transferred to Tzaneen to join Miss Simms and, apart from a short spell at Phalaborwa with Mrs. Christie, Miss Grossen spent the remainder of her ministry in Tzaneen.

Miss Simms also spent time at Phalaborwa, but health problems necessitated a return to Tzaneen. She undertook midwifery training between 1951 and 1953 and, after a furlough in the UK, transferred to Southern Rhodesia in 1956. (RGD)

In 1950, Miss Ruby Maplesden, from Croydon, joined the team in Transvaal, to be with Mrs. and Miss Christie on the field at Phalaborwa. Unfortunately, the extremely hot climate caused her problems and she transferred to Witwatersrand where she worked for a while in Sophiatown until its demolition by the architects of apartheid and its replacement by the new white suburb of Triomph. Shortly afterwards, she withdrew from South Africa on health grounds and returned to the UK. Having served in Transvaal until 1957, Ruby settled in Hull where she remained extremely active in the work of the City Temple. She received her home call in 1966.

Nevertheless, her short time on the Field was meaningful and beneficial. She was able to report that God was pouring out His Spirit and they were seeing His hand at work. One man had a vision that caused him to weep all night. In the morning, he sent for the missionaries and surrendered his life to Christ. A murderer was saved, and the mother of their house boy came to know the Lord. She recorded her weekly activities: Monday – night school and two meetings in the location at different places held at the same time; Tuesday – night school and a meeting in the location; Wednesday – a meeting in the church and a meeting in the location; Thursday – the day of prayer. Night school and a meeting in the location; Friday – a meeting in the compound and a meeting in the location; Saturday – a meeting in the church; Sunday – Five meetings in different places. She asked for prayer for the Chief that he might be converted and also for the many murderers who were in the district. In the midst of all the ministry, there was the added burden of physically building church buildings, a task that, undaunted, Mrs. Christie took on.

Miss Faith Christie left Phalaborwa in 1951 to join Miss Ruth Munroe at Legalies near Munnik. She married in 1954 and became Mrs. Haws, leaving Legalies in 1955 to take over the work in Pilgrim's Rest for a period and living in nearby Sabie.

The Francis family left from Pilgrim's Rest station having resigned from Emmanuel Mission, but retaining their Elim credentials for a further period. They took up a position with another Pentecostal denomination in Pretoria and Pilgrim's Rest was looked after by workers from Nelspruit until Mrs. Haws took up the oversight there. Her mother, Mrs. Christie, was replaced at Phalaborwa in 1960 by Pastor and Mrs. Don Norton, originally from Knottingley, who had been in Nelspruit since 1954, so she remained at Pilgrim's Rest with Mrs. Haws until 1967 when she retired to Canada. After a very valuable and sacrificial period of service in South Africa, she went to be with the Lord just a few days short her one hundredth birthday. The Nortons remained in Phalaborwa until 1973 when they transferred to work in Southern Rhodesia. (RGD)

A feature of the work throughout the region was the extensive use made of local evangelists in outreach. In Pretoria, for example, there were five full time evangelists, fifteen unpaid local preachers and three unpaid Bible women. They were very well accepted and much used for the extension of the Kingdom. Perhaps the most well-known was the Zulu, Nicholas Bhengu who conducted great crusades across Africa, and in the various townships, was helped by the missionaries in terms of organisation and administration. Signs and wonders followed all these workers as bodies were healed and demons were cast out. In one of Bhengu's missions, over 2000 professed salvation.

In 1952, the missionaries in Pretoria, including W.H. Francis, prepared for a mission with William Branham of the USA. Brother Francis reported that over 5000 attended one service alone and many were saved and healed. This mission presented an opportunity to reach out to the Indian and coloured people of Pretoria, an area that had hitherto been neglected.

From time to time, there were also visits to the Field by Mr. F. B. Phillips, brother of Hubert. F.B. would film during his visits and, when the films were processed, would show them at churches in the homeland to let the people see how the missionaries were living and working. People were impressed with the visual impact the films made as they portrayed the natural beauty and colours of Africa alongside the squalor and misery of the unsaved.

In 1952, Mrs. W. N. Hawley arrived from England and was appointed to work with Frieda Grossen at Tzaneen. During one of Frieda's furloughs, Mrs. Hawley found herself in charge of the station and was able to testify to the ongoing blessing being experienced both there and in other locations where opportunities not only presented themselves but were gladly seized and used for the glory of God. The result was the opening of two new churches within a one month period. A visit a little later by Sunny Blundell[XI] highlighted the great need for a vehicle for this station but it was not until 1958 that a new Volkswagen microbus was presented to Mrs. Hawley and Frieda Grossen as a gift from the Elim Churches of the UK.

In 1956, the biennial Conference was held and Hubert Phillips's report indicated that it was something of a watershed in the work. Nicholas Bhengu read a thesis on the subject of a National Church. After consideration in two meetings, his proposal was unanimously approved by both whites and non-Europeans. This marked the beginning of a new era in missionary work in South Africa. Africans would now be responsible for their own church. This had as much impact upon the missionaries, who would have to adjust their work methods, as it did upon the Africans themselves. Until that time, many Africans had not felt free to come into what was perceived as the white man's church. Now it would be different and there would be three or four sister groups – European, African, Coloured and Indian, all working "on parallel harmony through the one Spirit". There was a real feeling that this was God's plan and His timing.

About three months later, Bhengu held a mission in Nelspruit. Although the church was extended to hold 800 people in time for the mission, it proved far too small and most of the meetings were held in the open air. Night after night, hundreds stood to signify their desire to accept Christ as Saviour. Many hundreds were prayed for after each service and, although not all were healed, many were. One man, who had walked on his hands and knees for nine years, was immediately made whole.

There was an outstanding conversion. A leader of a gang known as Totsis (murderers, plunderers, thieves and everything that was evil) was gloriously saved[xii]. The following night, he publicly confessed Christ as his Saviour and called on his gang to follow him in the new and living way. At the end of his talk, eight of his confederates came forward and openly confessed Christ. Bhengu asked them to sit down by his platform until he had finished his message, then made an appeal to all the young men to accept Christ. One by one they came forward until between three and four hundred stood before him and prayed the sinner's prayer.

Some four months later, the effects of the mission were still being felt in the Nelspruit area as significant responses were being made to the Gospel as people were not only being saved, but were truly repenting of their past deeds and making restitution. One man had used a tape recorder while Bhengu was in town and now was travelling the countryside playing the tapes and seeing many respond to the messages.

In the late 1930s, the Emmanuel Mission had amalgamated with the Assemblies of God (SA) as an entity, but between 1955 and 1960, the association came under pressure and the tension was such that it became apparent that there would be a parting of the ways. The proposed plan of organisational groups working in their own right under an umbrella name began to evolve into something quite different. Effectively it brought the Emmanuel Mission churches and workers under the control of an Executive on which they had no representation.

Meanwhile, Nicholas Bhengu's ministry had generated a large number of churches bearing the name "Back to God". These assemblies joined the Assemblies of God and, in doing so, flooded the organisation and dominated the African section. Because of their numbers, they were seen to constitute a Group in their own right, with their own Constitution and, eventually, their own Conference. The Emmanuel Mission churches were not so organised and simply existed as Assemblies of God churches, subject to the overall Constitution of the Movement.

Ultimately, the tensions became too much to bear and were damaging to the work. Both ministers and missionaries working with Emmanuel Missions were denigrated and demeaned until, by 1970, plans were being made for a secession of the Emmanuel Mission from the Assemblies of God (SA). Meetings and discussions took place in many different places and with many different people over the next few years but, in October, 1977, a Conference took place at KaNyamadzane, near Nelspruit, where a number of men discussed the setting up of a new church body which became the Emmanuel Assemblies. A second meeting was held in the November and an inaugural General Conference was held in December, 1977 at a school just north of Bushbuckridge. Ron Gull, in his definitive record of those events, has done sterling work in reporting in detail the names of those who were initially involved.

It was recognised at an early stage that a means of forging an identity and providing a focus of activity would be the setting up of a Central Conference centre. Following many negotiations and not a few setbacks, the site at Bushbuckridge was acquired and a fine hall was built. Subsequently, dormitory blocks were added and facilities for cooking and toilets were installed. The churches in the UK were very much involved in this venture and remained so over the years when improvements were done.

Meanwhile, the work was continuing throughout the region in spite of the various political moves taking place. New missionaries were still arriving on the field and finding themselves fully occupied in assisting the local people in extending the Kingdom. In 1963, Anne Stephenson[xiii], a state registered nurse and midwife from Huddersfield, went to join Frieda Grossen at Tzaneen. She had completed two years training at the Elim Bible College and would be invaluable in working with Frieda who, at that time, was the only European missionary working in the area.

Don and Mary Norton were continuing their ministry with great effectiveness at Phalaborwa and in 1965, took a ten month furlough. On their return, they no longer had to use their old Morris Minor, but had the use of a new Land Rover which aroused great interest on their station. There had been a drought for about four years and, just as they returned, the rains came, so the Land Rover was a blessing, enabling them to continue to visit remote areas that otherwise would have been unreachable.

A new project was launched in 1965 entitled "Books on Wheels". The idea came about because of the unprecedented demand for literature. In local market places, Ron Gull was virtually overrun by people wanting to buy Christian literature, even to one man wanting to buy Ron's own Bible. The project asked people in the homeland to raise sufficient money to equip a vehicle that could take Christian literature anywhere on the Field. It was envisaged that the Transvaal unit would operate from Emmanuel Press and serve the whole region. It would act as a mobile centre for wholesale literature distribution to town and village shopkeepers as well as a retail shop in the bush areas. It would be used as a mobile evangelistic unit staffed by a team of national workers. The vehicle envisaged, together with stock and equipment, was a Volkswagen Kombi 1500. The price? £1000!

The breadth of the work was seen in a report in 1966 by W. H. Francis on a Field Conference which was attended by delegates from six different African tribes. The Conference was held at Klerksdorp, Western Transvaal and co-workers came from Cape Province, Natal, Free State, Transvaal and Bechuanaland (subsequently renamed Botswana[xiv]).

Having seen the work in Botswana established, there was then a call in 1967 to work in Natal, known as the Garden Province. This was some 500 miles from Pretoria where the Francis family was then based. The city of Durban was a beautiful city and presented a massive mission field in itself. A feature of this work was that there were Africans who, as evangelists, went to areas far removed from their own homelands and became missionaries in their own right.

William Francis was finding his parish expanding all the time, with contacts up to 1000 miles from his base in Pretoria. He was seeing growth of the work in Pondoland as the Holy Spirit set His seal on local men who had come out of darkness into the glorious light of the Gospel. His own feelings for Botswana were developing and he saw there a great need that was not being fully addressed.

In 1968, George and Betty Gemmell went to the Transvaal as Lightbearers[xv] and were appointed to Tzaneen. They remained there until 1972 when Betty was appointed Supervisor of Nursing Services for the Transvaal (excepting the cities of Johannesburg and Pretoria). This meant they had to move to live in Pietersburg and presented her with a wider sphere of services and, in addition to her nursing duties, she was able to conduct Bible studies and services in the evenings. They maintained a contact with the Teacher Training College in Tzaneen, returning about once a month to minister. George was instrumental in preparing the plans for the building of the church at Lenyenye, some 24 kilometres from Tzaneen.

Meanwhile, the number of missionaries from the UK was being augmented by the arrival of David and Maureen Butcher. David Butcher was a qualified printer so his expertise was much in demand at the Emmanuel Press. Their arrival in South Africa meant that the work also had the use of the Ford Transit minibus they had brought with them. David was a keen photographer, so photographs of the work began to flow back home and appeared, in many cases, as accompaniments to reports sent in by the missionaries.

Obviously, Hubert Phillips had a strong, vested interest in the printed page, recognising the impact this could make, especially in developing countries. He had seen the influx of massive distributions of propaganda from communist sources, and sensed that the Church needed to address the problem and, in some way, balance it at least. Thus, he followed the two-fold principle that there should be teaching by print and preaching by print. The work that the Press was able to do over the years could not be quantified this side of eternity, but the feedback received indicated that a most effective tool for the spreading of the Gospel was being mightily used by the Holy Spirit to reach people, even in the remotest areas of the nations of Africa.

Hubert retired in 1972 and was presented with an illuminated scroll by his fellow-directors. The scroll was signed by Mrs. Ingrid Chawner, widow of his first co-director, David Newington, Ronald. A. Gull, R.J. (Bob) Skinner and W.F.Mullan. Hubert was founder Chairman of the Press for thirty-four years, having started with a small press brought in by the Chawners from Canada years before. On December 12th, 1973, Hubert passed peacefully into the presence of the Lord he had loved and served for almost fifty years[xvi].

Ron Gull had the oversight of the church at White River but, at the same time, he and Betty were fully occupied with the work of the Press as well. Betty operated the IBM typesetter (sitting on a 'superchair' provided for her by EWMA!) and Ron took care of the artwork and layout. A new magazine was produced entitled *Tell* and this was distributed to many parts of Africa. In 1974, the Press needed a new machine so this became a project for the UK and also, Canada. Bob Skinner was returning to Canada on furlough and he determined that he would promote the project there. The sum of £6500 was raised and a new litho machine was delivered, taking the Press beyond the old system of letterpress printing; before long, the benefits were becoming apparent and life on the production side became much easier.

The passing of the Chairman of the Press did not in any way lessen the output or vision of the work. Gwen and Bill Kirby staffed the office with African helpers providing valuable back-up. At the opening of a new church 60 miles away on the Lisbon Citrus Estate, Mrs. Phillips spoke to the congregation on the basis of notes that Hubert had prepared before his death. The estate manager had accepted Christ as his Saviour and, while building accommodation for his workers, had incorporated a church building in the plans.

The scale of the work of the Press can be gauged a little by the report from Ron Gull:

The monthly tally in our mail is in excess of one thousand per month. Letters came from bakers from a Biscuit Factory, welders in a Bus Builder's workshop, smelters in the giant ISKOR Steelworks and workers with a well known Tyre Manufacturer. Their addresses included the names of a huge Sugar refinery, a Coal yard, a Paper Pulp Mill, Hotels, Motels and Restaurants; a Motor Spares centre, Supermarkets and Village Trading stores. They included Civil Servants, workers from a Magistrate's court, Dock labourers, porters from an International airport; prisoners from jail and patients from hospital; theological students, policemen and soldiers, refugees all wrote to say they had accepted the Lord. They wrote from Chrome and Copper Mines in Rhodesia; from Coal and Platinum mines in South Africa; from a tea plantation in Malawi; from an oil rig near Port Harcourt in Nigeria; from an Army battalion in West Africa and from an Air Force base in Rhodesia.[xvii] The new complex for the Press was opened at White River on July 2nd, 1977[xviii].

A highlight in the lives of the missionaries was always visits from folks from the homeland. Over the years, they had seen F.B. Phillips and his wife and Jean Ayling. From time to time, the President of the Elim Churches would visit, as well as members of the Missions Board. Among those who called were W. Ron Jones, R. B. Chapman, John C. Smyth and Fred Hodge. In many cases, they were accompanied by their wives.

The establishing, in the early 1970s, of the Emmanuel Assemblies led, in 1979 to a formal agreement between Elim and Emmanuel Assemblies in terms of fellowship and support. Letters of agreement were signed by David Ayling, then International Missions Director and Mack Mabitsela on behalf of Emmanuel. David reported that Elim and Emmanuel were now 'sister fellowships'. Ron Gull served on the Emmanuel Executive council and the plan was to continue to send out missionaries and to provide support for church planting and annual bursaries for Bible college students. In later years, when the number of missionaries had declined to a large extent, the support consisted mainly of an annual grant to the Africa Bible College at Lenyenye to help students from Emmanuel Assemblies. In due course, the numbers of students also declined and the whole situation was reviewed.

Ron not only served on the Executive Council but, because of his expertise, was always busily engaged in designing and building churches. Many of the permanent buildings are evidence of his handiwork and his drafting abilities were much used throughout the region. He was responsible, much of the time, not only for design, but for the preparation and marking out of the site and the organising of the work of building itself. When he and Betty retired to Graskop, the work did not diminish, but for many years, he maintained his input through the Executive Council, as Elim's representative, on the Board of the African Bible College and as the only person who knew enough about building to push the practical side of the work forward. His ministry was wide ranging and effective because of the great love God had given him for the African people.

In 1980, Tony and Beryl Leavesley arrived, bringing expertise in radio programming and the expectation of conducting Bible seminars throughout the Transvaal. Tony very quickly became involved in Youth Camps and saw them as having a major impact on the young people. They were initially stationed at KaNyamazane but the following year, moved to Tzaneen.

July, 1981, saw another new venture for the work in Transvaal. Negotiations were still under way for the acquisition of the site at Bushbuckridge for the Conference centre, but the ladies of the churches decided they would hold a Conference there anyway. There was a need to unite the northern and eastern women's groups and, for this, they established EWA – Emmanuel Women's Auxiliary. The word *auxiliary* was translated *helps.* Their intention was to use the labours of their hands to raise money to help with the building of the Conference Centre. Some 320 ladies arrived and their total contributions from the sale of their goods raised £500.

Lenyenye was also the base for a major church to serve the Lebowa Homeland. Pastor Mack Mabitsela and his congregation laboured long and hard on the project and the finished building was a credit to them. The opening, in 1982, was of special significance in that it was the first permanent building completed and dedicated to the Lord's service since the formation of Emmanuel Assemblies just over four and a half years previously. Honoured guests present at the ceremony included the Minister of Works from the Lebowa Government and the Mayor of Tzaneen. This latter emphasised that he was not there simply in his official capacity but as a brother in the Lord representing the Christians of

Tzaneen. Tom and Ruth Walker had recently attended a Conference in South Africa so were present at the ceremony and Ruth, as Secretary of the Elim Women's Missionary Auxiliary, cut the ribbon at the door and later unveiled a plaque commemorating the support given in the erection of the building by both Kensington Temple, London, and EWMA. Pastor Tom Walker was the speaker at the special afternoon services over the weekend and Pastor Oliver Raper of the Apostolic Faith Mission in South Africa spoke at the evening rallies.

Just before the Easter Convention, delegates in representative Session were shown artist's sketches done by Ron Gull of the proposed Centre. After discussion, the proposal to build was unanimously agreed. During the Convention of the Emmanuel Assemblies, the plans were announced to those attending and the delegates were taken from the Convention tents to the site for the new Convention Centre. The sides of the hall, measuring 20 x 20 metres were outlined on the ground by lines of ministers. The delegates were then asked to stand in the resulting space. They subsequently demanded that the size be increased to 25 x 30 metres and a steel erector was engaged to build the framework. It was designed as a five bay structure with 25 metres clear span and earthmoving equipment belonging to the local Government, under Ron Gull's direction, levelled the ground in June 1983. The necessary excavation for the footings was dug by a small local team. A detailed description of the work, including costings, was recorded by Ron Gull, in his document on the Emmanuel Assemblies.

Brian Edwards, International Missions Director, was present for the Easter Convention and recorded his satisfaction at the development of the work under the leadership of Pastor Luke Mjaji, Chairman, and Pastor Mack Mabitsela, Secretary. He paid tribute to the missionaries, Ron and Betty Gull at White River and Tony and Beryl Leavesley in Tzaneen, together with the indefatigable Frieda Grossen, then actively retired, but still enormously engaged in the work.

As the Convention delegates occupied the space that would become their Centre, God touched their hearts and a great shout of praise went up. The vast crowd sang and worshipped and then an offering was taken. The sacrifice of giving seemed to sanctify the area where they stood. Brian preached on *"Go in and possess the land"*. In subsequent years, the development of the site at Bushbuckridge was kept very much before the folks in the UK and much help was given and interest shown.

By 1985, the hall was well on the way to completion and it was decided to name it the "Phillips Memorial Hall". Donations had been received from churches as far away as Australia and Elim had produced a Rand-for-Rand scheme which enabled them to buy the steel window frames and to complete payment for the steelwork. All the building work was done by church members, Bible school students, ministers (including members of the executive Council) and missionaries. At one stage, over sixty men appeared to lay concrete blocks and install the door and window frames.

The local EWA were already raising money for the doors and glazing for the windows, while many assemblies had given sacrificially to finance the erection of their own permanent church buildings. Severe drought and a national recession held the work back to some extent and limited the potential, but not the will, to give.

A new thrust in evangelism was envisaged in 1985 when the Missions Board, backed by Cardiff City Temple, provided a new style of enclosure in which to preach the Gospel. Ron Gull described it as a new "Tabernacle in the Wilderness". It was an arena, like a large marquee without the roof. It had seating for 1000 and could be used throughout the dry season, about six months in the year. It was to be taken to open areas of ground where the sides would be erected and tiered seating arranged inside. This meant that crusades could be held without the need or cost of renting large halls. The Cardiff church undertook to raise the full £3680 needed which would include seating, lighting, PA system and platform. Ron Gull had a vehicle available for transporting the arena to the sites and Mack Mabitsela with his co-evangelists in Emmanuel Assemblies would be able to take full advantage of this new facility. The plan was to use it throughout Transvaal and also to reach out to other areas. The first of these 'stadiums' was dedicated by Pastor William Mullan, Irish Missionary Secretary, who was visiting for the Easter Convention.

The Leavesleys, in 1985, moved to Groblersdal at the request of Emmanuel Assemblies, to pioneer new works in that area. This was north-east of Pretoria and, by 1985, a small group of dedicated African pastors and church leaders had established about fifteen assemblies and meeting points. In 1987, they moved again to Middleburg, where they finally retired from the work. From this centre, they saw works established at Bosplas, Atok, Benoni and Kendal. Smaller works, without full time leadership, were established at Hammanskraal and Glen Cowie. A feature of the work here was the youth camp where many were delivered from the power of evil spirits and a number found Christ as Saviour. There was also an invitation to hold a mission some 75 miles away in Elandskraal. Despite many difficulties, they saw results and, after some significant conversions, later were able to minister to between 50 and 60 people in the home of a converted cult leader. They identified the need for more experienced ministers to take the work forward and to continue evangelism and church planting.

At the time of writing (2006), there are now no expatriate missionaries in South Africa. Frieda Grossen died; the Leavesleys retired and moved away from Middleburg to Natal and the Gulls retired to Graskop. However, the Gulls are still close to the central workings of the Assemblies and are called upon from time to time as required.

i For a brief overview of the Transvaal work, see *Elim Evangel* Vol. 60. Issue 3, pp. 7, 8. See also Vol. 62. Issue 27, pp. 8, 9.

ii Hubert's testimony was recorded in the *Elim Evangel,* Vol. 42. Issue 27, p.421.

iii Ron Gull prepared an unpublished document entitled *A Brief History of Emmanuel Mission and Emmanuel Assemblies.* This documents, with reference to minutes of those organisations, the reasons behind decisions that brought the two organisations into being. It is not possible to reproduce this in full but reference to it will be made from time to time under the credit (RGD).

iv See "An autobiography of Emmanuel Press" by Hubert Phillips in *Elim Evangel,* Vol.49. Issue 46, p. 725. See also Vol. 56. Issue 39, pp. 10, 11.

v For details of Austin Chawner, see the *Elim Evangel* report of his home call in Vol. 44. Issue 47, pp. 742,743.

vi Reported in *Elim Evangel,* Vol. 43. Issue 22, p.340. See also an extended review by H.C.Phillips in the *Elim Evangel,* Vol. 44. Issue 23, pp. 360-362. A further report is of interest published in Vol. 45. Issue 23, pp. 359, 364.

vii Brother Francis's background was reported in *Elim Evangel,* Vol. 44. Issue 5, p.74.

viii The background to these ladies was recorded in the *Elim Evangel,* Vol. 42. Issue 33, pp. 518,519. See also Vol. 47. Issue 25, p.396. Don Norton's tribute to these ladies was published in the *Elim Evangel,* Vol.49. Issue 48, p. 757.

ix Congo Evangelistic Mission, now CAM – Central African Missions.

x Child Evangelism Fellowship.

xi "Auntie" Sunny Blundell was well known in Elim as a Children's evangelist. She eventually married a South African, Tommy Connell and was known as Sunny Blundell-Connell.

xii In 1968, the Phillips's visited the church now run by this young man and numbering around 300 people.

xiii See the *Elim Evangel* Vol. 44. Issue 49, p. 782.

xiv See chapter on Botswana.

xv Lightbearers was a programme whereby lay people with particular skills could give some time to the work at their own expense.

xvi See the tribute by Leslie Wigglesworth in the *Elim Evangel* Vol. 55. Issue 2, p.6.

xvii *Elim Evangel* Vol. 57. Issue 4, p.11.

xviii Various reports highlight the developments in the work: *Elim Evangel*

CHAPTER 19

SOUTHERN RHODESIA / ZIMBABWE

About six hundred people gathered in the Elim Church, Graham Street, Birmingham on the evening of February 14th, 1949, to bid God-speed to Pastor and Mrs. Jesse Williams and their seven year old son, who were taking up missionary work in Southern Rhodesia and Portuguese East Africa.

The Missionary Secretary, Pastor George H. Thomas, gave a brief survey of the Mission Fields, stating that at that time there were forty-four missionaries working in various areas. There was a challenge for others to respond to the call of God on their lives and to offer themselves for service.

Mrs. Williams told how they had sold all their furniture ready for the move and she wondered if she would ever have a proper home again. Pastor Williams pointed out on a large map the black spot of Africa where, he said, over four million had never heard the Gospel and the door was practically closed to Protestant missionaries. His intention was to reach into Portuguese East Africa whenever permission was granted but in the meantime, he would be working on the Rhodesia side of the border.[i]

Safely arrived in Africa, Jesse based himself in Penhalonga in the vicinity of a gold mine where there were large numbers of workers in camps. He wasted no time in setting up a church and, before long, a school as well. There was a good response as people attended the meetings and some testified to both salvation and healing. It was gratifying that many had come from Portuguese East Africa and were therefore able to take the message back across the border with them. Within about fifteen months, the congregation was numbering around 120 and plans were made to build a bigger building that would seat about 300. To do this, the men dug the foundations while the women made mud bricks and the children cut and carried many hundreds of bundles of grass and reeds for thatching the roof.

The ladies were catered for and their meeting had increased from fourteen to forty, while the children's work continued to flourish. The children were a great help because they were taken to the villages and sang the Gospel songs lustily. Because of their valley location, they had had to confront fever on a wide scale. This allowed them to exercise their treatment skills and brought them a measure of favour with the people. Nevertheless, not long afterwards, Mrs. Williams had to have her appendix removed and, immediately on her return from hospital, Jesse and their son, Michael, succumbed to a bout of malaria. This was to be a regular feature over the years, as they were prone to suffer in spite of medication. Mrs. Williams also found herself hospitalised again, this time because of tick fever.

The new building was completed after many months of weary work, and it was opened on Christmas Eve, 1950 to scenes of great rejoicing. But in the early part of the year, the troubles started. Unusually heavy rain began to fall and torrential rain fell in the Penhalonga valley for almost a week, so that the valley became like a lake and they were marooned on the Mission station. To their dismay, they discovered that the plaster was stripping off the most exposed gable of the church and, as the unprotected mud bricks became soaked through, the gable end began to crack. They intended to repair it as soon as possible but, before they could, the wall collapsed, taking the roof with it. The building was so badly damaged that they had to take down the remaining walls. Only nine hours earlier, the church had been packed for the Sunday morning service.

Understandably, the loss of the building disorganised everything. There was insufficient room for the Sunday services, and the children's activities were badly overcrowded. Fortunately, they were able to use the old building and the veranda of their house. Other activities took place out of doors. But in the midst of all the hassle, they were encouraged and overjoyed at the coming of two new missionaries, the Drs. Cecil and Mary Brien. Dr. Cecil was a pharmacist and surgeon and his wife, Mary, was a physician and an anaesthetist.

The doctors had been working in Africa for two years with an inter-denominational mission and had led four hundred Africans to the Lord, but had also had contacts with Elim.[ii] Mrs. Brien was in touch with Elim in Belfast and took part in open air work with the young people from the then Apsley Street church (now South Belfast). They also had contact with Pastor Brewster during his Wigan campaign, where Dr. Brien was a surgeon in the Wigan hospital. They enjoyed fellowship with the Elim church in Swansea for some time, where the pastor, Leslie Green, had a great influence on them, particularly in relation to Pentecostal doctrine and experience.

They had read in the *Elim Evangel* of the coming of Jesse Williams to Africa and the Lord had stirred their hearts towards joining up with him, but they had hesitated to make any move until they were sure it was the Lord's will. The confirmation, in the form of a letter from Leslie Green suggesting that they go, was taken as a sure sign from the Lord.

At the beginning of his ministry in Africa, Jesse Williams had visited the unevangelised area of Inyanga; it was for this very area that they were negotiating with the Government. There was no mission of any kind in the district, but they were informed by the Government officials that the Roman Catholics had made application to enter and they had promised to supply a doctor within one year. It was felt that if Elim didn't get in first, the whole area would be closed to them.

When the Drs. Brien came, they were also able to tell of their intense interest in that same area, and also that they had a desire to reach Portuguese East Africa. The Katerere district in Inyanga North Region was in the low veldt and was known to be terribly hot, barren and fever ridden. This didn't in any way diminish the vision. Before long, the doctors had obtained the necessary permission to build a new station in this very needy area where there was no Gospel, no school and there were no medical facilities. Their description of their journey was reported in a letter to the *Elim Evangel*.[iii] They told how they were led by the Lord to find an ideal spot for their camp beside a stream. There they pitched their tents and used them for both living and operating as they began their labours among a people described by the District Commissioner as "neglected".

The place was a barren wilderness and it was the rainy season so they were unable to begin proper building, but they had a dispensary consisting of several corrugated sheets erected in tent fashion. The intention was then to put up a pole and mud hut that would serve until something more permanent could be erected. The rains that year were extraordinary. One African said he only once remembered such heavy rain. Fifty inches of rain fell in that one season making travel virtually impossible and just the business of living was, to say the least, uncomfortable. In spite of the weather, people used to come in from the villages and make themselves small grass huts where they would live while being treated at the dispensary. In the process of time, the Briens spent much time making and burning thousands of bricks so that they could build a proper hospital and a small dwelling.

Dr. Brien went to visit a village and described what he found as 'hell let loose'. There was a big beer drink in progress and he counted more than sixty people who were helplessly drunk. Satan had held sway in that region for so long, he would not easily give up, but the missionaries were determined that his kingdom should be attacked as strongly as they were able.

This was a feature of the work. The Brien's 'boy' Pauro visited one of the villages and after a talk about Christianity, the women told him, "We don't want to attend your church. We prefer the Roman Catholics because they allow us to continue drinking beer, etc." The challenges took many forms. In one village, the local store keeper had thirty-six children and another man had eighteen. Many of the men had multiple wives. All these things meant that anyone considering becoming a Christian had major difficulties to overcome if his lifestyle was to change.

Meanwhile, it took about twelve months to replace the church building at Penhalonga, but the work was finally completed and the new building was packed for the opening with rejoicing crowds. Jesse commented that it was relatively easy to get the Africans to confess their need of a Saviour; it was more difficult to get them to leave their sin. A major encouragement was to see whole families worshipping in the church. They were further encouraged when they saw real progress being made in Christian living. The evangelist came back from one meeting holding up a bottle and proclaiming that this had been Lydia's god which she had worshipped for many years, but now she was giving it up and meant to serve the true God. The meetings that followed were filled with blessing. So many people wanted to testify that it was hard to find the time to preach, but the power of God was so real that the whole night was taken up with people confessing their sins, others praising God for their deliverance and the believers helping and exhorting the weaker ones. Some were kneeling down with tears streaming down their faces, praying for deliverance from their sins.

The school work developed all the time, and Jesse was quick to see an opportunity for planting a school. By 1952, the local school had 200 pupils and six Government paid teachers. Other schools were opened as the needs presented themselves. In some cases, they were opened in response to a request by a Government official.

At Inyanga North[iv], there had been much concern about the influence of the Roman Catholics and special prayer had been requested. But as the doctors began to work, they saw the Lord working mightily through them and, as a consequence of both good doctoring and prayer, lives were changed, bodies were healed and the Gospel began to have relevance for the people.

In Inyanga, the doctors were beginning to see fruit for their labours. After many months of hard work and planning for their new station, the Africans from the surrounding villages were responding to the Gospel. People were coming to church on Sunday, albeit there was as yet no church building. But there were those who were beginning to dress for the Lord's Day, others knew the words to some of the choruses. People came on foot from all the villages within a radius of about five miles and many of them were accepting the truths of the Word of God. While about two hundred were gathered at Inyanga, another group of about 100 met at a school over five miles away; then, in the afternoon, they would travel to another new school building and hold a meeting for between 50 and 70 people. Later, Pauro, the teacher-evangelist would go to yet another venue to preach the Word.

It is difficult to imagine the physical effects on a trained surgeon whose hands were not only used for healing, but also had to become adept at the harsh realities of maintaining buildings and vehicles. We can only imagine what pressure he must have been under in trying to maintain a balance that would allow him to practice his medicine and also to ensure that the station was kept in reasonable order as well.

In order to do this, he would rise at 5 a.m. all through the dry season and spend the whole day hauling sand, water and building materials until sunset to get the work done before the rains came. In the evenings, he would take meetings and the dispensary work would largely be done by Mrs. Brien. It is not surprising that their own physical bodies were in danger of breaking down under the constant strain. Dr. Brien was afflicted with malaria and Mrs. Brien had boils on her back caused by a certain fly that laid its eggs on clothing and a maggot developed under the skin, causing boils.

But the end result was a hospital, house and a double classroom which could be used as a church, all made with red bricks and built by a local builder at reasonable cost. They had also built a two roomed house for occupation by Miss Winnie Loosemore, a nurse, who was expected to join them in the near future.

Day by day the work progressed as invitations were received from far and near to establish a school and a church in various villages. They tried to meet all the needs thus presented but obviously, were limited by the constraints of time and personnel. Gradually, however, the Africans themselves were able to take more responsibility for ministry. Teachers could also hold meetings and reach out to their own people. With growing maturity in the Christians, there was growing evidence of desire for spiritual things.

Women spontaneously organised themselves to hold prayer meetings and travelled sometimes many miles to a locale they had chosen to reach the people with the Gospel.

Winnie Loosemore arrived from England in 1954 and was taken, initially, to Penhalonga where she experienced a typical African welcome. Within six months, she was working with the Doctors Brien at Inyanga North and had learned enough of the language to be able to speak to the Africans and tell them about Jesus. The tribe amongst whom they were working had heard nothing of the Gospel until three years before. They were 'depraved and backward, dirty, uneducated, spirit worshippers, bound by witchcraft and superstition. Beer drinking sessions were common and it was not unusual for them to have fights and cut each other with knives'.

The burden was to reach them with the Good News. They wanted medicine and education, but not the Gospel. But in answer to prayer, the Lord broke through and, in one short period of a few weeks, sixteen surrendered themselves to Christ. It was a great joy to see over four hundred gather for the Sunday morning service and in the evening, they had a bonfire to burn the fetishes and idols people had brought in and surrendered.

The completion of the hospital was a great boon to the work in that it not only provided the team with better facilities, but it also served as a focal point for people to come and hear the Gospel. In one month, over eight hundred patients were treated at the hospital, several staying for many days and even weeks. One area which was proving most productive was with antenatal care as many women came for the birth of their child. This was in stark contrast to the normal way of doing things in the bush, which often resulted in the death of the child.

A young witchdoctor brought his wife who was expecting their first child. The condition was abnormal and, had facilities been available, the baby would have been delivered by Caesarean section, but this wasn't possible. The child was delivered with great difficulty, but died and the husband was told that had they remained at home, probably his wife would have died as well. The consequence of this was that he came back into the dispensary a little later and said, "I want Jesus. I want the white doctor who is like Jesus. I will leave my witchcraft and come to Jesus." He had walked thirteen miles on a Sunday morning and testified to his salvation.

Back in Northern Ireland, two young people had offered themselves for work on the mission field. William McKeown[V] had undertaken Bible school training at the Emmanuel Bible and Missionary Training College in Birkenhead, followed by a one year course at the Missionary School of Medicine in London. Vilia, his fiancée, had undertaken Teacher training in the Liverpool area. On returning to Northern Ireland, William took charge of a pioneer church in Belfast and pastored there for eighteen months. Both had sensed a call to overseas work at a missionary meeting with Leslie Wigglesworth, recently returned from Congo.

When it was known that Dr. Cecil Brien was quite seriously ill and had to be flown home, there was no other doctor to replace him. The Missions department therefore asked the McKeowns to go since William had had some medical training. They agreed to go, quickly married, did some deputation work in England and Ireland and then sailed to Africa. They farewelled from Camberwell on 15th August, 1955 and coincidentally, provided a homecoming setting for Archie Nicolson who had just arrived home from Senegal that afternoon. Some eight months later, the Nicolsons, now a married couple, were being given a good Elim send-off together with a young lady, Miss Anna Porteous, MA, of Edinburgh, a teacher destined for Penhalonga. She had been unwell and it wasn't certain she would arrive in time for the meeting, but part way through, she appeared. God had undertaken for her.

The Irish churches decided that the McKeowns would be better able to fulfil their call if they had transport so raised enough money for them to take a new Land Rover out with them. They disembarked at Durban where the Land Rover was assembled and then drove all the way north to Umtali, then out to Penhalonga where they stayed overnight.

Their destination was Katerere in Inyanga North region. Today, it is possible, on a good metalled road, to do the journey in just a few hours. In those days, it was cross country and took them from sun-up to sunset to make the journey. The distance was about 130 miles and they had to cross 13 rivers. Fortunately they were about two to four weeks ahead of the rainy season.

They arrived on the station to a good Ulster welcome from the Briens but no sooner had they arrived than they were called out to a man with a broken leg. The Land Rover proved a Rolls Royce compared to the Briens' old bone shaker, but when they arrived on the scene, they found a boy lying with both bones in his leg broken and sticking out through the skin.

Back in the hospital, Mrs. Brien did a mask and drop bottle anaesthetic while Cecil and William tried to pull the leg to bring the ends into line. So, without any further ado, they were plunged into the deep end and soon realised that most of the work would have the same sense of urgency about it.

The following day, Dr. Brien was taken to Umtali where he was ordered to have two weeks bed rest to strengthen him for the flight home. This left the McKeowns and Winnie holding the fort. Fortunately, Winnie now had a reasonable grasp of the language so they were not completely isolated. In a letter home, Vilia said, "We cannot speak too highly of the work the Doctors have done, and God has rewarded them by fruit for their labours."[vi]

The blessing of God on the work brought its own problems as schools multiplied and, in the course of time, as children grew older, the need expanded into a requirement for them to be taught by European teachers. With some sixteen schools to service, Jesse Williams was always stretched to find teachers. Fortunately, at primary level, he could use Africans and somehow kept things going. But with the need to develop secondary education, the requirement for European teachers became critical. By 1956, there was a call out for two women and one man to respond to the challenge.

One way to meet the challenge was to move Vilia McKeown back to Penhalonga and William went with her to oversee the spiritual side of the work. From time to time, William would return to Inyanga to inspect the schools. Meanwhile, Winnie had been joined by another nurse from South Africa. By this time, Jesse Williams had resigned from the Elim work and was now the minister of another church and living in their manse in Umtali, but continued to make visits to the Elim Mission in a holding capacity.

Around this same time, away in Senegal, a young Scot was labouring for God under the auspices of W.E.C.[vii], but recognised by Elim. He was Archie Nicolson from Greenock who went to Senegal in 1952 and remained there until 1955 when he transferred into the work in Rhodesia, where he remained for eight years. His work in Senegal entailed ministry and work in the dispensary. His application to language study meant that, before long, he could at least sing some of the songs and, eventually, hoped to be fluent enough to preach. While much of the time was spent in evangelism in the villages, it became clear that there was opposition as Moslem leaders refused to allow the preaching of the Gospel in their villages.

In Senegal, too, Archie had had his share of wild life. On one occasion he went to draw some water but found a snake lying in front of the bath. He quickly dispatched it with a heavy stone. His dispensary work also brought him into contact with victims. One young lad had been bitten by a donkey and another was bitten by a snake. Archie found himself busy stitching up wounds and sometimes, he also had to pull teeth.

At the Easter celebrations in London that year, Archie and his wife, who had recently qualified as a nurse and midwife, were presented to the congregation as the latest missionaries to be going to Southern Rhodesia and, with the help of the Youth Movement, £1300 had been raised to buy them a Land Rover for their work. The Land Rover was shipped to Capetown and was driven from there the 2000 miles to Inyanga North by Mr. F.B. Phillips, Managing Director of our Publishing Company, and a man who made regular trips to Africa making moving pictures of the work on 16mm film.

Archie soon fitted into the work and became involved in the administration of the schools as well as ministry in the villages around. A little later in the year, Dr. Brien returned to a rapturous welcome in Inyanga North, but had to move out almost immediately to Penhalonga to take care of school work that demanded attention.

They walked into problems for the schools, brought about by new Government legislation. School children were no longer to be allowed to live on site at Penhalonga. Classrooms and the necessary European missionary teachers were available, but would there be children to teach? The school did open on the correct day with classes from Kindergarten to Standard VI with full numbers. The Lord had answered prayer and various African homes had been opened to children who lived too far away to go home daily. At one stage, there was an attempt to remove all the African teachers as well, but representation was made successfully to the Native Education Department in Salisbury. At that time, there was no teacher training facility, so the supply of trained African teachers was problematical, but the Lord undertook and the supply was fully met. In 1957, the team was joined by Miss Brenda Hurrel, a trained teacher from the Essex churches.

Unfortunately, in the midst of all the hustle and bustle, Dr. Cecil Brien, feeling full of energy and ready for the work, broke his right ankle badly. He attended Umtali hospital where it was put in plaster and, later, when the plaster was removed, he was told by an orthopaedic surgeon in Salisbury that he would need an operation. The date was fixed for January, but he had to cry off because of pressure of work when the schools were due to open. He was again examined and told emphatically that there was no alternative to an operation.

Just a couple of weeks later, he went back to the hospital and had new x-rays taken, when the surgeon told him he wouldn't need an operation after all. The surgeon's view was that activity had moved the bone back into place, but Dr. Brien knew that Lord had touched him. He had been prayed for by Oral Roberts in the January and then by another Christian friend and was certain that the Holy Spirit had urged him to seek new x-rays before anything might be done. Friends in the UK had written to say that they too had had a witness that an operation would not be necessary about two weeks before the surgeon came to the same conclusion. Just after this, they returned to Inyanga North to continue their work there.

The following year, Margaret Gwynne left Swansea on St. David's day for Southern Rhodesia to become part of the teaching team at Inyanga North. She had offered her services to meet a short term need and stayed until 1963. She travelled by ship to Capetown and then had a four day train journey to Umtali. There, she was met by Dr. Brien and his three ton lorry which was loaded with all sorts of goods; bags of cement and drums of paraffin provided a platform for school desks, books, furniture, bicycles, grocery supplies and, high on top of it all, perched Mistress Joyce, a new African teacher taking over one of the younger classes.

Their journey to Inyanga was not without incident. It was the rainy season and the roads were treacherously rough. The lorry became stuck in the mud and everybody had to carry stones to block the mud bank and then cut down trees to provide a lattice on which to cross. Smaller vehicles just couldn't make the crossing. It was dark when they eventually arrived but the welcome from Mrs. Brien and Nurse Loosemore was warm and generous considering they had been up all night dealing with a demon-possessed woman who had broken into the dispensary. After the rousing worship of a Sunday in Pentecostal Africa, Margaret was ready to begin teaching her 15 – 20 year olds on the Monday morning. At around the same time, Mary Cooper went to Penhalonga to join the teaching staff there.

A highlight for the missionaries in 1958 was a visit from Pastors Bradley and Greenway. The delegation was met at Salisbury airport by Archie Nicolson and Dr. Brien. Archie confessed that that was the first time he had ever been to an airport. This writer was a Bible College student at that time and remembers well the subdued excitement of the dean, Mr. Bradley, as he prepared for his trip to Africa. On his return, the excitement was no longer subdued. He was thoroughly saturated with the experiences he had had, and spent no end of time regaling the students with stories. He was particularly excited by the fact that the benches used in the African churches were never full. It intrigued him that, no matter how full they appeared to be, any new person coming in simply squeezed themselves in where they wanted to sit. The fact that occasionally someone fell off the end was a source of great merriment.

Despite the gains made in relation to the work in the schools, there nevertheless was a crisis in that the number of teachers was insufficient to maintain the standards required. The children wept as they were told that there would be no follow-on to the next stage of their education the following year. Many appeals had been made in the homeland for teachers, but there had been no response and this mystified the missionaries. They maintained their prayer to the Lord that hearts would yet be moved to meet the need.

To add to all the misery, Ruby Simms, who had already served for period in South Africa, reported that the house of the head teacher at Penhalonga was struck by lightning and set on fire. He and his family lost all they had. His wife and seven children plus two boys who were staying with them so that they could attend school were all saved, but everything else was destroyed. The missionaries tried to set them up with some essentials, but they had only the clothes they stood up in, and they were wet through because of the hailstorm they had just witnessed.

In January 1959, Anne Renshaw had to leave Inyanga on account of her pregnancy and her place was taken by Margaret Gwynne. In addition, the Thomases leaving Tanganyika had created a vacancy there that the Renshaws were asked to fill. The consequence of that move was that Inyanga was left without a local director for the campus and Peter Griffiths was appointed in their place.

The Elim Church, Swansea, on April 10th, 1960, was the venue for a farewell service that would have far reaching ramifications, although no-one could have guessed it then. Peter Griffiths, a young teacher, was leaving to work with Dr. R. C. Brien in Inyanga North, Southern Rhodesia. The church was packed and it seemed that Peter was too young to be venturing forth on the world. But as he spoke in the service, people sensed an authority and wisdom beyond his years. At his final farewell in the Clapham Church, hands were laid on him and prayer made that he might be blessed of the Lord and used for His glory.

His arrival in Southern Rhodesia plunged him into an area that he thoroughly disliked – language study. He confessed himself no linguist, offering that his father had despaired of him because he couldn't or wouldn't learn his own native language – Welsh. But his call lay heavy upon him and he realised that only by being able to communicate with the people could he hope to make any impact on their lives. So, with 'rigid discipline', he applied his 'nose to the grindstone' and became fluent in the language, advancing through the years from being a school teacher in a mission school to the level of headmaster and a highly respected contributor to the national curriculum.

Around the same time, Winnie Loosemore was also saying her farewells in Southampton, ready for her second term in S. Rhodesia after furlough. Ruby Simms, just arrived home for her furlough, was also in the meeting and gave a short word. It was stated in the service that Winnie was "a very gifted person and all her talents are laid at the Master's feet. She gives herself untiringly to the work."

Back on the field, the work was producing fruit. Brenda Hurrel's class of standard six scholars in Inyanga all did well in their exams, with only one failing. The only girl in the class came top and three others, baptised Christians, went on to Teacher Training. Margaret Gwynne's students at Inyanga were likewise fulfilling expectations of them.

1961 saw the teaching staff augmented by the appointment of Joan Caudell to Penhalonga. From her earliest childhood, Joan had been nurtured in the Springbourne Elim church. She became a Sunday school scholar, then a teacher, then the youth leader. As pianist, organist or accordionist in the open air, she served wherever she was required. Being a gifted and experienced school teacher, in French as well as English, she was well fitted for the task to which God had called her. A meeting at the Royal Albert Hall with Pastor Archie Nicolson pointed her towards Southern Rhodesia and she learned from him at first hand something of the work there.

A short time later, as she considered her new position, Joan spoke of the beauty of God's creation in the landscape and weather patterns, but recognised the utter importance of teaching the people to read and to know Jesus. "From our schoolchildren must come our evangelists, pastors and teachers." This became very evident to her as she wrote the words of a chorus on a blackboard in the local language, but discovered that only about three or four of those present were able to read. She saw the moving of the Holy Spirit as a great necessity in the area.

An event took place in 1961 that was to have far reaching consequences for the Mission. One of the first schools to be established was at Mbiriadi. This was about five miles away through the bush and every other Sunday, Mrs. Brien walked to the district to preach the Word of God.

The headman there had been loyal to Elim because he had accepted Jesus as His saviour after a severe illness in 1959. One of his sons, James, who had been led to the Lord by Mary Cooper, had qualified for entry to an evangelical training college at Biriiri, and began a two year course. On one of his vacations, he returned aglow with the joy of the Lord and filled with the Saviour's love. He loved to tell others about Jesus. But a short time after arriving home, he collapsed and died at the Mission. His death shocked Africans and Europeans alike, and his funeral took place at the College, with Pastors Chiwara and Peter Griffiths present.

The Mbiriadi area was steeped in witchcraft and there had been much prayer for an evangelist to work there. A former pupil of the Mission and classmate of James, who died, volunteered to become an evangelist and work in that area. He was Ephraim Satuku, then working in Bulawayo. Those familiar with the Zimbabwe scene will know the name and recognise that for many years now, Ephraim has had an important role in the development and maintenance of the work.

While work on the mission station may at times sound mundane, there was a continual battle for the souls of men and women whose lives were steeped in the darkness of sin. Margaret Gwynne wrote that "fervent prayer, services on the mission station, the Sunday evening Bible class, the daily scripture lesson and personal work all played their part in winning souls for Christ. Rebellion against all things spiritual often preceded the final yielding to the Saviour and submission to His will. Many were the battles against witchcraft, parental opposition, extravagant ambitions and selfish desires. Glorious were the victories in the lives of the boys, wrought by the power of prayer."[viii]

Following the riots surrounding independence in Congo, several missionaries relocated. These included Catherine Picken, originally from Southend and Olive Garbutt.[ix] Cath gave herself to teaching while Olive was engaged in dispensary and nursing work. In a report in the *Elim Evangel*[x], Cath identified the rapid change that was then working in Africa. She observed that the kind of cultural and social change that took place in England over about three hundred years had taken Africa just seventy. Progress in education was staggering as African young people set their sights on education and, in many cases, on a higher education. Year by year, the control of education was passing from European hands into the hands of the Africans. Thankfully, too, many who were being taught in mission schools were hearing and responding to the Gospel.

She also recognised that the power of the witchdoctor was diminishing as the European doctors were being trusted more. Consequently, more people were coming to the hospitals and clinics, with the obvious benefit of hearing the Gospel at the same time. There was a change too in evangelism so that instead of the preaching being done by the missionary, there were African evangelists more than capable of spreading the Word.

In 1964, the Mission was granted permission to start a Secondary school and all the arrangements were in place. Unfortunately, one of the missionaries left the field and this meant a gap in the preparations. The new school would need a teacher and a manager to make sure everything went smoothly for the new venture. Alan and Anne Renshaw returned to Southern Rhodesia for their second term, after a period of service in Tanzania. They were joined by a young couple from the Bridge Street church in Leeds, John and Brenda Thomas. There is little information about the couple except to note that Brenda's activity was centred on the hospital at Inyanga as nursing sister, and her work was very highly regarded. Her husband, John, was appointed Inspector of schools and was required to make inspections of about 13 schools per term. They were involved in the preaching to some extent in the Kambudzi area. Brenda became pregnant and they moved to Penhalonga, leaving the field shortly thereafter.

A short furlough in 1965 allowed the Renshaws to extend their expertise in various skills. Alan had a course on the Land Rover and learned to weld, while Anne had driving lessons. They were also able to find, at the right price, an X-ray machine and an anaesthetic machine for the hospital. Having flown home to Gatwick the previous December, they found themselves on board ship the following November, and were relieved to return to the warmer climes of Mombasa and Beira, and thence to Umtali[xi] and Inyanga.

An important development in the work was the erecting of a secondary school at Inyanga alongside the Primary school already established there. Alan Renshaw had the job of designing and arranging for the construction of this building which stands today as a testimony to the faithfulness of God. Indeed, the site at Inyanga, with its hospital, schools, accommodation blocks and houses is a credit to the whole Elim work in Zimbabwe.

This venture was not without its problems, since the students had strong opinions and, when they were dissatisfied, they were not slow to show their feelings. Matters came to a head when, at the Sunday morning service, they refused to sing or take any part. The same thing happened in the fellowship hour in the afternoon and at the Bible study in the evening. The next day, the school did not open as, according to government regulations, by their action they had closed it. The government inspector confirmed the decision.

We can imagine the feelings of the missionaries as they pondered the future and wondered if the school would ever open again. Letters were sent out inviting the boys to reapply for admission and it was agreed that those who made application would be accepted. All but two applied and were accepted. It was felt that the two who had not applied were the ringleaders of the unrest, and so it proved to be. Happily, the school reopened a few weeks later, having lost a month of school time. The angry, rebellious spirit had disappeared and all settled down to work. The staff was able to testify to a wonderful work of grace being done in the lives of several of the boys, some of whom went on to serve the Lord. The school had been named, *Emmanuel* – God with us, and there was ample testimony that, even in the difficult times, He was always there.

It should be noted that, during his first term on the field, Peter Griffiths and Brenda Hurrel married. Towards the end of his first tour of Rhodesia, Peter provided a perceptive insight into the work in which he was engaged. He said –

> We have found the church work a far greater struggle than the educational work - our battle being on a higher plane. We have seen a few of our young people developing into fine Christians, some becoming teachers and a small number going to Bible school. On the other hand, many are a disappointment. The African church in Rhodesia is, not in my opinion, indigenous. The people, with very few exceptions, are not willing to give to support their own pastors, and most promising young people look for a more lucrative position than that of a pastor or evangelist. [xii]

During their furlough, Peter and Brenda Griffiths were able to take part in a valedictory service for another new missionary to Rhodesia, Miss Maisie Hopper from Ilford. Maisie had felt the Lord's leading for missionary work some twenty-two years before and had faced many frustrations while trying to reach the Field but, while waiting, had equipped herself fully in the nursing profession, gaining invaluable experience that would stand her in good stead in the mission hospital.[xiii]

The missionaries were encouraged in 1969 by a visit from the President of Elim for that year, Pastor Leslie Green. He visited Penhalonga where Miss Olive Garbutt and Miss Joan Caudell were working. A convention was held during his visit and was attended by about 300 people. Many were saved and filled with the Holy Spirit. He then travelled to Inyanga North and was impressed by the mission station which he described as an oasis in the desert – a "little village in no man's land." Here he saw the school work, headed up by Peter Griffiths with Anne Renshaw and Cath Picken. The medical side of the work was taken care of by the Doctors Brien and Alan Renshaw was school manager and general handyman right across the campus. The Sunday morning service was attended by over 500 people and many professed salvation.

In succeeding years, there were many reports of blessing as well as trial at both Inyanga and Penhalonga. At Inyanga North, the development of the Emmanuel Secondary school went on apace, as new buildings and facilities were added. The growth in the work of the hospital also demanded adequate staffing to maintain a ministry to the district. For many years, the great need was for a doctor so that the hospital's status could be maintained. Without a resident medical person, it would be downgraded to a clinic, with the consequent limitations on its impact. In the earlier days, the Doctors Brien had been in place and had done a magnificent job, but they were growing older and the hardships of the way were taking their toll. In October, 1970, Joyce Pickering of York flew to Rhodesia to take up a post at the hospital. She was a fully qualified nurse with several years' experience, and she also had had two years Bible school training.

The second of four girls, Joyce came from the Elim Church in York. She came to know the Lord when she was fifteen and, at sixteen, left home to take up nursing training. At the age of twenty-one, she qualified SRN and subsequently took her midwifery training to qualify SCM. Her experience gained in various hospital departments meant that she had a very broad knowledge to bring to the mission field. She heard a call when she attended a missionary rally at the Filey Convention, but rejected the idea. Some time later, she came to terms with the call and, following the Lord's leading, took Bible college training and ultimately agreed to go to Inyanga North at the request of the Missions Department.

At about the same time, Olive Garbutt was farewelling from Leeds for a return to the Field. Olive was, of course, a veteran missionary, having begun her career in Congo with Burton and Salter. She served there for fourteen years mostly involved in medical and maternity work and in ministry, but she had moved to Rhodesia at the time of Congo Independence and had served at both Inyanga and Penhalonga. Her time in Rhodesia had been spent in administration, much of the time as the Elim mission education Secretary and, from 1969, having sole care of the Penhalonga station.[xiv]

For much of the time, Olive laboured in great pain because of prolapsed discs in her spine. But she went to the annual Convention at Eldorado in South Africa and, on the Saturday, when brother C. Powell was ministering and telling of miracles of healing he had witnessed and experienced, he asked if there was anyone present who had spinal trouble.

Olive raised her hand and went forward for prayer. As she approached, he said, "Here is a lady with one leg shorter than the other. We are going to ask Jesus to lengthen it; if Jesus does not do it, it won't be done, but we believe He will manifest His power here today." Olive had never realised that she had one leg shorter than the other but, as he prayed, she felt it lengthening under the power of God. She stood up and immediately, her posture was different. All the strain and pain had vanished and she knew she was healed.

While Olive was on furlough, her place at Penhalonga had been taken by Don and Mary Norton. They had been serving in South Africa[XV] and transferred to Rhodesia to meet the need. They didn't waste much time in getting to work once they had arrived on station. There was much physical work to be done, as well as caring from the ministry side. The main mission house was badly in need of repair, so that became a priority – pulling down, building up, plumbing, laying drains, carpentry and electrical installation - were all necessary. The end product was well worth the effort and resulted in a comfortable home for the family. Before they knew it, Easter was upon them and they found themselves in the throes of an Easter Convention, with Alan Renshaw as the preacher.

Throughout the following year, they were visited by many folks, some from the UK, often with great blessing in ministry. During the August of that year, EWMA paid for them to be connected to the main electricity supply, so that made a huge difference to the quality of life. They had a visit from the Briens, which blessed both families, and Peter and Brenda Griffiths called before leaving for their furlough in England after five years at the Emmanuel school. Just a short time later, the Briens were present at the Missionary Convention in Cheltenham, their first visit home in seventeen years.

Over the next few years, the Field in Rhodesia was to be blessed by an influx of young, professional missionaries, all well qualified in their own specialities, usually teaching or medicine. Among the first were the McCanns, Peter and Sandra with their baby, Paul. Peter came with a B.Sc. (Honours) and was to become a teacher at Emmanuel school. A native of Huddersfield, Peter had struggled with Christianity through his university years, until finally, he was captivated by the Gospel. After working with a chemical firm for some time, he turned to teaching, but never felt really competent at it and wondered how the Lord had allowed him to go in that direction.

In the annual Conference in 1969, Cath Picken had made an appeal for graduate teachers for Rhodesia and Peter's wife, Sandra brought the news back from Conference with great excitement. Peter wasn't keen but when an advert appeared in the next *Elim Evangel* appealing for teachers, he sensed the Lord challenging him. The consequence was that he went to Elim Bible College for a term, then on to Rhodesia in January, 1970 to the beginning of what he himself called, "an exciting time of service for a wonderful God."

Sandra, also from Huddersfield, was the last of her family to find faith. In God's planning, she met Peter and they were married and had their first baby, Paul. Sadly, after just over one year on the field, Paul died, but they found new joy in the birth of their next baby in August 1972, a wee boy they named Philip. Philip was shortly afterwards joined by a wee sister, Joy.

When Olive Garbutt first went to Inyanga North, she was instrumental in opening a new church at Kambudzi village, where Dr. Brien had already established a clinic. There was a new Elim school there, but no missionary had been free to establish a work. Olive travelled the seventeen miles in a lorry, taking about two hours, over very rough roads to commence the work. The work developed to the extent that Ephraim Satuku was appointed Pastor and, after some considerable time, a church building was erected. Ephraim's appointment as the school's teacher had just come to an end but, although it meant a drop in income, he was delighted to remain in charge of the church and to do what was in his heart – to be an evangelist. Initially the church had used a school classroom to meet in but they longed for a building of their own. A suitable site was needed. The local Headman gave them a site and then the whole church membership became involved in making bricks and establishing their church. The first meeting in their own church was held at Christmas, 1972 and there was great joy among all present.

The shortage of trained staff was always an issue. The Secondary school needed qualified teachers and, despite many appeals for a resident doctor for the hospital, there had been little or no response from the homeland. Peter Griffiths felt it very keenly as he wrote for the *Elim Evangel*[xvi] setting out the needs and arguing that the need represented a call to those who were equipped to answer. While there have been occasions when doctors have been recruited, there has seldom been a comfortable situation when a regular doctor with an Elim background has had control of such a facility. At one stage, a very fine young man was employed, but he was an Ethiopian Roman Catholic. At school level, the work matured to the extent that most of the teachers were locally trained.

Joy Bath was the latest recruit. She left Salisbury in Wiltshire to fly to Salisbury in Rhodesia and, from there, to the hospital at Inyanga. At twenty-four and a trained midwife, she was an invaluable addition to the team. Joy's life fell into the pattern of work on the mission station, but later, was absolutely turned around as she was on furlough at the time of the massacre, went to India for a period and, finally, returned to Africa, only to contract Aids. She told her story in her own book, *No Greater Love.*[xvii]

Another well qualified team member was Mary Fisher, a school teacher engaged in the Emmanuel Secondary school. Mary came from Caerphilly, in South Wales. She took a general degree at Swansea University, and then a post-graduate Certificate of Education at Brunel. She became a maths teacher for a while until she entered London Bible College and obtained a Diploma in Theology. During her time at LBC, she applied to Elim for a teaching post at Inyanga and was accepted for Emmanuel Secondary school. She was an accomplished musician and during deputation work, often accompanied herself on piano or guitar. Despite her introduction to the great variety of wildlife on the mission station, she settled in well and began to enjoy the experience of working in the bush.

By this time, Ron Chapman, with his wife, had left England for Rhodesia to become Field Chairman for Southern Africa. Ron had been an Elim minister for many years and had held the posts of Field Superintendent for the UK as well as being Chairman of the Missionary Council. Now, in Penhalonga, he found his practical skills much in demand. He had the responsibility for administration and decision making at a time when there were many constraints on the work. The nation was in political upheaval as it sought independence. Guerrilla fighting was regular and, often, the mission station was approached by one side or the other seeking food or medical help. Trying to remain neutral was almost impossible and much effort was expended in letting it be known that the missionaries were there only to help the Africans.

Later, he settled into a house on the station at Penhalonga but continued his duties against the background of a dusk to dawn curfew, landmined roads – for which a specially adapted Land Rover was constructed[xviii] – the unpredictable presence of guerrillas and the uncertain attitudes of Africans to the white man. The world news was reporting involvements of the Russians in a bid to topple Ian Smith, while he was trying to keep order in the north eastern part of the country where African tribesmen were being beaten into submission. There were suggestions that Peking was about to supply arms to the guerrillas and a new name for the country had been chosen. It would no longer be called Rhodesia – after Cecil Rhodes who had pioneered there, but now its name would be Zimbabwe. Efforts to prepare the Africans for their own self rule were hampered by suspicion and an impatience to be in charge.

Around this time, Alan Renshaw had to return home because of recurring health problems. As station manager, Alan's work was indispensable, but a young man in Northern Ireland responded to the call for a replacement. He was Roy Lynn, a native of Cullybackey, but had been the minister of the church in Brookeborough, Co. Fermanagh for the previous six years. Roy's addition to the team was a cause for rejoicing. He fitted in well and was pleasant and obliging in all he was asked to do. Before very long, he and Joyce Pickering became close friends, a friendship that blossomed into love and led to marriage. They were married in the York church by the writer in July, 1977. In May, 1978, they were blessed with the gift of a baby daughter, Pamela Grace.

Another family to hear and answer the call to Rhodesia was Philip and Susanne Evans and their children. Philip was a teacher who became involved, not only in school activities, but also in the wider work of the mission, especially as it reached out to students and young people in the area.

The sense of trepidation can be understood when Peter Griffiths wrote of a "quiet weekend" they expected to have after a very busy week. After church on the Sunday morning, they heard the sound of automatic gunfire and rockets coming from about eight miles to the north. A little later, Peter met an African member of the Security forces coming from the hospital with bloodstains on the front of his shirt. He had been ambushed and chased by guerrillas and had a shrapnel wound in his chest. At about 10 a.m., three miles away, a European came running into the area where Brenda was conducting a singing competition. He was emotionally shattered having just experienced his first taste of combat. His African buddy sitting at his side in their vehicle had been hit and instantly killed by a rocket. He asked Brenda to take him back to his base. That was just the morning. The rest of the day was 'normal'. Peter and Pastor Ephraim Satuku visited, preached, prayed and counselled and saw the Lord at work. The following day, a policeman at Inyanga said, "You were lucky not to have been ambushed."

Last to join the missionary team was Wendy White, who had a wide variety of giftings, with experience in nursing, teaching and social work. Wendy had impressed with her care for those in need as she tended the sick, as well as her ardour and fervour in praying and serving.

In late 1977, with the pressure growing ever greater, there was discussion about the running of the school and hospital and it was felt that there would be an advantage if those in charge were seen to be local people. Pious Munembe was, at the time, a deacon in the church at Manjanja (Katerere) and a teacher in the school and it was agreed that he should become Headmaster. The view was also taken that his wife, Evelyn, a trained nurse, was well qualified to be given to oversight of the hospital.

Such discussions took place against the backdrop of a perceived need to evacuate the Inyanga mission station on account of the heightened threat of incursion and danger. Another school was found in the Vumba mountains, near to the larger town of Umtali (Mutare), but still quite near to the Mozambique border. Arrangements were therefore made to transfer students to the new school in the belief that it would be a safer position because of its proximity to a large town and a metalled road for access. Unfortunately, tragedy struck almost immediately.

The *Rhodesia Herald* reported:

Two African schoolboys were killed, a bus driver and nine children were injured, one seriously, when two busloads of children hit landmines north of Inyanga on Wednesday afternoon.

A nightmare journey for 180 children leaving Elim Mission Secondary school ended for some of them in Umtali yesterday.

Three buses set out to take the Elim children to Eagle school in the Vumba, where the school is to be re-established. Eagle school closed at the end of last year.

The first bus hit a landmine about 45 km north of Inyanga. The second bus stopped and took on board the injured children and carried on. The third bus hit a second landmine farther down the road and burst into flames. All the children escaped through the windows but the driver was burned to death. Bedding and luggage were destroyed.

Two boys died as a result of the first explosion, another was brought to Umtali hospital where his leg has been amputated, and others were treated at Inyanga hospital.

Last week, a truck bringing school equipment from the Mission hit a landmine and a relief truck overturned when trying to bring the baggage to safety, destroying much of the equipment.

Many of the pupils have now returned to their homes after being accommodated at other missions in the Inyanga area. Twelve pupils have volunteered to help get Eagle school ready for the mission to continue schooling next term. The principal of the Mission school, Mr. Peter Griffiths, said yesterday that the move to the Vumba was being made to keep the school going.

During this period of unrest and confrontation, Ephraim was severely beaten and the missionaries lost equipment to the value of £4000 from hospital, school and home. The hope was that the school could maintain its service to the students without interruption and in a position of relative calm and safety. Once the move had been accomplished, schooling continued. Peter and Brenda Griffiths went back to the UK for their furlough and members of the nursing staff made regular visits to the hospital in Inyanga, often by MAF plane. On the face of it, the move seemed sensible. With hindsight, it left the missionaries without an African backup. In Inyanga, they were known by the local people. In Vumba, they were strangers.

The events of the night of Friday, June 23rd, 1978, and which represented probably the darkest period in the history of the Elim Church, have been well documented.[xix] Rebels crossed the Mozambique border, roused the missionaries from their beds and, on the sports field, massacred them and their children. Those who died were –

Peter and Sandra McCann with Philip and Joy;
Philip and Susanne Evans with Rebecca;
Roy and Joyce Lynn with Pamela Grace;
Catherine Picken;
Wendy White;

Mary Fisher managed to escape into the bushes and was critically wounded. She died within a few days and was buried on July 4th, shortly after the main funeral took place.

As can be imagined, those involved in conducting the funeral found themselves wondering how they would get through the service. David Ayling reported:

We all feared we would not be able to carry through the service. There were naturally moments of great emotion, yet the grace of God was on us all. Leslie Wigglesworth spoke an appreciation of the missionaries. Then he and Mrs. Chapman sang, "We shall see His lovely face." Pastor Chapman had prepared every detail completely and led the service with confidence. The expression of thanksgiving and sympathy encompassed the world, with leaders from many parts of South Africa taking part. I felt the sympathy of all when I preached on the text - *"They loved not their lives unto the death".* Pastor Peter Griffiths spoke with deep emotion of his fellow-workers who had gained a martyr's crown. Pastor John Smyth took the Committal Service at the Umtali Cemetery where the earthly remains of our beloved missionaries were laid to rest beside each other under the shade of a large flowering tree.

Neither the Chapmans nor the Evans's older children, Timothy and Rachel, were on site when the atrocity happened and the children were later cared for by their grandmother in England.

A national memorial service was held in the Central Hall, Birmingham. Subsequently, regional services were held in Scotland, Wales, Huddersfield and York. The reporting of the various services in the pages of the *Elim Evangel*[xx] indicated how deeply the whole Movement felt about the situation. Needless to say, there was much comment and examination, and a measure of criticism, in the media. Elim was commended by some for their stance offering forgiveness; others condemned them roundly for failing to demand justice. The Anglican Bishop of Mashonaland contended that the British Government should have sent in troops, while the *Yorkshire Post* (June 26, 1978) reported that a revenge team from the Rhodesian army was tracking the rebels, although they had a ten hour start. One newspaper (*Northern Echo* June 26, 1978) blamed the British Government for being dilatory in arranging an internal settlement of the struggle in Rhodesia.

The whole ethos of Elim's mission and the background to the decision to move to the Vumba was examined by David J. Maxwell in his chapter on *Christianity and the War in Eastern Zimbabwe: The Case of the Elim Mission.*[xxi] In this chapter, Maxwell explored the relationship between the missionaries and the guerrillas, in the context of the local community. When opportunities presented themselves, the missionaries were open to speak with the guerrillas, Joy Bath and Philip Evans spending quite some time with them on different occasions. He noted that the Eagle school was very much a unit apart whereas the Inyanga station had been totally open to the community. As always, hindsight makes for 20/20 vision!

David Ayling and Leslie Wigglesworth were invited to the Foreign Office to receive personally from Dr. David Owen, then Foreign Secretary, the sympathy of both the Government and the House of Commons. The mail was full of letters and expressions of sympathy, together with gifts towards the Vumba Fund that had been set up. The Missions Board members not only visited the relatives throughout the country, but advised them of arrangements for many of them to attend the funeral in Umtali. Extraordinary help was received from South African Airways and the Passport Office to facilitate those travelling. There was an almost immediate reaction as people offered to go to Rhodesia to take the place of those who had died. Wisely, the Board held any response to this in abeyance until some of the emotion had subsided.

In the early 1980s, there were rumours that a number of those involved in the massacre had had remarkable conversions and Peter Griffiths was instructed to investigate the claims. He met the platoon commander who had led the group who gave him his reasons for the atrocity. He said that (1) he wanted to undermine white morale in the country; (2) he sought to close down institutions in the area to facilitate more effective routes for guerrilla infiltration and (3) the missionaries had not responded immediately to instructions to leave the site. It was subsequently established that many conversions *had* taken place and that some of those who had been involved were now engaged in Christian service.[xxii]

By the end of June, Ron Chapman had effectively handed over the reins of the work to the local people. Some felt that was a knee-jerk reaction to the events, but he was, in fact, simply confirming a situation that had been in place for about two years. In the event, it was to be the only way forward at that time. John Smyth, in his final report after the massacre, said, "I do not believe we should write off Rhodesia. . . The day of planting has been done. There must follow a harvest. In due season, we shall reap if we faint not."

It was essential that the Chapmans return to the UK and there was a delay before Peter and Brenda Griffiths could go back to the Field, so the Missions Board asked Archie Nicolson to go for a short time to maintain the contact and ensure the encouragement of the African believers. The Griffiths' finally returned in January, 1979. Although so much had changed, they would now be based in Salisbury where the sphere of Peter's influence would be greatly expanded as he maintained his contacts with the Inyanga team and former Emmanuel school students but, at the same time, began to make an impact on the national education scene. He became responsible for writing the new Christian education syllabuses for all the Primary Rhodesian education system, which touched millions of scholars.

In the aftermath, too, the question was asked if their deaths represented a waste. Events and information that flowed into the central office shortly afterwards assured the Church's leaders that it wasn't. There were testimonies of changed lives, new dedications, appreciation for ministry faithfully given and commitments to service. The seed that fell into the ground died, but it brought forth a harvest for the glory of God.

In the process of time, a church building was purchased in Umtali and designated the Memorial Church. This is now the central church for the region and provides facilities for the Headquarters of the Zimbabwe Elim Church. The work settled into its new way of working as Ephraim Satuku took the lead spiritually at Inyanga and David Tsvamuno became the pastor in the Penhalonga/Umtali area. The Primary school work continued with Pious Munembe involved, as his wife, Evelyn, continued to oversee the work of the hospital.

It was now becoming possible for plans to be made for Pious Munembe to go to the Elim Bible College for theological training, which he was able to do in 1981. It is significant that both Pious and Evelyn trace their Christian roots to the Elim mission stations in Rhodesia. Pious is today the Chairman of the work. That was the year, too, when the Emmanuel Secondary school at Inyanga was reopened with 84 Form One students. It was expected that, over the next three years, it would increase to between 300 and 500 pupils. There was a new Principal, Patrick Mukangara, a Zimbabwean who had obtained a Bachelor of Education (Honours) degree at Exeter in England. After teaching for two years in Wembley, he returned to open the Emmanuel school. There was great rejoicing in the area, as can be imagined. The Primary school, too, was making great progress, having increased in enrolment from 90 children and four teachers to 503, with ten teachers struggling to cope. The headmaster, Sanny Makanyanga, was an ex-student of Emmanuel and a church leader.

With the development of the work in its new phase, it was then opportune for expatriate teachers once again to make their way to the Field and one of the first was Jan Edgar. Jan was twenty-three, a school teacher and a member of Liverpool's Central Elim Church. While at University, our missionaries had been massacred and Jan had said to the Lord that she was willing to be a replacement for one of them if that was His will. Her call came in the form of a real desire to work in Inyanga. Initially, Jan accepted a Government teaching post in a secondary school in Bulawayo and remained there for one and a half years, and saw that as a missionary posting in answer to a call she had felt in University. Elim regarded her as a Pathfinder and she was able to work with Pastor Tom Hodge in the Bulawayo, the capital of Matabeleland region. Jan subsequently married Dudley Pate and they continued to serve in other parts of Africa, including Mozambique.

The work in Matabeleland was under the care of David Ndhlovu, who was at that time the Chairman of the Zimbabwean Executive, with a team of evangelists/pastors, and aided by Tom Hodge who once worked for the Oxford University Press, but at that time, was working as a printer producing a great deal of material for Global Lifeline. His wife, Nancy was working in one of the local hospitals. In Bulawayo, the main work was centred in the western suburbs where the main group met in a hired hall, while others met in smaller groups in homes. Many were being touched by salvation and healing and there were reports of people receiving the Baptism in the Holy Spirit.

The team in Bulawayo had no means of transport but there were other centres where the Gospel was making an impact. At the same time as the news of blessing was coming from Matabeleland, there were opportunities opening up to reach into Botswana[xxiii], just on the doorstep of Bulawayo. Some of the folks had already moved into Botswana to join the new outreach planned for there.

Meanwhile, with Government permission, Jan was allowed to transfer to Inyanga to use her skills at the Emmanuel school where, in conjunction with her teaching of English and 'O' level Bible Knowledge, she found herself engaged in ministry as well. Each week, she would travel out into the bush to Kanyimo, a school started by Dr. Brien and there, helped by some of her students, would conduct Sunday services. Her reports indicated that the Lord was blessing and young people were coming to the Lord and being baptised in the Holy Spirit. At Inyanga, too, there was much evidence of blessing in transformed lives.

Around the time of Jan's transfer to Emmanuel Secondary school, there was a new vocational missionary also appointed, Geoff Saunders. Geoff eventually became the deputy headmaster of the Christian Gateway School in Harare. For a short period, Peter and Margaret Wallace also served. It was exciting, too, to have on staff Virginia Nyaguzi because she was a former student of the school who had just completed a degree in Zimbabwe's University. Pious Munembe, with his wife, Evelyn, had just returned from Elim Bible

College to take up the reins as Headmaster of the school. Evelyn, with her SRN, had an important role in the hospital on the site.

The spiritual side of the work was being overseen by Pastor Ephraim Satuku who had expanded his role from that of a local pastor to a general oversight of the whole work. The local church was in the care of Pastor Mhlanga. Pastor and Mrs. Ian Wilsher were also active in the work and remained so for a number of years until Ian set up a counselling service in Harare, the capital.

With the passing of time, and following repeated appeals, the hospital had their prayers answered with the arrival of Sister Debbie Holman and Dr. Adrian Smyly, who was working with Oxfam on secondment. Their impact was seen in that, the following year, the hospital had about twice the number of patients. As a consequence of the war, much of the equipment had been lost, stolen or destroyed so, as always, there were shortages of material goods, including the money to buy necessary equipment. The operating theatre needed to be upgraded and there was an urgent need for a new ambulance. Appeals were made to the members in the UK for help and, from time to time, obsolete equipment from UK hospitals was made available and put to good use.

Brian Edwards became International Missions Director in 1983 following the untimely death of David Ayling. On a visit to Zimbabwe, he found himself in some difficulties at the border as he drove up from South Africa. The immigration officers were very officious, demanding all sorts of information. Initially, after supplying what seemed to be adequate information, he was asked the name of the person with whom he would be staying. His reply was direct: Mr. Peter Griffiths. When the officer-in-charge heard that, his response was immediate. "He was my Principal in Secondary school," and in a moment the whole situation had changed. What a wonderful testimony to Elim's work in Zimbabwe.

In 1986, Debbie Brown, a nurse from Northern Ireland, joined the staff at the hospital. From her salvation in 1972, Debbie felt a hunger for service. She sensed a call on hearing a testimony by someone from Zaire. She was already in nursing training by this time and followed her general training with experience in orthopaedics, midwifery and, later, tropical diseases. In the early 1980s, Debbie joined a Euroteam[xxiv], then went to Bible College and continued her nursing career until the door finally opened for her to go to Zimbabwe in 1986. She was able to work with Joy Bath, who returned to the Field in 1987 to work with Aids sufferers.

Joy had been working at Dehri-on-Sone in India, having left Zimbabwe in 1977 to undertake Bible College training. After a furlough in 1985, the Indian authorities refused to renew her visa, so she returned to nursing to update her skills. It was therefore proposed that she go back to Zimbabwe, a decision not to be taken lightly in view of what had happened to her former colleagues. On her return she was assigned to Outpatients so found herself well occupied. In addition there were clinics in the villages, around 16 per month.

Another Northern Irish girl also serving was Roberta (Bobbie) Marcus who had spent some time working in Hong Kong, but had offered herself to the hospital at Inyanga. She had, at one time, been involved with the Bridge Street church in Leeds. To some extent, this explained the interest Bridge Street had in Zimbabwe. So when nine-year-old Matthew Marsden, son of one of the elders, died, the church wanted to do something in Zimbabwe as a memorial to him. Initially, the idea was to erect a children's clinic, but the World Bank decided this was a worthwhile project and took it over. The outcome was that, following a fact-finding visit by Chris Marsden and the Bridge Street pastor, John Cave, it was decided to supply and install an electricity generator. This was accomplished a little later by Chris with help from J.B. McClelland and David Hamilton from the Ulster Temple in Belfast.

When the opportunity presented itself, Joy, Debbie Brown and Bobbie Marcus all travelled to Mutare to visit the graves of their friends. It was a moving experience and one in which they felt constrained to rededicate themselves to the work of the Lord.

An era in the Zimbabwe work came to an end in 1987 with the home call of Dr. Cecil Brien. He had remained Field leader until his retirement in 1974 and although he returned to his native Swansea, his heart ever remained in Africa. Elim Inyanga is a living testimony to his diligence and vision and the ministry he shared for so many years with his dear wife. Tributes were paid to him by Brian Edwards and Peter Griffiths[XXV]. In doing so, Peter made the point that Dr. Brien was so self-effacing that it was almost impossible to obtain personal information from him when a medical journal had asked for an article.

The following year, Beth Lancaster and Ruth Jarvis travelled to Inyanga to augment the teaching team on short term placements. From time to time, other teachers gave of their time for short terms. These included Brian and Sue Salter, Claire Odling and Helen Parsons. In June of that year, a special memorial service was held at the Elim Bible College, Nantwich to recognise the ten year period that had passed. The College sports hall was packed and Peter Griffiths was the main speaker.[XXVI] In November of 1988, Roger Drew with his wife, Joanne and their baby, Stephen, went to Inyanga. Roger would be the surgeon in charge of the hospital and many of the instruments he took with him had been donated by local hospitals because the operating theatre had been out of use for about ten years. Roger, a native of Norwich, studied medicine at Newcastle University and was converted during his first term in 1978. He met Joanne, who is from Northern Ireland, while she was studying for her BA at Newcastle. They continued in the Newcastle assembly from then on and were married in 1984.

From this time forward, the numbers of expatriate missionaries declined and the work was maintained by the efforts of the local people. In view of the growing Aids epidemic, it became necessary for the church to seek some means of helping those afflicted by it. Peter Griffiths had an association with an evangelical church in Harare, Northside, which produced a project entitled project 127, based on James 1:27. This was done in partnership with Elim and was based primarily on Inyanga. The intention was to raise money that could be used to support destitute families and provide basic food plus seeds and expertise on how to grow crops. In some cases, school fees for primary education were supplied together with help in obtaining the necessary uniforms. The scheme was administered by two members of the Manjanja church, based in an office on the Inyanga Compound. This was subsequently extended to a child sponsorship scheme, whereby children of secondary school age were sponsored at a regular rate on a monthly basis. Gradually, support for these schemes transferred from Northside to Elim funds from the UK and it was therefore mooted that general management and control should transfer to Elim. It is not known if this has yet been accomplished.

But the work in Zimbabwe goes on. A new church building has been erected in Harare and a city church is thriving. There is a strong women's work led by Erica Saunders, Geoff's wife and they are learning to be more and more self-sufficient. Church planting is seen to be a priority.

i The story of Elim's beginning was recorded by Jesse Williams in *Elim Evangel*, Vol.62. Issue 32, pp. 8, 9.

ii Dr. R.C. Brien told how he had come into Elim after serving in Africa for a number of years in the *Elim Evangel*, Vol.42. Issue 1, p.22.

iii *Elim Evangel*, Vol.32. Issue 49, pp578, 587.

iv Inyanga North was one of the regions where the Mission was working, centred in particular in the village of Katerere.

v Wm. McKeown produced an unpublished personal record of their call and experiences entitled *Marvellously Helped,* 1998. Used by permission.

vi *Elim Evangel*, Vol.36. Issue 46, p.545.

vii Worldwide Evangelisation Crusade.

viii *Elim Evangel*, Vol.43. Issue 22, pp.344, 345.

ix See chapter on Congo.

x *Elim Evangel*, Vol.45. Issue 23, p.357.

xi Now known as Mutare.

xii *Elim Evangel*, Vol.47. Issue 14, p.210.

xiii Maisie's testimony of the Lord's leading was published in the *Elim Evangel*, Vol. 48. Issue 6, pp. 90, 91.

xiv Following her 'retirement' from the Field, Olive gave many years of service to the International Missions Department at Elim Church Headquarters until she finally retired in 2005.

xv See chapter on South Africa/Transvaal for details.

xvi *Elim Evangel*, Vol.55. Issue 53, pp. 8, 9.

xvii Bath, Joy with Shirley Collins. *No Greater Love,* Kingsway Publications, Eastbourne, 1995.

xviii This was called a *Rhino* and was uniquely Rhodesian. It was constructed so that if a land mine went off, its blast would be diverted by the shape of the underside and the occupants would survive.

xix Thompson, Phyllis, *The Rainbow and the Thunder.* Hodder & Stoughton with Elim Pentecostal Church, Cheltenham, 1979.

xx See Vol.59, Issue 30.

xxi Maxwell, David J. in *Society in Zimbabwe's Liberation War*, Ed: Bhebe and Ranger, James Currey, Oxford, University of Zimbabwe Publications, Harare,

xxii Peter's report appeared in *Elim Evangel,* Vol.69. Issue 18.6.88, p.3.

xxiii See chapter on Botswana.

xxiv See reference in chapter on Euroteams.

xxv *Elim Evangel,* Vol.68. Issue 18, p.10; Issue 20, pp. 15, 16.

xxvi *Elim Evangel,* Vol.69. Issue 13.8.88, pp. 8, 9, 13.

SECTION THREE

CENTRAL & SOUTH AMERICA

20. Brazil 199
21. Guyana 213
22. Honduras 227

CHAPTER 20

BRAZIL

HENRY AND EDITH JEFFERY

The Elim work in Brazil was started in 1962 by Henry Jeffery under the auspices of the Elim Pentecostal churches (EPC), the title of the work in Essex at that time. Henry's wife, Edith, was formerly Edith Mynard, an Elim missionary to India for five years.[1]

Having lived and worked in Luton for a number of years, the Jefferys farewelled from the local Pentecostal church there before going to Leigh-on-Sea for their official send-off. The service there was blessed with a tremendous sense of the Lord's power as hands were laid on them and they were committed to His care. Their departure was from Tilbury on the RMS *Arlanza* on 24th February, 1962. Many friends travelled to Tilbury to bid them farewell.

From the very beginning, there were reports of blessing. The family settled in Saõ Paulo, negotiated the use of a hall, preached by radio to a potential audience of six million and shared in special meetings, seeing 35 profess salvation in just one week.

One of these, a murderer, had been released from prison three months earlier. He had been sentenced to 26 years for shooting a man, but was released after 12. Now he is filled with the joy of the Lord. Henry's expectation was to start a regular weekly radio broadcast lasting 30 minutes. He also had opportunities to go into schools. There had been an appeal for 1600 people to teach Scripture to Protestant pupils, but only 400 responded.

The work began on April 30th, 1963 in Santo Amaro, a suburb of Saõ Paulo. This is still the central church and headquarters today. At that time, there were three churches with 83 baptised members. One of these churches was in the interior, a 17 hour train journey away.

In a report from that time, Henry said:

Half of Brazil's people now live in urban areas, where there are offered to some a better way of life, a steadier wage, a decent house and schooling for their children, but there are also offered to others the disappointment, the immorality and for many, just a sordid slum. Over eighty percent of the population is illiterate and the majority of people are nominally Roman Catholic, but millions are turning to Spiritualism and black magic, endeavouring by all means to find peace and satisfaction, and to fill the emptiness that Rome has left.

The Spirit of God has been working and thousands have found Christ as Saviour, but the devil has used their illiteracy to divide the church into many sects, denominations and groups, many with man-made yokes that tend only to divide and not unite. The primary responsibility of the missionary is to evangelise in co-operation with the nationals and to teach them how to use God's word, teaching them by all means and methods - radio, Bible courses and literature. This task is one of extreme urgency, to reach the individual classes with the message of truth.

New mission fields are everywhere - around factories, mills and assembly plants, and the pace of industrialisation calls for a new concept of evangelism, one where every convert is a missionary. Evening classes for Bible teaching accompanied by practical team work are among the best and most productive ways of doing this. The teams thus created can move into the areas, ministering to the deepening of spiritual life, always emphasising the commission of the Master, creating by prayer and the fullness of the Holy Spirit a passion for the salvation of their fellow-countrymen, and then revealing the need for workers in other countries. They must also teach the necessity of Christian stewardship, working always towards the goal of indigenous churches and teaching other lay workers to accept the responsibility of leadership and of forming other cells of evangelism.

In 1964, Henry issued a challenge to Elim's youth. He was concerned that the shortage of workers on the field would result in a failure to capitalise on what he saw as fields white for harvest. Tracing the roots of Christian mission in the country, he said:

Just over half a century ago (around 1910), two young men[ii] arrived in the north of Brazil having received the fullness of God's Spirit, and through the gift of prophecy been told to go to Para. Having found that Para was in Brazil, they obeyed the Spirit's leading and arrived in thick clothing, totally unsuitable for the tropical heat and only God behind them. From this small beginning, the Pentecostal work has grown into a torrent of power and glory. God's protection from danger and harm reads like a story from the primitive church.

A small group of believers went out into the dark of an interior village to conduct an open air meeting and the service was abundantly blessed, but only after the evangelistic service that followed was the full truth known. In the dark of a village shop doorway six men stood determined to 'finish' the *crentes* (believers). With revolvers in pockets they awaited the commencement of the open air service, but this night was different. Around the small ring was a ring of fire, and as the believers began to sing and preach, so a small group of individuals clothed in sparkling white stood around them as if on guard. The murderers trembled with fear and slunk away, except for one who followed the group to the little local church and there surrendered to Christ, and then the story was told of the heavenly visitation.

It was the custom to hold a gospel service in the house of anyone who had a birthday, inviting the neighbours to attend. One young boy of ten in this same village had given his heart to the Lord. His mother was a fanatical Catholic and determined to kill her own son, as he refused to stop going to the meetings. We were invited to hold the anniversary service. A cake of meal flour had been made and after the service, as we stood around the table on which were the cups (Nestlé's milk cans polished with sand) and small enamel mugs and the cake, asking God to bless, one of the believers saw smoke coming from the cake. He touched his companion and soon we were all amazed watching the cake burn to a cinder. After some little time, the mother came bursting into the hut, broken in spirit and between her sobs, told the story of religious fanaticism and how she had mixed a whole tin of strong poison(to kill ants) into the cake, sufficient to kill twenty persons. That night, another soul was born into the Kingdom through the pain of persecution and the threat of death.

The same wonder-working God was in evidence in the Elim work in Santo Amaro. One of the workers, Agrario full of zeal and determination to take the full gospel message to his own folk in the north, was converted. He remembered a vow his grandmother had made and received an answer to prayer. His young wife was always ailing. Never a day passed without her having to purchase pills for a severe and constant headache. Making his vow that he would become a *crente* if the Lord healed his wife, he came to the meetings, received an answer to his prayer and soon, another young couple was following the Lord through the waters of baptism.

In 1963, the Brazil work was taken over by the Elim Missionary Society (EMS). For many years, the EPC and the EMS had worked closely together in missionary enterprise and endeavour. Mutual support had been extremely beneficial.

The sheer size of the country presented missionaries with a daunting task, but their vision was clear as they sought to proclaim the gospel "by all means". At that time, although there had been expansion along the coast, there were still tribes untouched by the gospel and some had never even seen a white person. Thousands living in isolated areas had never known the truth and waited to be led into the light. The powers of darkness were real. Hundreds were demon-possessed and still more were seeking in the lower forms of spiritism the way to life and light, only to become enveloped in deeper darkness and ignorance. Witchcraft and black magic were rife even in the largest cities of the land. And only the dynamic of the gospel of Jesus Christ could make a difference in liberating those who were bound by Satan's chains.

With the increasing numbers of churches, the need for Christian literature became more and more urgent, as did the need for more trained national workers for the spreading of the gospel. The situation is no different today. Despite the best efforts of missionaries of all denominations, there has never been sufficient involvement to make a major difference nationally, although obviously, individuals have been gloriously changed.

By the time Leslie Wigglesworth, the EMS secretary, visited the field in 1970, the work was well established and Elim churches were being planted between São Paulo and Brasilia, the capital.

In the beginning, children gathered for Sunday schools and this attracted the parents. National workers became available and expansion took place, accompanied by the evident working of the Holy Spirit.

In the Socorro church, at Santo Amaro, a small boy suffering from osteomyelitis and encased in plaster was prayed for. There was a sensation in the hospital when the cast had to be removed after prayer. Doctors and nurses were in tears as they realised what God had done. Needless to say, there was great rejoicing in the church when they received the news.

Around this time, there was some concern and a measure of strain on the Jefferys family because of anxieties about their children's education, their own health and new government laws affecting ministry. At a conference of workers, the Jefferys' return to England was a matter of concern and the brethren expressed strongly their need for someone to instruct them in the Word of God. They had grown up in Elim and felt they needed an Elim missionary to guide them.

Edith Jeffery tells the story of Maria, whom she called A Brazilian Jewel:

Maria was a tomboy who, at the age of seven, went to the local school. If corrected by the teacher, she would simply jump out of the window and go home. She loved to join with the groups who were invited by the priests to make fun of the Protestants and to get hold of their Bibles and hymn books and burn them.

One day, a new pupil joined the school and sat next to Maria. They made friends even although they were of opposite natures and soon, Isaura invited Maria to her home after school. There, Isaura showed Maria some of her favourite passages in the Bible and sang hymns and choruses to her. Maria would stay until it was nearly dark and her mother became very angry and asked where she had been. But Maria was afraid to tell her mother she had been with a Christian friend.

One day, her mother threatened her with a big stick because she was late home and that was the end of the visits. But the eternal seed had been sown. As she grew up, the seed lay dormant. Maria left home, having quarrelled with her parents and became a hairdresser until she married. She had two children seven years apart. At the birth of her second child, the midwife was a faithful Pentecostal who sowed more seed into Maria's heart. She told Maria she should confide in Jesus Christ and not in the crucifix over her bed, but Maria, strong-willed as ever, went her own way.

Her husband became ill and she also had heart trouble so she started to seek the aid of mediums. Then her youngest son swallowed a large fish bone which choked him. As she saw him turning blue, she cried out, "Oh, Jesus of the believers, save my boy." He immediately coughed up the bone and began breathing again. Because of this, she went to an evangelical meeting and gave her life to the Lord. Some time later, she found her way to a newly-opened Elim church and settled there to become a faithful worker for the Lord. The midwife also became a working member of the church.

The presence of evil is always evident where the Spirit of God is moving, and this is very much the case in Brazil. Henry told of an occasion when he was called to the home of a young woman who had been attending the meetings for about two months but who had been sidetracked by a fanatical sect of believers.

When he arrived at her home, it was evident that she was demon possessed and he began warfare with the demons until all had been removed. The authority of Jesus' Name brought the young lady deliverance, although it took a struggle lasting over one and a half hours to complete. Later, the lady was able to say that she believed her possession was because earlier that day, a black man had passed by who was a spiritist. He had asked her for water and she had refused and she felt that this was his doing. But the God of light is stronger than the prince of darkness and she was gloriously delivered.

Miracles marked the ministry! Levi Francisco was the fourth child of a deacon of the church and was a beautiful baby. At twenty days old, he became ill with what was believed to be bronchitis. He was treated with antibiotics and cough syrup to no effect, so was sent to hospital and given oxygen and other treatment. Despite all sorts of tests, no one could arrive at a definitive diagnosis of his condition. When the hospital bills reached £100 (in 1966), they felt unable to continue his hospital treatment so they took him home.

One night, they brought their "little bag of bones" to the prayer meeting, gasping for breath. Much prayer was made on his behalf. Then one of the doctors told the parents there was no hope for him and asked if they would let him go to the teaching hospital so that they could investigate and experiment to see if they could find a cure. The parents agreed.

After endless tests, lasting about three months, the parents were told to take him home to die. He had – in Portuguese: *muco-visidose* – and it was incurable. The mother's reaction was to tell the doctor, "He will not die, but live. God is going to operate." Their response was, "You have wonderful faith. We can do no more."

On arriving home, they continued to give him the extract of pancreas, which they said he needed to keep him alive, for eight days. His breathing was abnormal, the extract difficult to obtain. One day, they decided they would trust God completely and, from that day, when he was seven months old, he began to recover. The cough disappeared, appetite increased, breathing became normal within fifteen days and he began to gain weight. Twelve months later, he was the picture of health and normal in every way.

Miracles come in all sorts of ways and are not always recognised as such. But an examination of the history of events can very often show how the hand of God was miraculously at work to bring about His purposes. This was the case with Oswaldo who became the pastor of the church at Londrina in the state of Parana. Londrina church then had 160 baptised members and an active radio programme.

Brought up in a strict Roman Catholic home in Saõ Paulo, Oswaldo was always faithful to his church. Although religious, he was a smoker, drinker and gambler, but he was also a searcher for truth. One day, the second commandment arrested him. A boat builder by trade, he had many friends in the profession and one of these invited him to a Protestant church. He was greatly impressed by what he found there and, in spite of his being unconverted, he was invited to sing in the choir. He accepted and continued to do so until persecution from his family forced him to leave.

He returned to his idols but still had many doubts. One day, he pleaded with one of his idols to at least wink at him to assure him of her favour, but when nothing happened, he lost his faith and drifted. At twenty-three, he married a Roman Catholic girl but refused to go to confession. Meanwhile, one of his friends was converted and they both used to meet so that Oswaldo could hear the Word of God. One prayer meeting night, his friend found Oswaldo outside the church. He invited him in and he was soundly saved. He grew in grace and was appointed a deacon, reminding the missionaries of Nathanael – one in whom there was no guile.

After his conversion, his wife began to persecute him, tearing up his Bible, tracts and in general made his life miserable. But the church prayed and she began to attend the meetings. She didn't enjoy them because she had been taught that the Protestants were of the devil, but the Holy Spirit began to work. He convinced her of the truth and just before she had her first baby, she yielded her life to the Lord in her home and made her public confession as her baby was being dedicated. She then had to suffer persecution from Oswaldo's relatives but stood firm. At their farewell service to move to Londrina, they had the joy of seeing Oswaldo's mother in the meeting.

The World Pentecostal Conference was held in Rio de Janeiro in 1967 and, during that time, the Elim work in Brazil was visited by Pastor and Mrs. P.S. Brewster. In the central church, Pastor Brewster preached to a packed church of over 400 people, spoke to over 140 children, prayed for scores of sick people and visited three outposts where groups of adults and children meet several times a week. One of their visits was to Londrina where Oswaldo is the pastor. They preached to a crowd of hungry, cold people who sat and shivered in the church for two hours. There were converts and one man showed the congregation a dreadful ulcer that had been healed in the afternoon service.

In addition to travelling widely to see the work and minister in the churches, Pastor Brewster had the joy of opening the new church building in Socorro on July 9th, the anniversary of the Revolution and commemorated as a national holiday. This would also serve as the headquarters for the church in Brazil. The old temporary building was then moved to another location at Jardim Saõ Luiz. This was a church planted by a national evangelist in a hilly area where many poor families lived. The local lads loved to throw bricks at the building which was made of timber and compressed cardboard. By now, the building was looking much the worse for wear and the owner of the land asked for his land back.

The way for Pastor Brewster's coming had been prepared by Pastor Alex Tee, also in Brazil for the World Conference, who had conducted a short evangelistic campaign in the preceding days. He also spent time in Jd. Saõ Luiz where the old building from Socorro was in process of erection. The brick frontage had just been completed and Pastor Tee suggested that the whole building be built in brick, but funds were non-existent. Following his visit, Pastor Tee organised donations from Weymouth Vacation Venture and others and the building was completed on 6th December, 1967.

After some six years on the field, the Jefferys flew home on furlough in early 1968. The strain of their labours was evident, but a comfortable home had been provided for them by a member of our Ealing church. The children, Ann and Paul, seemed to be unconcerned by the rigours of air travel as opposed to the more leisurely transport that had taken them to Brazil on their outward journey.

The 1970 annual Conference in Brazil saw a number of changes that affected the ministry in the churches. There had been a period of consolidation and men were needed to take on additional responsibilities. Those involved had a chequered history, to say the least. Pastor Oswaldo Mengarda of Londrina was moved into the central church in Saõ Paulo after serving there for about three years. He endured much persecution from his family because of his stand for God. His place was taken by Pastor Norberto do Espirito Santo, an Assemblies of God worker before joining Elim two years previously. He laboured alone, his wife having left him some years ago to bring up five children on his own. The church at Jd.Saõ Luiz was in the charge of Moacyr Aguiar, a man who, before his conversion, was a wife-beater and a drunkard. Antonio Messias looked after the work at Narandiba, living by faith since there was no work in the township. The development of mechanised means of harvesting cotton did away with the need for manual labour, so the whole region was adversely affected. Others gave of their time and effort unstintingly in the service of the Master and against great odds. Indifference was rife and because of the economic climate, weeknight meetings almost died because people had to work so much overtime just to make ends meet. But God was faithful and so were they.

In Piraporinha, 80-90 children gathered every Sunday morning and their need was for a building of their own. The Pastor from Brasilia faced tremendous difficulties as the Government threatened to move some 56,000 people away from his region to resettle them further away from Brasilia itself. Their presence in their favellas[iii] was an embarrassment to the ultramodern city.

In 1973, the pastor in Londrina was appointed President of the Elim Work in Brazil and had to move to Saõ Paulo. His place was taken by Carlito de Oliveira. This man, four years before, had been suffering from TB, one lung having collapsed and the other being badly affected. He was haemorrhaging from the lungs and critically ill when the Elim pastor called to pray with him. First he gave him the gospel. Although unable to speak, Carlito nodded his acceptance of Christ. The haemorrhage immediately ceased, but the doctors insisted he should go to the hospital for an operation to save his life.

Although fearful about the operation, he remembered how the Lord had answered prayer. Soon he began to gain weight and to breathe normally. On his way home for a weekend, he asked the Lord for an assurance of his healing by arranging a baptismal service so that he could be baptised. As soon as he walked in the door, his wife told him there was a baptismal service in the Elim church right opposite where they lived.

On his return to hospital, further tests and x-rays were taken and he was declared to be completely healed. He began working for the Lord and was soon baptised in the Holy Spirit and making himself available for service.

Between 1946 and 1949, Henry Jeffery had worked in Londrina under the auspices of Peniel Chapel Missionary Society of London and on his return here in the '60s, he was invited to the area to open a new church. Because of the vastness of the country, one of the most effective means of evangelism was by radio. The work in Londrina had a regular radio broadcast. Soon after its inauguration, letters were received telling of conversions and healings. In response to the radio broadcasts, a paralysed lady sent in a prayer request for healing. As Pastor Carlito prayed on air, she was healed and presented herself at the radio station the next day to testify.

Through one of these healings, other centres were opened for the preaching of the gospel.

There were no financial resources so they worshipped initially in a rough tent made of canvas, then built a shaky structure in the front garden of a lady's home. The work progressed under Pastor Carlito's care and the radio programme was maintained by donations received from the UK. The writer had the joy of meeting and sharing fellowship with our brother during the early 1990s and he was still active in the work of the Lord.

STEPHEN and MAUREEN HUNTLY

On December 14th, 1974 Stephen Huntly with his wife, Maureen and his two boys, Mark and Stephen, farewelled from Smethwick en route to Brazil.

Most of the Brazilian churches are centred on the greater Saõ Paulo area but the work has extended 600 miles to the north to Brasilia, 200 miles west to Londrina, 100 miles south west to Curitiba.

In addition to the work of the churches, gospel radio programmes are broadcast daily over Radio Clube de Londrina and weekly over Radio Wenceslau. An outcome of these broadcasts is the planting of new churches as well as the winning of many souls for the Lord. Stephen Huntly reckoned that –

Gospel radio is one of the most effective means of evangelism. The message can reach people of all ages, in all walks of life, right where they are. It speaks to the man driving his car, the mother at work in her kitchen, the patient in hospital, the internee in prison. It goes into areas where the evangelist himself cannot go. . . We receive letters from children and teenagers, middle-aged businessmen and bed-ridden octogenarians. . . As a result of the Londrina broadcasts, six new congregations have been established. Another evangelist commenced a weekly broadcast. After six months, he had gathered a congregation of 150 on a farmstead fifteen miles from his other pioneer work in Presidente Epitacio. He has had letters asking him to open churches up to 200 miles away in Campo Grande.

One letter received from a young prison internee and counter-signed by the prison governor, said - "Before my conversion I was a spiritist. Many times before I was arrested and interned in the penitentiary, I passed by evangelical churches, but was afraid to go in because I thought I would not be welcomed. How glad I was to hear the message of pardon and forgiveness through our Lord Jesus Christ on your radio programme here in prison. Since surrendering to Jesus, I now devote my time to studying the scriptures and reading evangelical books."

The next extension to the work was the establishment of a Bible Institute built in Santo Amaro onto the headquarters building under the guidance of Henry Jeffery. It was anticipated that the Huntlys, after completing language study, would become responsible for this venture because it was felt, rightly, that the teaching and training of Brazilian workers would greatly enhance the work.

The system to be used was known as T.E.E. – Theological Education by Extension. Although there were many residential colleges for theology in Brazil, they were not scratching the surface of the need in touching leaders and workers who had little or no formal education. The financial considerations were enormous and the idea of leaving the locality for an extended period was just impossible. So TEE proved to be a viable means of extending the training to church leaders of all ages and educational backgrounds in the areas where they lived and worked. The Elim programme very quickly established itself with thirty-two workers and potential workers enrolled.

Shortly after his arrival in Brazil, Stephen visited Brasilia and was told of a meeting with Ronald Biggs, the Great Train Robber. While he was in the penitentiary in Brasilia awaiting extradition proceedings, he was witnessed to by another internee. This young man was arrested for allegedly being involved in the theft of guns from the local police headquarters. While there, he realised his lost condition and gave his life to Christ. During his time in prison, he had a number of conversations with Biggs. What fruit these produced eternity alone will reveal.

In the following year, Wesley and Marguerite Gilpin, on behalf of the EMC[iv], visited the work and were impressed by the progress made. Although the work was indigenous, Stephen Huntly had been appointed president for three years. The church's oversight is based on similar lines to that of the UK, with a six man Executive being elected annually and each church contributing 10% of offerings for the central funds.

The expansion of the work in Brazil was a major factor in the releasing of national workers for evangelism and church planting. In the annual Conference of 1976, Roque Arruda was set apart for just such a task. He had a vision for opening up the interior and he and Stephen made a start by obtaining a hall in the town of Campinal for a thirty day mission. During the first week, attendances averaged sixty, and thirty-two professed salvation. The following Sunday, the two evangelists did follow-up work and that night, 230 people attended the meeting, with 22 going forward for salvation. During the next two weeks, congregations were steady around 200 and all told, 120 decisions were registered.

When Roque went to see if they could hire the hall for another thirty days, the owner said he could have it free of charge for at least another two months!

It seemed as though this spark in Campinal ignited fires all over the nation as requests poured in for evangelistic efforts in the states of Matto Grosso, Minas Gerais and greater Saõ Paulo. The follow-up to one of these missions took Stephen and the evangelist to one of the favellas.

"Fragile - do not drop". I read the words as I knocked at the front door of Euclides' home. The other sides of the packing case made up part of the other walls of the shanty. On being invited to enter, I had to bend to get through the doorway and then continue standing in a stooped position because of the low ceiling. As I bent down to enter, the acrid smells hit me and I nearly vomited. On the bed in a corner was Euclides' wife, Ermelinda, where she had been lying for several months.

We were there because they had made a decision to follow Jesus and we were making a pastoral visit. We read and prayed and left them some clothing. It meant a lot to these people that someone had visited them in their home. There are thousands of people living like this in this area. Taking the gospel to them where they are is surely our task.

In 1979, the man who had been the first national President of the work in Brazil, Manoel de Melo, went home to be with the Lord. A report by Henry Jeffery describes his conversion as a miracle.

From infancy, Manoel was rebellious. His father died when he was eight years old and his mother soon had another lover. Manoel's heart revolted when he saw this man using his dead father's suits and so, at 13, he ran away from home and began a life of drunkenness and debauchery. He went to work in a manioc factory and slept on the factory floor. With his first wage, he bought himself a machete while his companions bought themselves hammocks to sleep in.

One day, the factory foreman saw the knife and Manoel was accosted; immediately the knife was out and there were three gaping wounds in the head and face of the man. A riot broke out and he had to flee. He had been brought up in a 'black magic' family and he said he knew prayers that enabled him to become invisible.

He refused to believe in God and said he believed only in himself. He had no peace, no light. He married a very fine Catholic girl only to give vent to his bad temper on her and their children. Moving to Saõ Paulo, he was soon planning an assassination. Through a very vivid dream, he was warned of the consequences of his crime and during this time, an accident occurred and he was taken to hospital with third degree burns. While there, he was visited by the man he wanted to kill, who said to him when he was leaving, "Trust in God". Thinking he would be scarred for life, he was discharged after only five days without a scar. "I knew then that there was a God," he said, "but I wanted nothing to do with the Protestant sons of the devil." This was the name given to Christians in those days.

During this time, the temporary headquarters of the Elim church was being built in the area where Manoel lived, and a friend of his attended the church. Much prayer was offered by the church for Manoel and his friends. One night, in a séance, he heard a voice saying, "Manoel, get out of here; this is not your place." He left the room and again heard the voice saying the same words. Kneeling in the forest for the first time in his life, he saw an angel in front of him who said, "Jesus is the One you must follow". He went to Elim the next night and accepted Jesus as his saviour. After a period of Scripture teaching, he became the pastor of the local church and, eventually, the first national President.

PAUL and ROSE JEFFERY

Following the return of the Huntlys to the homeland, Paul and Rose Jeffery took up the reins in Brazil. They had an appreciation of the work to be done from earlier exposure to the nation and spared no effort to carry the work forward. Their visitation of outlying churches was beneficial although extremely time-consuming. A visit to the church in Brasilia entailed a 20 hour drive!

One of the major problems they faced was syncretism which was so deeply embedded in the Brazilian psyche that it affected evangelical churches and had to be dealt with. Paul wrote at the time:

Though we preach justification by faith alone, to many of these people it seems incongruous that one should not earn favour with God by doing good works. Another sign of this throwback is that when prayer is made for the sick, whole families come forward. They seek not a cure for the body but a blessing such as the Roman Catholic Church gives. In spite of the immensity of the task, there were many tangible rewards and joy in service.

On Sunday, 24th May, 1981, Henry, Paul's father, had a heart attack and died. He had been feeling in his spirit a desire to return to Brazil to engage again in evangelism, but this was not to be. Just before church that morning, he had a heart attack and was taken to hospital where an injection brought him relief. In the afternoon and evening, he was feeling better, but at 10 p.m., he suffered another attack and died within two minutes. His funeral service was conducted by a long-time friend from Brazil, Rev. Mario Lindstrom[v]. Pastor Lindstrom described Henry as an apostle to Brazil and a glowing tribute by him was printed in the Elim Evangel[vi].

Elim in Brazil was founded by Henry and after twenty years, there were thirteen churches plus some smaller congregations. Many changes took place during that time because the churches had been blighted by the extreme fanaticism that assails many of the Pentecostal churches. There was a determination to bring Elim into line with a solid

Scriptural teaching but, unfortunately, many left as a result. Further changes were taking place in the recognition that they should address the needs of the whole man and, as a consequence, more emphasis began to be placed on the schooling and development of children.

The missionaries continued to perform a vital function to the Church. At that stage, Paul was visiting the churches, giving Bible studies, acting as Principal of the Bible school. There was an intention to open a day care centre for the underprivileged children of the city and the central church premises were altered to make this possible. World Vision was helping with information and advice at that time. Long term, there was a desire to open a Christian school although this never materialised. Overall, the commitment was to evangelise the unreached of Brazil and to ease the suffering of the underprivileged in any way that was possible.

One of the frustrations of the work was the readiness of some local authorities to make building sites freely available for the erection of churches. Sadly, lack of finance meant that many had to be refused. At that time, a building could be erected for about £2000 and appeals were made for support from the UK but there is no record of any significant response. Subsequently, the International Missions Board (IMB) became very involved in providing help as necessary for the support of the work in both fabric and ministry.

JOSE PEDRO FILHO

Following the return of the Jefferys to England, the work in Brazil was left largely to its own devices. Without an expatriate missionary, it learned to stand on its own feet, but always yearned for the back-up and support a missionary could give.

Jose Pedro Filho, who came from northern Brazil and was a worker in fibreglass, migrated to Saõ Paulo and became active in the church. He was subsequently appointed President and led the work until his untimely and tragic death as a result of accidentally falling from the roof of his house. Brazil was the first field to be unexpectedly thrown upon its own leadership resources. Pastor Jose Pedro Filho was leader of the Brazilian Executive, its Conference and pastors, seeking to further the work and establish new churches throughout the land. He became fully supported by the IMB, the first national leadership to be so.

In 1990, Elim entered upon a decade of evangelism relative to International Missions. Brazil was chosen as the first country to receive input and a strategy was devised for ministry. A survey of the work recognised that a major need was for a trained leadership. While some pastors were involved in correspondence courses, there was little practical help available.

The writer was delegated to address these questions and it was decided to arrange a series of teaching seminars addressing manifest needs. Teams of volunteers from ministers in the UK travelled to Saõ Paulo to lecture and minister and in all cases, their input was heartily received.

What was evident was that the earlier hopes for the development of the work had not materialised. The broadening of scope and diversification envisaged had never become a reality and recession was more the order of the day. There were various reasons for this. Partly, the economic climate all but dried up the financial base on which the church ran. Inflation rates were running at anything up to 60% and seemed to be increasing daily. While in principle, churches still paid their 10% to the central funds, that amounted to very little and the work was bolstered in some measure by Jose Pedro giving some of his UK-derived income for the benefit of the work.

Another reason was that, in the absence of a missionary, the indigenous church struggled with leadership questions. Some were placed in charge of churches who were, in effect, novices. Their Christian character was not fully formed and they were susceptible to outside influences in terms of doctrine, cultural factors and inducements. Many were educated to only basic secondary school level and few had any academic qualifications. They were working men who were launched on waters too deep for them.

There was also a measure of jealousy that the President received a stipend from the UK which they perceived made him very well off, while they were dependent on their secular employment with very little support from the church, if any.

A further problem was a dependency climate as some of the pastors were receiving support from central funds with no attempt at regulation or evaluation of their work. There was no restriction set in the time this might continue and this didn't provide any incentive for progress.

This was a subject addressed by the writer as relationships developed and the idea of a sliding scale, reducing over a period of years, encouraged people and pastors alike to take some responsibility for their situation.

i See chapter on India for early details.

ii Swedish ministers from the USA arrived in Belem, at the mouth of the Amazon.

iii Favella – timber and cardboard shanty towns built on the edge of cities. Some had electricity but few had sanitation of any kind.

iv EMC – Elim Missionary Council, the Executive committee of the Elim Missionary Society.

v Pastor Lindstrom was co-founder of the Bible Revival Churches in Brazil and was then a world-wide evangelist.

vi *Elim Evangel.* Volume 69, Issue 29, p.3.

CHAPTER 21

BRITISH GUIANA/ GUYANA

The work in British Guiana was commenced by John and Gladys MacInnes in 1949. Early indications for John's ministry were that he should go to China, but this was revised in the course of time and he found himself in South America in Georgetown, in the colony then known as British Guiana, now Guyana.

Their farewell from Greenock took place on 22nd March, 1949 as the church, packed with over 600 people, wished them God-speed. The preacher was Samuel Gorman who had been the minister in Greenock and had had the joy of leading John to the Lord. A donation from the Greenock Sunday school highlighted the interest that existed in the church at all levels and the MacInneses were assured of strong prayer backing as they set out.

Their voyage took them by way of Trinidad and there they were met by a pastor of the Pentecostal Assemblies of Canada (PAOC), brother A. Eggleton. This dear brother took them into his home where they enjoyed fellowship with his family, staying with them for almost a week and enjoying special meetings following a campaign by a PAOC missionary from Venezuela. They were invited to stay in Trinidad a further week, but a welcome service had been arranged in BG so they travelled on.

They arrived in Georgetown in May to a warm welcome from the few believers and a service in the home of Mr. and Mrs. Chow. There were about fifty adults and the same number of children present and decisions were made, among them eight year old Ian MacInnes. What a joy as the meetings were owned of the Lord and continued for a further two nights with further responses to the Gospel.

From the very beginning, John had an aggressive evangelism programme, involving himself not only in church work and open airs, but also in ministry to lepers, hospital patients and prisoners. Thankfully, he saw results in the open air and in the church and soon faced the dilemma of knowing how to accommodate the numbers attending church. Quite early on, he crossed the Demerara River (two miles wide at this point) on the ancient ferry to visit the only TB hospital in the colony. There he found hundreds of patients from all over BG and, among them, Indians from the interior. He visited all the wards giving out tracts and chatting with the patients, praying that the Word would bear fruit.

A further opportunity to preach the Gospel came when a children's dedication service was held. Mr. Chow had announced this before John arrived and on the day in question, twenty-nine children, from babies up to about age ten, were brought by their parents for dedication. The state of family life was abysmal and the plight of the children horrendous. Many brothers and sisters had different surnames; when parents split up, the children were often just turned out on to the streets and left to fend for themselves. In all

BG, there was not one single Protestant orphanage. Understandably, the crime rate was very high, many children being involved simply to exist.

The fact that there were no missionaries in the interior whetted John's appetite to spread the Gospel and although travelling was incredibly difficult, the work was nevertheless extended by all means. They were able to get right off the beaten track travelling by steamer, train, motor-launch, canoe, motor truck and on foot, sleeping in all sorts of places under all sorts of conditions. There was the added excitement of dealing with all the livestock – alligators, snakes, scorpions, centipedes, not to mention ants, spiders, cockroaches and a multitude of various beetles. River travel meant shooting rapids and dealing with waterfalls; land travel was on dirt roads that became quagmires in the rainy season; always there was the danger of falling into the ditches which were used for everything – irrigation of fields, washing dishes and people and sanitation!

But with perseverance, the villages were reached and the Gospel was preached. There was a response and there was also the encouragement of returning to a remote village and finding some who had previously decided for Christ going on with Him.

The work was developing rapidly and opportunities were multiplying. In a prison service, fourteen men stood for Christ, coming right out to the front before their watching wardens and fellow-inmates. Healings were taking place. One lady with sleeping sickness was brought for prayer then taken back to her village. Nothing was heard for some time and then the news came through that she was well. In the village of Anna-Caterina, a group of believers had been seeking the Baptism in the Spirit. A brother appeared a little later saying that five people had received an Acts 2 experience. One of the main themes promoted was that of the Second Coming, and the response was most positive. From time to time and in various places, services of water baptism were held. These were of great significance to the people because of their background. The people who came had made a verbal confession with their lips, then a practical confession with their lives. Now they were standing publicly to acknowledge their position in Christ. Locally, baptism marked the difference between those who were committed members and those who were not members.

According to some estimates, there were approximately ten million lepers scattered throughout the world, but no one had ever counted the numbers in BG. Just outside the small village of Unity, some twenty-two miles from Georgetown, there was a leper colony, but no one knew even there how many lepers lived in the colony. One nurse put the figure at over 300, while another simply said, 'hundreds'.

As John and another brother distributed Victory Tracts, many of the lepers had no hands to hold the leaflets and just stretched out two stumps to grasp them. Others had no eyes, some had no ears and others were affected in various parts of their bodies. As they conducted services in the wards, they came across one bright spot – a Christian. The disease had eaten away her fingers and her feet and was now affecting her eyes and ears, but there she was, sitting on the end of her bed praising the Lord for His salvation. She made no complaint concerning her condition, realising that it was better to lose parts of her body rather than her eternal soul. John described her as a light in a very dark place. They concluded their visit with an open air in the compound outside the main building where most of the men were lying. This meant that those confined to bed could still hear the service. The journey home took them about three hours, travelling on bicycles in the pitch dark of the rainy season. We can imagine their relief at arriving back in familiar surroundings, as John described it, weary, worn and GLAD!

Journeys were also undertaken by outboard motor boat as John visited Demerara, visiting various homes scattered along the river bank. In many cases, the only indication that there was a home was a pole stuck in the river as a landmark as the jungle appeared the same at all points. At the village of Alliance, some thirty miles up river, they held an open air, but the rain started so they moved under the largest of the houses – which were all built on stilts about four feet off the ground – and the service continued. The work was slow but productive.

Sometimes, he would travel by bicycle through a number of the Indian villages along the river and there he saw mosques and temples. The homes he saw were dirty, dilapidated wooden huts; the peoples' clothes filthy and ragged and there were open activities in looking for vermin in one another's hair just outside the huts. But these were the people for whom Christ died and he was determined to let them see that love personified.

Meanwhile, the work in their home, which doubled as the church in Georgetown, was going ahead with over sixty attending after about two years. Indeed people were turned away because there was no room and this emphasised afresh their need for a meeting place.

As a result of his open airs and vigorous activity, John's profile was raised to the extent that many who had no connection with the church sought him out to perform funerals for them. He saw this as a further opportunity to preach the gospel. Sadly, many of those he buried were victims of drinking, rum being a major curse in the country.

Despite difficulties in travel and weather, John maintained his programme of service to the prison. Indeed, on one occasion when the weather was so bad, he was tempted to stay home, thinking that he wouldn't even be expected. Nevertheless, he made the effort and, although soaked to the skin on his bicycle, was welcomed by the Warden who said he hadn't really expected him to come. But on that morning, after the service, ten men accepted the Lord as Saviour. One of the prisoners told John that the men had started a Bible class on Friday nights.

The breadth of John's ministry is indicated by the fact that he was asked to be the speaker at a National Young Life Campaign anniversary service in the Smith Memorial Church. This church was erected as a memorial to Rev. Jon Smith, known as Martyr Smith. He was a great friend of slaves and worked hard among them, leading many of them to faith in Christ. Because he taught them to read and write, the planters considered him dangerous and persecuted the slaves who attended his church. In 1823, the slaves rose in rebellion and were subdued only by force of arms. Smith was falsely accused, tried by Court Martial, found guilty and condemned to be hanged. While awaiting confirmation of his sentence from England, he was imprisoned in a garret and died as a result of the excessive heat. Later, the freed slaves built the church in his memory. Ten years later, the Emancipation Bill was passed in Parliament. The martyr had not died in vain. John counted it a privilege to preach the gospel from that pulpit.

Church life proceeded apace. Some 200 people, including parents and friends, attended the Sunday school outing and the day concluded with a service in the village of Buxton. People were being saved in the meetings in Georgetown. Travel was still difficult, even to the extent that the build up of mud forced John to clean it off his bicycle wheels three times on one journey. Eventually, he gave up and walked until he came to a better road. Even when using a horse, he had trouble and fell off, dislocating bones in his right hand. In resetting his hand, the nurse exerted such pressure that John fainted for the first time in his life.

One thing they had to contend with was the increasing effect of missionaries for counterfeit religions. Less than a hundred years before, there had been no Muslims or Hindus in the Colony, but by the end of 1951, over 56% of the population belonged to one or other of these two religions. The major so-called Christian religion was Roman Catholic which, at that time, controlled three daily newspapers in the country. In addition, there were four sects of 'Sabbath keepers' – Seventh Day Baptists, Seventh Day Church of God, Jordanites and the Seventh Day Adventists. The Jordanites, who were anti-white, held services in the open air. Their leaders wore long white robes and flowing beards, and they considered themselves a section of the lost tribes of Israel. Very few weeks passed without some new case of obeah (witchcraft) coming to light. A woman who had been killed in a road accident was discovered, less than twelve hours later, to have had her grave opened and her head tampered with.

One of the joys of ministry was to see the Lord answering prayer for healing. One lady was sick with a serious fever and unable to speak. After the laying on of hands she recovered and attended the prayer meeting the following night, testifying of her experience. In that same service was a lady who had had to use a stick for three years and had been unable to bend her knees because of extreme pain. After prayer, she was able to kneel in the prayer meetings. As the Lord confirmed His Word, so the requests came flooding in from Africans, Chinese and East Indians. As is so often the case, they were looking for a healer rather than a saviour.

A point of tension came for John and Gladys in 1954 when the time came for their oldest child, Ian, who was 13, to leave Guyana for Scotland for his continuing education. There was a tearful farewell on the quay as his Guyanese friends and his younger brother, Philip, wept to see him go.

Shortly after this, they were advised that they must stop holding services in the house within three months or vacate the premises. The church made this a matter of fasting and prayer and the Lord graciously answered. John was able to write home that 'since going to the new church, attendance at all services except the Gospel service has increased.' Sunday school rose to 154 and had ten teachers. The Government had imposed a ban on all open air gatherings of more than five people, but the church continued underneath the house and indoors. One of the greatest challenges was standing for the Gospel in the light of all the other religions had to offer, much of which was for the 'loaves and fishes' and not because of any religious belief.

A bright spot in the lives of the missionaries was a visit from Jean Ayling. Jean worked with BOAC and used some of her concessionary travel to visit various mission fields. Her visits were always welcome. Jean was exposed to the whole range of missions activities and was amazed to see what God had done and was doing. She was blessed and challenged by all she saw and sought on her return to present something of that challenge to the folks at home by means of slides. One of those major challenges was John MacInnes's desire to find a way to enlarge the new building. There were now over 200 attending and, once again, the place was rapidly becoming too small. Open air services, now free again, were attracting crowds of over 500 and were lasting for up to two hours.

By 1962, there were seven Sunday schools with twenty-two teachers associated with the work in Georgetown. At the anniversary services, over 400 Bibles, Testaments and books were given as prizes. There were twelve services every week at the main church and six branch churches. The young people's choir sang every night in the Gospel service. People were being saved, baptised and entering into a ministry for the Lord, sometimes at great personal cost.

After many years of faithful labour, John and Gladys needed to come home on furlough but this was delayed until John could find someone suitable to look after the work in his absence. Back in England, this need was laid on the heart of a young man recently out of Bible College and then ministering in the Elim Church in Lincoln. D.A. (Tony) Jones, a product of Cardiff City Temple, responded and offered himself to fill the gap for the period of John's furlough. He was excited to see the state of the work and discovered that there were opportunities to speak in school assemblies. He led a meeting fortnightly in a local day school when about thirty young people attended, mostly unconverted. He saw for himself the great impact that could be made by Christian literature and was keenly aware that the communists were flooding the country with their own propaganda. He appealed for supplies from the homeland so that the church would not be behind in reaching those in need.

During his furlough, John was able to visit the churches and, while in the Devon and Cornwall area, was presented with a cheque that enabled him to purchase a Gestetner duplicator which would be invaluable in the work on his return. The farewell took place in Croydon in October, 1964. Ian and Philip, their two older sons, remained behind as students at Elim Bible College and seven-year-old Joel accompanied them back to British Guiana. Some friends from BG were present and they testified that Pastor and Mrs. MacInnes were 'like mother and father' to them and to the many other Christians on the field. Undoubtedly, Gladys MacInnes was a help meet for her husband, maintaining the home and caring for the family. She was totally involved in the work and often played her piano accordion in the services and while travelling.

In the farewell service, John made reference to the young people and their commitment to Christ. He made special mention of Frank L. Douglas who, some time before, had surrendered his life to the Lord and had been in the church since it started some 15 years before. When he first started Sunday school, full attendance earned him a Bible as a prize. In his second year, his attendance was again perfect and he was told he could have a book, but he asked for another Bible – this time for his mother. By now, Frank had matured in his faith and had been appointed Director of British Guiana's Youth for Christ. He discovered in his work that young people were dedicating their lives to the Lord and seeking a closer walk with Him. His task was to seek to encourage more young people to take a stand against evil and for the standards of righteousness found in God's Word.

British Guiana, like India, looked forward to having its independence. Its new name would be Guyana, although it would take people a lot of time to become familiar with using just the one word. For many months, people had looked forward to independence and over 1000 Guyanese flew home from Britain, Canada, USA and the West Indies by less-than-half-price chartered planes. One of the benefits was that the MacInnes boys were able to pay a visit 'home', which greatly rejoiced the hearts of John and Gladys.

Independence took place around Easter and, in Easter week, there were five weddings to celebrate. The whole area was decorated and there were great festivities for both independence and weddings. Also in that week, John paid the last instalment on the mission church with the house above it. When it was announced to the church, there was great rejoicing because many years before, it was believed that if Elim was ever to have its own building, it would take a miracle.

In 1967, the Guyana field had a visit from Pastor and Mrs. P.S. Brewster. What they saw and heard astounded and humbled them as they considered the dedication that had brought the work into being. Pastor Brewster wrote to the *Elim Evangel* about what he had seen:

Our missionaries, John and Gladys MacInnes have laboured for God in South America for eighteen years. Undeterred by constant flies, mosquitoes and all kinds of insects, they have preached the pure Gospel of Christ in season and out of season. They are tireless and versatile in their dedication and have early morning prayer meetings at 6 o'clock. How they love these people; and nothing seems too much trouble for them to do for the aged members of the assembly.

When Pastor and Mrs. MacInnes obeyed the urge to go to Guyana eighteen years ago they literally started their pioneer missionary work from nothing. A few children gathered in their home, they preached in the open air, and eventually won a few precious converts for the Lord. Thus Elim was born in Guyana. Today they have a beautiful church, a home, and several out-stations run by the local men. They have a regular ministry in the local prison and a tremendous ministry in the leper colony. The church is very well attended and their thriving Sunday school fills the church to overflowing. But they have had so many setbacks, with some of their converts going for further education to Britain and the USA.

It is amazing how Mr. MacInnes can keep fresh, alert and on fire for God with all the variety of services and ministering. Undoubtedly, his passion for prayer contributes much to this.

It was such a blessing to stay in their home, to share ministry and to reap a little of what they have so faithfully sown. The visit to this missionary outreach is the highlight of a lifetime and can only make us thank God for such men and women.

Over 300 lepers, men, women and children, most of them in the advanced stage of this dreadful disease, will ever bless the day that Pastor and Mrs. MacInnes came to Georgetown. I personally spoke to almost forty lepers who could all testify to their personal salvation, and so many have been led to Christ through the ministry of our Elim missionary. How these unfortunate lepers love this compassionate man of God! He prays for them, lays his hands upon them, takes them in his car and has absolutely no fear of the disease at all. Some had no eyes, no hands, no legs. Others had shapeless bodies. Some lay on the floor; others hid behind curtains to hide their dreadful condition. In spite of all this, those who were saved were full of the joy of the Lord and thanking Him for His goodness in saving them.[i]

When Pastor Sandy Wilson visited in 1968 as part of his Presidential tour, he found much the same situation as described by Pastor Brewster. Having worked with John in the homeland for some years, it was exciting to renew fellowship and to see how the Lord had blessed these nineteen faithful years. Sandy was exposed to the full range of activities that made up the work of the church in Guyana and counted it a privilege to do so. His comment afterwards was, "The visit to this mission field has been the experience of a lifetime and has shown me that there are still some who 'count not their lives dear unto them'".

1969 – IAN MACINNES – MISSIONARY

Following in his father's footsteps, Ian MacInnes, with his wife, Valerie, was appointed a missionary to Guyana after training at Elim Bible College and a period of ministry in the homeland. His correspondence continued to highlight the ways in which the Lord was blessing the work, as well as the many challenges to be faced economically and politically. Churches continued to be opened and Sunday schools developed and grew, but the ongoing need was for workers and literature to counteract the many pressures brought about by the varying religions and philosophies encountered.

It was always a source of great blessing when the President of the Elim Churches visited the mission fields. In 1969, Leslie Green arrived in Georgetown on Saturday 26th

July. His welcome was warm – both in weather and in the temperament of the people. On the Sunday morning, he was impressed by the range of nationalities represented in serving at the Lord's Table – African, Indian, Portuguese and Chinese. During his visit, he held eighty-five meetings. He wondered if it was a coincidence that he preached sixty-seven times in twenty six days when he was sixty-seven years of age.

Always one for a laugh, he smiled when one wee fellow in Sunday school answered the question, "What was Isaac's father called?" with "Daddy". In one of his children's talks, two chickens began fighting and had to be wrenched apart. He thought that some might have considered that 'fowl play' but he saw it as an ideal illustration of his message.

The following year, it was Ron Jones's turn to visit as President. He was accompanied by his daughter, Glenys. During this visit, Ron had opportunity to visit and preach in the leper colony and in a youth camp that had eighty young people attending. Some twenty-seven responded to the appeal for dedication. In the leper colony, he listened to the testimony of seventy-nine year old Dorcas. She had first come to the colony at eleven years of age and had been responsible for several of the nurses accepting Christ. One of the things that impressed itself most on Ron's heart was the church's notice board which carried the legend – *Elim – The Mission with a message.* His desire was that this should be true, not only for Guyana, but for Elim worldwide.

Some years later, Ron returned, accompanied by Len Magee, arriving at 3 o'clock in the morning to be met by John and Gladys MacInnes. What a joyful reunion they had. Without any delay, they commenced their campaign that very night with Ron at the Middle Road church and Len some five miles away in Agricola. Their visit to the Leper Colony was a challenge and a blessing as they remembered saints who have left this scene of time and others who have come to faith in recent times. During the first six days of their mission, some sixty people indicated a decision for the Lord despite, in some places, being almost eaten alive by mosquitoes.

In 1973, during Ron's visit, Elim in Guyana had the opportunity to broadcast on Saturday 15th September from 9.15 a.m. to 9.45 a.m. It was an exciting, historic event. The service had been recorded earlier in the week and, although Ron and Len were to be involved for the first four weeks, John had to carry on from there for the next forty-eight. This also provided openings into other areas of broadcasting and interviews were set up over the period, with songs being played on air from Len's and Bristol's New Creation Singers' records.

In course of time, it was possible to gauge the impact of the broadcasts. Letters came in regularly and people approached church members to express their appreciation. In a baptismal service, two of the candidates had been saved through the broadcast. The Elim Half Hour was reaching far beyond the city boundaries and people along the coast and in the interior were picking up the broadcast and surrendering themselves to Christ.

Other areas of service included the Georgetown Prison where Ron preached and Len sang, and forty prisoners stood to indicate their acceptance of the message. They visited the Cambridge Academy and spoke to over 100 students, with five accepting Christ. On any given Sunday, at that time, Elim Sunday schools were teaching around 1300 children. At the leper colony they met with people who had lost various limbs and other parts of their bodies, but were shining brightly for the cause of Christ.

This visit was followed the following year by Archie Biddle. In the meantime, John and Gladys MacInnes had returned home for furlough and, at the Annual Conference that year, Mrs. A.V.Gorton, the E.W.M.A Secretary, presented them with a new vehicle, a Hillman Minx, bought by the ladies of EWMA.

Archie's first service was quite an introduction to Guyana. He was taken to the funeral of a high ranking police office who was buried with full honours including the police band and choir. Ian MacInnes conducted the service. The welcome service at night in the church was a little more normal! Archie had the great joy of ministering in the churches, Sunday schools and at the Mahaica Leper colony. Many of the services were held on street corners and under the houses which were built on stilts to help with ventilation and to protect from flooding.

One of the people he met who made a great impression on him was Sister Ten-Pow. She was in charge of the church at Middle Street, Georgetown and was responsible for a lively church filled with life and enthusiasm. Her testimony[ii] indicated that she had been won for Christ from the Moslem religion and, after much heart searching, as she was confronted by the life and witness of Christians, she came to know the Lord as her saviour.

Easter in Guyana was marked for the general population by two things – kites and picnics. These two activities occupied a major part of the weekend as people prepared themselves to leave the town and fly their newly made kites while indulging themselves in the prepared foodstuffs in the picnics. But in Elim, Easter provided opportunity for a wonderful week of services and celebrations with convention services and special speakers in the churches. The Good Friday communion service was always very special and it was encouraging to know that the majority of those taking part were local people.

The work continued apace as church buildings were erected to provide adequate meeting places for the work. In 1976, a "Build a Church" project was instigated in the UK and by the November, £2973 had been raised by the people of Elim at home. As a result, a good building was put in place and the work was enhanced. The church at Success was opened on April 4th, the following year. It was the culmination of many months of work and labour by the contractor and the men of the church. The opening day began with a march of witness from the place where the meetings had been held for the previous eighteen months. When they arrived at the new building, they found the members of the Mahaica church waiting for them. The congregation was truly multi-racial with East Indians, Africans, Europeans, Portuguese and Amerindians present. Roman Catholics, Moslems and Hindus gathered with many who had never been inside a Christian church before. It was estimated that over 90% of those present were from the immediate area. A subsequent evangelistic effort resulted in many coming to faith in Christ.

The work of Elim in Guyana was mainly among those of Indian or African descent, the former making up the main grouping in the population. Over the years, there had been strong cultural differences giving rise to major tensions and, while these were diminishing somewhat, they were nevertheless still a factor in ministry so that it was desirable that Indians reach Indians and African reach out to Africans. For this reason, part of the ministry was to see indigenous people saved and then commissioned as evangelists to their own people.

Besides the racial differences that had to be surmounted, there were also challenges from cults and isms, not to mention the pressure for people to accept a socialist view as the nation passed through a cultural revolution. This was taught in schools which were under total government control. Ian MacInnes stated that "there are problems with the divisions of race, but the problem of materialism, socialism and atheism are greater. These do away with the very thought and idea of God".[iii]

In August, 1977, there was a special need for Bible school seminars and teaching for the churches and Pastor and Mrs. Frank Frost responded to an appeal to serve. As a senior minister of many years' standing, Frank had much to offer the Guyana church. At this time, the Elim Church in Guyana had eighteen meeting places and other branch works for Sunday school and outreach. In two areas, there were thirty students in Bible school preparing for evangelistic work throughout the country. As a result of the ongoing radio broadcasts, two Bible correspondence courses were being offered. Their scope went far beyond the coasts of Guyana, reaching to other Caribbean countries. Children's Vacation Bible School was run by Valerie MacInnes, the numbers increasing daily until about one hundred children were attending.

Another minister from the UK who responded to the challenge of short term ministry in Guyana was Bill West with his wife, Ethel. Bill tended to go for short visits of about three months at a time, but he went often and those who knew him will remember his humorous reporting of his time there. His first report was entitled, "Shall all nature be vocal and sing?" and began –

The mosquito net gleams above me like a gossamer ghost as the moon shines into the bedroom window. Sleep will not come because I am not tired but all nature is having its say outside my indoor tent.[iv]

Then he talks about whistling frogs, dogs, then two donkeys that started braying and round-the-clock cockerels.

One of the things that impressed itself on Bill's mind was the proliferation of beggars. He found them in all arts and parts and was severely exercised in his own spirit as to his attitude to them. He came to the conclusion that many Christians who seemed to be physically well off were, in fact, spiritual beggars. They came for their few crumbs on a Sunday night but starved their souls for the rest of the week. They found themselves begging from the spiritual stores of others because they had failed to make provision for themselves.

In September, 1980, John MacInnes, pioneer of the work in Guyana, was suddenly called home. He had been pastoring the Elim Church in Armagh although some two years past retiring age. His death occurred during the annual Convention when the speaker was Pastor Bill Plowright. In a tribute to him, Pastor Tom Walker said:

Influenced in his Christian life by the ministry of the pioneer missionary to Mongolia, Joseph Payne, John MacInnes, who hailed from Greenock, used to spend nights out on his native Scottish hills in order to prepare for service in that land. His dedication to his call was an inspiration and a challenge. In the providence of God, he was not able to go to Mongolia but he was the founder of the developing work in British Guiana. Prior to going to the mission field, he had held pastorates throughout England and Northern Ireland from 1934 until he went overseas in 1949. On his return from Guyana, he became Elim's President in 1976 and returned to Armagh as pastor in 1978. He was a member of the International Missions Board from 1977 for a period of two years and his abiding cheerfulness and lively faith were a blessing to his fellow Board members.[v]

Needless to say, John MacInnes's departure from this life caused many who knew him to place on record their appreciation for his life and work. Ron Jones, who had visited the field in 1970, paid a glowing tribute to John and described him variously as a man of the Word; a man of his word; a man of vision and a man of work. He concluded by saying that the Elim Church in Guyana stands as a monument to his faithful ministry, his dedicated service and his sacrificial life.[vi]

David Ayling, the International Missions Director, described John as "one of those rarest of men, a legend in his own lifetime." He paid tribute to the extensive work developed as a result of John's vision and energy, to the extent that in all aspects of Christian service, Elim had a part to play. Churches were built, Sunday schools established, hospitals, leper colonies and prisons were all visited. Through the troubled days of independence, the church remained stable and quickly adapted to the new society, carrying forward the message fearlessly and with fervour. John was held in high esteem both inside and outside the church and was known by many as 'Brother Mac'.[vii] Bill West described John as "Guyana's great saint".

Although John died in Northern Ireland, the church in Guyana held its own thanksgiving service in memory of a beloved friend. The church in Albert Street, Georgetown was packed as the congregation sang, 'To God be the glory' and Sister Ten-Pow gave a tribute to the work that John had accomplished. She recalled the hardships and sacrifices of the early days and challenged all present to a new commitment to service. John's life was summed up by brother Ramdeen's opening remarks – A great heart has stopped beating; a shining light has gone out; the bugler has sounded the last post; another soldier of Christ has laid down his arms, not in surrender, not in defeat, but in death on the battlefield under the Captain of his salvation under whom he sought to bring others to life everlasting. In his memorial service in Armagh, the church elder indicated that written on the flyleaf of John's Bible was – "When I am dying how glad I shall be, that the lamp of my life has burned out for Thee."

Meanwhile, the work in Guyana continued to grow as the Wests maintained their input. One of Bill's major projects was to produce a Bible School course and having got a batch of students through to graduation, the course was then adapted as a correspondence course for the training of future ministers and workers. In 1982, Pastor Robert Robb and wife visited to see the work and stayed with the Wests. Needless to say they faced a massive culture shock as they took in the various sights, sounds and smells. Comparisons with the UK norm showed how challenging the work was as materials were sought and found to help the work. Robert and Sue were able to hold short campaigns which were blessed of God as souls surrendered themselves to the claims of Christ. They were particularly blessed by their final service, held in the prison chapel, when they saw almost the whole congregation respond to the Word.

The work at Georgetown Prison was founded by John MacInnes when the authorities gave permission to hold a service on any fifth Sunday in the month, which was about once in every three months. As time passed, the prisoners became familiar with Elim and as the ministers were escorted through the prison compound to the chapel, the officers would call, "Elim, Elim", and soon the chapel would be full. At the close of one service, the men asked that the Elim people come more often, so an approach was made to the Governor by Ian MacInnes and Sukhdeo Somwaru (Sam), who granted them permission to come once a month on the third Sunday. God richly blessed this area of the work and soon, many of the prisoners had not only accepted Christ, but were signed up for a regular correspondence course.

One of the significant aspects of the work in Guyana was the calibre of local men who became established in the leadership of the church. This was one of the factors that impressed Wesley Gilpin when, as Chairman of the Missions Board, he visited in 1982. In 1984, one of these men attended the annual Conference at Clacton-on-Sea. Bristol Carter was in his late twenties when he received Christ at a Crusade by the Full Gospel Fellowship in Guyana. His early Christian life was not easy due to parental opposition. His work and academic studies led him away from the rural community in which he was born and brought him into contact with Elim.

He spent three years in Trinidad and gained a B.Sc. degree in Agriculture at the University of the West Indies and, while there, was in charge of a small Christian fellowship on the University Campus. On returning to Guyana in 1977, he was a lecturer at the Guyana School of Agriculture for 1½ years before being transferred to work as an Agricultural Officer in charge of a drainage and irrigation project. He became the Lay representative of his home church in Guyana and a member of the executive Council in 1978. In 1982, he came to England to pursue studies for an M.Sc. in Agricultural Engineering at the National College at Bedford.

In 1987, the Guyana church lost one of its indomitable indigenous stalwarts, Sister Ten-Pow:

At the age of eighteen, she was married to Eric Victor Ten-Pow and God blessed them with nine children.

In July 1940, seven years after her marriage, she accepted Christ as her personal Saviour and, immediately afterwards, she became a glorious witness to the saving power of the living Christ.

Her ministry began in the early 1960s when she commenced counselling classes; she also convened inter-denominational prayer and fasting meetings, which moved the hand of God to bring many World Harvest Missionaries to join forces with us when our country was on the brink of political upheaval. God filled her with His Holy Spirit and, in 1968, the bottom flat of her building was partly enclosed to house just a few believers who originally met for prayers. Under God, Sister Ten-Pow single-handedly consolidated this work and, until the time of her death, was its God-appointed and anointed Pastor. She was used by God to pioneer three branch churches for Elim, and was also an able assistant in laying the foundations of other Pentecostal Assemblies in Guyana. Her ministry included the training of some workers and pastors, some of whom are Pastors today. On April 28th, 1972, she was officially ordained as a minister of the then Elim Mission in Guyana, and served uncompromisingly throughout her years as Pastor, Mother, Teacher, Counsellor and Servant. She was an example of a believer to all who really knew her; she led from the front and was filled with the Spirit.[viii]

Over the years, Bill and Ethel West travelled to Guyana several times, even following his retirement from pastoral ministry in the home land. The challenge of that nation was always on their hearts. In a very human sense, Bill asked himself why he did it.

Lying in bed one night, I thought, "I must be crazy. I didn't have to come. There are no rats to contend with at home; the water and electricity supply is reliable; cooking facilities are sure. Why leave all that?" His response to himself was interesting. "Apart from the spiritual challenge and the will of God, life is more than interesting. Lying under a mosquito net listening to a cockerel choir at 2 o'clock in the morning isn't everybody's idea of retirement, but it has its own spice of adventure. At least, we are not bored."

The bottom line for Bill was that Guyana needed Christ and, like so many other places, needed to see Christlikeness in the lives of men and women. Despite the difficulties and pressures, which included floods, shortages and sometimes earthquakes, the work prospered. The input of so many secured the work and allowed the indigenous work to develop and strengthen until, today, it is self-supporting and strong, filled still with a zeal for the lost and for the glory of God.

i Report by P.S. Brewster: *Elim Evangel*, Vol 48; Issue 39, p.620, 628.

ii Sister Ten-pow's testimony was printed in full in the *Elim Evangel* Vol.52, Issue 41, pp. 10, 11, but a tribute was paid to her on her death.

iii Ian MacInnes in *Elim Evangel*: Vol.57. Issue 52-52, p.7.

iv Bill West in *Elim Evangel*. Vol.60. Issue 28, p.16.

v Full tribute appears in *Elim Evangel* Vol.61. Issue 40, p.3.

vi *Elim Evangel* Vol.61.Issue 42, pp. 8, 9.

vii *Elim Evangel* Vol.61. Issue 43, p.6.

viii *Elim Evangel* Vol.68. Issue September 1987 Mission News. Report by Bristol Carter.

CHAPTER 22

HONDURAS

In 1979, David Ayling, the International Missions Director, on behalf of Elim, entered into negotiations with Dr. Ernest Soady, American President of the Evangelistic Missionary Crusade, based in California, USA. He had a work in Honduras that came about in the early 1970s after an evangelistic tour through Mexico and into Central America. He was accompanied by Josie Bullock and Avril Hopkirk, two English nurses and, together, they set up a work in the Red Light district of Tegucigalpa, the capital. Initially, this had care of four children, but the devastation caused by Hurricane Fifi caused the work to explode overnight, increasing the number of children to 75. Fortunately, a piece of ground was made available by the wife of the President and the work developed from there. The orphanage was based in the Valley of the Angels, known locally as La Finca de los Niños.

The agreement between EMC and Elim was that Elim would supply missionaries and workers, but that any evangelistic work would be done only under the direct oversight of the Soady family. The first missionaries to be sent out were Paul and Pat Cooper with their sons, Vivian and Michael. They hailed from Chippenham in Wiltshire and, in the first instance, spent six months on language study in Valencia in Spain.

The Coopers had felt a call to missionary service for some time and after seeing some photographs of Honduran orphans, they offered themselves for service there. At this time, Josie was running the orphanage, but on their arrival, was away on furlough. This made settling in somewhat difficult at the beginning because of cultural differences, but on her return, things soon settled into a working routine and the Coopers' expertise and abilities complemented others on the site to make the work run smoothly.

While the main work was church-based evangelism and teaching, the social needs that imposed themselves daily also demanded attention. So, much time was spent farming, building and associated legal work. But God's work is never easy! The death of the Missions Director, David Ayling, meant that some things were not proceeded with, and the delays caused by the interim settling down period provided frustrations for those on the field. The situation was not improved by Paul being run over by his truck and having malaria. Pat contracted hepatitis from one of the children and diarrhoea was a killer for the babies. A young man working for Tear Fund on the farming end of the work had an unfortunate accident when a child was run over and killed.

When the Coopers left the field in March 1983, there were no immediate replacements. It was not until 1987 that Andy and Sheila Graham offered themselves for the work. Andy had been the manager of an adult training centre for the mentally handicapped and Sheila was a nursery nurse. She later developed her expertise in counselling. Although they had no children of their own, they had been fostering for the

Local Authority over a four year period. Children aged from infants through the early teens had been placed with them.

They had first become interested in the Honduran orphanage in 1984 and, over subsequent years, the subject kept cropping up. Eventually, in 1986, they made enquiries of the IMB as to the possibilities of working in the region. Elim had, by this time, been working in the area for some years. The work of running the orphanage was in the hands of Josie and Roque Carrenza. The Grahams were accepted for the work, their first priority being to do language study, so they joined Andy and Yolanda Smith and Isobel Stormont in Figueres in Spain and received expert tuition there. So it was that, after months of preparation and language study, they flew out from Heathrow on Wednesday, 26th August, 1987.

In his first report, Andy told how, arriving in Tegucigalpa, they then had an hour's journey into the mountains to the orphanage. This would be their home for the next three years. On arrival, they were welcomed by a scrum of 130 children all wanting to say 'hola', carry a bag or just touch the new missionaries. Early adjustments included the climate – hot and humid – and time – up at 5 a.m. every day! A daily routine was established and Andy set about clearing up some outstanding jobs. The major priority was to repair and service the Land Rover.

Needless to say, the responsibilities were wide and varied. Sheila taught classes in sewing, cutting and caring for children's hair, making clothes, assisting in the clinic and teaching home craft. Andy's job was to run the local church, oversee the stores for the kitchen, feed the chickens, clean the drains, repair anything that was broken and supervise getting up and going to bed. Shortly after their arrival, Josie and Roque took a vacation, so the Grahams had to come to grips with the running and oversight of both church and orphanage.

There was limited support from the homeland. From time to time, Pathfinders[i] came for short term service periods. One of the mainstays of the work was Jennifer Cox of Derby. She made it her mission to organise the filling and transportation of 40foot containers. One container was held up in Customs for seven weeks and then delivered with just ten minutes advance warning.

The Grahams' time on the field, which ended in 1994, was not without incident. Sheila was injured in a bomb blast and Andy was involved in the shooting and death of a passenger in a car he was driving. Andy also fell off a roof and injured himself quite badly. While on the field, three out of four of their parents died, making for a great grief upon them both. On the up-side was the fact that they became involved with the expatriate community and found themselves invited occasionally to some rather upmarket social functions.

An insight into the variety of the work was given in a report in 1988:

The news from the church is encouraging this month as there have been two baptismal services with a total of six candidates. The service was held at night in the lounge and garden of Josie's house, using the swimming pool as a baptistery. Some of the tasks falling to my hand in recent months have been - tackled three forest fires, fitted a new pump to the well, installed windows in a workshop, put in a new water supply to the laundry, sorted about 4000 pairs of shoes into types and sizes and tackled some electrical repairs.

In addition to this, there are the normal duties involved in the running of an orphanage - dealing with broken bones, petty theft, staff replacement, buying in supplies and just giving a child a cuddle. There were also five services a week in Spanish. Now and again, he was able to say 'hello' to Sheila!

Sheila's side of the work had its challenges too:

Liseth's father brought her to the orphanage saying that her mother could no longer look after her. The baby, aged about 14 months, was undernourished, with the development of only an eight month old baby. She was unable to sit up on her own, and had not been weaned onto solid foods. It took a few weeks of care before she was able to take solids and for her condition to improve.

About one month later, Liseth's father returned saying that her mother had died and he had no hope of ever caring for her. Could a good home be found for her? Within a couple of days, the father returned saying that his wife had not died, but was half-dead. He meant that she was paralysed from the waist down one side. Then, he returned to say that his wife's family had accused him of selling the baby, so could he have her back for 24 hours to prove she had not been sold?

On another occasion, a grandmother brought her two granddaughters, aged 3 and 21 months along with her own daughter aged four. These children were fairly well looked after but the youngest one was badly undernourished. The orphanage cared for them for three months without hearing anything from either the children's mother or grandmother. Then, the mothers of the children suddenly appeared and, within 24 hours, had taken all three children away. These were typical of the frustrations and problems that were part of the day to day working of the orphanage.

After the Grahams returned from the field, the IMB conducted a review of its strategy in Honduras. After much deliberation and prayer, it was decided to sever the links with the orphanage and the Soadys. Part of the reason for this was the historical agreement that restricted Elim from doing evangelism and church planting. It was felt that this cut across what we saw as our main ministry.

It had become clear that the orphanage was only partly so. It was, to some extent, being used as a child care facility and it was not unusual for a child to become an inmate for a period of years, only to be claimed back by a parent once it was old enough to be used to generate finance for the family.

During the review, it was discovered that there was operating in Honduras a small group of churches calling themselves Elim. Investigation showed that these had come into being following a visit by David Ayling, but they had never sought official recognition. Discussions with the leaders indicated that their ethos was acceptable to Elim and it was therefore decided that we would remain in Honduras, develop an affiliation with the existing churches and that we would engage in church planting and the establishment of day care centres. This was set in motion under the leadership of Alex and Alethia Grannum and has proved to be most fruitful.

i Pathfinders: short term missionary placements encouraged by the IMB at individual expense. Usually lasted about 3 or 6 months.

SECTION FOUR

INDIA & THE FAR EAST

23. China/Hong Kong 233
24. India 245
25. Japan 273
26. Malaysia 277
27. Mongolia/Formosa/Taiwan 281
28. Thailand 295

CHAPTER 23

CHINA/HONG KONG

JOHN and MABEL McGILLIVRAY

While Elim, as such, never had a recognised field in China, there were connections that had a bearing and influence on Elim work. Specifically, John's two children, Ken and Vera became recognised Elim missionaries in works that, for political reasons, centred predominantly on Taiwan and Hong Kong. For this reason, it is appropriate that a short résumé of John McGillivray's labours be included in this work. There can be no doubt that his dedication to the Chinese people had a significant bearing on the later ministries of his children.

John McGillivray was born at Burntisland in Fife on 9th March, 1884. Left an orphan at four years old, his mother's dying prayer was answered twenty years later when he was converted at a mission in East Wemyss, this being followed by his receiving the Baptism in the Holy Ghost and a subsequent call for service in China.

In the autumn of 1910, he sailed for China, one of the first band of workers sent out by the Pentecostal Missionary Union (PMU)[i]. While studying the Chinese language in Honan Province under Pastor Stanley P. Smith, he met his future wife, Miss Mabel Seagrave. After their marriage in 1913, they laboured for six years in Choni, a Chino-Tibetan settlement in Kansu, in association with A. B. Simpson's Christian & Missionary Alliance (CMA).

Following the 1911 Revolution, missionary work was completely changed, but never monotonous. Co-labourer with the McGillivrays, Pastor Charles Coates, declared that "the thrills that redeem it (from monotony) are of a kind that Europeans would rather be without".

Those years witnessed the raids of White Wolf, the Honanese Brigand, who streaked the northern provinces of China with blood and ruin, varied with other disturbances by Chinese Moslems and Tibetan Buddhists together with epidemics of 'flu and pneumonic plague. The McGillivrays and Mrs. Coates, serving then on another part of the same frontier, waited with some trepidation the arrival of the raiders in their own city.

But God is faithful and news filtered back of blessing. One letter told of an evangelist who was being mightily used of God. He had a boy of 18 months who died. The custom in China was to bury the children at once, but he refused. Instead, he prayed to the Lord that He would raise him up and, after two hours, breath came back into his body and, some time later, the missionaries saw him, a sturdy, healthy boy, full of life.

This was the second person to be raised to life. The other was an old man in his coffin. The evangelist prayed for him, took him by the hand and he sat up. His relatives got an awful shock as they did not want him to live. However, he lived for a few days after that. The reality of Jesus' mighty power could not be denied.

While on furlough in 1919, Mr. & Mrs. McGillivray resigned their connection with the CMA, and the closing decade of our brother's service, for the most of which he was still accompanied by his faithful wife, in turbulent Kansu, is a record of heroic endurance in situations of upheaval and terror truly Asiatic.

Two great earthquakes, in 1920 and 1927, each accounting for some 100,000 Chinese lives, wrecked considerable areas of the province, while the people were further decimated by successive years of famine caused by harvest failures, aggravated by savage guerrilla warfare between Moslem rebels and Government troops, both of whom, in the intervals of fighting, behaved like brigands to the people, while pestilence again added its quota to the misery.

Much of the missionaries' time during this period was devoted to the wounded, the sick and the dying, both civilian and military, in a truly apostolic service which was so valued by the Governor of the province that he honoured our brother with a Chinese decoration.

The close of John McGillivray's service was further shadowed by a considerable period of physical suffering, endured in separation from his beloved life-partner, who had some time before left for England with their children, and who just then hoped to welcome him home soon. Working thus alone, it was while setting out in May (1928) upon a pastoral visit to a sick Chinese woman some distance away that his horse fell and threw him into a stream. Unable, under the conditions of travel, to change his soaking garments, he contracted a chill and was eventually carried back to Minchow on a cart.

Pneumonia and dysentery supervened and slowly, but surely, his strong frame was reduced to a mere skeleton in the weeks of suffering. Yet his continually triumphant faith and joy in Christ were such that Rev. W.W. Simpson, who had him in care, was hopeful even to the last that he would pull through. But it was not to be for on August 16th, at 10.30 p.m., with over 2000 miles of brown Asian soil between him and civilisation, he peacefully departed to his reward with only two faithful Chinese attendants at his bedside. He was laid to rest in a small graveyard belonging to the local Christians just outside war-wrecked Minchow.[ii]

Vera McGillivray

In early March, 1947, Vera McGillivray sailed for China, expecting to land at Shanghai on 3rd April and then travel onwards to Mongolia. Her vision was for the unevangelised people of Mongolia, but initially, she remained in T'ung-Hsien working with native Christians and seeking to minister to those in need in the local Chinese Military Hospital. Meetings were held throughout the hottest days, but the battle-scarred sons of China, despite horrendous injuries, responded eagerly to the Gospel. Many were so badly wounded that they were never expected to return to fight again and the concern was that there was no Government compensation for them and no home for incurables. Vera often thought of the scripture, *"without God and without hope in the world."* A campaign was held with open airs and meetings in the church at midday. These were well attended and, on the last Sunday, they held a baptismal service. The testimonies were a blessing, especially from those who were regulars in the Chinese army and who had come to faith. This was particularly poignant as the men were engaged in a civil war and knew that they might be killed at any time. Indeed, one such young man, just three weeks after giving his testimony in Church, was ushered into the presence of the Lord.

Some five months later, Vera travelled by train for about ten hours from Peiping to Kalgan, which she described as 'another step nearer to Mongolia'. She felt quite keenly the pain of parting from workers with whom she had developed a significant bond and a tie of love. But her vision was still for Mongolia and, she said, that kept the pull in her heart fresh.

Arrived in Kalgan, Vera's priority was to make her accommodation habitable, find furniture and clean it sufficiently to make it into a home. Despite a liberal use of DDT, she had to share her home with the hordes of wood lice that enjoyed her hospitality. Before long, however, she was being called into areas of ministry as she delivered two Chinese baby boys. She also had opportunity to visit the local jail where there was freedom to preach and sing the Gospel. An item for a radio broadcast was also required. Alongside these duties, she had to give time to Chinese language study and she also wanted to begin studying Mongol ready for when she would be able to go into the country.

One of the benefits of being in Kalgan was that there was a work already going on among the Mongol population of the city. Two years previously, the city had been freed from communist rule and a Norwegian Pentecostal missionary had been able to rent a building on a main road of the upper city. The meeting room at street level was used to bring Mongols into contact with the message of the Gospel and, for many years, this lady had been faithful to her calling. Now, though almost blind, she was still an inspiration to missionaries and Mongols alike. Although the work had been slow at the beginning, she had been joined by some Swedish Mongol missionaries and they had prayed that refugees would take advantage of the good opportunities to hear the Word of God. After a week or two, numbers began to increase until it was impossible to accommodate them all. In just a few weeks, numbers jumped from 10 or 15 to between 60 and 80. Finally, a new hall was rented that could seat 100 but, at the first meeting, 130 turned up. However, although numbers attending were encouraging, results were few and far between.

Kalgan was the gateway to Mongolia, while three hours north lay the city of Shan-Tu-Hsien, where she hoped to able to help a struggling work. Stories from that area were heart-rending as the communists moved in from the north, driving all before them. Many Mongols had fled to seek refuge in some of the large border cities, but many were killed and others lost all they had. Numbers were forced to sleep without shelter of any kind and without protection from the heavy frosts and autumn rains. In some places, snow had already fallen and the sub-zero temperatures of mid-winter made their position extremely dangerous.

Around the same time, Vera's brother, Ken,[iii] had ventured into Mongolia almost to the Russian border and had sent encouraging news that the people there were more open to listen to the Gospel than they had been in previous years. At this time, there were no missionaries north of the Great Wall in Chahar Province (Inner Mongolia) but this only made Vera more determined than ever to press on.

The continuing advance of communist forces in North China meant that all British nationals were being encouraged to leave the area while there was still transport available. Despite that, Vera continued to move on with the work and found it possible to visit a Mongolian encampment. She was called there to offer medical aid to several who were ill. In one tent, she and her interpreter found three families, about eight adults and six children. The tents were twelve feet in diameter and, opposite the door, was the tent altar. In the centre was a mud-brick stove and communal cooking pot, often used for other things as well. When Vera arrived, the pot was wiped out with an all-purpose piece of cloth(!) and then filled with water and some tea; to this was added rancid butter and one or two other indiscriminate ingredients. The wooden bowls were brought from among the dirty bedding and junk heaps and they, too, were wiped with the cloth. Vera fully expected that they would then be licked clean in Mongolian style, but they were spared this. Tea was then served with pieces of grey, wet, sour bread. Only then did she begin to dispense her medical help.

Passing from tent to tent, they were conscious that disease and poverty held sway. The following day, she returned, taking a Swedish missionary with her who could speak to them of the Gospel. The hope was that the people would see that Jesus was the answer to their needs despite their dreadful situation.

Unfortunately, the time came when the missionaries had to leave the area because of the continuing advance of the communists into northern China. Ultimately, this served their purposes very well because they found themselves involved with a relief convoy that took them further into Mongolia than they had previously expected. They travelled some way on the backs of the lorries and then the rest of the journey was accomplished by train. When they arrived in Kuai Sui, the missionary party split into two and Vera remained in the city for a short period of rest. There was a thriving Youth for Christ there and she was invited to take part one night. About sixty students attended and there was a real sense of the Lord's Presence. The following Sunday, all China united in a day of prayer and fasting, calling on God to bring an end to the chaos that was sweeping their land. This was the first time this had ever happened.

By now, Vera was feeling very much at one with the Mongol people. Arrived at their new station in the Patsebolong region, there was much to do. With Scandinavian missionaries away preaching, Vera and another ex-Kalgan missionary found themselves immersed in medical work at the clinic. They saw an average of thirty patients a day and dealt with all manner of problems, ranging from sores and abscesses to people suffering from VD. There were dental extractions, setting of a dislocated jaw and people who had been injured in fighting among themselves.

A party from the mission station travelled by camel, horse and donkey to a Mongol temple where a devil dance festival was being held. While the festival was in progress, the missionaries had a busy time preaching, selling Gospels, giving out Scripture portions and tracts and attending to sick folk. The desire was to bring the light of the Gospel into the darkness that pervaded these temple gatherings.

Unfortunately, less than a week after their arrival in Patsebolong, there was news of heavy fighting just 100 miles to the east and that the first line of defence was to be 100 miles to the west. This placed the missionaries right in the centre of the danger zone. Soldiers fleeing from the 'reds' passed them by on foot, horse, bicycle and with carts. Bridges were destroyed and dikes on the canals were breached. It was necessary for the missionary party to leave so they packed all their goods into the one lorry they had as well as on their camels and set off. The lorry provided a shuttle service while the camels travelled overland. In the process, the lorry was shot at twice and one of the camels was almost lost in quicksand. Rivers had to be crossed on rickety ferries. Finally, they arrived in Shih Tsui-Shan where they were accommodated by Swedish Pentecostal missionaries, Mr. and Mrs. Newman.

In spite of the political turmoil, the work continued and Vera moved on to Teng-K'ou where she reported much blessing and numbers being saved. They were sensing a real move of the Holy Spirit in their work. There was satisfaction too in seeing a hunger among the believers for a closer walk with the Lord. The uncertainty of those days was manifest as the missionaries sought the Lord's will as to whether they should stay or go. Their feeling was to stay and see what reaction there would be when the communists came, but others, who had been closer to the action, were advising that it would be wisdom to leave as their work would be seriously hindered once the 'new China' had been brought in.

In view of the impending invasion, other spheres of labour were sought and it was decided to move into areas of Mongolia not yet attacked by the communists. They therefore took a boat up river to Kansu and Tsinghai where they felt they could continue to spread the Gospel without too much hindrance. Because of the situation, communications and mail were at an all time low, so there was little news arriving in the UK to tell of the developments in the country. Once communications were re-established, it was obvious that there had been major developments in the nation relative to the missionaries and their work.

It was about six months before Vera was able to report that there were tight restrictions on the movement of foreigners but hoped this would be eased shortly. Nevertheless, the work continued with preaching, language study and, so long as there were supplies, the medical work was maintained. All the time, there was a desire to expand the work and, as soon as it was feasible, and depending on travel permits, Vera, with one of the Scandinavian Alliance missionaries, Angeline Bernklau, planned to move north east towards Paotou with a view to reaching out to the Mongols in that area. The major problem they faced was the effects of the total breakdown of law and order that had given rise to a widespread infestation of armed bandits and brigands who were killing and robbing all over the place.

By March, 1951, the situation in the country had so deteriorated that it was felt wise for Vera to leave the area, so she found transport that brought her to Hong Kong, a journey of twelve days which she considered good going! In Hong Kong, she met up with her brother, Ken and his wife, Wynn who were en route to Formosa (Taiwan). She expressed the feeling that she wouldn't mind going there as well but wondered if the communists might seek to 'liberate' Formosa as they had done China. But her concern was still for the Mongolian people. As the missionaries had retreated, for the first time in over one hundred years, there was not one missionary left in the thousands of miles of countryside.[iv]

For about three years, Vera worked in Formosa until her return to Hong Kong where she rented a hall and pioneered a church, and also gave herself to teaching. In the intervening years, she saw young people coming to faith in Christ and rejoiced with them at their baptism.

While in Formosa in I Lan, she saw the Lord at work and, side by side, the devil's strategy in ruining lives that had been committed to Christ. The Christmas period was particularly difficult as unsaved husbands demanded that their wives and families involve themselves in the merry-making. This led to some backsliding. There was also persecution and some soldiers had their Bibles taken from them. Senior people in army camps and hospitals ordered their workers not to attend the meetings. During a hospital service, the missionaries were told that a mentally deranged patient was a backslider who had once been baptised at their church. Demon possession was evident. Such were the discouragements that they faced, but God remained faithful.

Evangelism was always a priority and a visiting Chinese lady evangelist was much blessed in her labours among them. She and Vera spent many hours on door-to-door visitation followed by evening public meetings. There was also an encouragement when they found it possible to put down a deposit on a piece of land on which they could build a church. Indeed, it was regarded as a miracle and a direct answer to prayer. The money was supplied through the home call of a missionary-minded sister who, during her lifetime, sacrificed for missionaries. After she passed on, her daughter felt it right to construct a church in memory of her mother. The money was expected to be just the right amount.

A Mrs. Wang gave her heart to the Lord and began to learn that prayer really works. She was then the mother of four little girls, but her unsaved husband threatened that if she didn't produce a son, he would take another wife – a feature common in China. Almost a year later, Vera had the great joy of putting a beautiful baby boy into her arms after a safe delivery. That increased Mrs. Wang's faith and her belief in the power of prayer.

There were other encouragements too. One soldier, who attended the I Lan church, was saved about 18 months previously when the missionaries visited a military hospital at Nei-Yuan-Shan. At the time, he could neither read nor write, but since coming to the Lord, he learned to do both because he wanted to read his Bible. He was rising at 3 a.m. each day to read and pray and walked for an hour four times a week to attend the meetings. Always first there, he would sweep and dust the whole place. Then he came under an order which required him to be in the barracks by 9 o'clock every evening, which would have denied him access to the evening meetings, but he still turned up. When asked how he managed it, he replied that the punishment was only confinement in barracks for two or three days, so this meant that he would be free for the next meeting and he felt it was well worth the effort.

Ultimately, Vera's time in Formosa came to an end and she returned to Hong Kong on a more or less permanent basis.

HONG KONG

At one stage, she wrote asking for help for people who had been devastated by a typhoon and had lost homes, clothes and, in some cases, loved ones. She was also instrumental in calling Pastor Chang Tung Hua to the work of the church in Hong Kong. This man was active in Taiwan and had seen much blessing on his ministry there. He had pioneered a church and saw 400 people pass through the waters of baptism in a period of about eight years. On a visit to Hong Kong, he was invited to preach at Tsuen Wen church where Vera associated and, in the course of time, it was felt right that he should be invited to come as their pastor. Only when he felt the strong leading of the Lord did he consent and found peace in the will of God.

In 1971, Pastor P.S. Brewster held a crusade in the Province. Each morning, he also conducted a seminar for ministers and church leaders. It was gratifying to note that almost all the Pentecostal ministers from all denominations attended throughout the week. There were many moving scenes as veteran missionaries, who had spent over forty years on the mainland (now Communist Red China), joined with younger pastors in planning and praying for Hong Kong. One Conference delegate had swum for many hours through forbidden waters in his bid for freedom. He was then a pastor. In the public evening rallies, crowds packed the large Methodist church to capacity and multitudes came for salvation. Local churches provided bands, choirs, orchestras and singing items.

During his time spent with Vera, Mr. Brewster was staggered by her work load. He said, "In all my travels, I have never seen such a dedicated missionary with such a vision and such a passion for souls. How she loves the Chinese! Sister McGillivray's programme is almost unbelievable: twenty-one periods of teaching[V] every week plus services almost every night. She lives in an area packed with people. It hardly seems safe for a woman to live there by herself. She finds it necessary to move her home and she is planning to open her new home for Bible and salvation messages in a new area of some 60,000 people."

PAUL and DIANE SARCHET-WALLER

During Mr. Brewster's visit, one of his observations was that Vera would be helped if a 'young, dedicated couple from the homeland would feel the call to go and help her to open more churches in her area'. In 1979, Paul and Diane Sarchet-Waller took up the challenge and settled in Hong Kong to do a work for God.

Paul and Diane were serving the Lord in Jamaica in 1974 when God called them to serve the Chinese. Paul's reaction was, "I'll go, Lord, but don't ask me to learn the language. I'm too old!" However, they were obedient, returned to England and sold all their possessions and took a 'plane to Hong Kong. As they began to learn the language, they were still not too clear what God had in mind for them to do, but they could see a great need around them in training local brethren for ministry. Initially, they teamed up with the Revival Christian Church, which provided an outlet for Paul's teaching ministry.

Following a furlough in 1978, the return to Hong Kong provided more challenges, out of which came a burden to pioneer a church in Shatin. From 1980, the Lord worked with them to bring about the founding of a new fellowship in an area with about 500,000 inhabitants. A prophetic word from a sister in USA confirmed that this was God's will at this time. Subsequently, they saw the Lord bring together a team that would work for the Kingdom in bringing this vision to reality. In 1983, the building they had was too small and they were seeking to buy a new, three storey building to use as a church and HQ for the work. At this time, Paul was supported financially by the Elim Church in the UK, although the intention was to encourage the church locally to take responsibility for its own expenses. At an early stage, they were giving a tithe of their offerings to missionary work and helping to support a missionary in the Philippines.

In addition to the work in Hong Kong, Paul and Diane had a vision to see the Gospel making an impact on mainland China. So besides their involvement in language study and other missionary work in Hong Kong, they became directly involved in training the Chinese to take the ministry to their own people. It was the intention to take the Scriptures into mainland China and to distribute as they were able.

They were told that God sometimes worked mighty miracles to help His work and one case was cited. The Chinese border guard, instructed to inspect a Pentecostal pastor (they called him Pastor Wang, but not his real name) who was travelling at the time, seemed poised to make an arrest. Suddenly, the government official was prompted to ask the pastor if he had any medicine to relieve stomach pains. The guard explained that he had suffered stomach pains for more than twenty years and doctors couldn't find a cure. Courageously, the pastor told him that Jesus could heal sickness and prayed for him. Instantly, the man was cured and the grateful guard changed his attitude. The pastor was left praising God for this wonderful deliverance and his freedom.

On his first trip into China, Paul was able, with others, to take around 1,000 Bibles, testaments, concordances and hymn books and place them in the hands of pastors in Canton. Paul's ability to converse in Cantonese was a benefit and drew crowds as he began to speak to the people in their own language, whether in the open air or in shops. This became a feature of visits, as their communications skills drew people in to hear the good news. Because of the restrictions that had occurred since communism took over, it was difficult to preach openly, but many opportunities appeared in which believers were contacted and blessed with fellowship.

They met with pastor Wang and he told them of his five years' imprisonment. His daughter told them that the family had prayed twenty-four hours a day that his mind would not be adversely affected. He did not wish to dwell on the imprisonment or physical scars he still had, but rather told of the many times he had seen God working miracles for them. As the visitors prayed with him, his face was radiant as he rejoiced in fellowship with believers from outside the country. At one time, he had had opportunity to flee to Hong Kong, but refused saying, "God has called me to be a missionary to my people. I must stay where I am."

Persecution of the Chinese church was at its height when fanatical Red Guards arrested Sister Wong. When Sister Wong was put on trial, accused of being a counter-revolutionary, the move backfired against the hard line Maoists and revival swept the Chekiang Province. But Sister Wong was a dedicated and much-loved Christian who had broken no laws. Believers were greatly incensed when they saw this godly, elderly woman suffering persecution and being made to walk the streets carrying signs of her guilt. Then, a group of men, women and children was imprisoned for gathering to pray for Sister Wong.

But the next day, more than 1000 Christians from many parts of the State protested to the authorities, "Those people are part of our family. If you imprison them, you must do the same to us." The authorities showed them no mercy and threw them all in jail. Next day, however, several thousand more believers flocked in from all around the province and demanded that they, too, should be arrested. As the jails were full and the warders were having problems feeding them all, they decided to free everyone. This began a tremendous move of God in the area as Christians had seen the need to stop arguing among themselves and stand together.

In spite of Government opposition to Christianity, the church survived and became strong over the years. An American visitor[vi] saw the work at first hand and identified three reasons for the Church's survival. He discovered that when the church buildings were taken away, the peoples' homes became their churches. Then, he found that when their pastors and Bible teachers were taken from them, the Christians who survived learned to hear God speaking to them through His Word. And then, those who survived spiritually learned to appreciate their heavenly Father and their relationship to Him far more than the present life and the gifts that came from His hand. This was seen to be diametrically opposed to life in the west which was perceived as humanistic and self-centred.

One brother in mainland China in 1981 reported:

There are so many testimonies of the blind who have had their eyesight restored, the crippled who have walked and even those who have been raised from the dead and other outstanding miracles that it would be impossible for me to relate them all one by one.

Over a thirty year period, the church had been stifled and persecuted, but there was strong evidence that God's purposes had not been thwarted. The outlawing of all religion from 1966-1976 in fact created a great spiritual hunger in the people, especially the young. Pan Xiao (a young Chinese girl) wrote to the China Youth Magazine asking, "Life, is this the mystery you try to reveal? Is the ultimate end nothing more than a dead body?" The letter ended with the plea, "Does anyone else feel the same way?" The magazine received 60,000 replies from young people who had tried Buddhism, Taoism, 'forms' of Christianity, but failed to fill the spiritual vacuum. A new move of God was meeting the need in unprecedented ways.

Central to the survival and growth of the Church in China was the supply of Bibles. Because of the vast area and population size, there never could be enough Bibles for all believers, so it was customary for those who had access to the scriptures to memorise them and, subsequently, copy what they remembered into their own notebook. It will be clearly understood that the appreciation expressed by mainland believers when receiving their own copy of God's Word was an emotional affair.[vii]

One of the major questions facing the Church in Hong Kong was about its future when the Province was returned to Chinese rule in 1997. This was a concern for people in all walks of life and, for the Church, it presented a similar challenge to that faced by India when they recognised the changes that would be brought about by the communist invasion. A measure of indigenous activity was certainly called for and had to be planned. The various teaching and training programmes instituted by Paul no doubt contributed greatly to the effectiveness of the witness.

There was a measure of additional help available when Roberta Marcus, a native of Ballymena, joined the team. A trained nurse, Bobbie worked in a local hospital but gave time to the work of the church over a two and a half year period. She left Hong Kong in 1985 to take up a position with the work in Zimbabwe.

One of the ways in which the Church operated was in the use of home meetings, and leadership training focused on those who would lead such groups. Each group had two leaders and a helper, with Paul overseeing all of them. The numbers attending increased gradually until over sixty people were present at any given time. The benefit provided by such groups meant that there was a deepening and consolidation of relationships. The groups themselves had a five-fold purpose: caring for people, personal growth, fellowship, burden-bearing and outreach. In the context of Hong Kong's population explosion, this was probably the most effective way to conduct the church's business and see it prosper.

In addition to the work of the local church, teams were sent into China, to Canton, where they were very effective in sharing the Gospel. In the light of individual needs as well as community problems, the church was enabled to manifest the love of Jesus in practical ways and this had a good effect on their acceptance. A development of this vision was to set up Asiateams,[viii] much like the UK's Euroteams, with a view to reaching into Malaysia, Indonesia, the Philippines and other Far eastern countries. In later years, there was also a Hong Kong based outreach to India.

While the city of Shatin itself continued to expand, so too did the local church until it was necessary to hold two services on a Sunday morning. The first of these was attended by a number of Hong Kong-based missionaries, while the second service was almost 100% Chinese, representing a good cross-section of the people.

In the course of time, the work in Hong Kong became very broad, reaching out throughout the region and producing high quality publications and video material. Eventually, Paul and Diane felt that they needed to be free of denominational constraints and severed their links with Elim UK.

i The Pentecostal Missionary Union (PMU) began at a meeting chaired by Alexander Boddy on January 9th, 1909, at All Saints' Sunderland. See details in *Inside Story,* William K. Kay, p.43. Mattersey Hall Publishing, Mattersey, 1990.

ii From a report by Pastor Charles Coates in *Elim Evangel,* Vol.10, Issue 30, p.466,467.

iii See chapter on Formosa for details of Ken McGillivray's ministry.

iv A full report on the situation that had faced the missionaries was given by Vera in *Elim Evangel,* Vol.32. Issue 17, pp200,201.

v Vera was teaching G.C.E. "O" level Scripture at Tsung Tsin College, taking five lessons daily covering a total of 650 students.

vi Don H. Kaufman in the *Pentecostal Testimony* magazine, reprinted by *Elim Evangel,* Vol.61. Issue 41,pp8,9.

vii An overview of the development of the Bible in China was given in the *Elim Evangel,* Vol.63. Issue 15,pp8,9.

viii A report of an early visit by an Asiateam was contained in *Elim Evangel,* Vol.70.

CHAPTER 24

INDIA

Despite the challenge presented by the teeming masses of the Indian continent, India was one of the first to receive the input of the warm heart of Elim missionaries. Indian had a population of 375 millions, of whom only seven millions were Christians. The population was a collection of twenty-five to thirty different nations, speaking about twenty-five main languages and about 450 dialects. Consequently, the spiritual needs of India were immense. As early as October, 1919, during World War I, Miss D. Phillips, usually known as Dollie, whose base was Mahim, was in Chandur, Berar Province and reporting home of blessings received. She testified to the definite leading of the Lord as to her destination as she continued her language study and also had opportunity to live in and experience village life. She was expecting to return to Mahim a few months later at the end of her language study.

Dollie was part of the Phillips family and served in India until compelled to return home through ill health. In 1928, she became the minister of the Letchworth church in the place of her brother, Hubert, on his departure for South Africa to become a missionary. In 1947, she became the hostess of the Elim holiday home, Lascelles Hotel in Eastbourne, seeing this move as of the Lord and receiving no monetary reward. She passed into the presence of the Lord she had loved and served for so many years in 1961.

Each day, in India, there were testimonies of salvation. One Bible woman had been baptised in the Spirit and several other workers were actively seeking the blessing. There was already a small church in the village and that attracted people from the surrounding district each Sunday. In recent times, fourteen men and two women had come out of the darkness of Hinduism, had turned from their idols and were serving God. Their lives had changed; their faces had changed but they were standing firm against persecution and many hardships for the sake of the Gospel.

Ten years later, in October, 1929, a farewell service was held in London for another two ladies who were responding to God's call to India. They were Miss Marion B. Ewens and Miss Marion Paint. This was convened by the Principal, George Jeffreys, whose emphasis for a new move forward in missions endeavour was greeted with great enthusiasm by the gathered crowd. [An initiative of G. Jeffreys for missions was being promoted – Foursquare Gospel World Crusade]

Marion Paint had been born again just three years previously and had subsequently entered Elim Bible College for training in August, 1927. There she received the Baptism in the Holy Spirit, with a vivid intimation conveyed during prayer with a missionary from India that God would choose her as a vessel for His grace. At about the same time, she had a vision which seemed to be set on a Guernsey beach near her home. She saw herself bathing with others in the sea when they were menaced by a strong tide.

Making for the shore, she cried, "Now you will have to swim over this part as it is deep." They replied, "Oh, we cannot for we can't swim. And you – you knew of this dangerous spot and didn't warn us. Now we must perish."

The Holy Spirit applied this to her heart as a parable of her spiritual responsibility to the thoughtless and perishing. At the end of November, during a period of being laid aside through sickness, she felt that she had been providentially met by God and was given a vision of India with a black band stretching across its great expanse from Bombay to near Calcutta and with it, a deep impression that Jesus alone could bring light to that darkness. She was later to discover that the indicated territory covered the exact rail route over which she would now travel from Bombay to her station, Giridih, Bihar Province, near Calcutta. She was going to India on the strength of the great and precious promises of Scripture. Marion served the Lord with great distinction in India until her home call in 1972. Following her 'retirement' from the field, she joined the staff at Elim Bible College, helping many English Language students and touching student lives for Christ.

Miss Ewens was in a totally different position, having already completed six years service for Christ in China and four in India. She had been baptised in the Spirit during her time in India while working in Lahore in charge of school work. A work took place among the young girls in the school that showed clearly the moving of the Holy Spirit in individual lives. One young girl, overcome by a sense of her personal sin, came to Miss Ewens and sobbed in remorse, but saw a vision of Christ in heaven surrounded by angels who were rejoicing at her new-found peace. Miss Ewens was able to point her to the scripture that the angels rejoice when a sinner repents. This young girl received a gracious and powerful baptism in the Holy Spirit.

Great joy was evident in that valedictory service for the two ladies and a pledge was made for support in prayer and giving as they then proceeded to sail from Liverpool on 22nd October. The voyage took until 10th November and on the 11th, Remembrance Day, they found themselves standing in silence for two minutes in the local branch of the Imperial Bank of Bombay.

First impressions for Marion were multifaceted. Miss Ewens took her to a market where they were followed by several coolies all wanting them to use their services, and fighting among themselves for the right to carry the ladies' goods. The constant bargaining for everything was also something quite new to her. The scenes at the station brought home to her the immensity of the need and the task to which she had given herself. Three or four hundred people were sitting cross legged on the platform waiting for their train. As the ladies walked around studying the various groups, they became aware of the tremendous needs. There were what looked like bundles of rags just lying there, but they discovered they were a person who had just fallen asleep; beggars were there and one boy walked like a four-footed animal. Another was hideously deformed and painted. The darkness of the land was appalling. Marion was surprised to see the custom of the men in wearing their shirts over their trousers! (What would she think today?)

Exactly at 11 p.m. on the 11th day of the 11th month, they started their train journey across the continent, breaking their journey for a rest with a friend of Miss Ewens at Bhusoul and eventually arriving at the Maranatha mission on Friday 15th November. Their welcome was a splendid affair with *saris* laid on the ground and garlands of flowers hung around their necks. A thanksgiving service was convened at which speeches of welcome were given by all and sundry. Sadly, there followed for Marion a period of severe trial as she was laid aside for five weeks with malaria.

There were many needs for prayer. One was identified by Miss Ewens. The lady in question was a high-caste Bengali widow. Although she fully trusted Jesus, her home life was bound up with idolatry. Because she was a young widow, she had to do all the drudgery of housework; she was not allowed to wear any jewellery or nice clothes; neither may her children. But she was expected to make garments for her sister-in-law's children, all the while receiving their scorn and scoffing. She had indicated to the missionaries that she wanted to run away, but no one could see how that would be possible. Nevertheless, the church continued to pray for her release. Meanwhile, the pundit who had been teaching them Hindi had been converted and was actively seeking the Baptism in the Holy Spirit.

Rajubai, the Indian Bible woman, was returning from her vacation. On the train were two homeless boys begging their way to Calcutta. The ticket collector, finding the boys without tickets, was about to put them off the train when Rajubai pleaded for them and said she would take them to the Mission.

They were Brahmin boys and the elder, named Red Bird, had the sacred cord around his waist indicating that he had reached twelve years of age and had been invested with all the rights of the Dijo Brahmin. Settling in at the Mission was difficult because they had been smoking all their lives and couldn't give up, but the missionary weaned them off it with lemon drops.

In the evenings, they listened to Bible stories and then, the following evening, they would entertain and amuse the missionaries by retelling them in their own patois. Arrangements were being made to transfer them into a Pentecostal orphanage when, unfortunately, the Arya Somaj, a Hindu society bitterly opposed to Christianity, heard about them. They demanded to see the boys and accused Rajubai of kidnapping them.

But the boys, knowing the evil intentions of these men, hid themselves and wouldn't come out. When finally they were persuaded to come out, the men immediately grabbed them and physically carried them away despite much protest from the boys themselves.

The missionaries later heard that the boys' coats of English cloth had been torn from their backs and they had been given coarse homespun jackets. Their heads had been shaved, but a tuft was left in the centre to mark them as Hindus and they were taken back into caste. Their captors asked them why they had listened to the Christian teaching, so the boys told them the story of Jesus. What they would have refused to listen to from a missionary, they heard from the mouth of 'babes'.

A week later, the boys were found talking to Rajubai's brother as they bathed in the Ganges, so they were taken to another place that had very high walls. But at midnight, Red Bird planned their escape and he and his brother scaled the walls and made their way to the railway station, praying there would be a train they could board. They got on board, but not having any money, they were put off three times. Nevertheless, they finally arrived back at Giridih around midnight. They were later transferred to a Pentecostal school where they were kept safe. Red Bird wrote to the missionaries that they were going forward in the knowledge of the Lord and were seeking the fullness of the Spirit.[i]

In 1931, the missionaries moved to a new centre in Bihar Province, named Monghyr, the second most important town in the region, Patna being the first. At their first service, there were just five people present but one of them, a nurse with her baby, had a high fever and asked for prayer. The next day, she was seen in the street and both were completely well. This provided other openings to go and pray for the sick and opened doors for the Gospel.

Shortly after this, Marion Paint went alone to minister among some Bengali people in Calcutta where she was much used of the Lord in prayer for the sick. A boy said to be insane was delivered and the following morning took up his Bengali Bible and started to read it. Another lady with severe heart trouble had been unable to sleep lying down for many months but, after prayer, had a good night's sleep lying in her bed. There were many evidences of the Lord's moving and time was spent in seeking the Baptism. Needless to say, there was great joy among the believers in the city. Both in Calcutta and back in Giridih the Lord was pouring out His Spirit on thirsty souls and many were being introduced to a new power through the Spirit.

Meanwhile, Miss Ewens in Monghyr was calling for rejoicing because, she said, there was a sound of an abundance of rain. She reported that in other parts of India too, there was evidence of a move of God. In Purulia, a Mr. Munshie had been seeking the Baptism for so long that it was decided that they would have a week of prayer and pray until the answer came. Prayer started on a Monday morning and that afternoon, the man's three children came seeking to be saved. Under great conviction they all cried and asked for forgiveness. Soon, all three were testifying to assurance of salvation. On the Tuesday, Mrs. Munshie, who had opposed her husband's seeking for the Baptism for two years, was herself baptised in the Holy Spirit. Right up until late on the Saturday night, God continued to bless but Mr. Munshie still hadn't received. When all were about to give up, the Lord graciously touched him and filled him. Within minutes, his eldest son was also baptised and then the next son came in and was almost immediately touched as well. Jesus was given all the glory!

On June 1st, 1933, a special service of dedication was held for the laying of a foundation stone for a building for the small assembly in Calcutta where Marion Paint was in charge. A Christian family in the church had undertaken the construction of this 'House of Prayer and Good News'. The service, numbering about sixty people including four ministers, was interdenominational and much blessed by the Lord. There was great excitement that the assembly would now have its own premises for worship.

1933 also saw an increase in the missionaries on the field. Miss Ewens had taken a short furlough to recuperate after a period of illness and, following her farewell to return to the field, was joined by Miss H. Newsham whose call was to India as well. Miss Newsham was well known in the Croydon area, having been active in the church, in the home and at Elim Camp. Her long season of preparation and waiting was prayerfully watched and, suddenly, she was ready to go. A fellow missionary, just moments before the farewell service was due to start, wrote:

No rose-petalled pathway to walk on,
No velvety, grass-covered way;
But stones, and a desert and an outpost,
And a cross to carry alway.
There's sin to be dealt with, and sinning,
There's a fight to be fought, just by you;
But there's glory ahead for the follower
And a victory that's always true.
So pick up your armour and wear it,
Grip firmly the Sword in your hand,
And the power that has called you to battle
Will see that you also can stand.[ii]

Shortly after Miss Newsham arrived in India, she was in Calcutta for the opening of the new building on January 15th, 1934. This was a memorable occasion because this was the first Full Gospel church building to be erected in the city. But it was also memorable because at three o'clock that afternoon, an earthquake shook the city for eight minutes. People had gathered for the ceremony, but the house just swayed and the windows rattled as the gathered congregation rushed into the compound to see if the house would stand. In other places, there was loss of life and destruction, but Calcutta was saved. The service of dedication took place at 6 p.m. and for the two weeks following, there were special meetings at which the Lord was pleased to bless with the salvation of souls, the healing of bodies and the Pentecostal Baptism in the Holy Spirit.

After five years, Marion Paint went home on furlough to her native Guernsey where she was received joyously and welcomed by huge crowds who had travelled from all over the island to Vazon for her welcome home service. She rehearsed much of what the Lord had done in the past years and acknowledged that India, one of the most religious countries in the world, and one of the hardest from a missionary point of view, needed not another religion, but an encounter with the living Personality of Jesus. Marion was able to tell many stories of deliverance from evil spirits, sickness and persecution. She could identify people who, despite great hardship and at much cost to themselves, had trusted Jesus and become bright, shining lights for God.

While Marion was on furlough, Miss Ewens was bravely attacking villages where no one had ever preached the Gospel before. She and Miss Grace Brown found great opposition but were not to be diverted from the task. In one village, they found a group of women whom they thought might be willing to listen to them. But in these villages, the domestic animals occupy the entrance room that leads to the living quarters. At the time they arrived, a meal was being prepared and, so that their shadow wouldn't fall on it and defile it, they were led into the stable where a string bed was brought for them to sit on. They spent about half an hour speaking to about forty women and closed by leading some to the Lord.

Their 'follow-up' counselling was to teach the women the Name of Jesus – Yisu – and to impress on them the need to trust Him at all times rather than being involved with their idols. The Spirit enlightened the women and they gladly acknowledged Christ's lordship in their lives.

The following October saw Marion Paint once more leaving British shores for a further term of service in India. She farewelled from Clapham on October 22nd 1936 and in the service acknowledged the abundant provision she had known in response to fulfilled promises given to her on her first farewell.

A description of an Indian School

There are seventy five names on the roll in Alinagar School and, because all the girls come from good homes, they are escorted to and fro. The headmistress is a capable teacher and a very keen evangelist. The girls love her very much and consequently do not leave school as soon as they can read and write, but stay on until the ages of 14 or 15. At that age, marriages are arranged for them.

Many of these Hindu girls are true believers in the Lord Jesus Christ and have witnessed in their homes to the love of Jesus. One dear girl of eleven often leads the whole school in prayer. Recently, she was quite ill with malaria, but she testified to being healed in answer to prayer. One morning, six girls went to visit a sick schoolmate and prayed with her, leaving her 'in the Lord's bosom'.

All the older girls have bought separate copies of the four Gospels and in order to preserve the Word of God, many have had their Gospel portions bound by a bookbinder for the sum of two annas. The girls have shown great eagerness in purchasing the Word of God and so far, 148 books have been sold in this school.

Not only are the older girls interested, but a small girl of six, called 'The Queen', has been refusing to bow down to idols in her home. She has told her parents that three men called Shadrach, Meshach and Abednego pleased God by refusing to bow down to an idol. The parents were very upset and asked her why, if Jesus was God, He allowed His hands to be pierced with nails. The question was much too difficult for her, so she asked her teacher the answer. She went home prepared

to tell her parents that if Jesus' blood had not been shed, we could not be saved.[iii] How true it is that a little child shall lead them. The mothers of these children were reached through the efforts of the school to help their children.

On her return, Marion worked in both Bihar and United Provinces, mostly among village people whom she found generally to be delightful and friendly. Her approach to these was often by walking on the raised paths through the rice fields or by wading through streams. One village was populated solely by carpenters and Marion was impressed to see them working in the open air, making yokes for the oxen or wheels for the bullock carts. Jesus of Nazareth became very real to her in those circumstances.

One of the advantages of working in the villages was that there was free access to the women. In cities, they were always hindered by bolts and bars, but in the villages, if they were not too busy grinding misala or pounding grain, they were more than happy to sit and talk. While most of the villages were Hindu, there were some that were Muslim and in these, there was often quite a debate about the Gospel. But even here, copies of the Gospel were purchased and prayer was made that it might bear fruit.

The outbreak of war in 1939 urged Miss Ewens, who was on furlough, to hasten her return to India despite the threat of submarine attacks, this time accompanied by Miss Irene Snell, a young lady who had sensed a call some ten years previously and had been waiting for God to open the door. So rapidly were the arrangements made that Miss Snell was unable to itinerate around the churches to advise them of her vision.

In the Gorakphur region, Marion Paint spent time reaching out to pilgrims who attended the many festivals held throughout the year. One of the benefits of this was that pilgrims came from Nepal, which was closed to the Gospel. So the workers waited to meet them on their return and preached the Word to them, encouraging them to purchase copies of the Gospels for themselves.

Sometimes there was organised opposition and at others, there seemed to be a readiness to accept the Word. One young boy threatened his family that he would run away if they didn't allow him to buy some Gospels. The family yielded to his request and he bought eight Gospels. On another occasion, a Rajah, accompanied by his servants sent his servants to bring books to him and ended up buying all that were sent – sixteen in all – and also requested a Hindi Bible which he promised to put in his library.

Miss Ewens in Madhupur was equally busy with English meetings every Wednesday and on two Sundays each month. Using English provided a measure of relief as most of her work was in Hindi with a Bible study class three evenings a week for the teacher and colporteur. There was still no meeting hall at this time and some people felt a little diffident about coming to the mission bungalow where only women were resident. Some who had been reached were transient and did not provide a stable base on which to build. One young man made a profession but moved on when he found that the missionaries couldn't give him food every day and a place to live. Sadly, so many of India's millions were starving, out of work and unfit for work and yet, because of these, the population was greatly increased.

Miss Snell settled in well into her new role in India and was based in Jasidh. As part of a four day vacation, she walked ten miles to bring the Gospel to a hill village and the ministry was well received. On the way back, she just missed standing on a poisonous snake, but one of her companions killed it with a stick and they all thanked God for His protection.

After two months in school, she was asked to take a surgical case at the Landour Mission Hospital. Taking this to be from the Lord, she became involved, but hoped to return to the school in due course. As a nurse, she also used her dispensary work in the villages as opportunities to preach the Gospel. The people had great faith in the white man's medicine, but their trust was in God.

A note from Marion Ewens in 1941 indicated that she and Miss Alice Buckler, a retired school headmistress and an honorary Elim missionary, had moved to Giridih where the climate was much better, but the house was being renovated and there was dust and dirt everywhere. Miss Paint continued to work at the girls' school in Madhupur and Irene Snell was still nursing sick folk. There had been cases of typhoid on three of the mission stations that year.

On returning from the railway station one day, Irene saw a group outside the local police station. She would have ignored it since crowds were always gathering for something, but a servant came and told her there was a dead baby lying in front of the police station. She went to see and found a baby girl, about one month old, lying unclothed in front of the gaping crowd which included many children. She asked the policeman to cover the baby but he had nothing so she went to a little shop and bought some cloth to wrap the baby in. The baby's mother was in a cell, having thrown the baby into a pond. She was able to talk to the mother as well as the policeman, explaining what she as a missionary believed and what she was hoping to do with the resources she received from the UK.

Although India was such a large continent, the effects of the war in Europe were being felt, not least in Giridih, where Miss Ewens was. In the recent few months, a massive camp had been established for housing Italian prisoners of war. These were guarded by British and Indian soldiers and, as a result, a whole new town developed, swelling the population from about 20,000 to twice that number. The infrastructure of a city appeared almost overnight, with shops of every kind opening instantly. The missionaries were able to hold a meeting for the servicemen and it filled their hearts with joy to hear the singing and testimonies of many who confessed that they were soldiers of the Cross.

In the following weeks and months, circumstances became very difficult with trouble and unrest evident on all sides. Riots were common. During this time, Marion Paint sailed home on furlough, having been assured in a vision that it was safe for her to do so. Miss Ewens and Miss Buckler remained in Giridih and were thankful for the presence of British soldiers who gave them a feeling of security. They also held meetings for the servicemen at which a number received Christ.

During Marion's furlough, she arranged to meet with a number of prospective missionaries at Elim Woodlands so that they could get to know each other. These included Miss E. M. Mynard,[iv] Miss Coralie Paint, Marion's sister, and Pastor Aubrey Hathaway, an Elim minister.

Miss Edith M. Mynard came from the Elim Church in Ingatestone, Essex. She was converted at the age of thirteen and, under the ministry of Pastor John Woodhead, she was baptised in water and then in the Holy Spirit. She felt the call of God on her life and undertook nursing training, becoming a fully qualified general nurse and midwife. Thus, in April, 1945, she set sail for India to join Miss Ewens, assured of the Lord's smile upon her as she considered the many tokens of His provision in terms of money and equipment that had been supplied.

Some six months later, after waiting for thirteen years for God's timing, Miss Coralie Paint, sister to Marion, also set sail for India where she laboured for over twenty-five years until her home call in 1976. Coralie, like Edith Mynard was a trained nurse and midwife and would find much for her hands to do, but in her farewell service, she was reminded by Pastor George Thomas, the Missionary Secretary, that her main calling was to preach the Gospel.

VE Day and VJ Day were celebrated in India by Miss Ewens, Elim's senior missionary, in taking the challenge to the lost millions in Dehri-on-Sone, Bihar Province, a thickly-populated industrial area where the need was very great. This move followed much prayer and investigation and all the missionaries involved felt that this was God's move in God's time.

Dehri was a flourishing town with many factories working day and night, and multitudes had flocked there to find work. Thus the ladies lost no time in packing up their belongings and moving to find suitable accommodation. Their trip was no picnic, involving several train changes and an overnight wait in a train station just sitting in a chair. There was no guarantee of finding food on the journey so all had to be carried with them. The round trip covered four days and four nights on trains that were appallingly overcrowded.

In a town where all the factory owners had bought up the properties, there was not much hope of finding a house to rent, but God makes no mistakes and, after a long search, the missionaries were able to rent a suitable property, 'the most perfect Indian-built house I have ever lived in', according to Miss Ewens. By now, she had been joined by Miss Mynard and the work in Dehri quickly opened up with opportunities multiplying every day, but the great need was for a male missionary as it was not always appropriate for women to minister to men.

Marion Paint's seventeen years in India were celebrated at her farewell as she planned her return once again. This would be her third term of service abroad. When she first went out, her father was loathe to let her go but, being one of a family of ten, she was regarded as the 'tithe'! Then, when her sister, Coralie, went out, she was considered to be the family's 'freewill offering' to the Lord.

Marion made the point that, although she had seen many changes in her time in India, yet there still remained an immense work to be done. Millions had still never heard the name of Jesus, and so she appealed for others to respond to God's call to the Field. She clearly said that there was no romance in such a life, warning of loneliness, heat, dogged toil, vermin, real conflicts with the powers of darkness, but alongside these, the power of Him who has conquered all and promised never to leave His own. She told that once, in the midst of riots, she was hotly pursued and her oppressors shouted angrily, "Go away, little white monkey!" On the other hand, the missionaries were visited by Ghurkha soldiers who treated them with great respect and helped them in those violent, anti-Imperial days. They also took the scriptures back with them to territories where the Gospel could not be preached.

There were also some other encouragements. Miss Ewens and Miss Mynard, in Dehri had a visit from an army chaplain looking for a meeting place to hold a service. He had been told that Elim was the only place in town so a number of officers arrived and a great service was held in English, to the great satisfaction of the missionaries. After the service, some of the officers left, but others stayed for communion and remained for a time of fellowship. It turned out that the chaplain had met Pastor Woodhead in the church in Carlisle[V] and knew something of Elim. He also brought refreshments from his camp canteen which were appreciated by all present.

In May, 1946, Coralie Paint finally arrived in India but, about a month after her arrival, she was struck down with malaria and dysentery. Her journey was accomplished in the company of other missionaries whose itinerary had been changed at Bombay, meaning that Coralie had travelling companions all the way to Patna. Arrived there, she became involved in the local mission hospital and also in intensive language study.

The effective working of the lady missionaries in India was always a matter of great joy that they were accomplishing much for God, even although the task seemed overwhelming. Their constant prayer was for God to send out men because so much on the Indian continent was targeted on men and women were kept in a subservient role most of the time. Thus the farewell service in October, 1946 for Pastor and Mrs. Aubrey Hathaway en route to India was cause for great rejoicing. Their call had been with them for a long time but the doors hadn't opened until now and they were keen to serve the Lord.

The work in Dehri continued to develop with a constant demand on the missionaries to open a school for the children of the area. This presented problems with both space and teachers, but in due course, arrangements were made and the school became established. The workers in Dehri consisted then of three Indian bible women – Misses I.M. Biswas, N. Biswas, S. Daffadar, and the missionaries, E.M. Mynard, A.M. Buckler and M.B. Ewens. They were expecting the Hathaways to join them within a short period of time.

At this time, India was being rocked by riots and unrest in many areas. In Dehri, the missionaries used a lorry to rescue about 400 women. Whole families were being locked in their houses and then the house was set on fire. Marion Paint went to Patna and all but walked into a riot there. She was told she had to spend the night sleeping by the side of the Ganges river, but she managed to persuade police to escort her to the hospital where her sister, Coralie, was working and there found shelter and safety. The desire for revenge was likely to prolong the unrest but the missionaries just had to leave themselves in the Lord's hands.

The serious rioting and bloodshed gave occasion for ministry to those involved. Refugees poured into the hospital emergency room, injured and terrified. The city itself was spared the worst of the bloodshed by the arrival of the military. When the Government hospital was full (1000 beds), the mission hospital found room for fifty more, all Mohammedan women and children. Coralie told of one woman whose three children had been knifed, thrown into a well and then had been stoned until they died. It was hand to hand fighting with the crudest of instruments but, thanks to modern medicines like penicillin, most of those treated survived and were able, a little later, to listen to the Gospel story. Many received it gladly.

Once Miss Mynard had completed her language course and had her second year exams behind her, she moved back into Dehri where changes were being made. The original rented house was left behind and the new house where the school had been set up became their centre. It was unfurnished so they had great fun being 'pioneers' and finding the necessary furniture to make the place habitable and reasonably comfortable. Once established there, they set up a Sunday school and saw a measure of success. The dispensary was not reopened for the time being.

Meanwhile, another lady, Miss Elsie Wriglesworth, a Certified Midwife, had come into Pentecost in 1936 and entered Elim Bible College in 1946. She committed herself to work in India and farewelled from Croydon in January, 1947. Her first impressions were mixed but, as she arrived by train in Dehri, she was met by Aubrey Hathaway and taken to meet the other missionaries. She was touched by the sheer scale of need that presented to her eyes as she travelled along in a rickshaw. She saw the rich and opulent co-existing with the slums and beggars. She felt moved by the vision of children with sore-infested bodies and eyes running with pus, covered in flies. The small, squalid huts that served as housing brought a measure of concern as it portrayed India's great need. Alice Buckler, who had been on furlough for a short period, also returned in early 1947 for a further period of service in Dehri. She testified that since she had been serving the Lord in India, she had found more joy in her life than ever before.

By now, Coralie Paint had also joined the team in Bihar and was engaged in the work of evangelisation throughout the area. She and Miss Mynard were involving themselves with some American A o G missionaries in a camp setting, studying their methods. They were living in tents, wearing Indian dress and eating Indian food. Mornings were spent in Bible study and afternoons were given to visitation in the villages. Meetings were held in the evenings. Their plan was to master the language and then obtain the necessary materials to have their own camp. Just before leaving, they were advised that the Plague had broken out on all four sides outside the camp, so they had to take all necessary precautions.

Following this camp, Edith Mynard and Miss Biswas (the Indian Bible woman) had opportunity to speak with a high caste woman who had heard about the missionaries and wanted to know more. She had had contact with them through midwifery, but now, with her household, she was showing great interest in the Gospel. In course of time, she came to receive Christ and asked for baptism. Members of her household also had reason to seek the help of God for demon possession and healing.

The constant challenge of conditions in India was described by Elsie Wriglesworth shortly after her arrival in Dehri:

Two miles from here is a small compound of the lowest caste of all. Could I portray it as I saw it there would not be a dry eye or a heart unmoved in all the Elim family. The shacks would not have been a fit place to keep chickens, let alone human beings. The stench was nauseating. One filthy cloth covered their nakedness; their eyes were dull and listless, their bodies emaciated, their hair filthy and matted and teeming with vermin. These people are just existing. In the natural they are repulsive, yet they are the souls of men and women passing out into eternity. I long for the time when I will be able to speak Chojpuri and tell them about Jesus.

In May, 1947, the Wimbledon Elim church was packed as a congregation said farewell to another family destined for India. They were Pastor and Mrs. David C. Lewis. Although both Mr. and Mrs. Lewis testified to a positive call from God, they had had a remarkable experience just shortly before this service. They had been in a church in Torquay and David noticed a coloured man in the service. Thinking he might be Indian, he decided to talk to him and discovered that he was, in fact, Indian and came from the area to which they had been appointed. He was able to supply David with the name and address of a relative living in that district who held an important Government post.

In August, 1947, Miss Ewens was able to go home on furlough after a period of about eight years on the field. Also in August, there was a farewell service for Pastor Jack and Mrs. Grace Troke from the Elim Church in Winton, Bournemouth. The Trokes had been working in Bombay Province, Western India mainly among the Hindu people. These had a highly organised system of priests, temples, holy men, pilgrimages and devotees. During this time, Mahatma Gandhi was having great influence.

Although he wasn't a Christian, he used his power to combine religion and politics to hold the masses. He copied missionary methods and held prayer meetings every day, with attendances of between 10,000 and 15,000. He took portions from all the religious books, including the Sermon on the Mount and mixed them together in an attempt to hold all the peoples of India.

The Trokes found themselves dealing with various epidemics during their time there, including the plagues of smallpox and cholera. They also worked in an orphanage which cared for over 200 boys and girls, including unwanted babies that were brought in for them to care for. Just before they left for furlough, there had been a famine in the villages but the Orphanage didn't suffer. In the same area, it wasn't unusual to see 30-35 Sunday school classes on a Sunday morning comprising married men and women with their families who were living on the Mission compound. This number was swelled by children from the orphanage and Hindus from the villages all seeking to hear the good news of the Gospel.

August 15th, 1947 was Independence Day for India, and its coming was awaited with some trepidation by the missionaries. Gandhi had said that missionaries would not be asked to quit India, but most of the missionaries decided that it would be wisdom if they stayed indoors that day. However, Miss Buckler was visiting some American missionary friends and they had an Indian Christian man in their boarding school who wanted the school girls to take part in the celebrations as an act of witness. So Miss Buckler found herself the only British person in the great throng that gathered as the girls sang their song and were warmly applauded for it.

The move to Independence was accomplished relatively peacefully, but there remained some tension in certain areas. Missionaries to the Punjab were not able to return to their stations and this left some anxiety in those who were left behind to carry on the work. The disturbances were mainly between refugee Sikhs from the Punjab and Moslems who were poorer and more illiterate. Christians were not molested but had to find a way to identify themselves so that they were left outside the conflict.

The general strife that occurred in these times meant that nothing could ever be firmly planned so far as travel was concerned. David and Mrs. Lewis, with Elsie Wriglesworth and Coralie Paint were trying to reach Dehri and had booked tickets for the journey but coolies to carry the baggage were intimidated and had to be cajoled or bribed; when they arrived at the bus stations, they discovered there were no buses; the weather wasn't kind since it was monsoon time but all these things meant that necessity became the mother of invention and, after much trial and developing patience, they arrived at their destination, tired and weary but safe.

Meanwhile, the Trokes landed back in Bombay to be met at the ship by Aubrey Hathaway and his family. They had a safe journey and, with about forty missionaries on board, were kept busy with meetings and taking what opportunities there were to minister the Gospel.

Work on the field was limited initially by the lack of language, so language study was a major factor in the missionary's timetable. Each one had to give time to study and there were exams to pass. But how delighted they were, not only in passing their exams, but in feeling confident that they could now converse with the people they had come to reach. Despite their felt limitations, there was no shortage of opportunities to share the Gospel and, in most cases, a willingness to listen. Usually, an interpreter could be found and the message given. That message continued to be delivered in the power of the Spirit as bodies were healed and demons were cast out. It was not unusual for sick to people to ask for the prayers of the missionaries rather than the ministrations of the local witch doctor.

The assassination of Mahatma Gandhi led to riots in many areas and the missionaries were not immune, but were able to testify to the guarding and keeping power of the Lord in times of extreme difficulty and much fear. During this time, the Indian church sought to be in the forefront of helping those in need and this came to the attention of Pandit Nehru who commended those involved for their good work and for the fact that they had not made clamorous claims on the Government.

In the midst of all the strife, the missionaries were able to minister to the Parsees. These were highly intelligent, with a faith in God, but a refusal to accept Jesus as His son. But an impression was made and seven souls repented and believed the Gospel. Teenaged girls were reading books containing Old Testament stories and one seventeen year old, who had a hearing problem, was prayed for with some success.

The political unrest and uncertainty in the country encouraged many of the poor and homeless to turn to the Europeans for comfort. This helped greatly in the extension of the village work and Gospels and tracts were freely distributed. On one occasion, Jack Troke had to visit the District Magistrate, some thirty miles away. He left home at 8 a.m. and had completed his business by 5 p.m. Unfortunately, there was no return transport due to petrol rationing. With no food and nowhere to stay the night, Jack went back and explained to the magistrate. He was very polite and immediately wrote out an order allowing the bus company to obtain enough petrol to run another bus in the evening. The agent was very pleased with Jack and so were the other stranded passengers. From then on, he was their 'friend'. Thus another avenue was opened for the proclamation of the Gospel.

Literacy campaigns were developing rapidly in the newly independent India, in themselves, a mixed blessing. The missionaries were very conscious of the advantage of having a population that could read, but were also acutely aware of the steps being taken by other organisations to flood the nation with their own propaganda. Coralie Paint and Miss Mynard were ever vigilant in seeking to disseminate the Scriptures. They travelled by bicycle to village fairs and erected a Gospel booth as a base from which to distribute the Scriptures. Their wares were purchased by the illiterate and the wealthy; some seemed interested and disposed to buy until they were put off by less-interested friends and went away empty handed.

In another evangelistic venture, Marion Paint told of one worker selling 1800 Gospel portions, hymns, etc, in one day. In order to achieve this, the workers went out early in the morning, travelling by bus, train and on foot, reaching into villages that had never heard the Gospel. In all, several thousands of items of literature were distributed. Mostly, the workers had a good reception, but in some places there was opposition and their goods and money were torn from their hands.

In the Bombay area, the work was proceeding well under the guidance of Aubrey Hathaway. In a fishing village where the police were reluctant to go, they went and held an open air service in front of a Hindu temple. They had a good audience of tough fishing folk, but when they offered books and literature, they were mobbed and then followed to their car, to be left alone only when the car started to drive away.

Nearer to Bombay itself, they found a group of Telugu people. This was a colony of people who had come from the south to work in the Bombay mills. Their dwellings were constructed out of waste material and were the poorest of the poor. They had no windows and just a small door which the people crept in and the smoke from the fires came out. Several hundred people lived here, with about one hundred Christians among them. There was a very positive response to the message as Aubrey preached and the Telugu pastor interpreted. At the close, several people asked that they return every night, but this was impossible. Nevertheless, Aubrey did feel that they needed to be nurtured because the Hindus were out to recapture them for Hinduism.

In all, Aubrey was now working in English, Hindi, Telugu, Cannarese and Mahrati, and there were two Elim assemblies in Bombay. Native workers were taking their place in leadership and were giving valuable help to the work. In a six week period, forty eight were baptised in water throughout the region.

In August, 1948, Miss M.B.Ewens returned to India from furlough and was accompanied by the newest recruit, Miss Doreen Stanton. Miss Stanton had felt a call to India while quite young and determined to prepare herself for missionary service by qualifying as a State Certified Midwife, followed by a period of theological training in Elim Bible College. The two missionaries would sail to Bombay and then have a long and trying train journey to Dehri-on-Sone.

The missionaries constantly were engaged in spiritual warfare. Elsie Wriglesworth told of one woman who heard the Gospel through Misses Mynard and C. Paint and who had responded. Tetri was taken ill and rebuked by the women of her village for giving up pooja (idol worship) and for refusing to worship the sun in thanksgiving for the harvest. One evening, the missionaries found this woman in a stupor and felt it was a demonic situation. They prayed for her but she seemed little better. She was healed in body but not in spirit. As the missionaries continued to pray over the next 24 hours, the Lord appeared to her in her small mud hut. As Tetri saw Jesus, she wept and wept, pouring out her soul and crying, 'Cleanse me; cleanse me'. She found the peace of God that passes all understanding.

In 1949, the first Elim Field Conference was held at Dehri-on-Sone. By this time, Elim was working in four areas – Bengal, Bihar, United Provinces and Bombay. The gathering was a great uplift for all those attending because of the opportunity for fellowship, so often limited to just another missionary. The folks at Dehri had made arrangements for accommodation and meals and all appreciated what was done for them. Following the Conference, Aubrey Hathaway travelled with the Trokes to Calcutta to take part in their weekend services before returning to Bombay, a forty-two hour train journey.

The vastness of the continent makes it difficult for us to comprehend the challenges posed to the work. Over the years, the missionaries faithfully pushed back the borders, encroaching on enemy territory all the time as they sought to win the lost and turn them from their native darkness to God's glorious light. Journeys were often by train, bullock cart and on foot. In some cases there was a settled programme, as in the case of the dispensary work where Tuesdays, Thursdays and Saturdays were given over to a mix between work in the dispensary and sick visiting in the villages. There was only one doctor in the area, so the availability of trained midwives was a godsend. Mondays, Wednesdays and Fridays were given over to preaching in the outlying villages, usually in the company of an Indian Christian woman.

Because of the tremendous heat, sometimes rising in the summer to between 110 and 115 degrees, the missionaries were themselves subject to bouts of malaria and the debilitating effects of the humidity. An electric fan was one of their most treasured possessions and every now and then, a visit to the hills for a brief holiday was a lifesaver.

The dispensary work was varied as they dealt with sore eyes, scabies, malaria, coughs and scorpion bites. It also presented an opportunity for the Gospel and people responded. Gradually, a number of young men were becoming interested and Miss Ewens had seventeen young men's names on her Bibles Class register.

In July, 1949, the team was joined by Miss W.I. Burlinson who had worked in China for a number of years. She had gone from China to India and worked for a time among the Chinese in Bangalore and Nilgiris. At her farewell in Clapham, she talked about the work that had been done in reaching out to the Chinese in India, and described how opium addicts had been touched by the Gospel. She also told of one young man who had been saved and, subsequently, gave up his business in India to return to his native China with the Gospel.

Time and again, the missionaries had occasion to praise God for His keeping power as they travelled in the most primitive of situations. While at times they travelled by train or bus, they often had to use just whatever was available, which might include ox-carts, bicycles, palkis(a kind of sedan chair) or on foot. On one occasion, on a journey from Dehri to Dudhi, Pastors Hathaway, Lewis and Troke were travelling by train when, after just fifteen minutes, it crashed head on into another engine. Apart from bruises, they were all unhurt, so they rushed to the front of the train to see what had happened. The two engines were severely damaged and the drivers were seriously injured, thirty-two passengers and railway staff were badly hurt. They had to stay overnight in the station but moved on again next day. Their journey of about 100 miles took them over rivers and through floods, in ramshackle buses and on foot, and lasted 48 hours on the outward leg and 36 on the way back.

January, 1950 saw the missionary team augmented with the arrival of Pastor and Mrs. S.C. Law and Mr. and Mrs. Clifford Stockdale. The Laws went to work in Dudhi, having first arrived in Bombay in mid December. On the advice of friends, their journey took them by way of Dehri where the Stockdales had already settled in. Thereafter their travelling was typical, via train, lorry, bullock cart and their own feet. Roads were rough and rivers were deep as their luggage, and sometimes Mrs. Law, was carried by coolies. However, their arrival was much welcomed by Miss Ewens and Miss Wriglesworth. An idea of distances can be gained by Clifford Stockdale's description of their journey to Dehri. They left Bombay at 9 p.m. on a Wednesday and arrived in Dehri at 3 a.m. the following Friday. Their arrival coincided with the Sunday school Prize giving, so they became the guests of honour. Clifford was very quickly involved in the work, travelling with David Lewis to visit the villages and meeting some of the influential people in the area.

Meanwhile, the Laws were finding plenty to occupy them in Dudhi. His visits took him into the towns and villages where he saw the depths to which the people had sunk. He was confronted by smoking, heavy drinking and gross immorality. He saw bodies that were rotting away for lack of medical care, but whose owners were trusting in false gods they couldn't even name. His heart bled as he asked himself what Jesus might have done for such as these. His answer strengthened him for the work as he recognised that the only answer to all the needs he saw was a living relationship with the living God.

Reports indicated that God was at work as people were convicted of sin and the moving of the Spirit was much in evidence. Services were well attended and there were trophies of grace present in every service. Answers to prayer on behalf of people and situations were regularly reported and became a cause of great rejoicing. Hindus, Mohammedans and Christians were all attending the dispensary and Naomi Massih, the Indian helper, was always faithful to present the Gospel in both word and song.

In Dehri, there were signs of growth in the work. Coralie Paint and Doreen Stanton were fully engaged with midwifery duties, but they were seeing new people coming into the meetings and associating themselves with the Gospel. New families and young men were moving into the area and attaching themselves to the Mission. These included some young Christians who had been drafted to the Dehri Military Police along with their Commandant, who was also a Christian.

Also in the Dehri region, Miss Buckler reported that they had had the benefit of an aboriginal boy preacher. He had been with the missionaries for about eight months but had had to return to his village home. His name was Biraj Toppo. He was twenty years of age, had been to school and came from a family where his father had been a preacher. The young man was saved and seeking a deeper life with God, so he associated himself with David Lewis on his journeys to the villages, where he took turns in preaching, as he also did in the church. He was instrumental in selling large numbers of Gospels to people who didn't even know of the existence of the Bible, and to many who had never ever heard the name of Jesus. It was estimated that there were about 25 million aborigines in India, many of them in Bihar Province. They were not idol worshippers as such, but were animists, worshipping nature, trees, birds, etc. They lived in the forests and used long bows and arrows for hunting. They were described as a happy, lovable people, and many had become Christians as a result largely of the work of Scandinavian missionaries.

Meanwhile, the Stockdales were settling in well into the work as they pursued language studies that enabled them to take more part in the activities of the witness in bazaars and villages. On one occasion, when Clifford had taken Miss Paint and Miss Stanton to a village, he was waiting for them to return and was reading his Hindi Bible aloud. He found it relatively easy to do as the language was phonetic and he didn't need to understand the meaning. But as he read the Gospels, he found himself surrounded by a curious crowd. He discovered that they couldn't read, so there was no point in trying to sell them Gospels, so he just kept on reading, hoping that the words they heard might produce some fruit.

On a later visit to the mountains for a vacation away from the heat of the plains, the accommodation was near the language school at Landour. So Clifford decided that he would learn the Urdu language as well as Hindi. Urdu was a more difficult language since its script was based on Persian and was very different from the Dev Nagri script of Hindi. It was also read from right to left and books began at the back and worked forward. Nevertheless, he felt that this would give him opportunities to speak with many more people since it was the language of the Muslims and also of many Indians living in the Punjab and the United Provinces. Many Christians and Sikhs used it so he felt that it was another weapon in his armoury for reaching people with the Gospel.

The words of Paul come to mind when he said that he didn't want to build on another man's foundation. Pastor and Mrs. Law found themselves just there as they preached mostly to people who had never before heard the name of Jesus. The scope for such ministry seemed never ending. One report made this clear as they sought to go into a state that had hitherto been closed to the Gospel :

We are planning to leave in two days for an itinerary lasting about two months. My eyes are on the State of Surguja. The first two weeks will mostly be occupied in going from its north-east corner right down through the capital to the south-west, a return directly north to within fifty miles of this place, and then we move in an easterly direction and get the lie of the land. By that time we should know something of the prospects of getting a Mission Station established right in a new untouched field.[vi]

The Trokes in Bombay were acknowledging times of rich blessing in their sphere of labour as well. In a two month period, they had seen eight people saved, bringing the total for the year to 32. Fifteen had been baptised in the Holy Spirit and many healings had taken place. One lady had a hernia healed instantaneously after suffering for two years, while a child with infantile paralysis (polio), with one leg three and a half inches shorter than the other, was healed as the leg grew to equal length. A woman dying of pneumonia and pleurisy was healed immediately. Kid James, a former lightweight boxing champion of India, now converted, while serving in the Forces, injured his hands and fingers so that they could not be straightened. He was anointed and prayed for and was then able to use his fingers. He became a telegrapher in the central telegraph Office in Bombay. God was surely getting glory.

When the Lord's Presence is so clearly manifest, it's not long before the devil wants to make an entrance as well. Jack Troke had reason to deal with a woman who was demon possessed. She was an Anglo-Indian who was married to an Englishman, had been in the grip of the devil for many years and lived a life of debauchery. She practised witchcraft and was aided by Hindu worshippers who lived under her roof. Her husband died suddenly and this led her to enter more fully into devil worship. Her husband's savings, about £4000, were at her disposal and disappeared rapidly through her evil living and the cunning craftiness of those who lived with her. She had eight children but only three had survived the ordeal of the wicked life she led. Jack was led to speak to her and spent much time and prayer on her behalf. She had had a Sunday school upbringing and the Word reached her, but it took a further eight months of consistent care and prayer before she was finally delivered from all traces of her former life.[vii]

Missionary numbers were depleted by the fact that Miss Mynard, later to become Mrs. Jeffrey, did not return to India, but the team was again augmented in 1952 by the arrival of Miss Sylvia Beardwell from England, a trained nurse and midwife, to take up her post at Dehri-on-Sone. She was met at Bombay by Mrs. Troke and Miss Stanton, then accompanied by Miss Stanton to Dehri where they were met by Clifford Stockdale with the Jeep. Although it was almost 3 a.m., she enjoyed a hot cup of tea provided by Miss Buckler. From then on, she was learning each new day and yearning to get to grips with the language so that she could minister meaningfully to the people she had come to serve.

As Miss Buckler reviewed the work that had been done in Bihar Province alone, she was thankful to the Lord for all that had been accomplished:

- A church congregation had been established;
- A Christian girls' school where the scholars, mostly from Hindu homes, heard the Gospel daily;
- A starting point for many new Elim missionaries arriving on the field whose efforts had touched the nation in many far-flung corners of India;
- Hundreds of sick folk had been miraculously healed in answer to prayer as well as the many thousands who had received medical help and
- Thousands of Bible portions had been sold and taken into homes where the name of Jesus was unknown.

Many will have heard the stories of Sadhu Sundar Singh, but Sadhus were holy men who were given great reverence by the population, and there were many who loved the Lord. Marion Paint reported on one such man who was blessed in his ministry:

A Christian Sadhu has been holding a campaign in the village here. There are about 1000 professing Christians in the village but many are living in sin, drinking, immoral, etc., but God is working among them through the Sadhu who is Pentecostal. The campaign was overwhelming and thousands and thousands came. One night, there were twelve thousand attending. The meetings were held for men and women only on alternate nights. The people gathered hours before the meetings were due to commence and were seated in rows, the blind in one place and the lame in another. I went to the last meeting with a deaf and dumb girl and

saw between three and five thousand women (all heathen) sitting in rows with more people standing in the cold on the outside of the tent.
. . . The sick were prayed for, first the blind, there were rows and rows of them, about 50 in each row. The Sadhu walked down a row, anointing the people, sometimes rebuking an evil spirit, then placed his hands on their heads and said just 'Christ'. The whole row then went home and the next row moved up. The little girl was prayed for and was able to hear and speak a little, but she was to be taught how to speak over a period of time. He would pray for the dumb only when he felt the Spirit resting mightily on him. It was all very Indian but richly blessed of God.

As early as 1953, the missionaries realised the importance of indigenous workers. In the absence of missionaries from time to time, and for various reasons, the Indian Christians had to carry on with the services and Bible classes. It was encouraging to see the progress that had been made in the interim period. Requests from the local people that meetings be started rather than the initiative coming from the missionary was an indication that a sense of responsibility was growing.

In February, 1954, there was an interesting article in a national paper -
The President, Dr. Prasad, assured Christian missionaries in the country that they would be given full freedom to preach Christianity and do social service work among the people of India, but none of these activities should be inspired by a desire for conversions. He went on to say that their services should be given purely out of love for the people but not with the motive of conversion. He commented that the Gita told them to serve and leave the results in the hands of God, going on to say that if service were rendered in that spirit, it would be more than welcome. In response to the President's speech, the Chief Executive of the Garo Hills District Council replied: The standard that our people has attained at present is due to the work of the missionaries, to whom we owe a great debt of gratitude, and we would earnestly pray that restrictions should not be imposed on their work as our progress in all spheres of life will thereby be retarded. We also request that the good work done by these selfless people in the fields of education, social welfare, medical and other nation-building activities should be encouraged as heretofore.

From time to time, there were sad situations arising from the death of co-workers, and in 1954, the work lost two faithful women. Miss Indu M. Biswas was an Indian Bible woman who had worked with the Elim missionaries from as early as 1916 when she laboured alongside Miss M.F. Barbour. Latterly, she worked with our missionaries at Dheri-on-Sone where she was much loved and highly respected. Just a little later, Miss Ewens also had her home call after twenty five years on the field. Prior to coming to India, she had spent some time in China. Throughout her years of service, she ever displayed the indomitable courage and spirit of a pioneer missionary. Hardships she often and gladly endured; not for her a life of ease and comfort, but rather that dusty Indian road, a crude, jogging bullock cart and the humble hospitality of an Indian home. Her spirit of faithfulness and self-sacrifice endeared her to missionary and Indian alike. Over the years, she worked tirelessly to establish new works and to extend the Kingdom.

The whole question as to the validity of missionary work remains an issue for some. It was ever thus. Clifford Stockdale addressed the question at one time and laid out what he saw as the justification for overseas missions. He defined five reasons –

1. It is the command of Jesus (Matt. 28:19; Mark 16:15)
2. It is the only hope of salvation for those without the Gospel (Rom.10:13-15)
3. Heathenism is sending out missionaries – Islam, Buddhism, Hinduism and many other false cults
4. The open doors on the mission field and
5. God blesses the missionary minded. He cited the experience of Dr. Oswald Smith of the People's Church, Toronto as a case in point.

In 1940, two missionaries from India had been on furlough and were itinerating around the UK. In one service, they challenged the young people with the work of missions and one young lady who was saved and baptised in water and the Spirit, had had a desire to serve, maybe in Africa or China. In this service, the needs of India were impressed on her and she responded to the call. In preparation, she took up nursing training, believing that, on completion, she would immediately go to the field, but it was not to be. In fact, it was over eighteen years before she eventually arrived in September, 1958. It had seemed that every door was closed and the waiting period became a real testing time for her call. But Olive Jarvis never wavered and, in the intervening years, learned many valuable lessons, not least in patience and perseverance, and drew ever closer to the Lord. Having arrived on the field, she was soon immersed in the work.

In 1960, after more than thirty years of service in India, Pastor and Mrs. Jack Troke retired from the field, but not from the Lord's work. Mrs. Troke was a native of New Zealand and that is where they intended to spend their retirement. They had already had about twenty years' missionary endeavour behind them when they joined Elim in 1947. Labouring at first near Poona, they put enormous effort into the work. When they moved to Calcutta, their ministry was blessed and fruitful. Then, when the Hathaways left Bombay, the Trokes took over the work in the great bustling seaport and saw many saved, healed and baptised in the Spirit during their time there. Their ministry touched Hindu and Moslem, Parsee and Jew, as well as many nominal Christians.[viii]

As the Trokes' period of service came to an end, the Lord was already preparing that the numbers of missionaries should be maintained. Early in 1961, Frank Newey, who had felt called to China, but had seen the door close, was commissioned for the work in India and was given a royal send-off from the Graham Street church in Birmingham. Frank had been pastoring in Ealing and then Camberwell and, while there, made good use of the time for preparation as he attended the Missionary School of Medicine and the Wycliffe Language course. At this time, Elim was active in five areas – Bombay, Dehri-on-Sone, Ramanujganj, Dudhi and Rihand. The last four were scattered in a 200 mile square in the plains of north India, 900 miles north-east of Bombay, 300 miles west of Calcutta and 200 miles south of the Himalayas with the river Ganges in between.

Frank arrived in Bombay while the Trokes were on furlough but an Elim brother from New Zealand met him and looked after him until he was ready to travel on to Dehri-on-Sone. Over the period he was there, he was able to visit all the mission stations. About a year after his arrival in Ramanujganj, the Stockdale family went home to the UK and never returned to the field. Meetings there were held in the mission-owned bungalow. A church had not been built although land was purchased for the purpose. There was no gas, running water or electricity. They used paraffin lamps and wood-burning stoves, while water was drawn from a well as in Bible days. They toured the tree-covered plains in the four-wheel drive ex-army jeep, visiting all the villages and using the jeep's battery to show filmstrips of Bible stories.

One of Frank's happy duties was to accompany Jean Ayling during one of her visits.[ix] They travelled for three hours by train in third class to meet the Stockdales, enabling Jean to discover for herself how the missionaries normally travelled. The remainder of the journey was in the mission jeep to Ramanujganj. The journey was as eventful as ever as the jeep stuck in the middle of a river and the passengers had to get out and paddle to the bank. As always, Jean took many slides and was available to the churches at home to provide insights into the life and work on the mission field. While there, she reported that her visit was overshadowed by the arrival of a refrigerator that had been sent out with funds raised by Elim young people.

At the same time, the Lewises were on the Rihand station. Nearby, the Americans were building a hydroelectric dam and the local Indian farmers complained that the water would be no good to them if all the power was taken out of it to make electricity! On one occasion, Frank was travelling on a packed train when he started to eat his lunch of hard boiled eggs and chapattis. The men sitting opposite him became enraged and threatened to throw his luggage off the train until an educated Muslim explained to him that Hindus never eat any animal products and they were offended at his hard boiled eggs. A hasty apology saved his luggage and taught him a lesson he never forgot. But trains also provided opportunities for the Gospel as the missionaries would sit and read and the natural curiosity of their fellow-passengers gave them openings to explain what they read.

Part of the work being done by the missionaries was the planning and erection of church buildings. Clifford Stockdale had expertise in design and drawing and David Lewis and Frank Newey became involved in actual construction. On Easter Sunday, 1964, a new building was opened at Turra Renukoot. Forty five adults and twenty five children, two missionary ladies from Dudhi and one American family attended the ceremony. Some six months later, a new building was consecrated at Dehri and a local man, S.S. Sharma, was inducted as the pastor. Brother Sharma was a high caste Hindu who came to faith in Christ following a vision of Jesus.

Unfortunately, illness overtook Frank and he had to return home after four years. A poisoned foot meant that he had to be carried across a swollen river from Ramanujganj to catch a bus to Dehri and then a train to Dehra Dun, then by bus 7000 feet up into the mountains to Mussoorie to recuperate before he could travel home.

In 1962, following a period of study at I.B.T.I.[x] in Sussex, John and Sally Prentice, natives of Northern Ireland, went to Madras to help brother D.H.Joseph, a colleague from the Bible school, with his vision of training nationals for evangelism. As this work was in the south of the country and Elim's work was all in the north, the Prentices went out in faith without denominational backing. Before going to India, John had felt the Spirit of the Lord impress upon him that he would serve in the south for two and a half years and then move. In just that exact time, they found themselves moving north to join with the Elim work as a result of the influence of David Lewis whom they met while at language school in Mussouri in 1965. There they learned Hindustani and subsequently took the oversight of the church at Rihand.

During their time in the north, the missionaries were subject to the same famine conditions as the Indians, but John was able to arrange for unemployed people to come and dig the garden of the mission bungalow and some other land nearby that had not been cultivated for a while, and to sow them with vegetables and grain. This provided not only work, but food as well, money having been supplied by the Movement to help out in just such circumstances.

The Prentices' first furlough was in 1969. During this time, G. Wesley Gilpin, on behalf of the Elim Missionary Society, visited the field and saw at first hand the work of the Maranatha Bible Training Institute[xi]. He was impressed by the possibilities this work entailed, particularly in the light of the fact that many missionaries had been refused visas to return and new missionaries were not being given much encouragement about entry, and felt that association with this work was a means to evangelising India. Elim therefore negotiated an affiliation with the Maranatha work in Madras, which the Prentices had helped to found, for the co-operative training of national workers and, on their return, they therefore rejoined Henry Joseph, remaining on the field until their homecoming in 1974.

1965 saw the return to India of Jack and Grace Troke. They had sought to retire to New Zealand, but were unable to settle, so found the means to take up the reins again in India. Back in Bombay, they lost no time in involving themselves in the whole range of ministry to which they had been accustomed, with hospital visitation taking priority as well as reaching out to the villages. Jack's comment was that hospital visitation brings tears and smiles, but village visitation brings anguish and sadness of heart. Bombay itself was the seat of endemic infectious disease and the authorities had a mass vaccination programme in place, but people were dying all over the city and hospitals were full. Sadly, the Hindus believed that smallpox had some kind of religious connotation and refused to be vaccinated, so the health authorities were having great difficulty in stamping out the disease. The missionaries constantly claimed the protection of a gracious God to keep them safe.

In the following year, India faced its worst famine in 100 years. In addition to a lack of food, there was a scarcity of water as well. 450 million people throughout India were affected and in Bombay alone, there were five million people suffering. Food was rationed and there were regular reductions in the amounts. People living in high rise buildings were told to grow their own vegetables in plant pots as there were insufficient supplies coming in from the countryside due to a lack of water for irrigation. The country was on the verge of the hot season when heat would be the predominant feature and the situation could only get worse.

Because of the shortage of water, mills and business firms were closing down through lack of power, and thousands were being laid off every week. Many of the workers had large families, and rent to pay on their dwellings. The newspapers were daily reporting tragedies of suicides and whole families were destitute and hungry. Because of the difficulties, many were picketing, stealing and looting, sometimes murdering, in order to get money, jewellery and food that they could find. The streets were filled with people begging, hoping to find some relief. The missionaries tried their best to help those who came to them, but they themselves were also caught up in the situation.

The desperation of those days was caught in a newspaper report seen by David Lewis with the headline – *Wanted – Someone to care.* It told the story of a woman found lying in the middle of a road. A passer-by brought her to the safety of the pavement where she continued to lie. No-one knew her or where she had come from. She had had a piece of sacking for a covering but someone had stolen that. Driven by her hunger, she had stolen some food from a nearby stall and had been beaten by the owner.

Hundreds passed her by daily without a second glance. The reporter said that the good Samaritan who had lifted her from the middle of the road went to a local coal yard and found a sack that he brought back to cover her. As she shivered under the sack, she told that she had been forsaken by her family, driven from her home by her daughter and son-in-law and was now destitute, with only a stone for a pillow and the cold pavement for her couch. She was too old, too cold to beg or steal, but who cared? The police were informed but said it wasn't in their jurisdiction, they should try the S.P.C.A. but they said they only cared for animals.

David's point was that if there had been a missionary nearby, no doubt some arrangement could have been made, but in all of India's five hundred million, the number of missionaries was still woefully small. Jack Troke told of one old lady who had not eaten for three days. Food shortages resulted in many deaths and, in some cases, even the food rationing system had broken down. Police were reporting deaths on the streets of Bombay, ten in one day including three young children. As a consequence of this information reaching the UK, an appeal was made to the churches and money was sent to help to alleviate the suffering of some at least.

Meanwhile, the work of evangelism was continuing, especially towards those living on the edge of eternity. A work among the Jews in the area was producing results as people were responding to the Gospel. A feature of the work was the production of testimonies by those whose lives had been transformed and, over a period of time, several of these appeared in the Elim Evangel.

The Maranatha work in Madras was also seeing development that gave cause for praise. John Prentice, on his return from furlough reported that whereas there had been six churches established in the early years of Maranatha, there were now twenty-five and it was expected that this number would rise to thirty by the end of that year. The people had a mind to work and John spoke of one pastor, a shepherd boy before going to the Bible school, who had now built a good church out of his small allowance of £7.50 per month. He also reported that the Gospel was reaching out into the islands of the sea –

Brother Thankachan has now gone to the Andaman Islands. He wrote to say that, as the boat left the mainland, many became sick, so he ministered to them and pointed some to the Lord. On reaching the islands, which are in the Sea of Bengal, he felt so alone as he watched many being greeted by friends as they left the ship and he had no one to meet him. He stuck his head out of a porthole and shouted "Hallelujah!" Someone responded from the crowd on the quay and he made his first contact.

Evangelism was also taking place on a large scale. A mission was conducted by a local pastor and one of his elders which was supported by 3000 people and there were reports of many conversions and miracles of healing. As a result, John Prentice had the joy of dedicating a new Maranatha church.

But there were evidences of a closing door in India. Some years before, this writer recalls Aubrey Hathaway reporting to the General Conference his feeling that the encroachment of communism from the north would one day effectively close the door to the Gospel. The Missionary Society took the news seriously and sought to indigenise the work as far as possible from that time forward. The association with Maranatha had an impact on this in that it was committed to training national workers to reach their own people. By 1972, missionaries were being refused visas to return to the field and potential missionaries were being refused entry. When the door finally closed, the then International Missions Board decided to take a step of faith and lodge enough funding in the country to help the work for a five year period.

A young man who has made a significant contribution to the work in India is Augustine Jebakumar (often referred to just as Jeb!). The Province of Bihar, an area roughly the size of Great Britain, had been given up by many denominational missionaries as a lost cause because their work had proved unfruitful over a number of years. But the patience and diligence of the Elim missionaries began to pay dividends and by the early 1980s, the Elim work was the largest in Bihar and was making great gains. But such was the need that more than 40,000 villages out of a total of 70,000 had not been reached with the Gospel. Over a two year period, the missionaries in Dheri-on-Sone had been praying for a national worker. God immediately put into the heart of a young man who was praying for north India in general. He not only placed a burden but also told him to go. Since he was then working for English Electric and had heavy family responsibilities, he denied the call and gave many reasons for doing so. However, the Spirit of God maintained the pressure and through prophecies and the Word, reminded him of the call.

He had been born into a Christian family but came to faith in Christ when he was 21. A staunch member of the Church of South India, he was totally opposed to Pentecostal truth. But God revealed to him the need for fullness in his life and this led him to a Pentecostal group. He was baptised in the Holy Spirit and then in water by immersion and finally, resigned from his job. Through the Lord's guidance, he went to Bihar, to Dehri-on-Sone. Once there, he had to learn a completely new language; he didn't even know the alphabet, but God helped him and he learned very quickly.

In a very short time, he was making an impact on the region and, in particular, his involvement in major campaigns stimulated both him and the work. Many conversions and miracles of healing were reported, even including some young men, themselves recently saved, going among the sick to pray for them. At a later campaign in 1975, Olive Jarvis was helped in the mission by Pat Hinxman, Sylvia Beardwell being on furlough at that time. Again, there was news of much blessing.

The development of Augustine's ministry resulted in the formation of GEMS – Gospel Echoing Missionary Society, of which he became the General Secretary and Director of Missions. This was not only a Gospel outreach, but also a training facility for young people in the north of the country, and described by Patrick Johnstone and Jason Mandryk as making a major contribution[xii]. Training consisted of short spells of Bible teaching and then practical outreach. The teams were used to publicise meetings and to draw people into hearing the Gospel. On a visit by John C. Smyth and David Butcher, they saw much that had been accomplished as they were hosted by Olive Jarvis and Joy Bath.

Joy's presence in India had come about by a somewhat circuitous route. Initially called to nurse in Rhodesia (Zimbabwe), she had left there in 1977 because of the war and attended Elim Bible College, Capel, for two years. On her graduation, she then took up her post at Dehri-on-Sone. John and David were able to testify to the tremendous sense of God's Presence in fellowship and worship as they shared the Word with gathered crowds night after night.

In recent years, thanks to the wonder of television, we have been made very much aware of the devastation caused by tsunamis and hurricanes. In late 1977, the churches in the Madras area were assaulted by a cyclone that destroyed much of the countryside. At this time, Maranatha had 65 assemblies, with churches varying in size between 30 and 100. Their printing press had been supplied by the ladies of E.W.M.A. and there were seven children's homes run by the churches, with about 520 children in care. Radio work was also being undertaken through FEBA in the Seychelles in a twice weekly broadcast.

The cyclone was the worst calamity to hit India in 70 years. The coastal region was destroyed by 90 mph winds and there was extremely heavy rainfall that caused the breach of dams and the flooding of the area. Towns and villages were submerged and waves of from three to thirty metres were recorded. As a result, they left four feet of standing water and some boats were found inland 5 kilometres from the coast. Death of cattle and livestock had not been assessed but it was estimated that more than 15,000 people had been killed. All six Maranatha churches in the Andrha State were completely wiped out. David Ayling was Elim's President that year, and he was visiting the area. In fact, he escaped Madras just before the cyclone struck, but he was able to co-ordinate the appeal for help in the UK and the churches began to send in supplies to meet the needs.

Emergencies occur at the most inconvenient times. Olive Jarvis came home from Bihar and, at almost the same time, her co-worker, Sylvia Beardwell became ill and had to be taken to hospital in north India and then, to Delhi. This left Joy Bath on her own and the Dehri centre without adequate oversight and an appeal was made in the UK for someone to hold the reins on a temporary basis. Pastor and Mrs. David Dean, then in the Nuneaton church, responded. David was well known for his Bible teaching abilities and pastoral care while Mrs. Dean was an experienced nurse. Their lack of knowledge of the language meant that they needed much prayer but their ministry in Dehri was a blessing at a time of crisis.

But he was thrown into the deep end immediately as his arrival coincided with Graduation day for students in the GEMS Bible school and he was to preach the Word as 12 students were commissioned for the work. Before long, not only was he working in Dehri, but his ministry was sought by Maranatha in Madras. He was met by Henry Joseph at Madras airport and soon found himself preaching in David Dayanandan's[xiii] church, the newly-founded Headquarters' Church and various other Tamil churches. The student body in the Maranatha Bible School sat under his teaching for the next ten days as he talked to them about "The Life of Christ". Only then was he free to return to Dehri as the Madras folk testified to great blessing through his ministry.

The GEMS work in Bihar became the main focus of Elim's work in the north. Expatriate missionaries were limited and, often, non-existent, so the work of GEMS was supported to the full. Their development seemed to be never ending as they added an English language school to their outreach activities. Beginning in 1983 with just twenty-seven pupils, by 1984, it had one hundred and sixteen. There were six teachers, all but one Christians and, for a short period of time, the help of Olive Jarvis and Joy Bath. The ages of the children varied from three to eleven and all were from well-to-do families. Twenty-three of the children travelled 35 kilometres each day as this was the nearest English school.

Just the following year, the Indian government refused to renew the residency permit for Joy despite pleas from senior members of the Elim Church Executive. It appeared at that time that there was a concerted effort to refuse residency permits for Christian workers seeking to enter the country. It was in foreseeing this contingency that support had been directed to the GEMS work. It should be noted that the support of the Maranatha work in Madras was also continued.

It was an ongoing policy of GEMS to establish Hindi and Christian schools everywhere their workers went. They felt that if they simply went with the Gospel, people would not wish to hear them, but if they set up a school and placed a teacher in charge, he gained great respect in the district because of his position. They also required parents to sign a form stating that they were happy to let their children listen to the Gospel every day in school. Forty-five per cent of Bihar's population of 70 million were children. By 1987, GEMS had five schools and three orphanages with six hundred children in their care. In the summer of that year, many of the children in the homes were baptised in the Holy Spirit. Three discipleship training centres had been opened and an institute of evangelism with a one year course had been started. Fourteen students were in training and, in their field course, they had led 129 people to Christ, baptised 67 and a further 62 were waiting to be baptised. The GEMS vision was that there would be a dedicated Bible Institute in the area.

In the midst of God's blessing, there was much persecution. Communism was a challenge and underground factories were manufacturing weapons, but these things served only to strengthen their resolve. Women's teams were formed to reach the women and Bible camps were held for teaching and fellowship. Major crusades were undertaken with good results. Attendances ranged from 500 to 800 in different places, with responses to the Gospel and notable miracles adding to the Church.

The work in India continued to be blessed even although UK missionaries were no longer able to offer input. But the vision of both the GEMS teams and the Maranatha workers has meant that the Gospel is still the power of God unto salvation to those who will embrace it.

i *Elim Evangel*, Vol. 11, Issue 14, p.220.

ii Anonymous: *Elim Evangel*, Vol. 14, Issue 40, p.629.

iii Reported by Marion Paint. *Elim Evangel*, Vol. 20, Issue 6, p.93.

iv Edith Mynard married Henry Jeffery and went with him to serve in Brazil.

v Carlisle Elim Church had a very strong ministry to the soldiers garrisoned in the town during and shortly after the war. Pastor John Woodhead was the minister at that time.

vi A full report of the journeys and ministry was given in *Elim Evangel*, Vol. 32. Issue 24, pp. 282-284

vii *Elim Evangel*, Vol. 33. Issue 43, pp 666,667.

viii A retrospect of their thirty years in India appeared in the *Elim Evangel*, Vol.41. Issue 24, pp. 370,371,379.

ix Reference has been made elsewhere to Jean's visits to various fields on the basis that she had concessionary travel available to her through her employment with BOAC. Her report of her visit is in *Elim Evangel*, Vol.43. Issue, 48, pp. 760-763.

x International Bible Training Institute, Burgess Hill, Sussex, a Pentecostal training centre for ministry.

xi A full report about the founding and work of the Maranatha Evangelical Movement in South India was given by Henry Joseph in the *Elim Evangel*, Vol.54. Issue 8, pp.12,13. See also Issue 27, pp10,11; Vol.60. Issue 12, pp.8,9.

xii Patrick Johnstone and Jason Mandryk in *Operation World* (CD, 2001).

xiii David Dayanandan was the President of GEMS which had its inception in Madras before extending its work into Bihar in the north.

CHAPTER 25
JAPAN

MISS VIOLET W. M. HOSKINS

Violet Hoskins was a native of Bournemouth where she found Christ as her Saviour under the ministry of Pastor William Henderson. Some months later, she experienced the Baptism in the Holy Spirit and, with it, a renewed desire to serve the Lord. She began to witness effectively in her own locality mainly through the Elim Crusaders youth group. As she was praying, she had a vivid experience with God who laid Japan on her heart as a charge for future service.

Before long, the way opened up for her to attend the Elim Bible College, although she still had no direct connection with Japan and was intending to make her own way there, independent and unsponsored. But, in the providence of God, the Elim Missionary Society accepted her as a missionary and she made plans to go to Japan, there to associate with a Mrs. M. Taylor, a veteran missionary in Kobe, who offered her a welcome to fellowship and service in what was described as "a populous and fruitful field of ripe opportunity". Thus, in early January 1931, Violet set sail down the Thames estuary in thick fog with the sounds of singing ringing in her ears from the many friends who had attended to see her off.

She was met at Kobe harbour about one month later by Mrs. Taylor and a number of other believers, also singing, and accompanied on two drums and other instruments. As was the way with new missionaries, she was plunged directly into language study the following Monday morning, but not before discovering over the weekend that the Spirit of God was moving in a mighty way among the believers there.

Her association was with the Door of Hope Mission where souls, once bound by sin and superstition, with the deep marks of the results of sin on their very faces, broken and bruised in body, were finding freedom through the Gospel. Despite the advances made in the nation, with its high culture and achievements, it was still a land of spiritual darkness. Indeed, it had been described as the "midnight land," and beneath the cloak of all its Buddhism, it was a seething pot of iniquity, where flesh and blood were offered day and night on the altars of lust and passion. Violet found it to be a land of broken hearts and bodies, a land upon which the judgements of God had fallen more than in any other land as earthquakes had swept away thousands. But she saw the possibility of finding 'treasures of darkness' (Isaiah 45:3) as her burden from the Lord for the women of the land was brought more clearly into focus by her new experiences.

One of the main means of outreach was by holding open air services at which many hundreds would stop and listen. The very effectiveness of their witness was demonstrated by the surrender of lives to the Lord. Their own manifestation of the love of

Christ was a powerful means of reaching many who had never felt even human love. One young woman cried for joy when she heard that Jesus loved her and her kimono was wet with tears as she found peace with God. Her life was turned around and the missionaries watched as she blossomed and grew in grace under the influences of God's gracious sunshine. Others, believers, were rejoicing in the coming of the Spirit in power into their lives.

A baptismal service was held when nine people passed through the waters, including a family of four – parents and two grown-up children. These were people who had a bright witness for Christ despite having suffered severe persecution for becoming Christians. One of the needs for the fellowship was for a man able to lead the church and, after much prayer, such a one was found. Hayashi San heard the call to help to feed God's 'lambs'. He was a young man, earnest and Spirit-filled, who had himself, led others to the Lord. As the work developed, two further branch Sunday schools were opened in new districts, with a good number of children attending both. Through the children, parents were reached, some of whom came and were saved.

It was a great joy for Violet to be able to write home from time to time with news of growth in the work. Men and women were coming to the Saviour, some in the open air meetings. One old believer had been at death's door, but after prayer, was delivered and rose from his bed to find Jesus, not only as his Healer, but also as his Baptiser with the Spirit. With renewed energy and drive, he began to seek others to introduce to his Lord. Indeed, it was a mark of their witness that souls were saved, broken bodies were being instantaneously, miraculously healed and believers were being baptised with the Holy Spirit with signs following.

With Kobe as a base, the work sought to open up further preaching points in the surrounding villages. Violet's first outstation was Oshio, which took up most of her time, but she was also inundated with requests to visit other villages with the Gospel. In 1934, the Lord opened the door and Violet went to Kakogawa where she saw many blessed and some receiving Christ as Saviour. One young woman came from the village of Onomachi and she was persistent in praying that Violet would one day go to her village with the message of God's love. It had several large schools and a large population, but no missionary, no Sunday school for the crowds of children and no gospel meetings. On the other hand, it was a Buddhist stronghold where multitudes lived and died without hope of salvation.

Soon after arriving in Kakogawa, Violet had visited Onomachi with her Bible woman and although there was deep snow on the ground at that time, they had real joy in distributing gospel tracts and speaking to people who came running from all directions to see to them. When they had left that evening, there were many requests that they return to tell more of the Gospel.

At the beginning of 1935, Violet received a message from Nishimura San, the young woman from Onomachi, begging her to come to her village and hold a meeting in her home because all her people wanted to hear the Gospel; this message had come many times before, but this time, Violet sensed it was of the Lord and prepared to go. When she arrived with her Bible woman, she found the mother, sisters, brother and friends eagerly waiting to hear the Word. The Lord gave a mighty increase as they sang and praised, and tears fell freely as dry, hard hearts were broken by His love. They said, "It is all so wonderful. It is the first time we have heard and we want you to come here always and teach us more of this wonderful Book; that is what we have been wanting." After this very precious service, they went out into the village to hold an open air and distributed tracts to the large crowds that gathered. Their journey home that night was with much rejoicing and praising God for His wonderful leading, and believing Him for 'greater things'. They subsequently travelled twice a month to this village and saw the work develop despite continuing difficulties and opposition.

The following few years were marked by blessing and increase although, in the early 1940s, the spectre of war was beginning to raise questions about the continuing viability of the work. There is little further information on Violet's labours and her association with the work in Japan.

CHAPTER 26

MALAYSIA

No one could have thought, when they saw the headline in the Elim Evangel,[i] that they were reading of an event that would one day be instrumental in the opening of the Elim work in Malaysia.

At the age of 15, Rajindark Singh was invited to a Pentecostal church by a school friend. There, she found Christ and went home and told her mother. Her father was a Sikh lay preacher who expected his family to attend the local temple. Obviously, there was a strong negative reaction to Rajindark's news.

For the next five years, she was denied fellowship and had to survive solely by reading a Bible she had been given. But then an opportunity arose to go to England to train as a nurse and one of the first things she did was to find a good church. A friend took her to a Pentecostal church and there, she rededicated her life to the Lord. She became a State Enrolled Nurse and a member of Banbury Elim Church.

In the course of time, she met and married Richard Buxton, an Articled Clerk to a firm of Solicitors and, together, they entered the Elim Bible College in 1980. For some time, Richard had had a growing conviction that God was directing him into full-time service with an emphasis on missionary work. Rajindark was deeply challenged by hearing Augustine Jebakumar of India speak to the 1980 Elim Conference, and she and her husband began to seek the Lord about working in India. An initial application was made to the Missions Board (IMB) for work in the northern province of Bihar. Their application for India was accepted but the political situation changed before this could progress and the door to India closed.

Some time later, a need arose in Tanzania for someone to continue the Bible school work founded by Pastor and Mrs. Tate in Tanga. The IMB invited the Buxtons to consider this as a possible area of ministry and their response was positive. Thus, in early 1986, Richard and Rajindark, with their children, Esther and Rachel, found themselves being met by Alan and Anne Renshaw who took them to Arusha for preliminary orientation and language study. Following this period, they moved south to Tanga where they became involved in the work of the Bible school.

They spent about five years here[ii] in Tanga and were approaching the end of their term of service when they sensed in their spirits that there were problems in Rajindark's family in Malaysia. Part of their difficulty was that there had been little or no contact with the family since Rajindark had married a Christian and was one herself. However, their sensitivity and response to the prompting of the Holy Spirit resulted in a restoration of family relationships and the opening of an Elim work in Kuala Lumpur.

Let Richard tell the story as reported in Direction magazine:[iii]

" 'Some very strange things have been happening to me recently that I've not been able to tell anyone about, in case they think I'm mad. Could you please help me to understand what it all means?' This question was posed to Richard by his brother-in-law, Jagjit Singh, a leader of all the Sikhs in his region and president of his local temple.

"Towards the end of 1990, a couple of months before we were due to leave Tanga, having completed the work we were sent out to do, Rajindark kept saying that she felt impressed upon her that we must go to Malaysia soon to visit her family. So I wrote to them asking if we could visit at Easter, the earliest time we could travel there after our return to UK in December.

"Before receiving a reply, and while still in Africa, we got news that Rajindark's brother was in a grave financial situation. We had few details, but we knew the amount involved. It was a large sum. Having no house or furniture of our own in England, and our own future being uncertain, we had saved as we were able for the contingency that we may have to set up house again from scratch if we should settle again in England.

"We considered the situation and as we prayed, we had no doubt that the Lord wanted us to send everything Jagjit needed. Knowing it would take a long time to be processed through the banking system, we decided to send him a telegram informing him of what we were doing, followed by a letter telling him the reasons we were doing it, namely that that we loved Jesus and as we had prayed, He had directed us to send the money, that He had always met us in our times of need and so we could not stand by and do nothing in Jagjit's time of need. We heard no more.

"On arriving in Malaysia at Easter, the family welcomed us with kindness and understandable emotion after Rajindark's long absence. This was the first time they had seen their grandchildren or me, although we had been married for thirteen years. The next day, Jagjit kept asking questions about Christianity, like, 'As a Christian, to whom do you pray, God or Jesus?' and 'What rules do you have to follow as a Christian?' His questioning continued over several days until I eventually arranged to talk to him at a time and place where we could be alone.

"Then he told me that he had been sounding me out over the past few days to see if I was the kind of person he could talk to. He must have found me acceptable because he began to tell me of the 'strange things' to which he had referred.

"He said that at the end of last year he had gone through a terrible crisis. He had discovered a plot of land that belonged to no-one. Knowing the correct steps to obtain full title to the land, he went through the necessary legal procedures, but in the process, incurred substantial legal and court costs. It was necessary to borrow money to complete the transaction. Unfortunately, the money lender turned nasty. He sent round the 'heavy boys' who threatened to beat him up, imprison him, even to kill him. They also did the same to his widowed mother, who he looked after.

"He tried every avenue he could to borrow money, but could find help nowhere. This went on week after week and month after month. He couldn't eat and lost 15lbs. He couldn't sleep at night and just lay awake praying to God. His problem was he didn't know which god he should pray to. As a Sikh and a Sikh leader, he had come to realise that Sikhism was not the road to God. 'We were lost, like being in the jungle without a compass', he explained. So he prayed to every god he knew, crying out, 'If you are the true God, reveal yourself to me and solve my problem, and I will be your slave for life!'

"He tried the god of the Muslims, then of the Buddhists, then of the Hindus, and every other one he could think of, but nothing happened. Time passed and matters were growing worse, so he tried the God of the Christians. 'By now I was so desperate', he explained, 'I had said to God – Tomorrow is my last day. If you do not reveal yourself to me tomorrow, I can go no more. I will commit suicide!' The very next day, our telegram arrived. 'I knew then that the true God was the God of the Christians.'

"He had meant what he said when he promised to be God's slave. Then, as he would be praying alone, he would be conscious that someone else would be standing in the room. He said, 'I could never see him, but I always knew exactly where he was standing and I would feel constrained to go over and bow before him and worship him. Tell me, who could this be?' At the same time, he would feel surrounded by a spiritual 'presence'. He had had experience in the past with evil spirits and knew about them. But this was something quite different. It felt holy. It made him feel rapturous, not afraid. Not only could he feel it around him, but it arose within him too until he began saying things he didn't understand. When I asked him which language, he replied, 'Mainly in English, although I did also speak in a language that was quite unknown to me.'

"Not quite sure of the situation, I asked him to invite Jesus into his life, which he did, although I soon found this to have been unnecessary. He then went to a certain part of the room, bowed down eastern fashion with his head touching the floor and cried out, 'Jesus is Lord! Jesus Christ is Saviour!' and then, with a great anointing, began prophesying, 'This man needs you, help him. The people are in despair, bring as many as you can to the Lord.' He later went on to prophesy the same things that God had impressed on my heart nine months before while still in Africa. During a period of fasting and prayer, I had been seeking the Lord's direction about our future ministry after we left Africa.

"'This is what happens,' he said, 'I don't know why I say these things or what they mean. Can you help me to understand what it all means?' I had never before met anyone who had been saved and baptised in the Holy Spirit without anyone leading them into those experiences. But now that I understood that this is what had happened, I was able to explain that the Person appearing to him was the Son of God and that it was the Presence of the Holy Spirit that he felt. The words he was speaking were as a result of the gift of prophecy – and tongues in the case of the unknown language – which had followed upon his being Baptised in the Holy Spirit.

"This explanation gave him great peace of mind and with excitement, he exclaimed, 'My only desire now is to bring as many as I can to Christ; nothing means anything else to me.' Because of his standing in society, he was in a position to witness to hundreds about Christ."

The Missions Board then arranged for the Buxtons to be made available to this fledgling work and they served from 1991 to 1995 establishing a viable fellowship under the auspices of the Elim Pentecostal Church. The work is progressing up to the present, although external support has been frugal. Nevertheless, the Lord of the work is the Overseer of the work and will bring it to its fulfilment in His plan.

i *Elim Evangel.* Vol.62, Issue 11, page 8. " Sikh wanted same joy as Pentecostals."

ii See chapter on Tanzania for details of their work in this area.

iii *Direction* magazine. Issue June, 1991.

CHAPTER 27

MONGOLIA/FORMOSA/TAIWAN

JOSEPH and MINA PAYNE

In 1932, Joe and Mina Payne were students in the Elim Bible College when they heard the call of God to Mongolia. Without any kind of official backing, they responded and set out for the barren wastes north of China. When they reached Kalgan, the Chinese official told them that if they insisted on going further, they must make a declaration that they did so at their own risk. The Chinese Government could take no responsibility for their safety. They were told that the whole area was swarming with bandits, but after much quibbling, they were given permission to proceed on condition that they made the declaration.

At six a.m. the next day, having paid a protection fee for going at their own risk(!), carts were hired and they set out for the bandit-infested land of Mongolia. They passed through the Great Wall, saying goodbye to Kalgan which was the gateway to Mongolia, and leaving civilisation behind.

A few hours through the Russian Valley and a stiff mountain climb brought them to an overview of the plains of Mongolia. Joe said that he would never forget the first impression the plain made upon him. There was room on the vast expanse to move about freely in their quest for souls. In the next six and a half years, they would be adventuring with and for God, with many trials, many of which were unsought and often unwelcome.

One of the major challenges involved the climate, which at times ranged from the tropical with temperatures of 100 degrees to the winter of 30 degrees below zero. Another was the bandits who were not simply petty thieves, but men of blood and torture who thought no more of killing a man than of killing a fly. Perhaps the major challenge was in attempting to reach people with the Gospel who had never heard the name of Jesus. Some thought 'Jesus' was the name of a medicine. This was a nation that had, for many centuries, been steeped in superstition and evil-worship, to the extent that they had no concept of what was sin and what was righteousness. Sixty-five per cent of the male population was set aside for the Lama Priesthood. They were not supposed to marry but were permitted to commit the grossest of evils. These were the men to whom was committed the spiritual welfare of the people, tens of thousands living in hundreds and thousands of villages without God. So far as could be ascertained, the Paynes were the only representatives of the UK in the country.

At the end of their first term on the field, the Paynes returned to the UK and, during that time, were accepted by Elim officially as missionaries under the Elim banner. Following their furlough, during which they toured the country telling of their work, they returned to Mongolia[1] taking with them the young Ken McGillivray, at that time the pastor of the Elim Church in Penzance. The farewell services, attended by a crowd of some 300, occupied a weekend at the Hendon Elim Tabernacle where, eleven years previously, Joe had found the Lord. During the tea interval on the Saturday, Ken showed lantern slides[ii] taken by his father and in the evening service, Joe also used lantern slides to illustrate the work in which he was engaged. The Sunday service was led by Pastor Ladlow in whose home Joe and Ken had first met. Pastors Edsor and Darragh contributed musically to the proceedings and both Ken and Joe ministered the Word of God with great effect. The evening concluded with a celebration of the Lord's Supper, leaving a memory that was to be an inspiration for many in the days to come.

The last glimpse Ken had had of China was when, as a small boy of eight, he had left the country with his mother and sister to return to England, while his father remained behind on the China-Tibetan border. At that time, the idea of returning was repulsive, as was the very thought of becoming a Christian, and he looked forward to enjoying all the pleasures the world could offer. For some years, he sowed his wild oats, wasting precious time in sinning until God wrested his unworthy life from death's door after a serious road accident. Soon after this, the news of his father's home call reached the family and the repentant young prodigal returned to the Father. Two years later, the call came to go to the harvest field of China and, in obedience, he retraced his steps until, in sight of the Chinese coast, he found his heart filled with a great joy and sense of the Presence of God.

However, as the ship docked, he quickly became aware of changes in the country. There was a Japanese sentry at the dock gates and, as they travelled down deserted streets, they saw the charred shells of bombed houses and spaces where there was not one stone upon another. During the devastating aerial bombardment of Shanghai, one bomb alone killed 2000 people, yet in the day time, the streets were thronged with crowds. They had to wait in Shanghai for a week before they could obtain the necessary passes to travel northward across the great wheat-bearing plains to Peking. They had another brief stay of ten days before they were granted further passes to get them to Kalgan. But Ken, as a newcomer, had to remain behind to be inspected by the authorities while the Paynes proceeded to their mission station. It was noted that some returning missionaries had been held up in Kalgan for over a year and not permitted to return to Mongolia. The Paynes' progress was regarded as nothing less than miraculous.

They were helped in their return by Mr. and Mrs. Almblad (British and Foreign Bible Society) who lived in Kalgan and had both permission to travel in Mongolia and also a new lorry with fitted seats. They took the Paynes and their luggage to their station at no cost to the Paynes and stayed with them for several days. Although the Almblads had been working in Mongolia for over thirty years, they were amazed at the scope of the work in which the Paynes were involved. They kept saying to Joe, "You must have helpers; you must have a lorry." Joe agreed but didn't know where either might come from. He acknowledged that the need was great with hundreds of villages filled with thousands of people who had never even heard the name of Jesus.

The Paynes' destination was Shang Tu Hsien where they were given a very warm welcome on their return, not only by the members of the church, but by the townspeople as well. The meetings continued to be well attended, having been held together by Brother Chang, the evangelist. Not only did he care for the church, but he looked after the Paynes' house as well. This was necessary because the continuous, heavy rains had all but washed away their mud roof and the inside of the house was badly in need of cleaning.

By early 1941, the political situation was making life very difficult for missionaries and many were evacuating. All the Americans and some British had left, but the Paynes felt they should stay as long as possible. Ken didn't make it into Mongolia but was held back in Kalgan and he, too, had to decide whether to stay or go. In the event, he decided to stay and, with the Paynes, now in Kalgan, sought to plant a work there. By now, Mongolia was being considered a closed door for missions. This filled the missionaries with a sense of frustration that so little should have been done, but they were thankful to God that, at last, some seed had been sowed and would, in God's good time, produce a harvest for His glory.

As soon as possible, Ken associated himself with an American Methodist missionary who was planning a journey south to preach the Gospel. This was to be a tour covering nearly 1000 miles. In villages and towns they found a few believers and convened services, travelling in the day time and resting each night, usually in cold rooms. Every night, they had to drain the truck's radiator to stop it from freezing, filling it again each morning for the day's journey. Wherever they went, they found people willing to listen; they were able to encourage missionaries in remote areas; above all, they saw the hand of God at work in conversions and restoration of backsliders.

Back in Kalgan, the Paynes had settled into working for the Lord. They were excited to see that many, who at one time had shunned the Pentecostal experience, were now actively seeking it. They had sensed the dryness of their own situation and realised the truth of Scripture concerning the refreshing power of the Holy Spirit. Now, about seventy seasoned and mature missionaries were of one mind, all seeking the Lord for seven whole weeks, three meetings a day and each meeting lasting about three hours! All differences and misunderstandings had been swept away and it seemed as if sin and friction could not exist among them. But in course of time, wave upon wave of glorious power swept through the group and step by step, the Lord led them closer to Himself; doctrinal questions that had been barriers for years were all swept away.

No matter the denomination, many received their Baptism with the Holy Spirit; others received gifts of tongues, interpretation and prophecy. The Pentecostal missionaries had nothing to do with this move, but found themselves in great demand throughout the region for ministry. The Gospel was preached with power and in Bible schools, students were brought into contact with the move of the Spirit that had revolutionised so many. Borders were being enlarged and an outstation was established about twenty miles from Kalgan. One man was about to build a new village and reported that he intended to build a church in it at his own expense.

While all this development was taking place, the world was at war and, within a short time, the area where the missionaries were based was overtaken by the Japanese who interned many of the foreigners they found there. Initially, the Paynes and Ken were detained within their own homes, but subsequently they were placed in a prison camp. Around this same time, a report was received that General Chiang Kai-Shek[iii] had accepted Christ as his Saviour. He was heard to pray that God would help him in his government of China and help China not to hate the Japanese people. He prayed for Japanese Christians and all the suffering multitudes whose impoverishment was making this war on China possible.

Chiang Kai-Shek died in 1975. As Ken reported[iv] on the events surrounding those days, some of the statements attributed to the Chinese leader were very telling. In his will he stated:

There has never been a single moment when I have strayed from faith in Jesus Christ. . . (Then) I deeply wish to entreat all men to read the Bible, which is the voice of the Holy Spirit spreading forth God's justice and righteousness, and His love of mankind in the Saviour Jesus Christ. . . Life cannot exist without religious faith. That was my belief ten years ago and now I must repeat this emphasis to you, my brothers of the whole world, that life cannot be, even for a moment, without religious belief (addressed to the Methodist Centennial celebration) . . . Christians should have the answer to the crux of the evil in this generation. This salvation can be found in the hearts of men. We often become disappointed that we cannot live up to our ideals for it is a fact that often men's character cannot sustain the trial of history, resulting in the same errors again and again. Past sins are magnified; left to themselves, men will be sucked into the vortex of degradation and lost for ever, without hope. But is there no way out? Of course there is a way. Christ has provided that way. . . the conversion of the world begins in the human heart. . . In trials and tribulations lies the secret of spiritual victory. A full life will be tempestuous. A thousand trials surround those who live by faith.

Both Ken and the Paynes, with their children, moved from Kalgan to Shanghai in the early part of 1943, but from April 12th, they were detained with others under Japanese rule. A letter sent through Switzerland indicated that all were well, although the men and women were separated, so that Mrs. Payne had the responsibility of the three children. There were about 250 people interned and about 120 were children. This situation obtained until a letter was received in October, 1945 advising that a news broadcast had been made on 19th August declaring their release and that freedom had been regained. Needless to say, all were grateful.

In a brief description of the circumstances they had been through, Ken wrote:

We soon found that though walled around and kept under guard, we had not forfeited our access to God's Throne of Grace and mercy. We were in the hands of people who hated us. Our lives were spared by their humanity, it seemed; and though they took the credit for our daily bread, we learned that the phrase in the Lord's Prayer revealed the true Giver. We were taught to obey difficult and unreasonable orders in silence and with dignity; under their tutelage, we awaited their pleasure and possessed our souls in patience. For me, the days (1040 of them so far) sped rapidly by; the days were too short to do all I planned. The spirit and atmosphere of an Internment Camp, even to the best regulated community of civilians, is extremely irksome and trying. You feel the constant humiliation of being locked in cramped quarters by those who take pleasure in your misfortune. To be confined within corrugated iron and barbed wire, watched by armed men and hedged about with such restrictions and regulations is hard to endure.

Ken had severe questions as to his situation. He wondered if he were there because of bad decisions he had made. He wondered if he had stayed in Kalgan too long and if he had moved on with others, would he have been free to continue the Lord's work in "free" China. He chafed at the idea of not knowing when he would be free again, feeling that petty criminals had a better outlook since their sentences were for a fixed period. However, he had come to terms with himself and recognised that spiritual development had taken place in his own life through the hardships he had suffered. His association with Joe Payne had also highlighted the poor health of his (Joe's) family, so it was agreed that, as soon as possible, the Paynes would be repatriated and he would stay on in the hope that he would soon be able to return to Mongolia. By November, the Payne family was on its way home to England on the Hospital ship, Oxfordshire, and were appreciating the sea air and good food after their years of deprivation. They were met by a large contingent of Elim friends at the docks in Liverpool. Next morning, they travelled to London where, shortly thereafter, they joined in a combined welcome home service held in Bloomsbury Baptist Church celebrating the homecoming of the Paynes and Pastors Nosworthy and Tate from Africa.

Meanwhile, Ken stayed on in Shanghai since it was impossible to travel north at the time. He made himself useful to American missionaries there for a period until his own repatriation a few months later. The S.S. Strathmore docked at Southampton where Ken was met by Pastor George Canty; then he travelled on to Waterloo Station in London where his family, including his mother, had gathered to meet him. Although there was a reception in the Elim Bible College in Clapham, Ken was not allowed to be idle for long.

It was discovered that the UK was to give warships to China after the cessation of hostilities and that young men from China would come to Britain to be trained before the ships were handed over. This was immediately seen as an opportunity to continue witnessing to the Chinese and Ken became fully involved in the project. There were some sixty Chinese sailors training in Plymouth and 600 more were expected. The Plymouth church, helped by some Chinese Christians, made preparations to provide social facilities for these young men and for showing them aspects of Christian love that would impress them and offer them something positive to take home with them. A service, conducted in

Chinese by Ken McGillivray, was held and it was estimated that 90% of those attending were not Christian.

Naturally, Ken's desire was to return to Mongolia if possible, and although he returned to Kalgan, he was not able to go further. Indeed, within two years of the end of the war, China was once again in the throes of conflict as the communists invaded from the north, seeking to take over the country. This is how Ken described the situation:

Striking with lightning speed, the Communists isolated Kalgan from the west and surrounded Tatung. All Kalgan was agog with rumours and refugees began to pour into the city from all directions. Within a day of the thrust on Tatung came the word that the top of the Pass into Mongolia was in Red hands. Railway traffic between Kalgan and Peiping ceased and troops began to flood into the city. Aeroplanes appeared over the city and sleepy streets soon filled up with long convoys of trucks laden with troops. With these came tanks, armoured vehicles and artillery rumbling through on their way up to the Russian valley. Feverish trench work began on the lower hills, shops put up shutters and the city prepared for a siege.

There was no way out and we could only resort to prayer and doing what we could to calm the terrified native believers who came to us. One could quite understand their anguish when stories of how Red soldiers had nailed people to walls, the burning of people alive and other indescribable sadistic killings were filling the news daily. Matthew chapter ten was a source of great encouragement to them all.

FORMOSA/TAIWAN
KEN and WINNIE McGILLIVRAY

In September, 1940, Winnie Jessop sailed from Canada en route to Hsiangcheng, Honan in the interior of northern China, under the auspices of the China Inland Mission. After a period of service there, she was recalled to Shanghai to take over clerical duties because of sickness among the staff. During her time in Shanghai, she was interned by the Japanese along with many others. As volunteers were required for kitchen duties, she volunteered. Later, she was to work in the hospital and, for one six month period, as a goatherd on a farm.

Ultimately, the war ended and so did internment. With it came the time for decisions. She was quite healthy and therefore decided to stay in China for a short time rather than being immediately repatriated. The consequence of this decision was that she and Ken McGillivray were brought into direct contact and a friendship grew that deepened with time, until they decided they should be engaged.

In 1946, Winnie returned to Canada and Ken went to England. It was then that he discovered that the Paynes would not be able to return to Mongolia and the responsibility for the Mongolia Evangelistic Mission devolved upon him. He spent much time in itineraries throughout Elim churches in the UK as well as churches across Europe – mainly Switzerland – explaining the work in which he was engaged. When laid low by a bout of malaria, he was prayed for by Pastor John Woodhead and was instantly made whole.

In early 1947, he travelled to Canada for a reunion with Winnie and a wedding as they were married in the Christian and Missionary Alliance church in Winnipeg. The plan was for them to return immediately to Mongolia and they were hopeful of a successful trip as news suggested that trains and planes were moving freely. Ken had been trying to get into Mongolia for seven years, and he still lived in hope that his vision might be fulfilled. He was able to do this initially in company with some others who were planning an exploratory visit. Winnie quickly realised that her lot was to stay home while Ken was away for about ten weeks. The trip was in a Model T Ford!

The visit was deemed a success and the men returned to plan their strategy for future ministry. Ken and Winnie moved to Kalgan, the gateway to Mongolia, and set up house there while they waited for the necessary permits to move into the country. While working in Kalgan itself, they saw a measure of blessing, but this was short lived because of the changing political situation as the Communists moved in from the north. Despite this, the McGillivrays considered it essential that they stay. Eventually, they were forced to move and, for about two and a half years, they travelled through China until they reached Hong Kong in December, 1950. In June 1949, while still in transit, their first child, Ian Bruce McGillivray, was born.

Full details of the trials and deprivation suffered by the McGillvrays is contained in *Pastor Wheat,*[v] and shows just what an impact Ken's ministry had in bringing many Chinese to Christ despite the turmoil. Matters took a turn for the worse with the onset of war in Korea and Ken's unwillingness to sign papers condoning and supporting the Koreans and against America. The new regime in Peking prepared a manifesto decreeing that all foreign missionaries should be removed and that the Chinese church "must develop into a self-governing, self-propagating, self-supporting organisation – train its own leaders, develop its own methods of support and learn to do without foreign money." It became increasingly obvious that their time in China was rapidly running out and arrangements were made to move across the border to Hong Kong. But even then, their journey was a nightmare. Although they were required to leave, everything possible was done to make that virtually impossible. In the end, they arrived in the British Colony and found a welcome that sustained them. Later, Ken was able to put together an article that outlined the plight of the church in China and recognised the impact of the communist regime on Christian witness.[vi]

The expatriate missionary community in Hong Kong was swollen by expelled missionaries from China, and there was much discussion as to the way ahead. Some felt that Japan was beckoning, but on reflection, the McGillivrays were drawn to Taiwan or

Formosa as it was called by the Portuguese. Responding to an invitation by the "host" Presbyterian Mission, who suggested that they might come to the plains and work among the Chinese people, there they found the government of Chiang Kai-Shek in exile and an indigenous aboriginal church that was moving in the realm of the Spirit despite years of depression caused by Japanese rule. After the close of hostilities, the church no longer needed to be underground but became totally visible and built over four hundred churches in fifteen years.

The area that most appealed to Ken was in the north-east of the island, Yi Lan. They located in LoTung nearby and found much to occupy their labours. In one series of meetings, it was estimated that 20,000 people had heard the Gospel during the 19 meetings held over four days. Ken regularly had opportunity to preach to soldiers in the camps, sometimes with as many as 3000 present at a time. They also found opportunities to develop a radio ministry with four programmes per week over three stations. Literature brought its own encouragements as people responded to the written word. Regular weekly visits were made to prison and also to the U.S. Army camp just outside the city. By now, there were six Sunday schools and women's meetings, youth fellowship groups and camps and, in the hearts of the missionaries, a great cry for additional workers to help in the work.

Their biggest problem was a lack of workers. But despite this constriction, the work continued to expand as new centres were opened up, including settlements for soldiers' families. Help was forthcoming in these settlements as seven ladies from the Yi Lan assembly volunteered to go there and minister. Subsequently, there were positive responses and new Sunday schools were started at the request of people in the Settlements. Ministry was indigenous as local people took up the responsibility for looking after the fledgling works. Not until May, 1968 did the work have the benefit of another expatriate missionary as Kevin Brotton set out for Formosa via Canada.

Kevin was a bachelor from the Elim church in Bradford. He had spent some time working with Teen Challenge in Toronto and then helped to establish a new church in Saskatchewan following a crusade by Don Cantelon. He went to Taiwan under the joint direction of Elim and P.A.O.C. and launched immediately into language study in Taipei. During Ken's long absences in Hong Kong, Kevin was a great help to Winnie and when the McGillivrays returned to Canada in 1969, much of the responsibility for the church's work was laid on Kevin's shoulders.

Ken and Winnie's furloughs were spent between England and Canada and in 1951, while in England, the McGillivray family was augmented by the birth of a daughter, Margaret Jennifer. In Canada, Ken supplied the pulpit of Bethel Pentecostal Tabernacle in Ottawa for several months. While Ken had had a loose arrangement with the Elim Missionary Society in the UK for a number of years, during this furlough in Canada he made contact and developed a strong association with the Pentecostal Assemblies of Canada.

The return from furlough marked the beginning of a new sphere of labour without the hindrances of political intrigue or unnecessary travel. It was now possible to concentrate on the development and consolidation of the work. Word from the field told of growth as the church matured and went so far as to elect its deacons, bringing new life to the leadership of the assembly. Ken was one of them! The diaconate consisted of seven men and four women; among the men was a national senator, a local judge, two high school teachers and a lawyer. In the congregation there were at least a dozen high school teachers and an ever-growing number of high school students. With people of this calibre, they were able to have a choir, conducted by Winnie, and as a result, her Chinese-English Bible class had taken on a new lease of life.

New buildings were being erected and baptismal services were being arranged. Two Sunday schools were running and growing in numbers week by week. Other groups were writing asking for ministry and Ken's time was at a premium. At a week's special meetings on the other side of the island, Ken saw forty people respond to the Gospel.

As Ken went about the Lord's business, he came into contact with many people from all walks of life. One man, a soldier in the Chinese army for fifteen years, was in hospital with final stages of TB and consigned to die in a very short time. After prayer and the laying on of Ken's hands, and surrendering his life to the Lord, he was completely healed to the amazement of his doctors.

One of Ken's great frustrations was to hear from refugees from mainland China that the people there had not seen a copy of the Scriptures for more than thirteen years. The feeling of urgency in the situation was strengthened by the knowledge that Christians, still meeting in secret, were being singled out as targets by the Red Guards and were being ruthlessly destroyed wherever they could be found. A novel means was discovered whereby Bibles could be deposited on the mainland. A supply of giant balloons was made available at no charge. These were generally used for sending food, clothing and propaganda material from the island of Quemoy (three miles off the coast of China), to the mainland. Varying in size, these balloons could float on the prevailing winds for thousands of miles inland and might reach even Tibet or Chinese Turkestan. No Bibles had been printed in China since the Red revolution; paper was rationed and none was available for the printing of Bibles on the mainland. But young people in the UK were invited to contribute funds to send Bibles into China at a cost well within reason for those living in the West. The first Bibles were 'floated' by balloon on 22nd December, just in time for Christmas.

Kevin Brotton's arrival had meant that the work could be expanded, and although he spent some time, in the beginning, in Taipei, he moved down the coast to a country town on the east coast to open a work. There he would face the prospects of being on his own, dependent only on the Chinese words he had learned up to that point. His challenge would be to identify himself with overt idol worshippers while not compromising his allegiance to Jesus.

The home he found was Chinese in nature, with chopsticks and bowls rather than knives and forks. His diet included octopus and seaweed soup, but he confessed that he wasn't partial to fish eyes! But having settled in, he saw the work develop, especially among the young people who were keen to know Jesus and to pass on to their friends information about their new life. Entirely on their own initiative, six young people from the Fu Lung assembly decided to get up at 5.30 each Sunday morning and climb the nearby hills to give the farmers an hour of Bible readings and Christian songs. Despite the resurgence of Buddhism throughout south Asia, there was a hunger for the Gospel that could hardly be satiated.

A highlight of the missionaries' diary was a visit by Pastor P. S. Brewster in 1971. This was the first time an Elim pastor had come to visit Elim missionaries and his coming was a cause for rejoicing. In the following week, he ministered eight times, speaking five times in the central Ilan[vii] Mandarin church. Thereafter, he travelled around the north of the island meeting with and ministering to university students and reaching out to the congregations of other churches in the area. He broke the ground for a new church building and a kindergarten which was nearly half completed. The beauty of the countryside was not lost on the travellers.

In 1975, the work was extended in the city of T'ou Cheng and Miss Carol Wilson, who had gone to Taiwan under the auspices of WEC,[viii] went to work there. A little later, the workers there were joined, for the first time ever, by an Elim Pathfinder, Miss Cathy Owen, who stayed for one year working with Carol.

Ken was a traveller. Following one furlough, he found himself in New Zealand, a guest of the Elim churches and speaker at their annual conference. As he shared his vision and expressed some of the needs of his field, the delegates sensed the Spirit's confirmation of his ministry and pledged themselves to generous support for the work. They promised support for the national workers and assured Ken he would have enough money to buy land for a church in a town of some 50,000 where his was the only church. They also declared their intention to finance the building of the church in the near future. Ken had the opportunity over the following three weeks to address many different groups, including churches and Rotary clubs, to share with them the aspirations he had for the work in Taiwan.

Over the years, Ken saw the work develop and deepen, growing physically, spiritually and materially. In 1978, some 21 years after the erection of their original church building, it became necessary to build a new facility to accommodate the wide range of ministries now being undertaken. Despite seemingly insurmountable difficulties, the church was built on land acquired at a fraction of its value. The ground area was 3000 sq. ft. on three levels, including a spacious basement, giving a total floor area of over 7000 sq. ft. The sanctuary seated 800 and there was a Children's Library, Kindergarten and a pastor's residence in the complex. E.W.M.A. was able to help financially to complete the project.

The work in Taiwan was enhanced in 1978 by the arrival of Susan and Derek Le Page, a young couple from the Delancey (Channel Islands) Elim church. They were involved in pioneer work in Kaohsiung, the second largest city in Taiwan with a population of one million, some 250 miles away from Ilan and associated themselves with Pastor Chu

Hung. This man had served as a soldier in Chiang Kai-Shek's army but had had to flee to Taiwan as a result of the hostilities in China. From that time, he had no contact with any family members and had heard no news of whether they were alive or dead.

The work demanded a readiness to deal with all sorts of problems and questions. Frightening things appeared to Mrs. Lin at nights as Satan tried to win her back after she became a Christian. Although she had destroyed the family idols, an evil presence pervaded her home in Kaohsiung.

Mrs. Lin realised the expensive idol table would have to go before she could be completely free from past idolatry. She asked Pastor Chu, her minister, to remove it and 30 minutes later, he and Derek were on their way with carpentry tools to do the job.

Idol tables were made from quality wood and played an important part in Chinese life. All the idols and gods of the household were placed on the tables, which measured 6 ft. long, 2 ft. wide and stood about 4 ft. high. The most important god was given pride of place. Lesser gods or protectors were lined up on either side. Incense sticks were burned and daily food offerings were made to the gods.

It meant a lot to Mrs. Lin to allow the men to cut up her table. It would have cost her at least £250 (in 1979) to buy a new one, but she watched with a happy heart as the two pastors turned her table into firewood. She later testified that she no longer was troubled by any evil presence and was able to sleep peacefully at nights.[ix]

After many months of patient searching, the people of the Kaohsiung church finally moved into new premises. The church had begun four years before, always using rented halls, but these had become too small and they were situated in a busy area where the traffic noise was intrusive. Building work started in 1979 and made good progress. In March the following year, church members became involved in finishing work to complete the project. The church consisted of a ground floor hall with a pastor's manse above it. On the night of the dedication of the building, a thief broke into the manse and stole money and a ladies' handbag. The enemy of souls was busy, but nothing could dampen the enthusiasm of the Lord's people as they considered the glorious possibilities for the Lord's work in their new church building.

In 1981, Ken was found to be suffering from angina caused in no small measure by the level of strain he felt in his capacity as leader of the work. He therefore transferred all his administrative duties to Chinese nationals and took a furlough in Canada. In 1982, he reached retirement age, but he intended to move on to another sphere of labour among the Chinese. He and Winnie felt they would be better able to advise people about the work of the Chinese Children's Crusade programme which helped underprivileged children to attend church-run kindergartens. Ken intended also to continue teaching the first year class of students at the Ming Tao United Bible Institute.

The arrangement nationally was that the P.A.O.C. would have administrative responsibility for the work throughout the major part of the Island while Elim (both UK and NZ) would look after the work in Ilan district, both groups continuing to be represented on the Pentecostal Assemblies of China Executive Committee.

An interesting development as a result of Ken's involvement with Taiwan was an association that developed with the Heavenly Melody Singers who made their first visit to the UK in 1982. The Elim Church sponsored their visit and they toured the churches in England with great acclaim. The group comprised singers and musicians, mostly young people trained to virtually professional level, who had connections with ORTV – Overseas Radio and Television Inc. of Taipei.[x] This was a missionary organisation commenced by Doris Brougham of Seattle whose passion and vision was to reach the Chinese with the Gospel. Subsequent visits expanded their sphere of influence throughout the whole of the UK and they have always ministered with great acceptance. They have impressed by their deep spirituality, quality music, generosity and warmth of fellowship, developed wherever they have been, and especially towards those who have been their hosts. Links have been maintained over the years and have grown richer and deeper with the passing of time.

On Thursday, 18th August, 1983, Ken McGillivray was suddenly called home to be with his Lord after a ministry spanning some 42 years. Dr. Ku, a very important person in Taiwan, told Pastor Frank Lavender, who was visiting, "We in the Republic of China hold Pastor Ken McGillivray in the highest esteem, for he has been a good friend of the Chinese people." Many others were to provide equally stirring tributes to the man they called, Pastor Wheat[xi]. A fellow-missionary in the internment camps described him as the one whose humour kept up the spirits of the others and they called him Merry Mac of Mongolia. Pastor Gerald Ladlow told that in Ken's last letter to him, he had expressed his 'dream of making a visit back to China, Inner Mongolia and Tibet and find it is not as impossible as some might imagine'. Despite being 66 years old and having angina, Ken had continued to give himself to the service of the Lord in Taiwan, involving himself in many types of Christian outreach including the ministry of Heavenly Melody and broadcasting through ORTV. Over the years, Ken had also given attention to writing and many of his messages were printed in the Elim Evangel. In many cases he was able to illustrate the point he wished to make with situations he had encountered in the field. His last contribution was a short series on the life of the Judges of Israel.

With Ken's passing and Winnie's retirement in Vancouver a chapter on the work in China closed, but the development of ORTV's ministry has been phenomenal as radio and television have beamed the Gospel into mainland China and reached where it would otherwise have been impossible to make contact. The consequences of those lives that have been given for the sake of the Chinese people rest with God.

i They returned in the middle of 1940.

ii Lantern slides were photographic positives in black and white printed on glass to allow them to be projected.

iii Reported in *Elim Evangel,* Vol.23. Issue 12, p.133.

iv *Elim Evangel,* Vol.56. Issue 28, pp.8,9,12.

v The early contacts between Winnie and Ken were recorded in a book written by Calvin C. Ratz on behalf of the Pentecostal Assemblies of Canada. It was published in 1970 by the Overseas Missions Department under the title *Pastor Wheat* and was an outline of Ken's life. I am indebted to PAOC archives for reference to their copy.

vi See footnote iv.

vii *Elim Evangel,* Vol.45. Issue 10, pp.152,153.

viii Ilan became the name of the original Yi Lan assembly.

ix WEC: Worldwide Evangelisation Crusade founded by C.T. Studd.

x Reported by Derek Le Page in *Elim Evangel,* Vol.60. Issue 31, p.6.

xi The full story of the development of ORTV was produced in book form in 1998 entitled *ORTV – A Miracle Unique,* written by William and Dorothy Pape.

xii Ken's Chinese name translated to 'wheat'; thus his title.

CHAPTER 28

THAILAND

Surrounded by the troubled nations of Laos, Cambodia and Vietnam, Thailand is an important part of Elim's international outreach in South East Asia. In a country of some 45 million people, 93% are engulfed in the dark shroud of Buddhism. Every village, town and city is dotted with temples and shrines, and it is against this backdrop that Tony and Ursula Wilson labour.

In 1982, they first travelled to Bangkok to begin a pioneer work for God. Although Elim had no prior work there, there was already a Christian presence provided by the Assemblies of God of America (AoG) and the Pentecostal Assemblies of Canada (PAOC). The PAOC missionaries were to be the Wilsons' covering for the commencement of their ministry.

Arriving in Bangkok, the Wilsons were met by all the PAOC missionaries who were then serving in the capital. On the way to the city from the airport, they experienced something they had been well warned about – culture shock! First impressions were that they should turn around and go home, but realising that this wasn't a short term holiday, but a new life and ministry that would last for three years, they gritted their teeth and settled down.

A good night's sleep was called for, since they had been awake for about 36 hours, but even that was denied. Coping with the heat was difficult and the barking of dogs all night long made sleep a very scarce commodity. Tony discovered that the Thais believe that when the dogs bark, the spirits are passing through and with the howling going on throughout the night, he almost began to believe it.

It didn't take long for reality to set in. Their inability to read the road signs, and understanding that they wouldn't be able to do so for some months to come, in heat that was overwhelming, with traffic too dense and frightening for words, caused them to realise very quickly that this was no romantic, exotic land as portrayed in books and on television.

But they also discovered that the Lord had gone before them and prepared the way. They lived initially in a flat four storeys up, which they shared with the local livestock – lizards. The lizards became acceptable companions but they never did get to like the cockroaches.

One of their first tasks was to attend language school. This occupied six hours each day beginning at 6.45 a.m. and called for perseverance and application. They were able to adjust fairly quickly to their new situation and soon, they were no longer shocked by the presence of diseased dogs or repulsed by the smell of the open sewers. The beggars with leprosy or the mother who had been left to fend for herself who sat with a baby across her knee looking for someone to give her one baht (2p) still turned their hearts over. Wickedness abounded and, at the end of their street, there were two brothels with others evident about every half mile.

Shortly after their arrival, Tony was able to take a trip to the north to see some 'real missionary work'. He reported[1]:

The Lord has blessed me with a friend, an AoG missionary who has been here for five months. We travelled together, starting early in the morning for the bus station. The taxi driver had difficulty in locating the bus depot and we were travelling along a road when we came upon a section that was awash. A bus was coming in the opposite direction and was negotiating the water all right, so we endeavoured to continue but suddenly, the taxi sank into a large pothole. All who saw the incident laughed and so did we, but only hours later! The taxi driver demanded more money for repairs to his car.

The journey by bus took six hours. The bus drivers force other vehicles off the road without mercy, overtaking on bends and while going up hills. Arrived at our destination, we showed films in the small town in the evening then preached the Gospel through an interpreter. About 500 turned out that Saturday night and about 40 made decisions. Next morning, we held a counselling class and, although Sunday is a working day in Thailand, 20 men turned up and I taught them the basics of Christianity. We had questions for a further two hours.

The Thais, being Buddhist, have no concept of God, so Sunday night we followed the same procedure and saw 20 decisions in a congregation of about 300 people. God is really at work here, but it's not easy. The town had no restaurants of western standards so finding food was a challenge. We bypassed small eating houses one after another because they were too dirty and then discovered that they were all alike. I wondered if it would be costly to eat. It was! The meal was only about 40p but the pain afterwards was severe.

The eating situation got worse. On Sunday, we ate on the spot where we held the meeting. The Thais made us a meal. There was a fight to see who would eat it first - the flies, the cockroaches or us. There was no table and obviously, no table cloth, and definitely no knives or forks. The food was placed on straw mats on the floor and we all (Thais included) just kept dipping into the various pots. On the Sunday evening, we travelled back to Bangkok arriving at 5 a.m., just enough time to get an hour's sleep before going off again to language study.

A few months later, on a Sunday morning, Tony set off to visit a refugee camp some 3 hours away up country. The scenery on the journey was monotonous, flat as a pancake, stretching for mile after mile. One rice field looks much like another, so Tony turned his attention to some language study. But today, he was to visit people who were not Thai, but Vietnamese.

Shortly after arriving, they held a service for about 120. Over a number of months, several people in the camp had become Christians and Tony was excited by the singing. Even although he didn't understand the words, he did recognise some very familiar tunes, especially *He lives, Christ Jesus lives today.* The power of the Spirit fell and there was great praise and expressions of joy, to the amazement of some of the other missionaries. Tony was impressed by the fact that these refugees, who had nothing of this world's goods, had everything – treasure in earthen vessels, jewels that would be made up in that day.

When he asked if the singing was always so good, he was told that it usually wasn't but that a pastor and some of his flock had escaped and recently arrived in the camp. These were bright, full-of-faith Christians. The pastor's refugee status was evident by his dress, which was shabby, with trousers held together with wrong-coloured thread. But he was more presentable than one of the camp church committee men who had a bright coloured shirt on top of which he wore a flowered winceyette pyjama top. He said that he had been severely persecuted by the North Vietnamese communists. He had escaped with his wife and five children but they had been separated and now he didn't know where they were except for one son he had with him.

The camp, supposedly one of the better ones, was sparse. Rice was cooked in huge pots and then carried to a central point for distribution. Chicken was also available, but it was totally unappetising. To western eyes, it seemed completely inedible.

The children delighted to follow the missionaries, touching their legs and generally looking for a little interest to be shown in them. A visit to the huts they inhabited revealed these to be long, two storey dwellings without walls and just a 12' x8' space allotted to each family. There were no beds, wardrobes or chests of drawers, just a mat to sleep on. Furniture wasn't needed because those living there possessed only what they wore. Nearly 4,000 men, women and children lived in this camp.

Tony discovered that most of the men spoke good English and, in conversation with them, found government officials, policemen, etc. who had escaped persecution. They were truly displaced persons, since no one wanted them and they had nowhere else to go. Their future looked bleak and was not helped by a decision that the Thai government was going to ban the distribution of tracts and Gospel literature in the camps and refuse to allow further preaching visits.

Just a few nights later, Tony and Ursula were having a meal with friends when they heard the sound of a heavy bombardment and realised that the Vietnamese were making incursions over the border and were targeting one of the camps. It had been estimated that, in a recent attack, over 3,000 people had been killed during the hours of darkness. There had been news of the Vietnamese dropping 'yellow rain'[ii] in Cambodia, but this was always denied.

News had come in of blessing being experienced in a village to the north, so plans were made to visit. Four hours brought them to Petchaboon Province and then they had to travel through the mountains to Chon Daen. There were no made up roads, just dirt and rocks. Many a time, the edge had sheer drops to the ravines below without any form of protection. This part of the journey was extremely hazardous. After reaching Chon Daen, they had to travel a further thirty kilometres on atrocious roads and, at one village, the bridge was down, so they had to ford the river. Fording the river was easy, but the banks on either side were treacherous.

When they arrived at the village, instead of finding evidence of blessing and high spirits, the atmosphere was pervaded with pessimism and despondency. The reason was that the day before, the pastor's young child had been taken ill and needed an operation. The pastor had visited the whole congregation and, together, they had scraped up 200 baht (£5.75) to cover the journey and the doctor's fee. Before they left the village, the pastor returned with his daughter, tired but victorious and with an exciting story. The doctor had examined the girl and decided to operate. But the pastor now had only 90 baht left and the operation would cost 800 baht, so he began to pray and pray. On the day of the operation, the doctor re-examined the child and discovered that her problem had vanished and she was now quite well. There was now no need for an operation.

The morning service was good and had been well attended, but not at the level that had been expected. The reason was that a *Jesus Only* group had entered the village and engaged in sheep stealing. They had re-baptised those that had left the church to join the "new" gospel but the problem was that those who had been deluded by the false teaching soon became disillusioned altogether and returned to Buddhism.

A major problem faces the new missionary to Thailand. It is not a question of where the greatest need lies, but of where to start. Requests flood in to go here, there and everywhere. Although based in Chiangmai, the surrounding villages where there were small struggling churches sought attention. There were also many areas where there was no witness at all.

Tony therefore arranged to go and visit the few members of Pastor Nuan's church in Baan Mai Sawaan. This involved a trip of some 30 kilometres in order to gauge the spiritual temperature of the fellowship. Most of the members lived near the church so as soon as the car was parked, an instant congregation materialised out of the bush, apparently from nowhere. A special meeting had been arranged but no one thought to inform Tony, so he had to do some hasty praying.

It turned out to be a remarkable morning. Tony managed to preach for about an hour and a half, preaching a message that started in Genesis and ended in Revelation, leaving the preacher totally drained. Strangely enough, he was corrected only once during his talk, not on theological grounds but on his use of the language. Unsure of just how much was being taken in, he asked for assurance every now and then, to be encouraged that they understood what he was saying.

As he taught on the baptism in the Holy Spirit, he discovered that not one person had received the blessing. Because of the emphasis in the culture on spirits, they had been fearful that surrendering to the Holy Spirit would render them out of control and subject to the supernatural control of demons. Some also felt that they needed to achieve a certain level of holiness before they could receive. The following night was a prayer meeting and, before long, the Spirit of the Lord had come down mightily.

Two of the congregation received the baptism and spoke in tongues. Instead of frightening the rest of the congregation, it drove them to a great soul searching and confession of sins. The prayer meeting, which had started at 8 p.m., ended after midnight with hearts dealt with and turned over to God, from formalism to spirit and truth.

The second source of blessing came during a question and answer session at the end of the service. Tony had asked what occupation the men had. Most of them were rice or crop farmers. They told him that for some months there had been no rain so the crops were badly affected. In conversation, they admitted that their income often didn't even reach a daily 75p, hardly enough to feed a family, let alone clothe them. One felt that the Lord should give them an abundance of rain so that the Buddhists could see that it was worthwhile following Jesus.

Tony showed them that even during the earthly ministry of Jesus, there had been times when those that followed Him did so because He would supply bread or fish and for no other reason. He explained that real faith showed itself when enduring hardship. Nevertheless, they all prayed for rain. Just as they drove away, rain began to fall, but only a few drops. However, within a week the rains came.

While based in Chiangmai, Tony spent his time seeking to plant new churches as well as visiting and encouraging other established small works in the villages. Two crusades were held with this in view. In San Baa Dong, a very hard place, the meetings were planned for four nights in a local school. There had been much prayer and preparation by local Christians and on the first night, 200 people crowded into the school and many came forward for prayer. Wonderful healings were seen which included restored hearing for the deaf, freed arthritic joints and, in one man's case, the drying up of a running painful sore on his jaw.

Needless to say, where there was blessing, there was also opposition. Permission to use the school was withdrawn as a result and hasty alternative arrangements had to be made to use a local church. This presented a problem of space as the church could hold only about 30 people, but newspapers were spread on the floor and people sat everywhere, including outside, to listen to the Gospel. God's power continued to be evident in the meetings. After the crusade was over, 20 new people attended the church.

In San Don Muang, the crusade was again faced with opposition, this time from the head man of the village, but also saw great blessing despite heavy rains. Many were challenged to trust Christ and follow up work was ongoing. Further crusades were being planned for the following year.

In 1986, Tony and Ursula moved from Chiangmai to Korat. This is a large city of about 200,000 people, situated in the north east of Thailand. Its vast area contains about one third of the country's population, is largely undeveloped and regularly suffers from prolonged periods of drought. Most of the migration within the country takes place from here and many of the girls have ended up working in the bars and massage parlours, as well as children who work in prison-like sweat shops in factories in Bangkok.

When they first went to Thailand, they met a young man, Santi, who had heard the Lord speak to him about planting a church in Korat. At that time, Tony had felt no particular leading for the area. As it happened, the young man didn't pursue this call either, and their ways parted. But during their last six months in Changmai, Santi met up with them again and expressed anew his hope of starting a work in Korat. He was delighted to hear that the Lord had also been speaking to Tony about work in that region and that was where they hoped to work during their second term.

So, before the Wilsons' furlough, a work was started with cell groups and Tony had opportunity to preach twice. Soon there was a nucleus of people gathering for worship. The Scandinavian Pentecostals in Bangkok had a recording studio and were then broadcasting programmes to the north east and, having no work there, passed on their contacts for follow-up. This was productive and in a short time, fifteen converts were baptised in water.

The development of the work was not spectacular, but was making steady progress. Thirty adults attended on the Sunday morning service and half nights for prayer were held twice monthly. As part of the outreach, English was being taught and this touched four groups consisting of bank officials, policemen, soldiers and high school students. Forty people attended and the Gospel of Luke was used as a handbook. Not far from Korat was the famous Bridge over the River Kwai, and that was a site for camps that helped to develop fellowship within the group.

Since Korat was strongly Buddhist, there were no suitable schools for missionary children and so Ursula found herself home schooling her own children. This was not easy and the children lacked the inter-play with other children. Eventually, of course, Hannah went to boarding school in Penang, Malaysia. For this, she had to travel in August, returning home for Christmas. Her two brothers missed her at these times, but Hannah enjoyed her time at the Christian Mission School. Unfortunately, there was little for children to do in Korat. On Ursula's day off, there was nowhere to go, so usually the children roller skated around the house, went for bike rides down to the railway or played marbles with some of the Thai children. Ursula hoped for some friend who might be passing through to break up the day.

Tony, meanwhile, was giving himself to the establishment of the church and the training of a suitable candidate to take on the pastorate. The outreach of the church was based on a type of 'Evangelism Explosion' programme with a group of church people committed to reaching out into their city. Tony also heard around that time that it might be possible to buy time on the local radio station so that the full Gospel could be preached and the church advertised. With the radios in third world countries being switched on most of the time, this was a glorious opportunity. Music would play an important part and Ursula was well qualified to assist in this department. The only hesitation was that Tony would have to take a test to show that his use of the Thai language was up to broadcasting standard. The programme went out on FM for thirty minutes each Sunday morning at a cost of £60 per broadcast. From it, a postal Bible course was offered resulting in additional contacts.

Many believers struggle to know what God's will for their lives is. The missionaries are no different. And even when facing everyday events, it's always good to know that the

Lord has an interest in them as well. Ursula was feeling challenged because she wasn't as aware as she felt she should be about the needs of the Thai people with whom they were associated. But she consoled herself with what she did know and left the rest to the Lord.

While thinking about these things, one name sprang into her mind. She describes what happened[iii]:

The name, Doi, one of our members aged about forty, came into my mind and I therefore commenced praying for him. Not too long after, my husband, Tony, came home from visiting some church members with Pastor Wanlop. Tony told how he had met Doi that afternoon and Doi had opened his heart about a matter that was troubling him.

Doi's mother was a spirit medium and he had been brought up under her influence. He had married a Christian girl, but still was a Buddhist. After his marriage, he had visited a temple in Korat where there was a famous monk who, it was claimed, had special powers. Doi wanted special protection and strength from a guardian spirit. This monk chanted over two small pieces of gold, each about one cm. square, which had symbols engraved upon them, and then rolled them into two tiny scrolls. He took a nail, drove it through the skin of Doi's upper arms and then buried one in each arm.

Things did not go as Doi had wished however. Often, at night, he would wake up screaming and shouting. Sometimes he would shake all over and be unable to control himself. At other times, he would threaten his wife with a knife and shout, with a voice not his own, "I am the guardian spirit of the City Post" (This referred to a place in the city where people went to pray, chant and make merit.) After each occasion, he was totally unaware of what had happened. His symptoms grew worse and eventually, he began to lose the use of his arms and legs.

Doi subsequently became a Christian and started reading his Bible. He realised that the Lord was speaking to him about the matter of the two gold pieces in his arms. A small operation was arranged and Doi had the gold bars removed, but before the operation, his wife had the same dream on two consecutive nights. A thin old man appeared to her telling her not to sell the place he had lived in for so long. On describing the appearance of the man to her husband, Doi recognised the man as the priest who had inserted the gold bars into his arms.

There was a time of waiting on the Lord and then Doi was prayed for that the Lord would release him totally. The following Sunday, tears began to stream down Doi's face and he saw a vision of a nail-scarred hand outstretched towards him. Doi sensed complete relief and ease in his spirit, like a house that had been swept clean of all its uncleanness.

One of Tony's burdens was to minister to prisoners in the local jail. His opportunity came about in a most unusual way. Hundreds of tracts were distributed at a fair in the town and one of these found its way into the hands of an inmate doing life, who then contacted Tony. He then began to visit four men and had the opportunity to hold an open service within the prison. Each of the inmates was a long term prisoner, doing between 45-50 years. The prison conditions were better than might be anticipated, but still pretty grim. It was a cause for praise that this opening presented itself.

Persecution within families was an ongoing problem. Two Chinese/Thai girls were particularly affected. Their mother fell sick and the usual thing happened. The older son took the father to the local spiritist medium. These people had 'real' power – a challenge to the local church. The medium attributed the illness to the fact that the Christians refused to pay homage to the ancestors. Real anger was expressed by the family, who were calling the mother's spirit to be with them. Obviously, such situations created great tensions within the church and in the hearts and minds of the missionaries, but God remained faithful and His power was evident among the people.

i *Elim Evangel*, Vol.64, Issue 17, page 4.

ii Chemical warfare.

iii *Elim Evangel*, Vol.68.

CHAPTER 29

CONCLUSION

Following the close of the record in 1989, the work continued to expand, but reports and records became much more difficult to find or preserve. The demise of the *Elim Evangel* meant that missionary matters were given less prominence and hence the gathering of information relative to the various fields became much more piece meal.

In course of time, Brian Edwards retired as International Missions Director and the Missions Board was disbanded, its place taken by the National Leadership team. For a period, the Regional Superintendents were expected to make decisions relative to the Fields, guided by input from the Missions Director, but his position too was made redundant. However, it soon became apparent that the RSs had quite enough on their plate without having to make crucial decisions regarding areas that they knew comparatively little about. It was therefore judged prudent and necessary to have one individual, reporting to the NLT, who would take overall control of the International work. This resulted in Chris Jones being appointed.

In the meantime, the work was still developing, with new fields being introduced and changes being organised in existing areas. With the approach of the 1990s, a decade of evangelism was introduced and the writer carried the mission forward to Brazil, where there had been a dearth of trained leadership and therefore, of growth. Several teams of three went to Brazil on regular occasions during the decade and a measure of improvement was seen.

An emphasis was placed, too, on evangelism and church planting, not to the exclusion of "social" caring programmes, but as a recognition of our priority in ministry. Some rearranging took place in order to facilitate this view.

At the same time, the Field Superintendent, T. Gordon Hills, was active in foreign parts, especially the Philippines, where he registered existing organisations under the umbrella of ECI.[i] In 2002, Paul Sarchet-Waller had resigned from Elim Missions, but continued to pastor the Elim Full Gospel church in Shatin, Hong Kong. This church was not regarded as an Elim church and therefore, Paul's ministry with Elim was deemed to have concluded, since he had not been in charge of an Alliance Elim church for at least two years. Meanwhile, generally the number of expatriate missionaries declined. Since the turn of the century, however, this has been redressed and new fields have been opened up, in many cases because individuals felt the call of God to be there, not necessarily with IMB financial backing, but with the responsibility of raising their own support. Their ministry has been given recognition by Elim, and they therefore hold credentials from, and labour under the aegis of, the Movement.[ii]

It is clear that the desire to serve overseas and the strong sense of call is still very much in evidence in the Movement, and this is seen, not only in young, impressionable people, but often in people of middle age who want to give something to the work in their remaining years. There seems also to be a sense of time running out.

On the home front, Regional Missions Directors have been appointed and given much more authority than heretofore. In some cases, these have been established as full time appointments and the consequence has been a raising of the profile of Missions, which can only bring good.

If, in the natural, Global Warming is given urgent consideration, so too in the spiritual, the time must inevitably be short since world events seem to indicate that political moves across the globe are setting the scene for the soon return of the King. The commitment of every believer to evangelism, wherever they are able to do it, will hasten the day when the King comes.

i Elim Church Incorporated, the body which allowed independent groups to be in registered fellowship with the Elim Movement.

ii At September, 2006, there were 36 expatriate missionaries working in 39 countries according to the Elim Church year book. There were 26 National leaders reported with a further 28 credentialed national workers.